11/5/92

To Kurt

Happy Birthday!

Love,
Mom

THE
FALCONS
OF THE WORLD

THE
FALCONS
OF THE WORLD

by
TOM J. CADE

with paintings by
R. DAVID DIGBY

COMSTOCK

Cornell University Press
Ithaca, New York

R. DAVID DIGBY

Acknowledgements

The author would like to acknowledge the many standard references used for details of about half of the species in this book for which he has had no personal experience, such as Friedmann's *Birds of North and Middle America,* Part 11, Falconiformes (1950); Dementiev's chapter on Falconiformes in *Birds of the Soviet Union,* Volume 1 (1951); Brown and Amadon's *Eagles, Hawks and Falcons of the World* (1968); and the excellent and scholarly compendium by Cramp, Simmons *et al., Handbook of the Birds of Europe, the Middle East and North Africa* (The Birds of the Western Palearctic), Volume 2 (1980); and many others. He has benefited much from access to unpublished information, and particularly wishes to express his appreciation to Ludlow Clark, Nick Fox, Gary Falxa, Devora Ukrain, Dave Whitacre, Dean Hector, Peter Jenny, Nick Mooney, and Hartmut Walter, for sharing with him their knowledge of falcons. Lastly he would like to thank his copy editor, Tessa Board, whose sharp eyes have no doubt saved him from embarrassment.

The artist wishes to thank all those who made it possible to produce paintings of falcons little known to him. He is indebted to I. C. J. Galbraith, Dr P. J. K. Burton, and D. Read of the British Museum (Natural History) at Tring; to J. Heath of the Natural History Museum, Colchester; to R. Hartly and G. Engelbrecht of Zimbabwe for help on some African species; to Dr H. O. M. King for material on the aplomado falcon; to Dr N. C. Fox for information and photographs on the New Zealand falcon; and to Dr T. J. Cade for information on the bat and orange-breasted falcons. He would also like to thank Tom Deas for designing this book.

The distribution maps were prepared by Ron Hayward.

First published 1982 by Comstock/
Cornell University Press
Reprinted in 1987

Library of Congress Catalog Card Number 81-68743

International Standard Book Number 0-8014-1454-7

This edition produced by
Nicholas Enterprises Ltd.
70 Old Compton Street,
London W1V 5PA

Printed in Italy
by Grafiche Alma - Milan

PLATE i
(previous pages)
Common Kestrel
Falco tinnunculus
Male bringing food
to the young

Contents

TABLES AND FIGURES

Preface

Falcons can be observed and studied in all parts of the world, excepting only Antarctica and some remote oceanic islands. It is appropriate, therefore, that the thoughts for this preface came to me on a recent field trip to northern Iceland, where I was visiting my student, Olafur Karl Nielsen, who is making a study of the gyrfalcons of his native country.

We had climbed to the top of a steep, brushy, birch-covered slope to some lava rocks where the local farmer had told us a pair of merlins was nesting. Olaf wanted to ring the young, but they had already flown from the nest when we arrived – four of them scattered about among the rocks and heath-covered mounds on the slope. The parents screamed and dived at us, but the youngsters seemed not at all perturbed by our presence. They were not yet strong on the wing, still stubby-tailed, and they were wet and so all the more reluctant to fly. They allowed us to climb up very close to them – within a metre or two – and just sat there looking at us with mild curiosity or scolding us just a bit, especially when their parents became highly agitated.

I always feel a special kinship standing so close to a wild creature that shows no fear of me. The night before, we had had a similar encounter with the local brood of young gyrfalcons. I had actually been able to sit down on a rock only two metres away from a handsome, light-coloured tiercel who had been on the wing perhaps a week at most. There was a light drizzle and a cold northwest wind, and he was in no mood to be disturbed by the likes of me. We sat looking into each other's eyes for a few minutes in the dim light of the Arctic summer night – how wide and trusting those brown falcon eyes can be – and then he roused, pulled one foot up under his belly, fluffed out the feathers under his chin, and proceeded to doze off in the gentle rain, as though I no longer existed. Certainly I was perceived as no threat to his existence. Despite the miserable weather, I felt warm and good sitting in the rain, looking out over the rushing river Laxá beside my feathered companion. . . .

Now these young merlins displayed the same gentle, unsuspicious tolerance of my close presence. Had I appeared in the form of a fox or a raven, they would have reacted immediately with instinctive alarm and flight, but I apparently looked more like one of the innocuous sheep grazing near by.

Suddenly my reverie was interrupted by a rude commotion on the hill. I looked up to see Olaf running about wildly, waving his arms and yelling, chasing after one of the young merlins and throwing his hat at the poor bird. For an instant I thought he had gone berserk like one of his Viking ancestors, and rage began to well up in my throat, so at variance were his actions to my quiet communion with the friendly merlins. But just as quickly I realized what he was up to.

He was deliberately scaring the young merlin to teach him to fear man! We do the same thing with the captive produced peregrines that we release in the USA – sometimes shooting off guns near them at a certain stage in their development or otherwise making loud noises and frightening movements, so that they learn to keep a safe distance from men. Young falcons survive better that way, for not everyone enjoys being close to a falcon. Too many people still prefer to see them dead.

Standing on that remote hillside watching Olaf going through his antics to teach the young merlins their first fears of man, I was struck by the shame of it all. Why should some of us have to go about the world frightening young falcons so that they will be safe from others of us? Would the world not be a better place if all men could learn to appreciate the existence of falcons and to find joy in their presence on earth, as a few men always have? Instead of teaching falcons to be afraid of men, we should teach men to cherish the opportunity to be close to falcons – to see them eye to eye as creatures equally as deserving of some of earth's space as we humans.

I believe there is currently a strong trend toward such acceptance by many people. This tolerant attitude should produce a happy result, for when they are left alone many species of falcons readily adjust to the close presence of humans. American and Eurasian kestrels, and some other species, accept a variety of man-made structures as their eyries and often nest in cities and towns or around farmsteads in the country. They also take to nest-boxes eagerly and in many other ways actually benefit by association with humans.

Even the haughty peregrine and the elusive gyrfalcon can and will become commensal with man when they are given the chance to do so. Peregrines have a long history of nesting on buildings and other structures in Europe and Asia – even in America – and can live out their lives in the constant presence of human activities when left unmolested. In 1972 I had the good fortune to visit 20 peregrine eyries in Spain through the courtesy of the late Felix Rodriguez de la Fuente. Not one of these successfully producing nests was more than a few hundred metres away from some centre of human activity – a farm, roadway, town, village, or airport. It must be the same over most of Europe. In Scotland along the river Spey, Doug Weir has a lovely old home, where I once spent a pleasant night, from which one can look up to a peregrine eyrie on a crag just a few hundred metres distant. Every man should be so fortunate!

Nor is the peregrine singular in this respect among the large falcons. In India laggars frequently nest in villages, and in Iceland many gyrfalcons have eyries near farmsteads. Most of the farmers know about their falcons and keep a close watch on them, for foreigners often come to Iceland to steal eggs or young. Despite the suburbanization of the Antelope Valley in the Mojave Desert of southern California, there are still prairie falcons nesting in some of the buttes which I knew as a lad in the 1940s, in some instances now literally in people's backyards.

Mankind dominates the earth. There is no such thing as a completely unmarred, natural environment left anywhere. Despite our best efforts to preserve some fragments of "natural ecosystems" for the benefit of future generations of men, animals, and plants, man-induced alterations and degradation of habitats will continue as long as the human population remains at its present level or becomes larger. Increasingly in the future, the survival of species will depend on the extent to which they can make adjustments to radically changed environments and to existence in close proximity to man. A few species have already been very successful at making such adjustments – mostly pests such as cockroaches, houseflies, Norway rats, house mice, starlings, and house sparrows – but there is no reason why man cannot deliberately create places – new niches – for other species that he wants to preserve in the out-of-doors. Some species will be able to make such adjustments on their own, as long as man is willing to accept their close presence in the world which he has overpopulated. Still others will be able to do so with a little intelligent and sympathetic help from men – by creating some special situations and new opportunities to allow species to fit into the modified ecosystems of earth. The conservation ethic compels thinking men to do what they can to save animal species, but we must also face the fact that many forms of life are doomed by man's presence on earth.

Fortunately for those who admire and enjoy falcons, many species can adapt satisfactorily to altered environments and to the close presence of man. It only requires a desire on man's part to let the falcons live out their lives unmolested – to see that they have secure nesting haunts and a sufficient supply of uncontaminated food to raise their young and replenish their numbers annually. Respect and tolerance from human beings are the keys to the future survival of falcons and all wildlife. Such attitudes cannot be forced upon the majority of men by the authoritarian dictates of the few, however right the latter may be. They must come from within, from a true, inner appreciation by all men that other forms of life are infinitely interesting and wonderous expressions of the earth's prodigious creation and that the dimensions of our human experience are lessened each time a species becomes extinct.

I shall consider this book to have served some purpose if it provides the stimulus for others to seek the satisfactions in contemplating and learning about the lives of falcons that I have found in more than forty years of captivation by this superlative group of raptors, which, more than any other, combines form and function in a perfection that can hold men in spellbound wonder.

Part

I

Biology of Falcons

Table 1

THE SPECIES OF FALCONS

Common Name	Latin Name	Relative Size★	General Breeding Distribution	Main Habitat
1. Peregrine Falcon	*F. peregrinus*	Large	Worldwide	Open lands; sea-coasts
2. Barbary Falcon	*F. pelegrinoides*	Medium-Large	N. Africa; Middle East	Desert; arid scrub
3. Pallid Falcon	*F. kreyenborgi*	Large	S. South America	Cold desert and pampas
4. Gyrfalcon	*F. rusticolus*	Large	Holarctic	Tundra; forest-tundra
5. Saker	*F. cherrug*	Large	Eurasia	Steppe; forest-steppe
6. Lanner	*F. biarmicus*	Large	S. Europe; Africa	Desert; dry savannah
7. Laggar	*F. jugger*	Large	India	Arid scrub; open forest
8. Prairie Falcon	*F. mexicanus*	Large	North America	Desert; dry prairie
9. Black Falcon	*F. subniger*	Large	Australia	Dry, open woods
10. Grey Falcon	*F. hypoleucos*	Medium	Australia	Dry, open woods
11. Orange-breasted Falcon	*F. deiroleucus*	Medium	Neotropics	Tropical forest
12. Bat Falcon	*F. rufigularis*	Small	Neotropics	Tropical forest
13. Aplomado Falcon	*F. femoralis*	Medium	Mexico; S. America	Tropical and desert scrub
14. New Zealand Falcon	*F. novaeseelandiae*	Medium	New Zealand	Grassland and scrub
15. Merlin	*F. columbarius*	Small	Holarctic	Open lands; forest edge
16. Red-headed Falcon	*F. chicquera*	Small	India; Africa	Savannahs; open woods
17. Teita Falcon	*F. fasciinucha*	Small-Medium	Eastern Africa	Wooded gorges; mountains
18. Hobby	*F. subbuteo*	Small	Eurasia; N. Africa	Open woods; forest edge
19. African Hobby	*F. cuvieri*	Small	Africa	Savannah-forest edge
20. Oriental Hobby	*F. severus*	Small	India; S. E. Asia	Open forest
21. Australian Hobby	*F. longipennis*	Small-Medium	Australia	Open forest
22. Eleonora's Falcon	*F. eleonorae*	Medium	Mediterranean	Islands and sea-coast
23. Sooty Falcon	*F. concolor*	Medium	N. Africa; Arabia	Desert and islands
24. W. Red-footed Falcon	*F. vespertinus*	Small	Eurasia	Open woods; forest-steppe
25. E. Red-footed Falcon	*F. amurensis*	Small	Asia	Open woods; forest edge
26. Common Kestrel	*F. tinnunculus*	Small	Eurasia; Africa	Open lands; forest edge
27. Moluccan Kestrel	*F. moluccensis*	Small	East Indies	Open lands; forest edge
28. Australian Kestrel	*F. cenchroides*	Small	Australia; New Guinea	Open woods; parkland
29. American Kestrel	*F. sparverius*	Small	New World	Open lands; scattered woods
30. Madagascar Kestrel	*F. newtoni*	Small	Madagascar; Aldabra	Open lands; forest edge
31. Mauritius Kestrel	*F. punctatus*	Small	Mauritius	Native forests
32. Seychelles Kestrel	*F. araea*	Small	Seychelles	Clearings in forest; open palms
33. Lesser Kestrel	*F. naumanni*	Small	Eurasia; N. Africa	Steppe; forest-steppe
34. Fox Kestrel	*F. alopex*	Medium	Africa	Dry savannah; semi-desert scrub
35. Greater Kestrel	*F. rupicoloides*	Small-Medium	Africa	Dry grasslands and scrub
36. Grey Kestrel	*F. ardosiaceus*	Small-Medium	Africa	Savannah; tropical forest edge
37. Dickinson's Kestrel	*F. dickinsoni*	Small-Medium	Africa	Savannah; tropical forest edge
38. Barred Kestrel	*F. zoniventris*	Small	Madagascar	Native tropical forest
39. Brown Falcon	*F. berigora*	Medium-Large	Australia; New Guinea	Open lands; sparse woods, etc.

★Small – under 250 g; medium – 250 to 500 g; large – over 500 g. (In some species the male falls in one size range, the female in another.)

Introduction

ALCONS ARE SMALL to medium-sized, compact, long-winged, diurnal birds of prey, all of which are included in a single genus, *Falco*. They range in size and variety from the brightly coloured, buoyant, wind-hovering kestrels, some weighing less than 100 grams ($3\frac{1}{2}$ oz), to the sombre, grouse-hungry, arctic gyrfalcons, some of which weigh more than 2,000 grams ($4\frac{1}{2}$ lbs). There are some 25 to 40 species, depending on just how one decides to divide them, but they are all rather closely related populations, differing mainly in body size, proportions, and coloration. Thirty-nine different forms are considered in this book (see Table 1).

Falcons are powerful fliers with well developed pectoral muscles, and they include some of the swiftest and most spectacular fliers among birds. For this reason falcons have been much admired for the precision and sheer audacity of their aerobatics, and even the redoubtable Leslie Brown (1970) averred that "nothing equals the sight of a large falcon in full stoop". That is quite a testimony from a man whose first love was eagles!

Indeed, some of the aerial manoeuvres of falcons in hunting and courtship flights are so spectacular that words fail to convey their impact on the observer, and they must be seen to be appreciated. Perhaps J. A. Hagar's description (in Bent 1938) of a courting peregrine at an old eyrie in Massachusetts comes closest to conveying an adequate verbal impression. "The culmination of these flight displays depends much on the weather, but eventually the patient watcher will see an exhibition of flying that is literally breath-taking . . . again and again the tiercel started well to leeward and came along the cliff against the wind, diving, plunging, saw-toothing, rolling over and over, darting hither and yon like an autumn leaf until finally he would swoop up into the full current of air and be borne off on the gale to do it all over again . . . Nosing over suddenly, he flicked his wings rapidly 15 or 20 times and fell like a thunderbolt. Wings half closed now, he shot down past the north end of the cliff, described three successive vertical loop-the-loops across its face, turning completely upside down at the top of each loop, and roared out over our heads with the wind rushing through his wings like ripping canvas. Against the background of the cliff his terrific speed was much more apparent than it would have been in the open sky. The sheer excitement of watching such a performance was tremendous; we felt a strong impulse to stand and cheer."

Hagar's description tells us why falcon-watching has been such a popular pastime down through the centuries, and why so many naturalists have claimed the peregrine or some other falcon as his or her favourite bird. It also, I believe, tells us why the sport of falconry has had such an avid following for more than three thousand years and why it has experienced such a resurgence of interest recently, for as I shall argue later falconry is really a specialized form of bird-watching and not the "blood sport" that some have tried to denigrate it.

Falcons make their living by catching and killing other animals in the air, on the ground, and occasionally in the water. Most of their special features are adaptations related to their predatory mode of existence, which depends to a greater extent than for any other group of raptors on far-ranging aerial search and aerial pursuit of prey.

Special Characters of the Genus *Falco*

How does one tell a falcon from any other bird of prey? Those who are experts at identifying raptors in the field develop a certain "feel" for characteristic shapes, attitudes, and mannerisms that enable them to recognize a falcon from any other bird with high accuracy even at great distances, and yet when the systematist tries to set down a list of the diagnostic traits by which species of the genus *Falco* can be separated from all other species of raptors, he is unable to find any single trait, or set of related traits, that is absolutely unique to falcons. What is unique is a functionally integrated suite of characteristics which together make up what I call the "falcon *gestalt*" and which the field observer has trained his eye to perceive as a whole; yet any given trait may be shared with related species in one or more other genera.

Figure 1
Tomial teeth

Falcons share some similarities with other familiar groups of raptors such as eagles, buzzards, kites, short-winged hawks, harriers, and other "accipitriform" taxa. For example, they have typical raptorial feet with a hallux acting in opposition to three forward toes, all with a powerful grasping ability and armed with sharp, curved talons; they have hooked bills with a strong bite; fleshy ceres at the base of the upper beak; and remarkable powers of vision with lateral and binocular foveae in the retina of each eye. They are also similar in having a furcula (wishbone) that is not fused to the sternum, the same pattern of moulting the secondary feathers on the wing, the same taxa of feather lice, and "reversed" sexual size dimorphism, females being larger than males.

Falcons differ, however, in some fundamental, phylogenetic ways from the accipitriform raptors. For instance, while falcons have raptorial feet highly adapted to grasping prey, they lack the powerful, spasmodic clutching mechanism of accipitriform birds of prey and do not often kill their quarry by penetration with their talons. Instead, their rather short beaks and jaw muscles are specially modified to deliver a powerful bite, by which falcons sever or disarticulate the cervical vertebrae of tetrapod prey. Special structures associated with this biting mechanism are the so-called "tomial teeth" on the cutting edge of the upper bill and the corresponding "notches" on the lower bill, features that have been independently evolved in the shrikes, a group of passerine predators that also kill vertebrates by biting into their necks. (Figure 1.)

The nostrils (nares), which in falcons are a small circular to oval apertures in the cere, each possess a prominent, central bony tubercle, which is an extension of the septum that produces a whirled, conch-like passage in the anterior nasal cavity. It has been said to function as a baffle to slow down the stream of air through the nasal passages as an aid to proper respiration when a falcon is flying at great speed in a stoop (see Grossman and Hamlet 1964, Peterson 1948). There is no experimental evidence for such a function, and it seems unlikely in view of the fact that eagles and other raptors, which have large nares lacking such tubercles, also stoop vertically at high speeds, while the slow, largely cursorial savannah hawk (*Heterospizias meridionalis*) of South America has independently evolved a very similar structure in its nares. Perhaps the tubercle functions in some as yet undetermined way in olfaction, or an even more intriguing possibility is that it could function to indicate air speed by sensing changes in pressure or temperature produced by differing external air-stream velocities, in much the same way that Mangold (1946) suggested for the valve-like pockets in the nasal chambers of fulmars, shearwaters and albatrosses. Such a sensory system would doubtless be highly adaptive for a predator that depends so much on speed for success in capturing prey.

Falcons have long, pointed, distinctively proportioned wings with moderately stiff to very stiff quills. There are 10 functional primaries, no more than the outer two with emarginated tips, and 11 to 15 secondaries (Friedmann 1950). The longest primaries exceed the distal secondaries by much more than one-third and sometimes by more than one-half their total length. Primary number 9 (second from the outside) is usually longest, but sometimes P8 is; P8 is always longer than P7, while P10 is variable, sometimes longer than P8 (*peregrinus*), often longer than P7, and always longer than P6 except in two species (*novaeseelandiae* and *punctatus*, which have short, relatively rounded wings for falcons). These are all features related to fast flight. (See Figure 3.)

The pectoral region shows some modifications associated with the special requirements for high speed flight too. For example, the coracoids overlap one another where they articulate with the sternum (the precise functional significance is unknown). The sternum has a deep keel, which projects well forward, as in doves and pigeons, another fast-flying group of birds, and which accommodates large, powerful flight muscles. Exact quantitative measurements of the pectoral muscles mass are few (see Hartman 1961), but it is likely that the flight muscles range from 12 to 20 per cent, or more, of total body weight, depending on the species. Weaker flying species such as kestrels have relatively smaller pectoral muscles than rapid powerful fliers such as peregrines.

The axial skeleton has several distinctive features. Falcons have rather short necks with only 15 cervical vertebrae, and the body is otherwise strong and rigid owing to fusion of the thoracic vertebrae (sometimes also the posterior-most cervical). The pygostyle (tail bone) has a pair of accessory bones attached to its base, and these afford a greater surface area for the insertion of powerful tail depressor muscles (Richardson 1972). They apparently aid in transmitting and concentrating the force of several depressor and abductor muscles of the tail to the pygostyle and its closely associated series of rectrices (tail feathers). Such features, again, have obvious adaptive advantages for birds that must brake, shift, and manoeuvre quickly in fast flight when pressures on the tail are extreme.

The tail itself consists of six pairs of rather short to moderately long rectrices, ranging from less than 50 per cent to more than 70 per cent of the standard wing measurement, depending on the species. The width is relatively narrow and tapers toward the end owing to a pronounced inward curvature in the shafts of the outer pair of rectrices. The tip is usually slightly rounded, the outer pair of rectrices being shorter than the inner pairs, but the shape varies from distinctly graduated in some species (e.g. *berigora*) to squarish, to slightly emarginate in a few forms (e.g. *severus*). The faster flying falcons have squarish to emarginate tails, while the slower species have more rounded to graduated tails.

Falcons also differ from accipitriform raptors in the way their feather tracts are arranged over the surface of their bodies (pterylosis). For details interested readers can consult Compton (1938) or Friedmann (1950), but one important consequence of this difference is that brooding falcons have two incubation patches by which the eggs are heated, one on either side of their breasts in the apteria between the axillar and sternal regions of the ventral feather tracts (Willoughby and Cade 1964), whereas accipitriform raptors have one large, central patch. The reason is that in falcons the sternal and abdominal regions of the ventral tract lie close to the mid-line, and there is little space in the median ventral apterium for the development of a brood patch, but in accipitriform raptors the main trunks of the sternal and abdominal regions are in lateral positions, producing a very wide mid-ventral apterium. In falcons the incubation patches form in the apteria on either side of the breast by loss of down and the characteristic increase in vascularization and thickening of the skin which are seasonally mediated in birds by prolactin and the steroid sex hormones (Drent 1975). Both male and female falcons have patches, but the male develops his later in the breeding cycle than the female, and his are not as large as hers.

Falcons have a distinctive pattern of moulting the remiges, as the German ornithologist Vesta Stresemann (1958) first noted. The primaries are moulted in both ascendant (toward the outermost) the descendant (toward the innermost) directions beginning with P4. The same applies to the secondaries, starting with S5. The tail moult begins with the central pair of rectrices (deck feathers) and progresses outward, except that the outer pair R6 falls out before R5, which is typically the last pair to drop. Depending on the species and sometimes on the individual, R6 drops at different positions in the sequence from R1 to R5, the sequence varying from R1-6-2-3-4-5 to R1-2-3-4-6-5.

Falcons produce eggshells with a distinctive chemical composition, convergently similar to that of the osprey (Pandionidae), and the outer layers of the shell lack vacuoles (Tyler 1966). When held up to the light, falcon eggs produce a characteristic reddish-yellow translucence, not seen in the eggs of other diurnal raptors.

Falcons have small but functional nasal salt-excreting glands, which can secrete a sodium chloride solution several times more concentrated than that in their blood (Cade and Greenwald 1966). The nasal glands of falcons are ovoid in shape and lie partly in the orbital sinus and partly in the orbit itself, a location described by the German anatomist, Technau (1936), as position IIa, preorbital-interorbital, features again differing from all described examples of accipitriform raptors, whose glands are flat and lie entirely within the orbit.

Since falcons, like most other birds, have a limited ability to excrete sodium and chloride ions in their urine, the nasal gland functions to regulate these electrolytes in the blood and tissue fluids by reducing excessive concentrations resulting from ingested salts in food or from evaporative loss of ion-free water during thermoregulation in hot weather. Falcons characteristically sneeze out their nasal gland secretion in a fine mist rather than drooling from their nares and shaking their heads the way accipitriform raptors do; however, when the parents are feeding their downy young, they do drool out a clear, salty-tasting fluid that collects in droplets at the tip of the beak and falls on to the bites of flesh being fed to the young. It has yet to be determined whether this fluid is nasal gland secretion, and whether it has an importance in the nutritional requirements of the young.

The traits so far described do not exhaust the list of technical features that taxonomists use to define falcons, but they include the more important and interesting ones. For further details see Friedmann (1950) or Cramp and Simmons (1980).

13

Classification

The true falcons (genus *Falco*) share many of their fundamental characters with nine species of New World caracaras, scavenging forms in the subfamily Polyborinae (4 genera); the snake-eating Neotropical laughing falcon (*Herpetotheres cachinnans*), subfamily Herpetotherinae; four species of accipiter-like Neotropical forest-falcons (*Micrastur* spp) in the subfamily Micrasturinae; and nine species of pygmy falcons or falconets in the subfamily Polihieracinae (3 to 4 genera). The homologous similarities among these genera and species – and their many differences from other groups of diurnal birds of prey – have long been recognized. For many years ornithologists have represented these similarities and differences among the diurnal birds of prey in formal classification by placing all the falcon-like genera into one family, the Falconidae, within an order, Falconiformes, which includes all the other families of diurnal raptors, such as the true hawks, buzzards, eagles, kites, harriers and so forth (family Accipitridae), the osprey (Pandionidae), secretary bird (Saggitariidae), and New World condors (Cathartidae). Often the degree of difference between members of the Falconidae and members of the other families has been further emphasized by placing the Falconidae in a separate suborder, Falcones. This system of classification, which is supposed to reflect actual phylogeny, has not gone unchallenged, and as long ago as 1953 Malcolm Jollie questioned whether the Falconiformes represents a monophyletic order. In particular, there are questions about the phylogenetic relationships of the condors, the secretary bird, and the falcons.

As knowledge about the many basic differences between members of the Falconidae and other diurnal raptors has increased, avian taxonomists have begun to think of the falcons and their allied genera (family Falconidae) as constituting a separate order, the Falconiformes, parallel in evolutionary development to the accipitrine taxa which are consequently placed in a separate order, Accipitriformes (see, for example, the recent treatment in Cramp and Simmons 1980). This means that the similarities between members of the two orders are superficial and convergent. Such an arrangement of these raptorial taxa is further supported by some evidence suggesting that the falcons are more closely related to owls (Strigiformes) than to other diurnal birds of prey, based on the close similarities of their jaw musculature and details of its innervation by the trigeminus nerve (Starck 1959) and on egg-white proteins (Sibley and Ahlquist 1972). Whether this "relationship" between the falcons and the owls should be represented in classification remains an open question. Again, the similarities could be merely convergent. At the other extreme Cracraft (1981) places all the raptorial birds, including owls, into one order and reduces the falcons to a subfamily under Accipitridae!

There is no doubt, however, that all the species of true falcons are more closely related to each other than any is to other falconiform species, although the gap separating them from the pygmy falcons and falconets is not great. The evolutionary origin and history of the genus *Falco* cannot be worked out in much detail owing to a poor fossil record. There is no fossil that can be assigned with certainty to the genus *Falco* earlier than the Pleistocene, although the name *Falco* has been given to some bones of earlier date; however, it seems reasonable to suppose that species with the characteristics of the genus existed by the Miocene some 20 million years ago, and primitive species with the family or ordinal characters much have existed still earlier. There is no way at present to know which of the existing genera within the Falconidae are oldest or retain the most primitive characteristics, but again it is logical to think that forest-adapted species, or possibly scavenging forms, preceeded the true falcons, which are primarily adapted to open landscapes, habitats which were not abundantly represented on earth before the late Miocene.

If this scenario is correct, then South America may well have been the region where the first falconid raptors originated, and the existing caracaras, forest-falcons and laughing falcon could be descendants still possessing characteristics of the ancestral forms. Nick Fox (Ph.D. dissertation) has suggested that the evolutionary history of the Falconidae encompassed two waves of adaptive radiation. First, species similar to the caracaras, forest-falcons, laughing falcon, and some unknown ancestor of the falconets and falcons spread through most of the tropical regions but failed to reach Australia or at least failed to survive there to the present. A second radiation of falcons and falconets occurred as climatic and ecological changes reduced the extent of tropical forests and greatly expanded grasslands and parklands – changes which would have worked to the disadvantage of the highly forest-adapted falconids and which would have favoured those with pre-adaptations for life in open habitats. In this view, the falconets and a few later species of falcons became secondarily adapted to the remaining tropical forest habitats, after most of the original falconid populations inhabiting forests had become extinct, a few forms only surviving to this day in the Neotropics.

14

Darlington's (1957) studies of zoogeography led him to think that the dispersion and diversification of species in the genus *Falco* were rapid and multiple, once the combination of characters adapting these birds to aerial hunting in open habitats had been perfected by natural selection. The late Miocene or early Pliocene would seem to have been about the right time, just when things were starting to go well for another group of open-country inhabitants, the early hominids. It is musing and somehow prophetic to think that falcons and men both derive from the same evolutionary stimulus – the creation of open grasslands and savannahs with new and unexploited opportunities for both winged and bipedal hunters.

As a matter of fact, it is tempting to point to Africa as the geographic location for the origin of falcons, as well as for men. More species of *Falco* occur there today than on any other land mass, indicating the presence of many favourable ecological conditions for falcons, and its continental position in the Miocene-Pliocene period was central and still close enough to the other fragments of Gondwanaland and of Laurasia to make it a likely source of dispersal to the other continents and some islands.

Thus, it appears that the association between men and falcons is deep-rooted indeed. What did "Lucy" and her kin (*Australopithecus afarensis*) experience when they looked up into the azure sky over the Afar Plains and saw hunting falcons? Did they pirate prey away from their feathered competitors, which had evolved the ability to kill animals larger than they could carry away? How many generations of men stole from wild falcons before some enterprising human hunter got the idea of training a falcon to co-operate in the hunt?

What were the first true falcons like? Again, we can only speculate, but most students of the group, from Suschkin's (1905) early attempt to construct a phylogenetic tree to Brown and Amadon's (1968) monographic treatment, have agreed that the present-day kestrels are closest in form and habits to the ancestral falcons, while the peregrine and other large falcons represent more recently derived forms. If this is the case, then the ancestral populations were probably made up of small to medium-sized falcons with marked sexual differences in plumage but little or no sexual size dimorphism (Cade 1960). They were generalized predators taking prey from the ground as well as in the air and fed on a wide variety of insects, as well as on small vertebrates, including reptiles, birds, and mammals. The common kestrel (*tinnunculus*) may be a fair approximation of what these early falcons were like.

From these ancestral falcons several basic adaptive subtypes evolved during the Pliocene, and they in turn speciated often enough during the Pleistocene so that a number of species groups or subgenera can be recognized among the extant species. For easy reference I use subgeneric names for these groups. Their hypothesized relationships are shown in the following Figure.

Figure 2
GROUPS AND RELATIONSHIPS

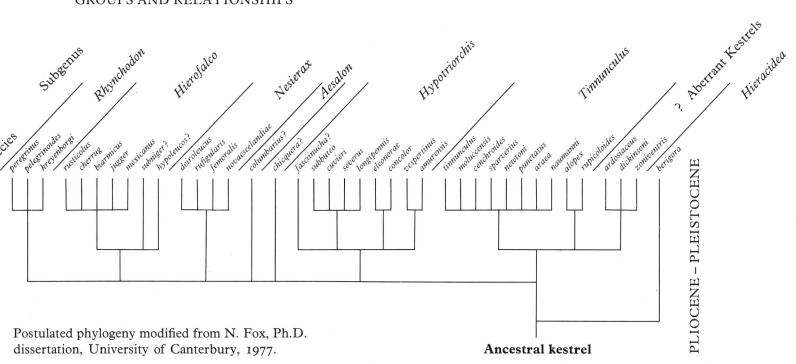

Postulated phylogeny modified from N. Fox, Ph.D.
dissertation, University of Canterbury, 1977.

Ancestral kestrel

PLIOCENE – PLEISTOCENE

The Australian brown falcon (*berigora*) is set apart from all other falcons in a subgenus of its own, *Hieracidea*, owing to its aberrant, buteonine (buzzard-like) characteristics. It is a generalized predator, which shows some similarities to kestrels in the scalation of its feet and in the proportions of its wing elements. It probably branched off early in the evolution of the genus from the basal "kestrel" stock and was probably the first falcon to establish itself in Australia, where it became widespread and abundant but owing to its many unfalcon-like characteristics posed no serious competitive block to the later colonization of Australia by more specialized species (eventually five additional ones).

Ten species of kestrels are grouped in the subgenus *Tinnunculus* and presumably are derived more or less directly from the ancestral "kestrel" lineage. They are rather long-winged (except *punctatus*), but with the manus relatively shorter than forearm, and long-tailed falcons (tail 60 per cent or more of wing length), which have the habit of hunting more or less frequently by hovering in the air and watching for ground-dwelling prey. Most are highly sexually dimorphic in plumage but show little difference in size between males and females. Four species (*tinnunculus*, *sparverius*, *moluccensis* and *cenchroides*) are disjunct allopatric equivalents which may constitute one "superspecies"; three (*newtoni*, *araea* and *punctatus*) are endemic to islands in the Indian Ocean and may belong to the same superspecies as the first four; two (*alopex* and *rupicoloides*) are African; and one (*naumanni*) is a socially aberrant species with highly developed colonial nesting and roosting habits.

A group of three "aberrant kestrels" (*ardosiaceus*, *dickinsoni*, both African, and *zoniventris* of Madagascar) are less clearly and certainly more distantly related to the *Tinnunculus* group. They may or may not be closely related themselves, but there has been a tendency to ally them on the basis of their similarities in plumage, which emphasizes grey.

Six species of hobbies form a rather distinctive group, *Hypotriorchis*, with the red-footed falcons (*vespertinus* and *amurensis*) probably being closely related also, and possibly the Teita falcon (*fasciinucha*). The latter has usually been allied with the peregrines because of its bird-eating propensities and its rather long toes, but it seems to be proportioned and coloured more like a hobby, and its size falls in the range with hobbies. Four species (*subbuteo*, *cuvieri*, *severus* and *longipennis*) are disjunct allopatric equivalents, which may comprise a superspecies, and two other essentially maritime and insular species (*eleonorae* and *concolor*) are also close counterparts with unusual trophic specializations and social behaviour. The hobbies have the longest and narrowest wings and the shortest tails of all the falcons, although the surprisingly short manus of *concolor*, as described by Suschkin (1905), needs further study. Hobbies are highly aerial hunters, catching flying insects, birds, and bats and often feeding on the wing.

The Holarctic merlin (*columbarius*) is usually placed in a subgenus of its own, *Aesalon*. The red-headed falcon (*chicquera*) is sometimes included, but I agree with Brown (1970) that there is no compelling reason for doing so. The exact affinities of neither species can be cogently argued on the basis of existing information.

The relationship of the four species grouped in the subgenus *Nesierax*, though not at first obvious, was first proposed by Boris Stegmann (1933) and has been ably argued most recently by Nick Fox (Ph.D. dissertation). The species are rather different ecologically and in their morphological adaptations for catching prey, ranging from the big-footed, peregrine-like orange-breasted falcon (*deiroleucus*), to the hobby-like bat falcon (*rufigularis*), to the accipitrine aplomado falcon (*femoralis*) – all Neotropical – and the New Zealand falcon (*novaeseelandiae*), most accipitrine of all. Nevertheless, there are some peculiar morphological traits shared in common. They all have laterally compressed beaks with a more (*deiroleucus*) or less (*femoralis*) well developed keel on the upper bill; they possess some basic similarities in colours and pattern of plumage, including the fact that they alone among falcons have tails with a dark greyish to black ground colour interrupted by *narrow, white bars*. They also apparently share some peculiar behaviours. The young of at least three (data for *femoralis* is not recorded) eject their excreta in a forceful lateral trajectory like the accipiter hawks do, rather than voiding in the more typical, relaxed falcon manner, in which the mutes drop vertically. The same three also sunbathe with a full spread-wing and spread-tail posture with back to the sun. I believe no other falcon is known to sunbathe in this manner. Peregrines, gyrfalcons, merlins and American kestrels that I have watched sunbathe by half-spreading their tails and by drooping the wings slightly with the primaries separated, but I have never seen any of them spread their wings fully in a perched position while sunning, though I have seen some of them do so in a prone position on the ground.

Hierofalco is the subgenus that includes the "great falcons" or the "desert falcons", species that appear to be recently evolved to exploit dry environments and arctic tundras of the late Pleistocene. Five species (*rusticolus*, *cherrug*, *jugger*, *biarmicus* and *mexicanus*) are disjunct allopatric equivalents

16

that comprise a well recognized superspecies. Two Australian species (*subniger* and *hypoleucos*) are less certainly related to this group, although the plumage of *subniger* is very similar to the rather unusual, dark immature plumage of *jugger*. The grey falcon has a decidedly short tail to be included in *Hierofalco*, which otherwise consists of rather long-tailed species with broad-based wings. These falcons include the largest species in the genus, and they are generally adapted to hunting rather large reptiles (*Uromastix* lizards and chuckwallas), birds (grouse and waterfowl), and mammals (ground squirrels and hares) on the ground or in the air just above the ground. Much of their hunting is done by a fast, direct, ground-hugging approach combined with a surprise attack before the quarry can react with an appropriate escape tactic.

The peregrine and the closely related Barbary (*pelegrinoides*) and pallid (*kreyenborgi*) falcons – which may only be forms of *peregrinus* – make up the subgenus *Rhynchodon*. They are largish falcons with long wings (long manus), and medium length tails, with large, over-sized, grasping feet. They are supremely adapted to catching other birds in the air. Peregrines are probably about equally related to hobbies and *Nesierax* falcons on the one side and to the great falcons on the other.

Distribution and Migration

The genus *Falco* is virtually cosmopolitan, as one or more species can be found breeding on all continents, except Antarctica, and on many oceanic islands as well – as far out in the Pacific as the Fijis (*peregrinus*) and New Zealand (*novaeseelandiae*), and as far out in the Atlantic as the Cape Verde Islands (*tinnunculus*) and the Falklands (*peregrinus*). Falcons breed at least from 82°N in Greenland (*rusticolus*) to 55°S on islands in Tierra del Fuego (*peregrinus* and *sparverius*), but the numbers of individuals and the diversity of species are greatest in north temperate, subtropical, and tropical latitudes, especially where grasslands or other open habitats are interspersed with sparse woodlands or small patches of forest. Migrants and vagrants can be expected to occur anywhere in the world from time to time.

Many falcons have great dispersive abilities, and 13 species have breeding distributions on two or more continents. The peregrine is notable for having a worldwide breeding distribution virtually coextensive with the distribution of the entire genus, but two other species (*rusticolus* and *columbarius*) have large, circumpolar, Holarctic ranges, while the American kestrel (*sparverius*) occurs throughout most of the Western Hemisphere, and the common kestrel (*tinnunculus*) has a vast range over Eurasia and Africa. Twenty species have breeding ranges restricted to a single continent, and six species are endemic to islands.

Among the classical zoogeographic regions which A. R. Wallace defined in the late nineteenth century, the great Palearctic Region of Eurasia and northern Africa has the largest number of breeding species, 13, while the smaller Nearctic Region has only seven. Three are shared in common between these two regions; only one (*mexicanus*) is restricted to the Nearctic, and it is an allopatric, ecological equivalent of the Palearctic *cherrug* in the same superspecies. The Palearctic, by contrast, has seven (eight if *concolor* is counted) breeding species restricted to it, and it has obviously been one of the main regions for the proliferation of species and for their dispersal to other regions, especially to the Nearctic, Oriental and Australian regions, having probably supplied them with members of the *Tinnunculus*, *Hypotriorchis*, *Hierofalco* and *Rhynchodon* subgenera.

It is puzzling to note, however, that no member of the hobby group has become established in the New World (unless *femoralis* and *rufigularis* are true hobbies), nor does the Western Hemisphere have any colonial nesting species comparable to *vespertinus*, *naumanni* or *eleonorae*. Walter (1979) has reasonably explained why the New World has no falcon like Eleonora's – the necessary environmental conditions for such a niche simply do not exist – but it is more difficult to understand why the North American prairies could not support a colonial nesting kestrel or why Nearctic woodlands are unsuited to the hobby. Perhaps these forms simply have never dispersed to North America in sufficient numbers or under the right circumstances to become established.

The Ethiopian Region of Africa (excluding Madagascar) provides habitats for 18 species of falcons; 11 are resident breeding species, and seven are migrants from the Palearctic. Six of the breeding species are restricted to the Ethiopian Region, four are shared with the Palearctic, and one (*chicquera*) with the Oriental. Various kinds of small to medium-sized falcons called "kestrels" reach high species diversity (5 species) in the African savannahs and arid grasslands between 20°N and 30°S, and two "hobbies" also occur in the ecotones between grasslands and forests. Despite the fact that all of these species have overlapping food habits (principal items being flying insects,

17

locusts, small birds and small mammals), this same general region is also host to four migrant species with similar feeding habits (*naumanni, vespertinus, amurensis* and *subbuteo*) and to a migratory segment of the Palearctic population of *tinnunculus*. In addition, *concolor* and *eleonorae* occur coastally. Thus, in the period from November to April eight resident breeding species of falcons in the size range from 150 to 300 g (5–10½ oz) are joined by seven migratory species in the same size range. In addition, three large species also occur (*peregrinus, cherrug* and *biarmicus*). No other region in the world has such a diversity of falcons, a situation no doubt made possible by the numerous open to semi-open habitat formations and by superabundant prey populations of insects, small birds and small mammals. It seems likely that these favourable conditions have existed in Africa at least since the beginning of the Pliocene – with some variations owing to climatic fluctuations (Moreau 1966); and it is for this reason that Africa is a likely region for the origin of the first members of the genus *Falco*.

The Oriental Region has only five breeding species of *Falco* and three migrant species from the Palearctic. Two of the five breeders (*severus* and *jugger*) are restricted to the region, and the breeding peregrine population (the *peregrinator* race) is rather different from other peregrines and could be an incipient species. The region also shares one other breeding species (*tinnunculus*) with the Palearctic and one (*chicquera*) with the Ethiopian. Each of the breeding species is drawn from a different subgeneric lineage (*Tinnunculus, Hypotriorchis, Hierofalco, Rhynchodon,* and *chicquera* of uncertain subgeneric affinity).

The Australian Region has an extremely interesting group of six resident breeding species, all but *peregrinus* being endemic to Australasia. No falcons are known to migrate into the region from beyond its boundaries. The brown falcon (*berigora*), which is not closely related to any other species, probably represents the first falcon to colonize Australia, perhaps from an African source early in the development of the genus. The Australian hobby (*longipennis*) is closely related to the *subbuteo* group and is probably derived from some individuals of the *Hypotriorchis* lineage that dispersed from Asia after Australia reached a position close to Asia in the Pleistocene. The black falcon (*subniger*) may be similarly derived from an Asiatic *Hierofalco* stock, while the Australian kestrel (*cenchroides*) is quite clearly only slightly modified from *tinnunculus* and is doubtfully distinct as a species. The peregrine is probably the most recent species to arrive in Australia. This leaves only the grey falcon (*hypoleucos*) unaccounted for; on present evidence it cannot be related to anything for sure, but it seems unlikely that it could have evolved as a geographic isolate from one of the other falcon populations in Australia, and it may represent a second, perhaps earlier dispersal of *Hierofalco* or *Hypotriorchis* stock into Australia from Asia or Africa.

The Neotropical Region supports six breeding species and three migrant populations from the Nearctic (only one of which is a different species). One of the six breeders (*kreyenborgi*) is doubtfully distinct as a species from *peregrinus*. Three species (*deiroleucus, rufigularis* and *femoralis*) are Neotropical in origin, although the latter two just penetrate the Nearctic at the northern extremities of their ranges (at least historically). They belong to a subgenus, *Nesierax*, which must have differentiated rather early in South America, probably from an African source, and which is otherwise represented only by the geographically isolated New Zealand falcon (*novaeseelandiae*), whose occurrence in those islands remains puzzling.

The western Indian Ocean islands possess a number of endemic species of kestrels: two on Madagascar (*newtoni* and *zoniventris*), also a slightly differentiated population of *newtoni* on Aldabra, one on Mauritius (*punctatus*), and one in the Seychelles (*araea*). The only other distinctive insular form is the Moluccan kestrel (*moluccensis*) in the East Indies.

How many species of falcons can be found nesting in the same locality, say within a radius of 10 km (6 miles)? Obviously this number will be determined in part by the diversity of ecological conditions within the 10 km radius and in part by how many species of falcons have adapted to different niches within the particular biome considered. In arctic tundra only two species are likely (*rusticolus* and *peregrinus* or, locally, *rusticolus* and *columbarius*); but in the taiga there is a possibility for four (*rusticolus* – *peregrinus* – *columbarius* – *tinnunculus* or *sparverius*). In parts of Central Asia where forest, steppes, and montane habitats come together in complex mosaics, as many as six or seven species might occur together (*peregrinus* – *cherrug* – *columbarius* – *subbuteo* – *vespertinus* – *tinnunculus* – *naumanni*), although I am unaware that any such locality has ever been identified. Similarly, despite the species diversity in Africa, owing to the fact that several species are allopatrically distributed there, no more than six or seven species could be found breeding in a circumscribed area (a possible combination in Zimbabwe might be: *peregrinus* – *biarmicus* – *fasciinucha* – *cuvieri* – *chicquera* – *tinnunculus* – *dickinsoni*). In all of North America the maximum possible is only four; the same is true for South America. All six Australian species may occur in the same locality, although again I know of no such actual case. Four species is the maximum for an island, Tasmania (*peregrinus – longipennis – cenchroides – berigora*).

It appears that species packing – the number of species that can occur together in a locality – has definite limits in the genus *Falco* despite considerable worldwide speciation. The limit seems to have been fixed early in the history of the genus by the evolution of several major adaptive subtypes that have speciated into groups now recognized as subgenera or superspecies consisting mostly of allopatric populations. One seldom finds two species of *Rhynchodon*, or *Hierofalco*, or *Hypotriorchis* occurring together in the same habitat, but one often finds single species from five or more of these subgeneric groups co-inhabiting the same area. Exceptionally two species from the same subgenus do occur together (*tinnunculus* and *naumanni*; *deiroleucus* and *rufigularis*), but in such cases very significant ecological and morphological differences have evolved between the daughter species. Apparently the major adaptive variations on the falcon theme occurred early in the history of the genus and partitioned the ecological possibilities for falcons so precisely that it has been difficult for further adaptive radiation to take place, except among isolated allopatric populations which nevertheless remain too similar ecologically to permit much sympatry.

Falcons frequently have breeding ranges that are geographically separate from areas occupied the rest of the year, and several migratory patterns can be discerned among the different species and their geographic populations. Species nesting in subtropical and tropical latitudes are more or less resident the year round within the same range, although some local dispersive movements by particular birds may occur after nesting, while in a few cases regular movements over short distances have been observed. This kind of occupancy applies to 24 of the 39 species: lanner, laggar, black falcon, grey falcon, orange-breasted falcon, bat falcon, aplomado falcon, New Zealand falcon, red-headed falcon, Teita falcon, African hobby, oriental hobby, Australian hobby, Moluccan kestrel, Australian kestrel, Madagascar kestrel, Mauritius kestrel, Seychelles kestrel, fox kestrel, greater kestrel, grey kestrel, Dickinson's kestrel, barred kestrel, and brown falcon. It also applies to some southern populations of species that are migratory in the more northern parts of their breeding ranges: some peregrines, some Barbary falcons, some gyrfalcons (Iceland), some sakers, some common kestrels, some American kestrels, and some lesser kestrels.

Other species are long distance migrants that make regular annual movements to and from the breeding grounds; they all breed in northern latitudes and "winter" to the south. Five species (Eurasian hobby, Eleonora's falcon, sooty falcon, western and eastern red-footed falcons) have breeding ranges widely separated from their non-breeding quarters, and one other (lesser kestrel) is virtually the same. These are trans-equatorial migrants, which spend the non-breeding season in the southern latitudes of Africa, or coastally around Madagascar (Eleonora's and sooty falcons). Other species with populations that perform long migrations have overlapping breeding and wintering distributions: peregrine falcon, Barbary falcon, gyrfalcon, saker, prairie falcon, merlin, common kestrel, and American kestrel. Often, as in the peregrine, those populations that breed farthest north sojourn farthest south, so that the arctic-nesting peregrines are also trans-equatorial migrants in both the Western and Eastern Hemispheres. (See Maps, pages 184–188.)

As with most other birds, the migratory movements and seasonal changes in range of falcons appear to be adaptations related to temporal and spatial changes in food sources (prey populations). In some cases the migratory movements of the falcons are directly tied to movements of their principal prey, for example, gyrfalcons and ptarmigan.

Feeding Adaptations

The basic advantage of the raptorial mode of feeding is that it allows the raptor to obtain relatively large packages of food, so that fewer captures are required to satisfy its daily energy needs than is the case for an insectivore, for example. Counterposing this advantage, however, are the greater difficulty of catching and killing large, active quarry and the necessity to render the large bodies into swallowable bites, both energy- and time-consuming activities. Falcons have evolved their own modifications of beak, feet, alimentary tract, and aerodynamic design in response to selection pressures associated with pursuing, capturing, killing, eating and digesting large, active prey.

The beak, as already noted, is typically raptorial in that the maxilla (upper beak) is strongly decurved and ends in a pointed hook, while the lower mandible is truncated and comes into apposition with the upper beak posterior to the hook. In addition, however, the beak has become shortened and deepened at its base, relative to the condition in many other raptors, and the "tomial teeth" on the maxilla and corresponding notches in the mandible are always well developed in true falcons.

These special modifications plus a set of powerful jaw muscles enable falcons to bite into objects with great force, and they are quite capable of killing birds and mammals larger than themselves by delivering hard bites into the neck and disarticulating the cervical vertebrae. In fact, the tomial teeth may allow falcons to kill prey considerably larger than would be possible, or easy, without them (Cade 1967). It is most impressive to see how effectively a peregrine falcon weighing 800 grams (28 oz) can kill a drake mallard weighing perhaps twice as much. When caught in the hand by a human, falcons fight by biting with their beaks as well as grasping with their feet, whereas an accipitrine raptor never uses its beak in defence but clutches spasmodically and powerfully with its feet and long, knife-like talons instead.

Before they leave the nest, young falcons, without any previous practice or experience with living animals, know how to use their beaks in defence and in killing prey by biting into the neck. Neck-biting is an automatic, neuromuscular co-ordination that is usually triggered whenever the falcon has suitable prey in its feet, whether dead or alive. Parent falcons are, however, able to inhibit this killing-response on special occasions when they deliver living quarry to their fledglings. It would be most interesting to know the neuro-physiological basis for this inhibition, for the response is otherwise so rigid and automatic.

Some falcons have especially large beaks for their size, and this heavy beak may be an adaptation related to capturing and killing difficult quarry, such as parrots in the case of Australian peregrines and the orange-breasted falcon. Falcons that are primarily insectivorous (kestrels, red-footed falcons) have relatively small and weaker beaks.

Falcons also use their beaks to tear up carcasses into bite-sized portions. They prepare large insects by biting off the wings and elytra and at least the lower portions of the legs of locusts and grasshoppers. A small insect may then be swallowed entire; otherwise, the falcon tears it apart starting with the head and proceeding to the thorax and abdomen. Falcons begin eating vertebrates by decapitating the carcass (sometimes the head is eaten, sometimes not), and then eating the neck and working posteriorly. If the prey is a bird, the falcon will pluck off many of the body feathers with its beak to get at the flesh, sometimes flight feathers too. If the prey is a mammal or reptile, the falcon also uses its beak to strip away enough of the skin to expose the flesh. Most of the flesh is bitten off or stripped away from the skeleton, which is left more or less intact if the prey is large, but on smaller vertebrates the falcon usually breaks up the long bones of the appendages and swallows them. The tomial teeth and notches may be involved in this process too. Falcons also frequently eat portions of the skull, jaws and beaks of vertebrates. In the case of small vertebrates, falcons eat most or all of the viscera, but they are more selective about eating the viscera of large animals, taking organs such as the heart and liver but rejecting the stomach and guts. They are more likely to eat the digestive tracts of birds and reptiles than of mammals.

The falcon's feet, which include all of the bare portion of the hind limbs, also play important roles in capturing, killing, and handling prey. The feet are basically designed as grasping and holding devices. Falcons may kill very small prey by squeezing with their feet or by penetration of talons into vital organs; but this is not the usual way, and falcon feet lack the special clutching mechanism and dagger-like talons of accipiters and owls.

Falcons do use their feet in another entirely different way to stun and occasionally kill large prey. When falcons attack prey by stooping (diving vertically from height to gain speed), they frequently strike the quarry with their feet instead of grabbing. When delivered with the full power of a stoop, this strike has sufficient force to stun a bird and cause it to fall to ground, or in some cases to kill it outright. In other instances the rear talon gashes into the prey and may produce a mortal wound.

PLATE ii (overleaf)
Prairie Falcon
Falco mexicanus
Female feeding
young

There has long been argument as to just how a falcon uses its feet in the strike. Louis Agassiz Fuertes, whose paintings of falcons have seldom been excelled, in a famous article published in the *National Geographic* magazine wrote that falcons kill their prey "by a terrific blow with the half-closed foot . . .". Like many another young devotee, I grew up with a copy of the December 1920 *National Geographic* by my pillow, and I was fully prepared to accept that this is the way falcons strike (Cade 1960), not only because Fuertes and all falconers said so, but because having been struck in the head several times by "playful" trained falcons and by angry ones at the eyrie, it always felt to me as if they were using their fists. Studies by Goslow (1971) and later by Morlan W. Nelson, using slow motion cinematography, have shown quite clearly that when falcons and other birds strike with their feet they do so with all four toes fully extended! How they keep from breaking their forward projecting toes is a mystery. There is an advantage: with the toes extended the falcon can strike or grab as the situation warrants.

Falcons also use their feet to carry quarry in flight. A falcon grasps the carcass firmly in both feet and tucks it up under its tail, in a position where it meets the least resistance to airflow and produces the least drag, and also where its weight is best distributed to interfere least with the aerodynamics of the falcon's flight. Depending on wind conditions, a falcon can lift off the ground and gain altitude carrying an object weighing about 50 per cent of its own body weight. A large animal is partly stripped and gutted before the falcon tries to pack it away. Olafur Nielsen and I watched a female gyrfalcon deplume and gut a male ptarmigan, while she was being harassed by a group of irate parasitic jaegers, whose young were hiding near by. Finally the gyr got off, packing perhaps 300 to 400 g (12 oz) of meat, and flew straight away rising steadily toward the mountains, where she finally disappeared in the telescope some 10 km (6 miles) away, despite being mobbed in the air by half a dozen jaegers all the way.

When feeding, falcons hold large prey down against the ground, a branch, or some other surface with their feet and pull it apart with their beaks. Typically they hold large prey down with the inner toes of both feet, while smaller prey may simply be grasped around the body by all the toes of one foot. Still smaller objects, such as disarticulated legs, wings, and insects, may be held in the space between the pads of the inner toe, and the foot is then held in the air while the falcon eats. Flying falcons also eat small prey held in one foot. These are mostly insects, but small birds and bats are sometimes eaten, too, while the falcon is in flight.

Table 2
FOOT PROPORTIONS

(Middle toe as percentage of tarsal length × 100) Species	Males	Females	(Middle toe as percentage of tarsal length × 100) Species	Males	Females
Aerial Bird Specialists			*Aerial Insect and Bird Feeders*		
Peregrine (North America)	93.9	99.1	Sooty Falcon	98.2	98.3
Peregrine (Europe)	100.6	100.4	Eleonora's Falcon	96.3	96.2
Barbary Falcon	98.6	94.7	Hobby	94.9	94.5
Orange-breasted Falcon	97.9	100.0	Bat Falcon	88.4	92.6
			Western Red-footed Falcon	80.2	81.7
Great Falcons					
Gyrfalcon	79.4	81.9	*Ground-hunting Kestrels*		
Saker	83.4	84.1	Common Kestrel	66.9	68.2
Lanner	83.1	86.4	Lesser Kestrel	71.1	71.8
Prairie Falcon	78.2	83.7	American Kestrel (Lesser Antilles)	63.0	64.7
Accipiter-like Falcons			American Kestrel (North America)	59.7	60.5
Merlin (East North America)	77.8	80.7			
Merlin (Europe)	80.0	81.7			
Red-headed Falcon (E. Africa)	78.8	86.1	*Ground-hunting Generalist*		
Aplomado Falcon	78.3	79.5	Brown Falcon	51.2	53.1

Data from Friedmann (1950); Cramp and Simmons (1980); and R. Bierregaard (Ph.D. thesis, 1978).

The structure of the feet varies considerably among the species of falcons, and these variations show some relationship to differences in predation. (See Table 2, page 21.) For example, bird-eating specialists, such as the peregrine, Barbary falcon, and orange-breasted falcon, have extremely long toes and relatively short tarsi. Such toes appear to be best adapted to grasping birds in flight, and the short tarsus may better withstand the shock produced when a falcon strikes from a stoop. The great falcons, which take a high percentage of large prey from the ground – particularly reptiles and mammals – have shorter and heavier toes and also rather short, stout tarsi, a type of foot better designed for striking large objects than for snatching. Kestrels and the brown falcon, which frequently strike into ground cover (short grasses and weeds) for mostly small prey, have short, stubby toes and long tarsi, the latter perhaps allowing for a deeper reach into hiding places than would be possible with a short, peregrine-like tarsus. The toes and tarsi of these ground-strikers are also covered with large, scute-like scales, which are a better protection than the small, reticulate scales on the feet of bird-catchers.

The accipiter-like falcons have feet proportioned much the same as the great falcons, although relative to body size I believe both their toes and tarsi are longer than those of the great falcons, which are almost as squatty-legged as peregrines. The hobby-like aerialists comprise an instructive series, ranging from the sooty falcon, which has a foot proportioned like a bird-snatcher and does, in fact, feed on birds to a large extent, through the more intermediate, partial bird-predators, Eleonora's falcon and the hobby, to the red-footed falcon, which has a foot approaching that of kestrels and is the most highly insectivorous of this group.

While the differences may not be statistically significant for any one species in Table 2, there is nevertheless a strong trend for females to have longer toes relative to tarsi than males. Only the European peregrine, Barbary falcon, Eleonora's falcon, and hobby show the reverse condition. Just how this small but consistent difference between the sexes relates to prey-catching is difficult to puzzle out, but it suggests that for most species the females may be relatively as well as absolutely more heavily weaponed than males.

Like other diurnal raptors and unlike owls, falcons have large crops or thin-walled, sac-like, distensible out-pocketings of the oesophagus, in which food is stored prior to entering the stomach. The crop allows a falcon to consume a large quantity of food in one meal, about 25 to 30 per cent of its body weight, so that fairly large prey can be entirely consumed on the spot. This capacity is no doubt advantageous in at least two ways: it allows the falcon to get the most energy back for the effort expended in capturing a large prey before potential pirates or scavengers can move in to capitalize on the falcon's efforts in hunting and capturing food. Secondly, the full crop, which is more than enough food to meet the daily energy requirement, is a hedge against starvation when hunting is poor by aiding the process of accumulating fat reserves or stored energy. A fat falcon can easily survive for 10 days or more without eating, depending on its size. For example, in winter gyrfalcons may be forced to go without food for several days during bad weather, but gyrfalcons also have a tremendous capacity to store ptarmigan meat in their crops and to build up body fat from the excess intake of food.

Another form of food-storage involves caching the uneaten remains of prey in special hiding places. Food-caching is probably universal among falcons, but the occurrence of this interesting behaviour went virtually unnoticed for a long time. Harrison B. Tordoff (1955) observed both captive and wild American kestrels caching prey, and Helmut C. Mueller (1974) has studied the influence of hunger on food-caching in captive individuals of the same species. I first saw a wild, male American kestrel cache a deplumed brown towhee (*Pipilo fuscus*) in the forks formed by two main branches of a eucalyptus tree, at a height of 10 m (30 ft), in Los Angeles, California, in November of 1954; and at the Sepulveda Reservoir in San Fernando Valley, where members of the old Southern California Falconers' Association used to fly their falcons in the 1950s, a female kestrel had a winter territory that included a telephone pole with an open utility box attached to it at a height of about 2 m (6 ft). The kestrel used this box as a caching site, and we frequently found the carcasses of mice and small birds tucked into the corners on the floor of the box. Breeding Eleonora's falcons have long been known for their habit of storing carcasses of small birds in caches near their colonial nesting sites (Walter 1979), and Nick Fox (1979) made a special study of caching by New Zealand falcons, as well as nicely reviewing the existing literature on the subject.

All species of falcons held in captivity for breeding have been observed caching extra food in special hiding places in their chambers. The list includes at least the following: peregrine, gyrfalcon, saker, lanner, prairie falcon, orange-breasted falcon, bat falcon, aplomado falcon, New

Zealand falcon, merlin, red-headed falcon, Eleonora's falcon, common kestrel, American kestrel, Mauritius kestrel, and greater kestrel. The following species have been observed caching food in nature: peregrine, gyrfalcon, prairie falcon, bat falcon, aplomado falcon, New Zealand falcon, merlin, Eleonora's falcon, common kestrel, and American kestrel. Falcons cache prey most frequently during the breeding season, but at least some species make caches throughout the year.

When about to cache prey, a falcon approaches the hiding place slowly and furtively on foot, holding the food in its beak. It does not fly directly to the spot. It may look around several times before thrusting the prey into place with its beak. The falcon then steps back a short distance and visually examines the site. Often it goes back to readjust the prey or to pick it up and hide it somewhere else. There is good reason for such caution and secrecy, for other birds do find the falcon's caches and rob them – crows and other corvids in particular, but also other raptors including other falcons.

Once satisfied with a site, the falcon usually walks around it or may fly up and hover over it, as though fixing the location in its memory. Falcons do have excellent memories for these cache-sites and do return to them to retrieve the prey at a later time – at least up to 10 days later (Fox 1979).

Locations for caches vary greatly both within and among species. Nick Fox (1979) recorded small, dense bushes, grass tussocks, tree-stumps, and small trees as caching sites of the New Zealand falcon. Cliff-nesting species often use small cavities or ledges in the rocks, tropical forest species use bromeliads and other epiphytes, and the peregrines that have become established as breeders in the coastal salt-marshes of New Jersey usually cache prey right on the ground, often under a small bush, at the base of a wooden post (a convenient marker?), or in driftwood.

Caching occurs in several fairly well defined circumstances, as Fox (1979) has noted. When an adult male returns to the nest with prey and meets no response from the female or young, he usually hides the prey near by. When a parent has fed the young and some food remains, the adult will either consume what is left or cache the remainder near the nest. When the male returns to the nest with food and encounters an intruder, he will often retreat to hide the food before engaging in nest defence. When vulnerable prey are clumped or hunting is especially easy for some reason, a falcon will kill one animal, cache it, and return for others, one by one. It is interesting to note that trained falcons, which have developed an especially co-operative rapport with their falconer, sometimes cache their quarry instead of eating it. Fox (1979) mentions one trained New Zealand falcon that caught and cached five house sparrows in a row without eating any of them, and Dan Cover's (1977) famous cast of tiercel peregrines, "Speedy" and "Tiger", showed the same behaviour with mourning doves.

There is one other special circumstance involving caching. In the breeding season, food transferring ceremonies from male to female ("courtship-feeding") sometimes begin as an activity that R. Wayne Nelson (1977) refers to as "remote food passing". The male caches prey deliberately within view of the female. After he leaves, she then goes to the cache and retrieves the item and eats it. Otherwise, retrieval from the cache is most likely to occur when the falcon returns to the nest or perching area after an unsuccessful hunt. Females with young evidently watch where their tiercels cache food, for they are able to find the carcasses on their own.

The various factors that promote the tendency to cache prey are no doubt complex and only partly understood. Mueller's (1974) experiments with captive kestrels show that birds which had been deprived of food for a time were more likely to cache surplus prey than those that were not so starved, a result similar to experiments on food-hoarding behaviour in rodents. Starvation or "hunger drive" can hardly explain the caching behaviour of courting males in spring, or the parental food-storing behaviour during the nesting season. Winter caching may be stimulated by the onset of cold weather, photoperiod, or other factors that signal a period of need for extra food and induce neuro-endocrine mechanisms associated with seasonal hyperphagia (overeating) and hoarding.

The adaptive advantage of caching seems obvious enough. Caching provides the falcon with a store of extra food for periods (hours to days) when the repeated capture of sufficient prey may be difficult or impossible for one reason or another. For example, the peregrines that Wayne Nelson observed in the Queen Charlotte Islands fed mainly on ancient murrelets (*Synthliboramphus antiquuum*), which the falcons caught in numbers as the murrelets left their burrows at dawn for the open ocean and cached for subsequent use during the remainder of the day while the murrelets were away at sea. Similarly, the autumn migratory birds passing over islands of the Aegean Sea are only available to Eleonora's falcons in the early morning hours, and the falcons in the Aegean colonies concentrate on catching and storing prey early in the day for use later (Walter 1979). Winter caches can no doubt be a hedge against periods of bad weather when prey are less available to falcons. It is interesting to note, however, that falcons are generally heavier and fatter in winter than in summer, and food-storing may certainly be related to the wintertime hyperphagia associated with this fattening. Again, falconers have long known that they can fly their birds in higher condition in winter than at other times of year, especially in spring when a fat bird is sure to fly away.

Falcons have powerful digestive systems capable of reducing a meal to its constituent amino acids and other nutrient molecules in short order (Duke *et al.* 1975). The gastric juice in the muscular stomach, which is a large, thin-walled organ by comparison with the typical gizzard of seed-eating birds, has a pH of about 1.5, highly acidic, and is capable of digesting not only flesh and other soft parts but also much of the ingested bone, in contrast to owls and some other raptors with a limited ability to digest bone (Cummings *et al.* 1976). Other ingested materials, particularly epidermal derivatives such as feathers, hair, scales, toe nails and horny beaks, the gizzard linings of birds, and the chitinous exoskeletons of insects are not digested, and one of the functions of the muscular stomach of falcons is to separate these materials from the digestible fraction of the meal and to compact them into an elongate pellet or casting, which is regurgitated some hours after digestion has been completed.

These pellets are mostly wads of hair or feathers in which harder fragments are embedded – bits of bone, toe nails, horny beaks, and the entire feet of birds encased in their scales, which prevent digestion of the underlying bony elements. If the falcon has been eating insects, then the pellet consists of compacted fragments of chitinous parts. Pellets of insect remains are much more friable than those consisting of vertebrate parts. These castings provide one means of assessing the food habits of falcons and other birds of prey, although they are of less use in studying the diets of falcons than for other species that regurgitate more intact bones and other identifiable parts.

Falconers have long known that trained falcons and hawks pick up and swallow stones, or "rangle" as they term it, and Symon Latham's (1615) adage has more than a little truth to it, as Nick Fox (1976) has recently reminded us:

"Washed meat and stones maketh a hawk to flie,
But great casting and long fasting maketh her to die."

Gilbert Blaine (1936) was a believer in the use of rangle to keep falcons healthy, and he considered pebbles about 20 mm ($\frac{3}{4}$ in) in diameter suitable for a female peregrine, while a jack merlin should be given smaller, smooth stones about 4 mm in diameter.

All species of falcons we have kept in captivity for breeding at Cornell University have been observed to swallow stones. Incubating birds are especially prone to pick at stones on the nesting ledge and occasionally swallow one. Wild falcons no doubt take stones as well, but only a few observations have been made. Nick Fox (1976) found cast up rangle stones at perching places of New Zealand falcons; the females produced stones about 15 mm ($\frac{1}{2}$ in) in diameter, while those from males were about 7 mm. Recently when I visited "Scarlett", the famous female peregrine which has her eyrie on the 33rd floor window ledge of a skyscraper in Baltimore, I discovered four, smooth, polished pebbles deposited at one of her favourite perching places on a granite balustrade. They were about 20 mm in diameter!

What is the function of rangle? Falconers generally believe the stones help in removing grease and mucus from the stomach lining. Fox (1976) observed mucus on regurgitated rangle, while he feels that other material loosened by the stones passes through the gut, producing oily and discoloured droppings for a day or two.

Like other birds, falcons periodically shed the inner lining of their muscular stomachs – the so-called "koilin" lining – which is a non-living coating secreted by special tubular glands in the walls of the stomach (Ziswiler and Farner 1972). According to McAtee (1906) falcons regurgitate the shed lining, while some birds pass it through the lower digestive tract. It may very well be that falcons swallow rangle as a means of aiding in the removal of the old koilin. This is a subject ripe for study. It is also interesting to note in passing that eastern falconers often dose their falcons with sal ammoniac to "physick them" and sharpen their appetites for prey. Sal ammoniac (ammonium chloride) causes the sloughing off of the koilin lining.

Size and Flying Performance

As Nick Fox has shown (Ph.D. thesis), the hunting performances of raptors can be compared along a gradient of characteristics from those that define birds predominantly as "searchers" to those that define them predominantly as "attackers". Searching raptors spend most of their hunting time looking for small, numerous, relatively sluggish prey over large areas, and the attack, when it comes, is simple, direct, and usually successful. Typical examples are the harriers and kites, the snail kites (*Rostrhamus* spp) being an extreme case, as are the vultures and condors which search for dead animals. Attacking raptors prey on small numbers of relatively large, less numerous, more agile prey. They spend less time searching, but the attack is usually highly complex, sometimes prolonged, energy-demanding, and is less successful on average than the attacks of a searcher. Eagles, accipiter hawks, and most falcons are attackers, although kestrels are intermediate in their hunting characteristics, as are many other kinds of raptors, while the barred kestrel of Madagascar, when hunting chameleons, may be basically a searcher (see page 178).

The wing-loadings (weight carried by any given unit area of the wing) of falcons and typical "searchers" and "attackers" are compared in Figure 4 on page 31. Clearly attacking raptors such as falcons come under strong selection pressures related to aerial agility and speed, as well as to ability to subdue and kill large prey as discussed in the previous sections on adaptations of feet and beaks. These selective forces become reflected through generations in adaptive modifications of the morphology of the falcons, their shapes, sizes, and proportions of appendages.

According to the quasi-steady-state aerodynamic theory of avian flight propounded by Colin Pennycuick (1975), several aspects of aerial performance that are critical for attacking raptors are importantly influenced by body mass, so that a scaling effect of size can be deduced for *birds of similar geometric design*, such as falcons. Using this theory, Andersson and Norberg (1981) examined six parameters of flight that they consider especially important for capturing prey: linear acceleration, horizontal speed, diving speed, rate of climb, and manoeuvrability, which depends on angular roll acceleration and turning radius (Howland 1974). From equations based on Pennycuick's mechanical and aerodynamic models, Andersson and Norberg show that under the given assumptions of the equations, maximum linear acceleration in flapping flight, maximum speed in horizontal flapping flight, maximum rate of climb, and manoeuvrability all decrease with an increase in body mass. Only terminal diving speed increases.

They conclude that because flight performance decreases with increasing mass in five respects and increases in only one, the former five should be of "overriding importance" in determining the raptor size most efficient for hunting. Small size of the raptor *relative to the size of its prey* should be selected for the more capture depends on acceleration, speed, rate of climb, and manoeuvrability; therefore, the more agile the prey, the closer the raptor should approach the size limit below which subduing and transporting it become difficult and counter-selective.

It is pertinent to note that falcons are among those raptors that do frequently capture quarry near their own body sizes, or even larger than they are. The larger falcons are quite capable of catching and killing animals three to four times their own mass, and all falcons can take prey near their own body weights, although the prey most frequently taken, in all cases, average smaller in size than the falcons catching them. Newton (1979) provides other examples of mean weight of prey in relation to mean weight of raptors for accipiters and harriers. It does seem to be the rule that raptors preying on the more agile prey, especially birds, select quarry closer to their own body size than do raptors preying on more sluggish animals. If Andersson and Norberg are correct, it would be even more advantageous for a bird-hunting raptor to pursue prey larger than it is, if the raptor has the capability of overpowering and killing such a bird, because the larger bird would have less acceleration, horizontal speed, climbing rate, and manoeuvrability than its smaller pursuer. One could argue that the excessively large feet and massive beaks of the bird-hunting falcons have evolved in relation to this advantage.

Andersson and Norberg have proposed an interesting hypothesis that will no doubt stimulate much thought and new research, but it probably depends too heavily on the assumption of "geometric similarity", for there are many other morphological determinants of flight speed and performance to be taken into account in addition to body mass. It should be stressed at the outset, however, that most falcons rely on the "stoop" as their main tactic in capturing prey, and large falcons *do* have the advantage over small ones in this important respect, as terminal diving speed is positively related to mass.

While acceleration and manoeuvrability no doubt decrease with increasing mass in the way Andersson and Norberg have explained, it seems likely that the speed of horizontal flapping flight and rate of climb vary somewhat independently of body mass and are more precisely determined by wing-loading characteristics and power output from wing-flapping. These depend importantly upon wing surface area and the mass of the pectoral muscles relative to total body weight, features which are not necessarily geometrically similar in falcons of different body sizes, including even males and females of the same species. See, also, Mueller *et al.* (1981) for similar conclusions about age and sex variations in accipiters.

As Figure 4 (page 31) shows, attacking raptors have heavier wing-loadings than searchers over quite a range of body weights, and while wing-loading is positively related to body mass, owing to the fact that surface area increases as the square, and volume (mass) as the cube, of linear dimensions, it is also associated with horizontal flapping speed at any given body weight. Searchers may spend long hours on the wing looking for prey, but they do not require great speed to capture their quarry; thus, a light wing-loading and low energy expenditure for flight are advantageous, but they have sacrificed speed and are therefore limited to taking relatively sluggish animals. Attackers need high speed and agility for short periods when pursuing quarry; they attain speed in part by a reduction in wing area relative to weight, thereby reducing the moment of inertia of the wings and profile drag on the wings and gaining a faster flapping rate, and in part by investing a greater percentage of total body mass in energy-demanding pectoral muscles. Attackers use up a great deal of energy in fast, flapping flight, but they gain the advantage of being able to capture large, agile, fast-moving quarry that are unavailable to searchers. Again, it should be noted that stooping falcons reduce the metabolic energy required for high speed attacks by taking advantage of the potential energy gained by rising to high altitude and subsequently transformed into movement by diving (gravitational falling).

While the adaptive trade-offs between high speed, heavy wing-loading, and high energy-demanding performance on the one hand, and low speed, light wing-loading, and low energy demanding performance on the other hand, are rather easy to understand and even quantify when one compares a typical searcher, such as a kite, with a typical attacker, such as an accipiter hawk, the distinctions become much more subtle and difficult to specify in a homogeneous group of species such as the falcons. One difficulty is that there are very few solid data on wing-loading, flight speed, relative size of pectoral muscles, wing flapping rates and stroke amplitudes for species of *Falco*, and one is left mainly with impressions from observations of falcons performing under field conditions.

Table 3
WING-LOADING, BODY WEIGHT AND PECTORAL MUSCLE MASS (Actual Measurements)

Species	Sample No.	Sex	Body Weight (Grams)	Wing-Loading (Gms/Cm Sq)	Pectoral Mass (% Body Weight)	Source
peregrinus	2	?	762	0.62	—	N. Fox
peregrinus	1	M	712	0.62	—	Poole
peregrinus	1	F	1,223	0.91	—	Poole
peregrinus	1	F?	813	0.63	—	Brown & Amadon
peregrinus	2	F	825	0.59	19.2	Hartman
rufigularis	1	M	150	0.51	17.0	Hartman
novaeseelandiae	5	M	334	0.43	—	N. Fox
novaeseelandiae	18	F	531	0.55	—	N. Fox
columbarius	2	M?	169	0.40	—	N. Fox
columbarius	1	M	145	0.33	20.2	Magnan *fide* Greenewalt
columbarius	1	M	173	0.42	—	Poole
subbuteo	1	M?	165	0.30	19.0	Magnan *fide* Greenewalt
tinnunculus	14	M&F	193	0.31	—	Brown & Amadon
tinnunculus	1	M?	129	0.20	—	Mullenhoff *fide* Greenewalt
tinnunclus	1	F?	260	0.38	—	Mullenhoff *fide* Greenewalt
tinnunculus	1	M?	147	0.27	—	Mullenhoff *fide* Greenewalt
tinnunculus	1	M	172	0.24	13.3	Magnan *fide* Greenewalt
tinnunclus	1	F	245	0.35	12.2	Magnan *fide* Greenewalt
sparverius	11	F	113	0.29	15.0	Hartman
sparverius	1	F	137	0.37	—	Poole
rupicoloides	1	M	280	0.35	12.9	T. Cade

The limited data in Table 3 show that wing-loading and pectoral muscle mass do vary considerably among species of falcons. Owing to the surface-to-volume relationship, small falcons generally have proportionately larger wing areas and lighter wing-loadings than large falcons. The calculated wing-loadings (Table 4) for males and females of 33 species of *Falco* suggest other interesting trends not necessarily related to body mass. For example, kestrels ranging in size from 60 to 300 g (2–10 oz) have lighter wing-loadings, and presumably relatively smaller pectoral muscles, than small bird-catchers (bat falcon, merlin) in the same size range. Among large species, the desert falcons (*Hierofalco*), with relatively shorter but broader wings, appear to have lighter wing-loadings than the peregrines and their relatives (*Rhynchodon*), which have relatively long but narrower wings. Although considered very fast fliers by most observers, hobbies have light wing-loadings for their size, about comparable to kestrels, but their shorter tails make them less buoyant than kestrels.

Falcons have wings which Savile (1957) categorized as "high speed wings" as do shorebirds, pigeons and doves, swifts, hummingbirds, and swallows. Such wings have a flattish profile (low camber) and a rather high aspect ratio (long relative to width). They show the sweep-back and

Table 4
CALCULATED WING AREA AND WING-LOADINGS FOR MALES AND FEMALES

Species	Wing Area (Cm Sq)* Males	Females	Av. Body Weight (Gms) Males	Females	Wing-Loading (Gm/Cm Sq) Males	Females
peregrinus, European	1287.0	1708.3	666	1129	0.52	0.66
babylonicus	1102.5	1888.9	359	663	0.33	0.48
rusticolus, Palearctic	1835.3	2221.8	1115	1735	0.61	0.78
cherrug	1766.3	2145.9	840	1135	0.48	0.53
biarmicus, Palearctic	1415.0	1795.7	550	800	0.39	0.45
mexicanus	1205.0	1585.8	554	863	0.46	0.54
subniger	1766.3	2178.3	600	750(?)	0.34	0.34
hypoleucos	1110.2	1441.2	336	500(?)	0.30	0.35
deiroleucus	829.0	1064.3	345	600	0.42	0.56
rufigularis	481.5	652.4	128	210	0.27	0.37
femoralis	890.3	1133.6	260	407	0.29	0.36
novaeseelandiae, eastern	883.8	1188.9	330	531	0.37	0.45
novaeseelandiae, bush	750.5	1004.5	264	474	0.35	0.47
columbarius, European	533.8	634.7	162	212	0.30	0.33
chicquera, African	533.8	688.5	170(?)	250	0.32	0.36
fasciinucha	555.5	757.1	212	306	0.38	0.40
subbuteo, European	883.4	968.2	182	241	0.21	0.25
cuvieri	688.5	789.4	166	200	0.24	0.25
severus	628.9	744.4	175	229	0.29	0.31
longipennis	789.4	953.7	225(?)	305	0.29	0.32
eleonorae	1011.9	1094.9	350	390	0.35	0.36
concolor	1012.0	1094.4	300(?juv)	340(?juv)	0.30	0.31
vespertinus	802.5	815.7	147	164	0.18	0.20
amurensis	725.5	738.1	136	148	0.19	0.20
tinnunculus, European	815.7	883.4	156, summer	193, summer	0.19	0.22
			213, winter	252, winter	0.26	0.29
cenchroides	815.7	946.6	185	200(?)	0.23	0.21
sparverius, N. American	451.4	512.5	109	119	0.24	0.23
sparverius, Nicaraguan	378.2	422.3	73.4	81.0	0.19	0.19
newtoni	502.1	600.1	105	144	0.21	0.24
punctatus	412.8	461.3	178	231	0.43	0.50
araea	299.2	319.7	70.0	87.0	0.23	0.27
naumanni	769.9	776.4	131	173	0.17	0.22
rupicoloides	1012.0	1072.0	250(?)	280(?)	0.23	0.26
ardosiaceus	688.5	744.4	222	247	0.32	0.33
berigora, Tasmanian	1503.8	1880.4	430, summer	630, summer	0.29	0.34
			545, winter	740, winter	0.36	0.39

*Calculated by the formula, wing area = (wing chord/0.62)²/1.93, from Greenewalt (1962). *Note:* Comparison with measured values in Table 3 indicates that this formula underestimates the actual wing-loading by 0.05 to 0.10 grams per cm. sq., but the method allows instructive comparisons between species and between sexes. (Data from Cramp and Simmons 1980, R. Bierregaard 1978, Brown and Amadon 1968, and Friedmann 1950.)

Figure 3
Comparison of
primary wing
feathers of (from
left to right) New
Zealand falcon,
common kestrel,
and peregrine

  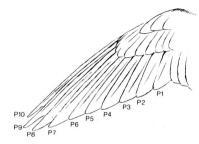

"fairing" to the body of jet fighter-plane wings, and they taper to a slender tip, usually without slots, which, when present, increase the lifting power of the wings. (See Figure 3.)

Falcons do have wing-tip slots, which are more characteristic and more highly developed in the "slotted, high-lift wings" of static soaring birds such as condors, vultures, and eagles. Savile (1957) suggested that falcons have slotted primaries in consequence of their need to carry heavy prey; falcons also soar on occasion, and the slots then help to transform their wings into the slotted, high-lift form. In rapid, flapping flight falcons hold their primaries in a partly closed, swept-back position, in what J. A. Baker (1967) refers to as "that cloud-biting anchor-shape", and the slots are then closed, so that falcons have the ability to gain some advantages of both types of wing.

The slots are produced by distal emarginations in the inner vanes (P9 and P10 only) and by sinuations on the inner or outer vanes of the outermost three to four primaries. These features and the relative lengths of the outer five primaries vary among different species of falcons and no doubt influence the aerodynamic characteristics of the wings. Fast flying falcons such as peregrine, bat falcon, Teita falcon, and orange-breasted falcon have less slotting and more pointed wings than the more buoyant, slower flying kestrels. Accipiter-like falcons (New Zealand falcon, Mauritius kestrel, aplomado falcon) have more rounded wing tips and also deeper slotting than the high speed falcons; typically their longest primary is P8, and P10 is no longer than or even shorter than P6, whereas in fast fliers, P9 is longest, and P10 is longer than or no shorter than P8.

The length and shape of the tail also correlate with flying performance, especially in relation to soaring, hovering, and manoeuvrability. Tail length varies from 40 per cent of the standard wing measurement (Teita falcon) to more than 72 per cent (Mauritius kestrel), and the shape of the tip varies from markedly graduated in the brown falcon and some kestrels to squarish or even slightly notched (bat falcon, Teita falcon, oriental hobby). Fast fliers have short tails (40 to 55 per cent of wing) with squarish tips; slower fliers and hoverers, and accipitrine falcons, have long tails (60 to 72 per cent of wing) with rounded to graduated tips.

Figure 5 shows the range of relationships between relative tail length and relative wing width for most species of falcons and compares them to other basic kinds of raptors. Most falcons fall in the narrow-winged, short-tailed category, where other major taxa of diurnal raptors are largely absent, but a few kestrels converge toward the narrow-winged, long-tailed category, which is occupied mainly by harriers and various species of kites, while two falcons (*punctatus* and *novaeseelandiae*) have converged markedly toward the wide-winged, long-tailed accipiter axis. No falcon falls in the wide-winged, short-tailed category.

Although extremely difficult to quantify, the texture of the feathers also appears to vary with different abilities to fly. The fastest fliers have exceptionally stiff wing and tail feathers. To a degree stiffness is associated with the intensity of melanization and usually also with degree of sheen or gloss. The bat falcon, orange-breasted falcon, Teita falcon, oriental and African hobbies are some of the species with the stiffest flight feathers – very swift-like in their texture – while peregrines and hobbies have slightly less stiff feathers. The great falcons have much softer, more flexible primaries and rectrices, as do the kestrels and the accipitrine falcons. True accipiters also have rather soft, flexible flight feathers, apparently an adaptation to prevent breakage when the birds fly through dense cover and thickets. The brown falcon and the Madagascar barred kestrel have the softest feathers of all falcons.

Juvenile falcons frequently show characteristics of flying that differ from adults. In most species the first year birds have softer, more flexible feathers than adults. Could this be an adaptation to compensate for the greater clumsiness of young birds and the greater likelihood that they will encounter situations in which their feathers could be damaged?

Although the difference is not well reflected by the measurements of museum skins, nevertheless in some species of falcon the wing and tail feathers of juveniles are slightly but consistently longer than in adults. This difference becomes readily apparent when one compares moulted feathers from the first and second moults. Each adult primary, secondary, and rectrix is a few millimetres shorter and also slightly narrower than its first year counterpart. At least the following species show this difference: peregrine, gyrfalcon, saker, lanner, prairie falcon, orange-breasted falcon, bat falcon, and New Zealand falcon (Cramp and Simmons 1980).

This means that in these species, first year birds have lighter wing-loadings and "tail-loadings" than adults, a difference that is exaggerated even more by the fact that first year birds also generally weigh less than adults. It seems likely that this greater wing and tail surface area compensates the juvenile falcons for their weaker and less well developed pectoral muscles and allows them to subsist on a lower energy intake than the more heavily wing-loaded adults. Mueller *et al.* (1976, 1979, 1981) have described a similar case for North American accipiters. On the other hand, the data summarized by Cramp and Simmons (1980) and others, indicate that kestrels and hobbies show the reverse relationship, adults having longer tails and wings than juveniles. This difference could be related to the greater specialisation of these species for hovering and for buoyant aerial pursuit of insects and the concomitant advantage of light wing-loading and low energy demanding flight for this type of foraging.

Many of the differences in proportions, relative size of muscles, feather texture, and other features discussed in the preceeding paragraphs as having significance in producing differences in flying performance are quite subtle. In sum they no doubt do modify the aerodynamic capabilities of falcons, but it should also be pointed out that great redundancy seems to be built into almost all aspects of the mechanical parts involved in avian flight. For example, a falcon can lose quite a few tail feathers or wing feathers and still fly and catch quarry with evident ease. The alula (so-called "bastard wing") is supposed to be an important slotting device to prevent stalling at slow speeds when the bird lands or takes off, but a falcon can still fly quite effectively with both alulas missing or damaged.

The hybrid falcon called "Crazy Legs" that Jim Weaver and I (1976) produced at Cornell by inseminating a female gyrfalcon with peregrine semen is living proof that subtle differences in form and proportions may not always be as significant as students of microevolution like to believe. Crazy Legs has a genetic or epigenetic defect that produced marked bilateral asymmetry in the length and size of the wing and tail feathers on her right and left sides. The wings are perfectly shaped, except that each primary and secondary on the left side is smaller than its counterpart on the right. The same is true of the left set of rectrices, so that the left wing is overall about 25 mm (1 in) shorter than the right, and the left side of the tail is about 20 mm shorter than the right side. This falcon has now been flown in falconry for six years, and if she has any impediment it has never been revealed by her performance in the air.

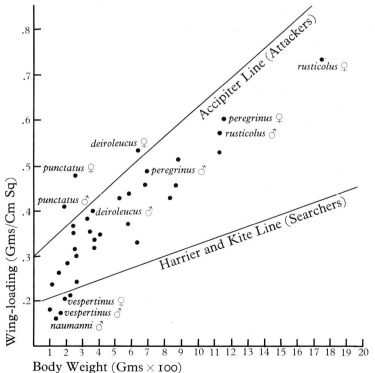

Figure 4
ESTIMATED WING-LOADING
PLOTTED AGAINST BODY WEIGHT TO
SHOW LIMITS OF VARIATION IN FALCONS

Each point represents the male or female of a species of *Falco* (total of 20 species). The limiting line below which most accipiters (attackers) fall, and the line below which most harriers and kites (searchers) fall, are based on data from Mueller *et al.* (1976, 1979, 1981), and N. Fox (1977). (Wing area estimated by Greenewalt's 1962 formula.)

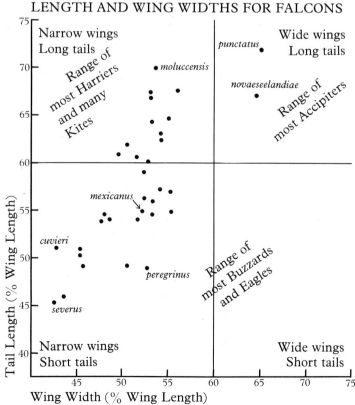

Figure 5
RELATIONSHIP BETWEEN RELATIVE TAIL
LENGTH AND WING WIDTHS FOR FALCONS

Each point represents one species of *Falco* (total 34). Based on an original figure by N. Fox (Ph.D. dissertation, 1977). Data from Fox, from G. J. Nielsen (Verslag van een Onderzoek Naar De Relatie Tussen Voedelkeuze en De Grootte van Bepaalde Lichaamsdelen In Het Genus *Falco*), and from R. O. Bierregaard (Ph.D. dissertation, 1978).

Hunting Success

In order to maintain itself, and to engage in productive activities (courtship, mating, egg production, care of young), the energy which a falcon expends in obtaining food (searching, capturing, killing, and processing) must be less than the metabolizable energy to be gained from the food. This is of course particularly true in the breeding season when there are young to be fed. The best measure of foraging efficiency, then, would be the ratio between energy used to energy gained per unit of time hunting. Does foraging efficiency vary significantly with the size of falcon, age, sex, type of prey, and environmental circumstances? Under field conditions it is, unfortunately, difficult to obtain the required data to determine foraging efficiency in terms adequate to answer these questions.

Hunting success (percentage of all hunts that end in capture of prey) is recordable and does vary widely among falcons. (See Table 5.) Students of raptors have usually assumed that hunting success varies with type of prey, particularly with the agility of prey and size of prey relative to size of raptor. For example, insect-hunting falcons may have higher success rates than bird-hunters, or as Nick Fox would say, searching raptors have higher capture rates than attackers. It is also generally believed that young falcons in their first year are less successful than adults; certainly the experience of falconers with trained birds bears out this generality, as does a comparison of Gustav Rudebeck's data for autumn migrating merlins and peregrines with data for a wintering adult and for breeding adults.

One of the most frequently stated generalizations is that male falcons, being smaller, are more successful and efficient hunters than their big females, because being smaller they concentrate on sizes of prey lower down on the Eltonian pyramid of numbers – that is, on prey species that are more numerous than the larger classes of animals on which the females concentrate their efforts. Furthermore, a small falcon requires less total energy per unit of time than a large falcon, so that he expends less energy per unit of time searching and hunting than his female counterpart.

The available data, which are admittedly limited, suggest that the hunting success rates of searching raptors and attacking raptors, as represented by insect-catching falcons and bird-catching falcons, may not be as different as some people have maintained; and when it comes to actual foraging efficiency, there may be no difference at all, or conceivably some bird-catchers may even be more efficient than insect-catchers. A 150-gram kestrel feeding on grasshoppers averaging 1 gram might have to catch 30 insects to meet its energy requirement for one day. Even if it were 100 per cent successful in capturing, unless grasshoppers were superabundant, the kestrel would have to spend a large fraction of the total day searching for food. A 150-gram merlin, on the other hand, only has to catch one 30-gram bird to gain the same gross energy as the kestrel. Even if he is only 20 per cent successful in his hunts, he devotes much less time (and energy?) to his daily foraging routine.

Questions about "efficiency", therefore, are not so simply answered. They may also be essentially irrelevant: sufficient performance is the only demand that natural selection really places on an organism, and it can be a relatively efficient or inefficient user of energy so long as it gains a competitive advantage in the way it uses energy.

The actual records of the breeding male peregrine and the breeding female listed in Table 5 are interesting to compare. He had a capture rate of 93 per cent one year; she had a capture rate of 31 per cent. He caught almost exclusively blue jays weighing about 90 g (3 oz); about 70 per cent of her captures were coots weighing 500 g ($17\frac{1}{2}$ oz) and 30 per cent were Australian little grebes weighing 150 g (5 oz). They both hunted on average within a radius of 1 km (3,300 ft) of their eyries and launched all of their attacks from the vicinity of their nests.

Consider the results of 100 hunts for each bird. The male brings back to the nest 93 jays for a total food mass of 8.37 kg (18 lbs), or approximately 16,740 kilo-calories of metabolizable energy (average of 2 kcal/gram of prey). The female brings back 22 coots and 9 grebes for a total food mass of 12.35 kg (27 lbs), or 24,700 kcal.

What has been the energy cost of this hunting effort for the male and the female? Assume that the male weighs 600 grams and the female weighs 900 grams. His standard, resting metabolic rate (SMR) can be calculated from the empirical, weight-relative equation derived for non-passerine birds – SMR $= 78.3 \times W^{.723}$ (Lasiewski and Dawson 1967) – as 54.12 kcal per day. The female's is 72.56 kcal.

When flying at maximum speed the falcons are probably using energy at a rate at least 10 times greater than the SMR (Tucker 1971) – probably higher (see Copeland et al. 1980) – or a minimum of 3.8 kcal/min for the male and 5.0 kcal/min for the female. Assume that each hunting foray

Table 5

HUNTING SUCCESS RATES OF SOME FALCONS

Species	No. of Cases	Prey and Conditions	% Success	Source
peregrinus	252	autumn migration	7.5	Rudebeck 1951
peregrinus	113	racing pigeons on coast	16.0	Parker 1979
peregrinus	55	coastal eyries, pigeons	62.0	Treleaven 1980
peregrinus male	81	nesting, coastal marsh	73.0	Sherrod and Cade
peregrinus male	102	nesting, coastal marsh	93.0	Sherrod and Cade
peregrinus female	32	lakeshore eyrie, Australia	31.0	S. K. Sherrod
femoralis	174	singles hunting insects	82.2	D. Hector
femoralis	37	singles hunting birds	18.9	D. Hector
femoralis	68	pairs hunting birds	44.1	D. Hector
novaeseelandiae	20	hunting birds	55.0	N. Fox (1977)
columbarius	139	autumn migration	5.0	Rudebeck 1951
columbarius female	343	winter seashore, birds	12.8	Page and Whitacre (1975)
sparverius male	246	insects and reptiles from ground, Costa Rica	39.4	Jenkins 1970
sparverius	403	still hunting from a perch	52.0	Collopy 1973
sparverius	95	hovering	23.0	Collopy 1973
sparverius	199	attacks on insects and other invertebrates	85.4	Collopy 1973
sparverius	34	attacks on vertebrates	23.0	Collopy 1973
sparverius	47	still hunting	36.2	Sparrowe 1972
sparverius	7	hovering	14.3	Sparrowe 1972

begins from the eyrie and involves flying one minute out to make contact with the prey and one minute to return. An unsuccessful hunting foray costs the male 7.6 kcal; it costs the female 10 kcal. If the falcon catches prey, however, there is an additional cost involved in transporting it back to the nest. I have assumed that it costs the falcon as much on a per gram basis to transport the additional weight of its prey as it does to transport a unit of its own body weight. (In fact, it would be more owing to changes in drag and other aerodynamic variables associated with the shape and mass of the prey added to that of the falcon.) Thus, it costs the male at least 0.57 kcal to carry a 90-gram jay for one minute, while it costs the female 2.8 kcal to pack a 500-gram coot and 0.84 kcal to carry a 150-gram grebe.

Summing up, seven unsuccessful hunts and 93 successful ones cost the male a total of 813.01 kcal, for a cost to benefit ratio of 0.049 kcal expended for each kcal gained. Sixty-nine unsuccessful hunts, 22 captured coots, and 9 captured grebes cost the female 1,069.2 kcal for a cost to benefit ratio of 0.043 kcal per kcal gained. Under these two sets of conditions, to deliver 1,000 kcal of food to the eyrie cost the male 49 kcal, while it only cost the female 43 kcal.

The female was actually more efficient than the male in terms of energy used per unit of energy gained, despite the fact that she had a much lower rate of success in capturing. The large size of her prey more than made up for her low rate of capture. The female could have increased her hunting efficiency still more either by increasing her capture rate or by catching more coots or even larger prey such as ducks. The male, which hunted near the maximum possible rate of capture, could only have increased his efficiency by capturing birds larger than blue jays.

The male had a higher rate of food delivery to the nest than the female, and he probably actually delivered more food, more kilo-calories, per unit time to the nest than she, a critical consideration for the normal development and survival of the young. Neither searching time nor non-hunting time have been included in the above comparisons of male and female, but the male would only have had to deliver jays five times more often than the female delivered coots and grebes in order to have slightly exceeded her overall rate of food delivery. It is likely that male falcons deliver food much more than five times as frequently as females, not because females are poor or inefficient hunters but because of their sedentary role as guardians of the nest and young during the breeding season. A true comparison of male versus female success rates and efficiencies of capture awaits study of the hunting performances of males and females in non-breeding situations.

Finally, consider a 200-gram hobby foraging on the wing for flying termites weighing one-tenth of a gram. The hobby's calculated SMR is 24.46 kcal/day or 1.02 kcal/hour. If the hobby has to

PLATE iii (overleaf)
Gyrfalcon
Falco rusticolus
Male (grey phase)
striking down a
ptarmigan

33

fly at $10 \times$ SMR in order to capture termites (10.2 kcal/hour), then it would have to catch and eat about 51 termites per hour just to break even. Since the hobby has a light wing-loading and often soars, it may be able to reduce its energy expenditure in foraging flight to about $3 \times$ SMR, or the equivalent of 15 termites per hour. To gain significant amounts of energy to feed a brood of young – four needing a minimum of 200 kcal per day – the hobby would have to catch an additional 1,000 termites per day (200 per hour for five hours). When one considers the energetics involved in such a foraging effort by a bird the size of a hobby, it becomes easier to understand why hobbies switch from insects to preying on birds to feed their young.

Copeland *et al.* (1980) have provided an instructive model for predicting the daily energy expenditure of raptors, and they give measured and predicted values for *cherrug*, *mexicanus*, *columbarius*, *tinnunculus* and *sparverius*.

Reversed Sexual Dimorphism

Most female birds of prey, including all falcons (see Table 4), are larger than their respective males, in contrast to the great majority of bird species in which males average slightly to considerably larger than females. Other than in predatory groups of birds (falconiform, accipitriform, and strigiform raptors, jaegers and skuas, frigate birds and boobies), reversed sexual size dimorphism (RSD) occurs in a few groups of birds with sex role reversal or with peculiar mating systems such as polyandry (tinamous, various shorebirds such as phalaropes, jacanas, and some sandpipers, and button quail). Ornithologists agree that the latter instances of RSD can be explained as special cases of sexual selection through competition among females for mates, following Charles Darwin's original ideas. No such general agreement exists regarding the explanation for RSD in raptorial birds, and since the subject was first broached by Hill (1944), a considerable literature has developed with a diversity of explanations, none of which has achieved universal acceptance (Rand 1952; Storer 1955, 1966; Amadon 1959, 1975; Cade 1960, 1980; Perdeck 1960; Selander 1966, 1972; Earhart and Johnson 1970; White and Cade 1971; Reynolds 1972; Snyder and Wiley 1976; Balgooyen 1976; Newton 1979; Walter 1979; Andersson and Norberg 1981; Susan Smith, in press).

In their considerations of RSD, most workers have used the standard wing measurement (cord of the primaries) as the indicator of "size" (a trend begun by Storer 1955), or some other linear measurement such as length of tarsus, because such measurements are readily obtained from museum study skins. Body weight is, however, the best measure of overall mass, although its accurate determination can be complicated by the amount of fat deposits or by food in the digestive tract at the time of weighing. It is important to emphasize that differences in linear measurements between males and females bear no precise relationship to differences in body weight. For example, in species such as the jaegers, *Stercorarius* spp (Maher 1974), and the lesser kestrel (Cramp and Simmons 1980) there is no statistically significant difference in wing length between males and females, but there are pronounced differences in body weight. Each measurable trait showing dimorphism between the sexes should, therefore, be considered independently of the others. Some workers have presented figures on an "average dimorphism index", which is the mean of the means for several mensural traits. Such averaging can obscure important differences between species. Conceivably a species with a large RSD for weight and a small RSD for length of tarsus could have the same "average RSD" as another species with a small RSD for weight and a large RSD for tarsus; yet these species would surely be dramatically different in their actual phenotypic expressions of sexual dimorphism. Amadon (1977) has considered other aspects of the problems involved in measuring sexual size dimorphism in birds.

Since pronounced RSD has evolved independently in three different lineages of true raptors (Falconiformes, Accipitriformes, and Strigiformes), and to some degree in other predatory birds, it seems most likely that the nature of being "raptorial" is linked in some way to the selective advantages of RSD in these otherwise phylogenetically divergent groups. As Amadon (1959, 1975) has continually emphasized in his studies, raptors are *special* because their talons and feet have become modified into powerful instruments for seizing and killing other animals, including in some cases animals as large or larger than the raptors themselves. Their hooked beaks are also adapted to a carnivorous diet and are capable of tearing into and rending the bodies of large animals. They have a fierce, predatory disposition that makes this weaponry effective, and they use it against enemies as well as in attacks on prey (Cade 1960, Willoughby and Cade 1964).

Specifically which aspects of the raptorial mode of existence are likely to be acted upon by natural selection to produce the observed differences in size between males and females? Two have been considered, usually as alternative or competing explanations, although it is more than likely that several factors work in concert to produce RSD in raptors and other birds. One has to do with the social relations of the male and female during the reproductive period, and the other has to do with the feeding niche and the possibility that intraspecific competition for food has been a driving force for niche-partitioning through divergence in body size between the male and female of a given species (Storer 1966, Newton 1979, Snyder and Wiley 1976, Andersson and Norberg 1981).

Unlike the tinamous, phalaropes, jacanas, button quail and other birds of their sort which have evolved RSD, falcons and nearly all other raptorial birds are strictly monogamous, and the mates have markedly different roles as parents. The male is essentially a food-provider to the female during her period of rapid follicular development and ovulation, during incubation (usually), and throughout at least half the time the young are in the nest; and he also catches and delivers to the nest most or all of the food required to raise the young. The male does relieve the female at the nest for variable periods of time during incubation and brooding, but usually just long enough for her to eat, perform other essential bodily functions, and obtain some exercise. The female does most of the incubation, she broods and feeds the young with the food provided by the male, and she guards the nest and young and provides the first line of defence against predators. Some males also join in defending the young, depending on circumstances. Also, some females join the male in catching prey for the young during the latter part of their development as nestlings and after they become fledglings. Conceivably RSD could have evolved in falcons and other raptors in relation to this division of labour between the male and female parents (Andersson and Norbert 1981).

It has long been noted that falcons and other raptors with the most pronounced RSD are species that catch relatively large, agile prey, mostly birds, and that the bird-eating accipiters and falcons show the greatest difference in size between males and females (see Newton 1979). In some of these species males and females also tend to take different sized prey and different species of prey, whereas in raptors with little or no RSD, such as the highly insectivorous or scavenging forms, males and females feed on the same kinds of food. The tendency toward differences in the diets of males and females as RSD increases no doubt has advantages in reducing intraspecific competition for food and, particularly, in expanding the numbers and kinds of prey available to a pair of raptors during the critical breeding season when they and their young are forced by restriction to the nest-site to make the largest demand on a local supply of prey (White and Cade 1971).

Two basic features of RSD require explanation: why has natural selection consistently favoured *large* females relative to their males among diverse groups of raptors; and why is the degree of RSD so variable among different species of raptors?

Amadon (1975) has pointed out that when he surveys the Animal Kingdom generally, he finds that sexual dimorphism in size (regardless of which sex is the larger) is nearly always related to mating behaviour, and one's first inclination is to suppose that RSD in raptors has something to do with social relations between mates. Birds with such lethal weapons and fierce, aggressive dispositions as raptors have might pose a serious threat to each other in the close encounters involved in mating and in co-operating as parents, unless some mitigating factor can be brought to bear on the potential of each mate to do bodily harm to the other. RSD might have its selective importance in this context.

Following Amadon's lead, some years ago (1960) I proposed that female falcons are larger than males in consequence of their need to exert a clear-cut social dominance over their partners as part of the mechanism for maintaining the separate roles of the sexes in the reproductive process, particularly the role of the male as food-provider to the female and young. Female falcons definitely are dominant over their males: they have first rights to favourite perches or roosts and to the food obtained by their mates; they control the occurrence of copulation; they can supplant their brooding mates on the eggs or downy young but not vice versa; and I believe that they can also control or stimulate the hunting efforts of their mates through behavioural and vocal means (see, also, Monneret 1974).

Unfortunately, I was not able to articulate this hypothesis in a sufficiently concrete way to be convincing to a majority of my colleagues 20 years ago, and ideas about "niche expansion" have predominated. Many may agree that Andersson and Norberg (1981) delivered the final *coup de grâce* when they concluded that . . . "hypotheses based on pair formation and dominance relationships between the mates have been severely criticized, and may be regarded as refuted . . .".

Recently, however, Monneret (1974), Amadon (1975), and especially Susan Smith (in press) have helped to rekindle thinking about the role of social dominance as a selective factor in RSD. R. J. Monneret, studying the agonistic behaviour of both wild and captive peregrines in France, explains the agonistic behaviour between male and female, as well as the male's food-providing behaviour, in relation to changing dominance between the sexes during the breeding cycle and to changing hormonal influences. He believes that the male's submissiveness to an aggressive and dominant female early in the prenuptial phase of pairing results in displaced or redirected attacks on other birds, so that the male is able to accumulate a cache of prey beyond his own requirements. Once the female has become used to being fed by the male, he is able to achieve a short period of social dominance, or perhaps equivalence, which enables him to come in close contact with the female in courtship and to effect copulations. During incubation the female's attention is narrowly centred on the nest and eggs, and she is not very aggressive; but after the young hatch, she becomes more outwardly orientated and resumes her highly aggressive character, as manifested by her frequent defensive attacks on other birds and by her dominance over her mate, who becomes essentially excluded from the immediate environs of his eyrie. This exclusion by the female activates his aggressive tendencies and again results in a high rate of predation on other birds and food-delivery to the nest, primarily as an appeasement to the female to gain access to the centre of his territory but resulting secondarily in providing the necessary food for the young. Certain aspects of Balgooyen's (1976) concept of male and female "centrifugy" and "centripidy" at the nest fit into this scheme as well.

Smith (1980) has made the further important point, not sufficiently recognized before, that female dominance during the breeding season is the rule among the vast majority of monogamous birds regardless of sexual size dimorphism. It occurs, for instance, among songbirds in which the males are typically somewhat larger than females and dominant to them in the non-breeding season. According to Smith's view, in order to assert the required degree of social dominance over their mates, female birds of prey must be larger than males because both sexes possess dangerous weapons that can be used in intraspecific fighting as well as for predation. The large female body size and greater associated strength and aggressiveness allow her to establish a necessary and clear-cut social dominance over the male with a minimum of actual physical aggression, which otherwise, if the male and female were evenly matched in size and strength, could easily result in physical injury to one or both mates, as Willoughby and Cade (1964) suggested for falcons some time ago.

One of the expectations from this hypothesis is that those raptors which are most powerfully armed and most capable of killing large-sized quarry, and hence also most capable of inflicting serious injury on a mate, should show the most pronounced RSD. This relationship should be especially strong in those raptors that prey on other birds near their own body size, as the prospective mate could well possess many of the stimuli associated with the image of the prey. Raptors that are more weakly armed and that prey on relatively small prey, especially on species of insects, rodents, or other animals whose images are far different from the image of a bird, should have little or no RSD. On the whole there is a remarkably close relationship in raptors between degree of rapaciousness – as indicated by relative size of talons, feet, and beaks and by prey size relative to raptor size – and the degree of RSD (see Amadon 1975). Certainly the data on the morphology and behaviour of falcons and other raptors are consistent with this prediction and with the hypothesis that the requirement for female dominance in the pair bond has been the primary selective force producing RSD.

Other adaptive advantages of large female size relative to male size have no doubt been involved in determining the precise degree and character of RSD for particular species. The "big mother hypothesis" proposed by Katherine Ralls (1976) to explain RSD in mammals should also apply to birds. Big mothers are better mothers because a large female is more likely to produce a greater number of surviving offspring than a small mother. A big raptor mother produces larger eggs, which hatch out larger chicks better able to survive than small chicks; owing to her greater thermal insensitivity to cold weather, she can lay earlier in the season than a small female, and she is a more efficient incubator; she is also more effective in nest defence; and she can store more energy and, when necessary, fast for a longer time during incubation and care of nestlings than a small female.

There does, in fact, appear to be a strong selection for energy storage in female falcons and other raptors during the breeding season (Newton 1979). An essential part of the male's role in reproduction is to provide the food on which his sedentary female fattens prior to laying. Under these conditions large body size will be favoured (Downhower 1976). The reason is that metabolic expenditure of energy increases by an exponent of body weight that is less than 1, about 0.723 for raptors (see previous section), whereas functions related to the storage of energy – food intake, digestive capacity, and fattening – have a nearly linear relation to body weight.

Other aspects of RSD in raptors may be more directly under the influence of selective factors associated with requirements for effective pursuit and capture of prey for individual raptors of a given mass. Differences between male and female in size of appendages – wings, tail, beaks, feet, and talons – and parameters such as wing-loading and "tail-loading", which are influenced both by mass and by linear dimensions, are likely candidates. Differences in body weight (mass) may also have been exaggerated in some cases – particularly in bird-eating raptors – as adaptations that allow males and females to take different sized prey to feed themselves and their young while the family is restricted to a limited nesting area (White and Cade 1971).

Because a large female requires more energy for all biological activities than a small one does, and because the male raptor obtains nearly all of the food for himself and his mate (as well as the young) during the breeding season, her larger size is a definite and measurable tax on the male's prey-catching abilities and must be countered by strong adaptive advantages. This consideration of the energy demand on the male is another reason for thinking that natural selection has produced RSD in raptors by working to push the female's body size upward and away from the male's, rather than the reverse. Part of the reason for observed degrees of difference between males and females may well have to do with balancing the advantages of large female body size against the limits of the male's ability to provide food to his mate during the breeding season.

The male's size probably is adjusted to allow him to catch the most available sizes and kinds of prey for which his basic predatory adaptations are fitted, and with the least competition from other predatory species. The female's size has been adjusted upward from his to the degree that best adapts her to her *domineering* "big mother" role and, in some cases, to her role as a supplemental food-provider to the young late in the breeding season after the male has depleted the available prey for which his size is best suited.

Social Behaviour and Reproduction

Like other raptors, falcons have basically aggressive dispositions, and they often have to contend with antagonistic individuals of their own species, as well as with the members of other raptorial or piratical species and with potential predators. (See Olsen *et al.* 1979 for Australian examples.) Even advanced nestlings respond with aggressive defence to intruders. These aggressive encounters perhaps most often involve disputes over captured prey, but also, favourite perches or roosts, hunting areas (territories), nest-sites, defence of eggs and young, and self-defence against predators such as eagles, larger hawks and falcons.

A falcon must know when to be the dominant aggressor in a given encounter and when to submit and break away. Consequently, a falcon has a whole gamut of agonistic behaviours ranging from outright attack and fighting, involving bodily contact with the antagonist and the possibility for injury or death, through a variety of threatening and submissive displays and vocalizations, to escape by fleeing. The agonistic displays are most likely to occur in ambivalent situations, when the falcon is not clearly motivated either to attack or to escape, or when the falcon is influenced by other conflicting drives, especially sexual motivation, as during pair formation and other interactions between mates.

Falcons are most prone to attack and do their fighting in the air, and they are reluctant to close with an antagonist on the ground. If a falcon is down on the ground with quarry when a potential pirate or enemy appears in the air, its first reaction usually is to crouch over its prey and to remain motionless in this "intruder crouch" in an apparent attempt to remain unseen; it is the same reaction nestlings make to the sight of a large predatory bird in the air. If the intruder indicates that it has spotted the falcon on the ground, then the falcon will attempt to fly away with its prey. If the quarry is too large to carry, the falcon will leave it and fly in pursuit of the intruder and attempt to drive it off, uttering aggressive cackles – "kek-kek-kek" or some species-typical variant thereof. If the intruder persists and finds the quarry and lands on it, the falcon will usually break off its attack and depart, should the intruder be a large bird. Wintering peregrines, for example, not infrequently lose their kills in this way to harriers and buzzards.

Aerial attacks on antagonists are basically like pursuits for prey. The falcon attempts to gain the advantage of height and then to stoop down over the back of its opponent and to rake it with its talons. The attacked bird attempts to avoid the strike by rolling over at the last instant and presenting its own feet and talons to the attacker. A perched falcon under attack will sometimes jump up and do the same thing. Occasionally the two birds actually lock talons together and fall, cartwheeling through the air, usually breaking apart before they hit the ground; but two fighting tiercels may actually go to ground locked together and continue the contest on the ground, scrapping with beaks and feet, until the defeated bird can break away and escape by flight.

39

Figures 6 and 7
Upright Threat
(above)
Horizontal Threat
(right)

When a falcon goes for another bird flying with quarry in its feet, it will usually first attack by stooping in an attempt to force the other bird to drop its booty, in which case the falcon deftly snatches it out of the air as it falls and flies away with it; or the falcon may fly in under the other bird, roll over, grab hold of the quarry and try to pull it away from the other bird (crabbing).

When cornered on the ground or otherwise faced with an especially formidable opponent, whether a potential predator or a conspecific, all falcons employ an Upright Threat display, in which the bird orientates its body vertically, spreads its tail, holds its wings out from the body, and fluffs out all its feathers to the maximum extent, especially those on the breast, the cheeks, nape and crown. The bird hisses and cackles and strikes out with its feet or its beak. This is the most extreme form of aggressive display; adult falcons use it in defence of the nest and young and, exceptionally, to defend food from competitors. By the time they are well feathered, nestling falcons employ the same defence against nest-intruders, flipping over on their backs when really hard-pressed.

Being aggressive and predatory, many falcons lead a solitary existence outside the breeding season, usually frequenting a regular home range or feeding territory, although in some species, particularly tropical ones, mates maintain a loose pair bond even when not breeding, hunting together and defending their territory from intruders. Night roosts are also usually well isolated from others used by members of the same species and may be remote from the feeding area and separately defended.

A few species are social – *naumanni*, *vespertinus* and *amurensis* in particular – but also *subbuteo*, *eleonorae*, *concolor* and *tinnunculus*; and they often hunt together in mixed aggregations for swarming insects in the non-breeding season and form large roosting associations sometimes numbering several thousand birds.

In all large species of *Falco* and in most others, too, the breeding pairs are solitary and rather widely dispersed through suitable habitats. Often the dispersion is fairly uniform for a given habitat (see Newton 1979 and Ratcliffe 1980 for examples), suggesting that territoriality or some other form of intraspecific spacing mechanism is at work to hold the breeding density to some level related to prey density or prey availability. The same species that form social foraging and roosting aggregations in the non-breeding time of year also show varying degrees of colonial breeding. Thus, while *subbuteo* is usually a solitary breeder, occasionally several pairs cluster in a particular patch of woods, forming a semi-colonial aggregation with overlapping hunting areas; *tinnunculus*, which is also most often solitary, has an even greater tendency to form small, loose colonies; *concolor* is sometimes a solitary breeder in the North African desert, but on islands in the Red Sea and Arabian Gulf it aggregates into loose colonies of a few to several dozen pairs, again with overlapping hunting spaces; *vespertinus* usually nests in small to large colonies in tree rookeries, but occasionally pairs are solitary, especially near the northern limits·of the breeding range where food resources become sparse; *eleonorae* forms small to large nesting colonies on islands; while *naumanni* is apparently the most social of all the falcons, nesting in colonies of two to more than 500 closely spaced pairs, which show little or no territorial defence of their nest sites and hunt together in flocks.

40

Colonial nesting in falcons seems to be related to two aspects of the environment: limited and patchy distribution of suitable nesting sites and, perhaps most important, the coextensive occurrence of a superabundant food supply (swarming insects, mouse plagues, migratory streams of birds). Obviously in such species there has also been an increase in behavioural tolerance for close nesting by adjacent pairs; however, while overt fighting and aggressive intolerance of near neighbours have been selected against in species such as *naumanni, vespertinus* and *eleonorae*, Walter's (1979) detailed studies on the social system of the latter species have shown that agonistic displays nevertheless form a prominent part of the social interactions among colonial nesting Eleonora's falcons. The same is no doubt true of red-footed falcons (Horváth 1975) and lesser kestrels, and in these species it is likely that relations involving social dominance (dominance hierarchies and the like) among closely spaced individuals replace the strong territorialism and aggressiveness of the other falcons.

Social dominance is also clearly manifested in the pair bond of all falcons. In most situations females dominate males, as discussed in the section on RSD, and much of the communication between mates has to do with signalling different levels or degrees of threat or appeasement to each other. Falcons indicate their aggressive tendencies to each other by a variety of postures and calls. The "kek", "kak", or "klee" call which falcons use in aggressive encounters with interspecific antagonists is also used as a high intensity threat toward conspecifics, including the mate at times, but most signs of aggressive intent are conveyed by postural changes, which vary in sometimes subtle ways from high intensity to low intensity forms of threat.

Threatening postures involve some degree of fluffing or erection of feathers away from the body, pointing the beak toward the mate, and possibly gaping or even hissing. At high intensity, the falcon orientates its body horizontally (Horizontal Threat), puffs out the feathers on its upper back, crown and cheeks, and points its face and beak directly toward the other bird. It is in a position ready to charge forward on its feet and may do so if the other bird does not respond by moving away or with appropriate appeasing displays. A falcon may indicate only mild threat by slightly flaring its cheek feathers, turning its face toward the other bird, and gaping momentarily, for instance when its mate flies up to a perch and lands near by.

Submissive and appeasing displays in the main involve postures and feather positions that are directly opposite to those used in threat. The feathers are depressed tightly against the body, the head is held below the body axis, often pointed down, and the beak is directed away from the dominant bird. Any vocalization is a soft, peeping, chick-like call.

In close encounters, paired falcons frequently bow to one another, and bowing forms a conspicuous element in many courtship displays. The bowing varies from a slight forward and downward bending of the head and anterior body to frequently repeated deep bows in which the head is lowered to foot level and the tail is elevated at about 45° above horizontal. There has been considerable speculation about the significance of bowing in falcons (Mueller 1971; Wrege and Cade 1977; R. W. Nelson, Ph.D. thesis). Sometimes the bows are performed with some degree of feather erection, indicating aggressive intentions, and at other times with the feathers sleeked. I believe that bowing results when there is a conflict between agonistic tendencies and sexual motivation; it is mainly appeasing in its effect on the other partner, and mutual bowing ceremonies in courtship allow the two mates to come in close, face-to-face contact – billing often occurs with bowing – so that each can assess the other's readiness to copulate. Courtship displays on the nest,

Figure 8
Head Low Bow

Figure 9
Courtship-feeding

nest-cup and nest-scraping displays, often incorporate bowing and chupping or chipping calls, as do food-presentation ceremonies.

While the female dominates the male in close encounters, the tiercel is clearly the more active and conspicuous partner in aerial display. Often the male arrives on the nesting territory ahead of the female and makes himself conspicuous by perching in prominent places, by loud calls (the same used in aggressive attacks), and above all by spectacular, aerial acrobatics over and around the prospective nest. These aerial displays take several forms and probably function partly as territorial advertisement and partly to attract a mate. Soaring and calling high over the nesting territory is one such activity, but the more energetic and visually impressive displays involve various fast dives along the face of the nesting cliff or over the nesting tree, undulating flights and loop-the-loops in the vertical plane, and horizontal figure-of-eight patterns. In these display flights, the tiercel frequently rolls 180° from one side to the other, producing a conspicuous "flash pattern" by alternating the positions of his dark back and light underparts in rapid succession. (See Cramp and Simmons 1980.)

In several species of falcons the male also flies about the eyrie with slow, deep, halting wing-beats, dangling a conspicuous prey in his lowered feet, apparently as an enticement to his prospective mate, or he may perform the same flight without prey (called 'buzzard flight" by Cramp and Simmons 1980). This display is probably an incipient form of courtship feeding, and it may be of more general occurrence among falcons than presently understood. The male ends some of his display flights by landing in a conspicuous manner at a prospective nest-site, cliff ledge, stick nest, tree cavity, etc., an action that apparently functions to reveal the location of a suitable nesting site to his mate. He may also stand in the nest and utter courting calls, usually a "chip", "chup", or chitter of some sort.

Once the female arrives at the eyrie, she joins the male in some of these aerial displays. The birds may soar and dive together, or dive at each other, often calling loudly. When one mate stoops at the other, the latter often rolls over and presents its talons, and occasionally paired falcons lock talons briefly in these encounters, but not so frequently as eagles and some other accipitriform raptors do. Some falcons also touch beaks in flight, and it seems likely that both talon-grasping and the so-called "aerial kiss' are ritualized or presumptive forms of courtship-feeding.

After the mates have formed a workable bond, the female soon becomes much more sedentary than the male and restricts most of her activities to the immediate vicinity of the eyrie. She no longer hunts much, if at all, and the male provides her with most or all of her food. Food transferring ceremonies ("courtship-feeding") become prominent activities at this time, and it has become increasingly evident to students of falcons and other raptors that these interactions between male and female involving the transfer of prey and adequate provisioning of the female in the pre-laying phase of the cycle are critical for successful reproduction (Cade 1960, Cave 1968, Balgooyen 1976, Newton 1979).

Courtship-feeding takes a variety of forms in falcons. Often the female begs for food like a juvenile, fluffing out her feathers, spreading her tail, and quivering her wings, while uttering a plaintive wail. If the male presents himself without prey, the female sometimes charges at him in an aggressive version of this begging display. The female also uses an aerial version of food-begging just as the young do. At other times, she simply sits calmly on a perch in a hunched posture and wails. These begging behaviours of the female appear to stimulate the male to hunt and to return with prey.

Especially early in the season when the male is still trying to entice and attract the female, he may engage in prolonged, ritualized plucking of the prey, especially if a small bird, stopping frequently to look at the female, before finally presenting it to her or caching it conspicuously in a place that she can observe. Later in the season, the transfers become more routine and automatic, but they are nearly always accompanied by characteristic, species-typical vocalizations – "eechips", chips, peeps, chitters, etc. Transfers can take place in the air from foot to foot, from foot to beak, or from beak to beak, or the male may drop the prey while flying above the female, and she then catches it in her feet as it falls. Generally when the birds are perched, the male transfers the prey from his feet to his beak and then walks up to the female presenting the prey to her in his beak, and she takes it in hers. An aggressive or hungry female, however, will charge up to the male and grab the food from his foot into hers.

While all these food transferring ceremonies are no doubt important in adjusting the male and female to each other and in socializing them to accept the close bodily contacts required for mating (and hence the term "courtship-feeding" is appropriate in this context), nevertheless it is true that in most species of falcons (all except *naumanni* and *vespertinus*?), the male continues to feed the female right through the egg-laying, incubation, and early nestling phases of the breeding cycle, so that her nutritional state is largely determined by the male's ability to catch prey. Some writers prefer terms such as "production-feeding" (Balgooyen 1976) or "supplementary feeding" (Newton 1979) to emphasize the nutritional importance of this activity for the female. It is, of course, not unique to falcons or raptors but does seem to be especially well developed in them.

Ian Newton in his book on *Population Ecology of Raptors* (1979) has pointed out the importance of the female's body condition for successful reproduction, not only to produce eggs but to enable her to accumulate sufficient reserves of fat to help tide her over the incubation and nestling periods. Since the male provides most of her food, as well as food for the young, there may well be an adaptive advantage for him to feed her as much as possible before the young hatch, so that a greater proportion of the food delivered to the nest after hatching can go to feed the nestlings.

Newton has made the important observation that female raptors reach their heaviest seasonal weights during the laying period, and then tend to lose some weight but to remain relatively heavy through incubation and into the nestling period. It seems likely from this observation that increased feeding prior to laying results in an improvement in body and gonad condition, which in turn influence such reproductive parameters as date of laying, number and quality of eggs. The ability to utilize fat reserves during incubation and parental care increases the chance for successful rearing of young, while if food is insufficient body and gonad development may be so retarded that laying does not occur at all.

Thus, the male's ability to catch prey and provision the female can be sorely taxed, and he tends to lose weight steadily through the breeding season, so that by the end of summer he is often quite thin. His food-provisioning capability is related in part to his intrinsic physical ability as a hunter and in part to the quality of his territory, particularly to the abundance of prey animals in it. It is likely that the food transferring ceremonies early in the season provide the female with a means for assessing the overall quality of the male and his territory (including, also, the nest-site) and determining whether it is to her advantage to stay or seek another situation. There must be a very high selection on males to locate optimum nesting territories and to perform with high proficiency as food-providers.

Reversed sexual size dimorphism fits this division of labour between male and female falcons. A large, dominant female can force her mate to hunt at his maximum capacity, while her lethargy and large size are both adaptive for maximizing the storage of energy reserves for use during laying, incubation and brooding. RSD in falcons provides another example of Downhower's (1976) bioenergetic explanation for normal and reversed sexual dimorphism in birds and mammals.

Another striking feature of the pre-laying phase of the breeding cycle in falcons is that copulation, or copulatory mounting, occurs frequently and for a rather long time before eggs are laid. Males sometimes mount females before they begin courtship-feeding and nest-site displays, particularly in old, well adjusted pairs, and it is not at all unusual for copulations to occur for a period of four to eight weeks before the first egg. Mounting occurs several times a day, and in some

43

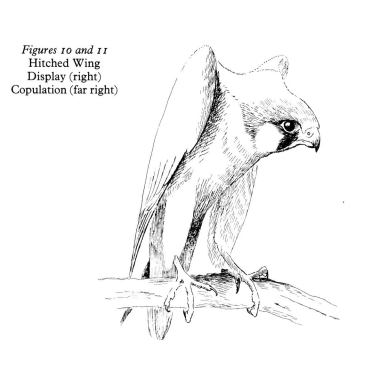

cases as often as several times an hour. Matings appear to be particularly frequent in the early morning hours in the days immediately prior to laying.

Most male falcons have a pre-copulatory display which they use to test the female's readiness to mate. This display usually has an aerial version as well as a perched version. The aerial display incorporates some special aerobatic move, such as a slow landing swoop up to a perch near the female with the feet conspicuously extended in flight. The perched element involves standing up tall on extended legs (showing off the sometimes brightly coloured pantaloons, as in the hobby), sometimes arching the neck and lowering the head, or hitching the wing butts above the plane of the back, and staring intently at the female. The male may run in a tip-toe fashion along a tree branch or cliff ledge holding this awkward posture, stopping abruptly to stare at the female, who, if she is receptive, turns her back to the male. These precopulatory displays are rather self-assertive and somewhat aggressive looking, and the male may actually achieve a temporary dominance over the female during these copulatory sequences, as Monneret (1974) has indicated.

A female falcon indicates her readiness to mate by turning away from the male and by bending forward and elevating her tail at about 45° or less above her back, assuming a kind of Stationary Bow. The male mounts the perched female directly from an extended flight, in some cases, or from a nearby perch. Sometimes he jumps on her back from a standing position by her side. As he lands on her back, she shifts her tail to one side, and he depresses his tail down between her wing and tail to achieve cloacal contact, while balancing himself on his tarsi and closed toes by flapping his wings, which are usually held high above his body.

Statements that falcons sometimes copulate or attempt to copulate in flight require careful confirmation. To my knowledge only swifts are capable of such a feat, and they do it by locking feet together in a belly to belly embrace, as the couple falls through the air.

Vocalizations during copulation, which lasts only a few seconds, vary greatly even among individuals of the same species, but usually both the male and the female vocalize, and the female's wailing calls are unusually loud and persistent. On a calm morning, the copulatory wailing of the large falcons can be heard from more than a kilometre away, and it seems likely that this loud calling is another kind of signal to neighbouring falcons that a successfully bonded pair is on location.

Close observations of falcons mating in captivity reveal that only some of the copulatory mountings result in actual cloacal contact with the possibility of insemination. Especially early in the season, the mountings are often brief and incomplete, and it is also likely that even later on, ejaculation does not occur every time there is cloacal contact. These observations and the frequency of mountings over an extended period suggest that copulation in falcons has become ritualized into another form of courtship display, which may be particularly important in synchronizing the gonadal maturation of the male and female, so that the male's potency is at a peak at the same time the female is ovulating. (For details on copulation see Cade 1960, Willoughby and Cade 1964, Balgooyen 1976, Wrege and Cade 1977, and Cramp and Simmons 1980.)

Compared with other birds, falcons lay somewhat larger eggs than average for their body sizes (Rahn *et al.* 1975), from about 10 per cent of female weight in small kestrels to 5 per cent in the large falcons. The eggs are rather blunt, rounded ovals with dull surfaces, which are usually intensely blotched or speckled with brown and red pigments, although occasionally they can be almost unmarked in hole-nesting species.

The interval between eggs in a clutch is usually from 48 to about 60 hours, but intervals of 72 hours or longer are not uncommon in individual females that typically lay at shorter intervals. Completed clutches are most often three to four eggs, but normal clutches of two are not uncommon, particularly in tropical species, and five to six eggs, exceptionally more, are laid by some Northern Hemisphere species, particularly kestrels. Most falcons will replace a first clutch lost after a week or two of incubation; the interval from loss to beginning of the replacement clutch is around 14 days in most cases. Some kestrels are known to re-lay and produce two broods per year, but the vast majority of falcons are single-brooded.

Falcons typically begin incubation with the penultimate egg of the clutch, but depending on environmental conditions, some covering of the eggs may occur sooner. True incubation, as distinct from sitting on the eggs or sheltering the eggs, is revealed by the adult's posture, particularly by the fact that the rump and lower back feathers are always fluffed out in an apparent heat-dissipating position.

Even in the same species there can be considerable differences among nests in the interval from hatching of the first to last eggs. Most often the eggs of a clutch hatch out within a 48-hour period, although it is not unusual for one or two eggs to be delayed significantly beyond the time the other eggs hatch, giving rise to a runt in broods of three to four, or sometimes to two runts in larger broods. In most falcons, however, hatching is more synchronous than used to be surmised from the apparent staggered ages of young in the same nest. It has only recently been realized that males develop more rapidly than females, particularly in species with pronounced RSD, and much of the difference in body size and, especially, feather development among siblings results from this sexual difference in rate of growth rather than from a difference in age.

Both parents incubate and possess paired brood-patches on their breasts, although the male's patches are relatively less well developed than the female's in most species. (Dementiev 1951 states that there are three brood-patches, while Cramp and Simmons 1980 say there is a single median brood-patch, but I have never been able to see any indication of a third or a median patch.) The male's participation in incubation is quite variable within and among species of falcons. He seldom incubates at night, and in species with pronounced RSD it may be difficult for him to warm the eggs adequately for an extended period. Typically his role seems to be to relieve the female for short intervals, during which she feeds, perhaps takes a bath, and performs other maintenance activities; however, even in large falcons it is not uncommon for the male to spend up to one third of the daylight hours on the eggs, and apparently the males of *naumanni* and *vespertinus* share about equally with their females in incubation. It is also interesting to note that in these species the females catch their own food during the incubation phase of the breeding cycle.

The incubation time for hatching of eggs varies somewhat among falcons, depending mainly on body size and egg size, but it is generally longer than has often been stated. Incubation times of 28 to 29 days for the eggs of large falcons are all suspect, and any incubation time of less than 27 days for even small species is probably erroneous. Kestrels and other small species typically hatch their eggs after 28 to 30 days of incubation; medium-sized falcons, after 30 to 32 days; and large falcons, after 32 to 36 days.

Young falcons are said to be "semi-altricial" and nidicolous. Their eyes are closed at hatching but open in one to five days. At hatching, the ear opening may be closed (*rufigularis*), indicated by a pinhole (*peregrinus*), or fully developed (*mexicanus*). Depending on the species or geographic race, the talons, beak, and fleshy parts may be lacking in pigments, or they may show varying degrees of coloration (for example, the white phase gyrfalcon hatches with colourless talons and beak, which gradually develop a degree of melanization, but the darker phases hatch with jet black talons).

PLATE iv (overleaf)
Lanner Falcon
Falco biarmicus
Male (right) bowing
to female (left)
at the eyrie

45

R. David Digby

Nestling and juvenile falcons usually have fleshy parts that are coloured differently from their adults – typically a pale fleshy yellow to greenish yellow, or some shade of bluish grey. Most adult falcons have bright yellow to chrome yellow fleshy parts, which become even more intense in colour during the breeding season – especially in males – but the red-footed falcons (*vespertinus* and *amurensis*) are unusual in having bright crimson-red parts (male) or orangish to yellow-orange parts (females and juveniles), while the adults of *subniger* and *berigora* have greyish white to bluish fleshy parts.

Falcons hatch with a thick, white, first downy coat made up of prepennae, which originate from the follicles of the later contour feathers. Beginning at 9 to 12 days of age, this covering is soon overgrown by a denser and longer second down made up of preplumulae, which develop from the follicles of the later, definitive down feathers. It often has a greyer colour than the first down and appears quite smoky in some falcons (e.g. Icelandic merlins). At 14 to 17 days of age the contour feathers (remiges and rectrices) begin emerging from their follicles, and depending on the size and sex of the falcon, it is fully feathered and ready to fly at 30 to 50 days of age.

The plumage of juvenile falcons, regardless of sex, usually resembles that of the adult female in dimorphic species, *sparverius* being the only exception; otherwise, the juvenile plumage is usually a rather plain, brownish colour with streaks on the underparts instead of bars. According to Baumgart's (1975) ideas about the functional significance of patterns and colour signals in raptors, the typical juvenile plumage of falcons lacks the sign stimulae denoting intraspecific aggressiveness and spatial intolerance of conspecifics. Falcons essentially achieve their definitive adult plumage with the completion of their first annual moult when they are somewhat more than one year old.

Some individual falcons, particularly among the small species, attain sexual maturity and breed in the season following their hatching when they are slightly less than one year old; but most falcons do not gain access to a mate and nesting territory until they are two or more years old. In the peregrine and other large falcons males apparently reach sexual maturity, on average, about a year later than females (Cade and Fyfe 1978). A few females breed in their first year, more in their second or third, and some not until their fourth or later; whereas, no males breed in the first year, some do in their second year, more in their third and fourth years, and some not until their fifth or later years. Obviously the average age of first breeding will vary depending upon the population status of the species in relation to available breeding opportunities, including nest-sites and food resources. In an expanding population the average age of breeders will be less than in a stable population.

Parental care is highly developed in falcons, and there is a rather complex system of communications between parents and their offspring to promote the latter's survival with minimum risk to the adults. At hatching the young are able to emit distress calls not unlike those of domestic fowl and many other birds, a kind of high pitched, rapidly repeated chirp, often given when a chick is cold or isolated from its mother and siblings, and also, comfort notes, a softer, slower peeping, which the chicks utter when they are warm and huddled together under their mother. They do not at first call for food, and while gaping is more or less automatic in response to any movement or disturbance around the chicks, the female does usually give a food-presentation call as she offers bites of flesh to her young, a kind of soft, low "chip", which stimulates the nestlings to gape.

Usually only the adult female feeds the downy young chicks, by stripping off small bites of flesh from the carcasses brought to her by the male and offering them on the tip of her bill, but the male's role in feeding the chicks directly is highly variable from nest to nest. He usually helps the female more in the later stages of nestling life, when the young require more food and are more demanding. There often appears to be a deliberate effort by the parents to ensure that each chick receives food, and beak to beak feeding continues even after the young are well feathered and fully capable of feeding themselves, unlike the situation with accipitriform raptors. The parents will avoid a food-begging young with a full crop to feed another that has not received food.

The young begin their food-begging wail at 7 to 10 days of age, and this call becomes progressively louder and more persistent with age and continues well into the post-nesting period of dependency. The full food-begging display with lowered and quivering wings, spread tail, and fluffed plumage, accompanied by incessant wails, begins before the young leave the nest but is most prominent after the young have started to fly. As with the adult female, the young also employ an aerial version of food-begging, a slow, almost stalled, cuckoo-like flight ("flutter glide" of Cade 1960), with spread and depressed tail, wings flapping rapidly in a position below the body axis, accompanied by food-begging wails. The fledged young often chase after their parents using this form of flight.

The intensity of food-begging appears to be related directly to the nutritional state of the young.

48

Fledglings that have been consistently well fed and have never experienced severe hunger are much less demonstrative than youngsters that have been starved on occasion or that are in generally poor condition. Hungry young become aggressive toward their food-delivering parents and will actually attack them for the prey. Once starved, the young falcon becomes compulsive in its aggressive food-begging and will continue the behaviour even after it has been satiated. (The birds that falconers refer to as "screamers" are eyasses that have been reduced in weight too early in their period of development.) It is probably for this reason that the parents stop feeding the young directly in the late stage of nestling life and begin delivering and leaving intact carcasses at the eyrie; also after the young start flying, the parents avoid direct contact with their offspring as much as possible, often dropping the prey to their young in the air or placing it quickly in a location where the young can get to it after the parent has departed. Depending on the species, the fledged youngsters remain dependent upon their parents for food for two to eight weeks, or even longer, after they leave the nest.

Relations among siblings are usually rather peaceful in a brood of falcons. The extreme "Cain-and-Abel" conflicts or deliberate fratricide recorded for certain eagles and other accipitriform raptors (Meyburg 1974, Newton 1979) is unknown among falcons, although it is likely that in a severely food-stressed brood, when a chick dies from starvation or disease, it will be eaten by the remaining siblings (see Cade 1960, for an apparent case at a gyrfalcon eyrie in Alaska).

The young begin their socialization as newly hatched chicks, huddling together and peeping in contentment under their mother. As long as they continue to be well fed by their parents, they get along calmly together, often sharing the same prey item together when they become well feathered nestlings and fledglings. They often engage in mutual preening and billing and in playful behaviours, such as footing mock quarry. After they begin flying, the young indulge in a great deal of contagious and exploratory activities. If one sunbathes or preens, the others do the same. If one calls for food, the others call, even if they have full crops. If one flies off to bathe in a puddle, the others join in. If one chases after a large bird, the others follow, and so on. There is also a great deal of chasing after each other, diving and stooping and flipping over to present talons. They race past trees or bushes on the wing and grab off sprays of leaves in their feet, or they dive down and grab sticks or dried dung from the ground, and then they contest over these objects in the air, as though crabbing over prey. It is hard to escape the conclusion that all these playful behaviours serve as practice for catching prey, and, indeed, the young soon begin catching insects and other weak prey as part of these early exploratory activities. Their prey-catching inclinations and abilities develop rapidly with further maturation and practice in the ensuing days before dispersal from their natal territory, aided in part by interactions with their parents as well as with each other.

In well fed and well adjusted broods this fledgling period is an active and exuberant time in the young falcon's life, and one imagines that many of its later social capabilities become established during this period of maximum interaction with its siblings and parents. Often, too, the young remain together for a time as a loose hunting party after they have begun to hunt on their own and leave their parents' territory.

A food-stressed brood shows rather different behaviour in the fledgling stage. The young are less active. They remain perched near the eyrie, giving food-begging solicitations and waiting for their parents to appear with prey. There is no sharing of food; the youngster that receives food from a parent flies away to a distant perch, and if a sibling approaches, it mantles over the prey, spreading and depressing its tail and drooping its wings around the food and constantly turning its back to the intruder in an effort to keep the food away from the other bird. Scuffles and fights over prey are frequent. Playful and exploratory activities are little in evidence.

Are such youngsters socially maladjusted in adulthood? Certainly there are great variations in the way adult falcons act toward one another in the pair bond, and as parents, and it could well be that the amount and kinds of socializing versus antagonistic interactions with siblings and parents during this formative period predetermine the degree to which a falcon can function successfully as a mate and parent in later life. There is a whole investigative field of "social psychology" yet to be explored in these birds, whose lives and social relations are influenced so much by the abundance and availability of food.

Figure 12
Mantling over food

Falcons and Men

Falcons and men have inhabited the earth together for several hundred thousand to a million years, depending on just when one fixes the origin of the genus *Homo*. During all but a fraction of that time species of both genera have occupied ecological niches that were determined by the blind forces of natural selection and that were integral, functioning parts of the global ecosystem. No one knows just when individuals of *Homo* became self-conscious, acquired cognition, the ability to foresee the consequences of events and actions, and attained the supreme capacity to break away from the forces of nature that control the lives of all other animals, but populations of *Homo sapiens* were probably already beginning to exert irreversible influences on the numbers and survival of other species at least 20,000 years ago. Today, modern, technological man is the dominating influence on earth, for better or for worse, and the destiny of falcons, like the destiny of all wild animals, is now inextricably bound by the actions of men and by the decisions these uniquely rational creatures make.

The accelerating destruction and degradation of natural habitats by an expanding human population, ever in need of more and more of the earth's resources, is the greatest threat to the continued existence of falcons and most other wildlife. The "Global 2000" report commissioned by President Carter predicts with awesome credibility the consequences to be expected by the turn of this century: more species of animals and plants will become extinct in the remaining two decades of the twentieth century than in all of man's previous history on earth, and the losses will be particularly heavy in the rich tropical forests of the world.

How many species of falcons will be included in the list of extinctions by AD 2000? Surprisingly perhaps, in my view, with a little luck none will be, although some of the island endemics such as the Mauritius kestrel and the barred kestrel of Madagascar are candidates that need careful tending. Some species, however, are likely to exist only in greatly diminished numbers by then.

Even so, the prospects for the continued survival of falcons are better than for many other comparable groups of animals. The reasons lie in part in the intrinsic capacity of falcons to adjust to environmental changes and to reach some accommodation with man-dominated lands (see remarks in the preface), but more importantly they lie in the fact that falcons have a special place in man's regard for other animals. Falcons have always been popular and admired birds – often even by those who kill them – and especially today there are a great many people who like falcons and who are determined not to let them die out.

This new determination to save certain especially valued species has found particularly strong expression in the example of the peregrine falcon. From the time it became clearly understood in the mid-1960s that the broad-scale use of DDT and some other organochlorine insecticides had been responsible for unprecedented, continent-wide declines in the breeding populations of this species in both Europe and North America (Hickey 1969), concerned scientists, conservationists, and falconers mounted efforts to increase the legal protection afforded to still existing populations and to secure reasonable limitations on the further use of DDT, dieldrin, and related chemicals for control of pests. Concern over the fate of the peregrine in Europe and North America was in no small measure responsible for the effective controls placed on use of DDT and dieldrin in most industrialized nations of the Northern Hemisphere by 1970 (see Ratcliffe 1980 for a full account). In Great Britain where voluntary restraints on DDT and dieldrin began earlier than in other countries, the peregrine has shown a gratifying natural increase in numbers and soon may well exceed its pre-World War II population there (see page 67).

At the same time falconers and others troubled by the possible extirpation of the peregrine from much of its historical range and by its increasing unavailability for falconry began a crash programme to learn how to propagate the species on a large scale in captivity and to re-establish breeding pairs in nature through the release of captive-raised individuals (Cade 1974, 1980; Cade and Fyfe 1978; Newton 1979; Ratcliffe 1980). Institutional programmes associated with Cornell University, the Canadian Wildlife Service, the University of California at Santa Cruz, and others in Europe joined with various private breeders in what has become an outstanding international and co-operative effort. By 1981 considerably more than a thousand peregrine falcons had been produced in captivity in North America alone, and nearly a thousand had been released to the wild (Harper 1981). Several pairs of released peregrines were breeding successfully on their own in the eastern United States, where the species had been completely wiped out in the 1960s, and also in the Rocky Mountains, California, and northern Alberta where only remnant wild populations remained by the 1970s. At least one released pair was breeding in Germany, and release programmes involving significant numbers of falcons were well launched in West Germany and Sweden.

Figure 13
Hooded peregrine
on a block

The combined cost of these programmes has been several million dollars, and they have involved several thousand persons, not to mention supporting governmental agencies, conservation organizations, foundations, and corporations. It would be hard to identify a parallel effort devoted to a single species in the entire annals of conservation.

The global endeavour to save the peregrine and other endangered raptors is, I believe, a phenomenon deeply rooted in man's past relations with falcons and other birds of prey and particularly with the cultural heritage of falconry. It has been a chequered past, but on the whole falcons have benefited from the veneration that some men – especially falconers – have always bestowed upon them.

The origins of falconry are lost in prehistory, but it is likely that techniques for training hunting hawks were invented independently two or more times, probably in the Far East (China or Mongolia) and in the Middle East. Several writers have suggested that hawks were being trained in China as early as 2000 BC, but the earliest acceptable historical record is the bas-relief depicting a falconer and his hawk from the ruins at Khorsabad during the reign of the Assyrian king, Sargon, around 750 BC. Falconry is not likely to have been practised in any consistent way by hunting-and-gathering peoples, as the luxury of keeping and feeding falcons requires a level of culture above that of bare subsistence. Hawking, on the other hand, fits especially well with pastoral nomadism, and most of the nomadic peoples of Asia probably practised falconry as far back in time as they had been herding domestic stock, riding horses, and keeping dogs. It may well be that the Mongolian horsemen were the first to train hunting falcons, but the Arabic tribes may have had an equally long tradition. The sport was probably first introduced into Europe by restless horsemen invading from the east, perhaps the Scythian and Sarmatian riders from the Russian steppes and certainly by Attila the Hun.

Falconry subsequently reached its zenith as an institution in the medieval feudal societies of European Christendom and Islam, from about AD 500 to 1600. During this long period falcons, or the "noble hawks" as they were termed, were among the most valued possessions of the aristocracy, and there were strict rules and laws about ownership. Severe punishments were meted out to those who harmed wild falcons, robbed eyries without proper authorization, or stole others' hawks. (There would be few poachers of falcons in the world today if hands were still being chopped off and eyes gouged out for such offences.)

Each rank in feudal society had a falcon or hawk as its symbol. In the *Boke of Saint Albans* (1486) one reads that the golden eagle is for the emperor; the gyrfalcon and jerkin (male), for the king; the falcon gentle (female peregrine), for the prince; the rock falcon (another form of peregrine), for the duke; the typical peregrine, for the earl; the bastard or tiercel peregrine, for the baron; the saker, for the knight; the lanner, for the squire; the merlin, for the lady; the hobby, for the page or youngman; while the "ignoble hawks" designated the lower classes in society – female goshawk, for the yeoman; male goshawk, for the poor man; female sparrowhawk, for the priest; and the muskayte or male sparrowhawk, for the holywater clerk.

Every manor had its mews in those days, and the office of falconer was accorded high rank. Vassals always took their falcons to court functions, but above all falcons were a part of the retinue of armies. They figured prominently as peace offerings and articles of trade during the Crusades between the Christians and Saracens; and during the first Hundred Years War falcons crossed the Channel with the English armies and witnessed the battles of Crécy, Poitier, and Agincourt when the English longbow men destroyed the flower of French knighthood with their armour-piercing, cloth yard arrows. For a thousand years or more falcons enjoyed a popularity and a degree of protection from human molestation that have seldom been accorded to any other animals.

The use of guns for hunting and the intensive management of game preserves, among other factors such as the Cromwellian Commonwealth in England and the French Revolution on the Continent, brought changes beginning in the seventeenth century that led to a decline in the popularity of falconry. These social trends culminated in the eighteenth, nineteenth, and early twentieth centuries in a reversal of the medieval veneration of falcons, and for a considerable time the noble peregrine falcon and all her relatives – merlins, hobbies, and even kestrels – came to be considered "vermin" by the gamekeepers and their landlords in Europe and by the waterfowl and gamebird hunters in North America. Falcons were ruthlessly shot, trapped, poisoned, and their eggs and young were destroyed in the nests. During this time, also, especially in the United States, hawk shooting became a sport just like wildfowling, and many peregrines, merlins, and kestrels, along with hawks and buzzards, fell to hunters' guns at such famous hawk-shoots as Hawk Mountain, Pennsylvania, before it became a sanctuary in the 1930s; Cape May, New Jersey; Sodus Bay on the south shore of Lake Ontario; and Fisher's Island, New York, where one famous and formidable lady used to hoist her 12-bore at many a migrant "duck hawk" and "pigeon hawk" winging its way southward from its boreal nesting grounds. The keepers of homing pigeons became determined and unrelenting enemies of the large falcons, especially peregrines, during these centuries as well.

In addition to all this carnage, egg-collecting became a favourite hobby of many naturalists, and falcons' eggs were especially prized because of their great beauty, relative rarity, and because of the physical challenge involved in their taking. No doubt many thousands of sets of falcon eggs have been collected in the last 250 years; often the same nest was robbed two or even three times in the same year, and some famous eyries yielded up their treasure year after year for decades. Certain species such as the peregrine, merlin, and hobby were especially hard hit by an excessive zeal for egg-collecting.

During this period, too, a handful of falconers continued to practise their sport in Europe, mostly as members of small, exclusive clubs, such as the Royal Loo Hawking Club in Holland (1771–1853), and in Britain, the Falconers' Club (1770–1838), the High Ash Club (1792–1830), and the Old Hawking Club (1864–1926). In 1927 the still extant British Falconers' Club came into existence. In 1923, a German organization, the *Deutscher Falkenorden*, was founded in Leipzig; it is the oldest still existing club devoted to the sport. Falconry began to be practised on a very limited scale in North America following World War I (Fuertes 1920); but the first club did not come into existence until the 1940s, and American falconry did not flower until after World War II.

While these falconers trapped a certain number of haggard and passage falcons from the wild and robbed nests for eyasses – or paid gamekeepers to take eyasses that they would otherwise have killed – their impact on wild populations was miniscule by comparison with that of the game-keepers, farmers, hunters, and pigeon fanciers. From about 1700 to 1930 falconers were virtually alone in speaking out against the wanton destruction of falcons and other birds of prey and in attempting to persuade other groups of people that wild falcons are beautiful creatures as deserving of their places in nature as any others. Falconers often clashed with gamekeepers, egg-collectors, and pigeon fanciers in ways that were unpleasant and counterproductive; but on the whole it must be fairly stated that falconers have always been, and continue to be, among the most ardent conservationists of wild falcons.

However disgusting from an aesthetic standpoint and biologically unnecessary the destruction of falcons is, it remains arguable as to whether all the killing and molestation over the past 250 years had any lasting impact on the size and distribution of falcon populations, except possibly in very local circumstances. Certainly the effects of direct mortality on individuals have been far less significant than the massive alterations of natural environments by agriculture, timbering, mining, suburbanization and the whole host of human-induced degradations of nature included in the contemporary concept of "environmental pollution". I personally feel that all the shooting and trapping and other direct actions to "control" the numbers of falcons and other raptors have been essentially without result in permanently reducing *breeding populations*, owing to the fact that only the expendable surplus from the annual production of young birds has been removed or partially removed by these means (Cade 1974, 1980a; see also Newton 1979; and Bijleveld 1974, for a different point of view).

It was not until after World War II, when the new technology of synthetic chemical pesticides and other aspects of modern "throw-away" society in the industrialized countries, and the whole-sale destruction of tropical forests and other natural habitats in Third World countries began to cause serious environmental problems and consequent reductions in the numbers of falcons and other wildlife, that a new public sympathy and appreciation for the value of falcons began to emerge. The prominence with which the peregrine and some other birds of prey figured in the public debates over the use of DDT and dieldrin rekindled interest and concern for the survival of threatened raptors in a way that all the old statistics on killing had not been able to do. Now most states, provinces, and nations afford full legal protection against the killing and the unauthorized taking of falcons. In the United States the Endangered Species Act of 1973 gives additional protection to those species most critically threatened with extinction and further authorizes the Secretary of the Interior to take whatever actions are necessary to effect the recovery of decimated populations. The International Convention on Trade in Endangered Species of Wild Fauna and Flora lists the peregrine, the Barbary falcon, the Mauritius kestrel, the Seychelles kestrel and the Aldabra race of *newtoni* on Appendix I, those species subject to the most stringent regulations in international trade, and all other species of *Falco* are included on Appendix II, the next most stringent category.

At the same time, various raptor societies, raptor rehabilitation centers, and raptor propagation programs have sprung up all around the world. The Raptor Research Foundation, Inc., an American based group of professionals and amateurs, frequently attracts more people to its annual

52

meetings than the august American Ornithologists' Union has at its. At no time in history have falcons and all their feathered kin with hooked beaks and taloned feet been so much in the public eye and such popular subjects of admiration and study as they are at the present time.

Falconry has never been more popular than it is today either. Although I cannot prove it with hard figures, I believe there are more falconers now than at any time in the past (Cade 1968). No one knows how many practising falconers there are in the world, but I consider the figure lies between ten and twenty thousand individuals. Most of them are in North America, Europe, and the Middle East, with scattered numbers in South America, Australia, New Zealand, Africa, the Indian Subcontinent, the Asiatic parts of the Soviet Union, Korea, Japan, and possibly China. Their numbers are steadily increasing in the affluent countries.

Falconers, like other hunters, have not been without their critics in recent years, and I think it is important to examine briefly the pros and cons of falconry in a book about falcons. How does falconry fit with the current predictions about declining raptor populations in the coming decades? Is falconry an anachronism that is no longer justifiable in a world where billions of people already over-utilize the renewable resources of the biosphere? Or does it have a continuing place in man's culture?

Some people object to falconry on ethical or religious grounds just because it *is* a form of hunting – it is a "blood sport" involving the killing of other animals. I am not a philosopher of the hunt; I am a practitioner, and I have never really questioned the "rightness" or "wrongness" of hunting because it has always been a part of my nature from earliest childhood days. For those who require a philosophy to justify hunting, I can do no better than refer to the essays of the American sports-writer, Ed Zern (e.g. *Audubon* 1972), or to the lyrical philosophy of José Ortega y Gasset in *Meditations on Hunting*, an English translation by Howard B. Wescott (1972).

Both of these writers say that the reason they are hunters rather than observers or, God forbid, photographers, is that true communion with nature is not a spectator sport; rather one has to participate in some integral way in nature's activities. Since man's primal occupation was hunting, it is most natural for him to function as a predator when communing with nature. As Zern puts it: "When I am there as a predator I am there as a part of the natural scene, and I feel a oneness with nature that I never feel except when hunting . . . When I kill a sharp-tailed grouse or bobwhite quail I become a part of the process of life, accepting and fulfilling my role as predator and rejecting the destructive Old Testament concept of man as something separate from nature."

Ortega also believed that hunting and the killing of animals are essential elements of human nature and that from these ancestral pursuits arose all of the most advanced aspects of human behaviour, intelligence being a highly specialized function by which natural selection perfected the hunter's capacity to foresee consequences and to plan the successful outcome of the hunt. Moreover, he felt that sport hunting has to be a contest between the hunter and the hunted. It involves all those manoeuvres and stratagems by which the hunter attempts to capture and kill his prey and all the tactics that the prey employs to escape. "It is not essential to the hunt that it be successful. On the contrary, if the hunter's efforts were always and inevitably successful it would not be the effort we call hunting, it would be something else . . . For all the grace and delight of hunting are rooted in this fact: that man, projected by his inevitable progress away from his ancestral proximity to animals, vegetables, and minerals – in sum, to Nature – takes pleasure in the artificial return to it, the only occupation that permits him something like a vacation from his human condition."

Obviously I largely concur with Ortega and Zern. I believe that to hunt and to kill are impulses deeply rooted in the biological make-up of both falcons and men, and to deny their expression is to deny the fundamental nature of being a falcon or being human. There is an urge to hunt and to kill prey that goes beyond the need to acquire food. Falcons and dogs, for example, show this urge quite clearly, and I believe that when human beings are completely honest with themselves, they come face to face with the same imperative. Some psychologists say that the ability to suppress this urge or to sublimate it in some "socially acceptable way" is what separates man from beasts and makes us truly human. Such repression may also be one of the chief factors promoting constant, genocidal warfare among men, a truly human trait that absolutely separates us from the lower animals.

In the worst interpretation, it can at least be said that falconry is the most benign of the various forms of hunting, as well as the most exacting and the most satisfying. It is essentially a contest, only slightly contrived, between a superbly adapted aerial hunter – the falcon – and its almost equally well accomplished quarry. The pursuit and the escape, which in Ortega's view make the

53

hunt, involve spectacular aerial manoeuvres, which are visually exciting and aesthetically pleasing to behold. The falconer is removed from the actual capture and kill, in which he can participate only vicariously. Falconry is, therefore, partly a "spectator sport", and that is why I maintain that it is basically a special form of bird-watching. It is also participatory in that the falconer trains the falcon and exercises a degree of control over what the bird does. He and his dogs may also actively co-operate in the hunt by locating and flushing the quarry for the falcon. The co-ordinated action that can be achieved among man, falcon, dog, and sometimes horse, in pursuit of an illusive quarry becomes a high form of artistic expression, as aesthetically satisfying as the performance of ballet, figure skating, or Olympic gymnastics.

There is something more . . . When the falcon is waiting on just right, high overhead and a little upwind, the dog is frozen on a hard point, and the falconer makes his move to flush out the grouse, at that moment he may achieve an ecstatic communion with the animals – something I believe they also feel – a heightened sense of proportion and awareness that allows the falconer to know the successful outcome of the hunt before the falcon strikes. It is the same sense of correctness that the expert bowman feels in every muscle and sinew of his body at the instant his arrow leaves the string, and he knows that it will fly true to its mark . . . Not every hunt results in such heightened perception, but once experienced it has to be sought again.

Others object to falconry on the grounds that it is inhumane or cruel to keep a wild creature in captivity; but I suspect there are many more who agree that there are legitimate scientific, technological, educational, and recreational reasons for keeping wild animals in zoos, research laboratories, breeding establishments, classrooms, and, yes, private collections, so long as they are properly tended. Trained falcons, of course, are not captive in quite the same sense as zoo animals. They are flown free in the out-of-doors, and they are able to perform many of their natural functions, especially their chief function as hunters. They have the choice, so to speak, of remaining "captive" with the falconer or reverting to a wild existence, and that choice is often exercised. According to statistics compiled by Kenward (1979) over 40 per cent of all birds flown in falconry in Great Britain are eventually lost to the wild, while another 30 per cent are liberated voluntarily by the falconers.

There are a number of redeeming values of falconry. Hawking is generally recognized to be the most intellectually demanding and educational form of hunting ever devised, and it requires a high degree of skill and devotion from the falconer. It leads the hunter to a deep appreciation of nature, to a practical study of natural history, and quite often to serious scientific research on birds of prey. Its techniques offer possibilities for detailed observations and studies that would otherwise be quite difficult to make. All of these values were reflected in the life and work of the greatest falconer who ever lived, the Emperor Frederick II of Hohenstaufen (1194–1250), the first truly modern man to sit on a throne in Europe and the man who first introduced scientific thinking into writings about birds in his famous treatise, *De Arte Venandia cum Avibus*. Many falconers have followed in his tradition.

Falconry is also a completely safe method of hunting. No falconer has ever killed another person or harmed livestock with his trained falcon. One can now hunt with a falcon in many areas where it is unsafe or illegal to do so with a gun, and long after overpopulation has finally rendered shooting an unfeasible and socially unacceptable practice, it will still be possible to go hunting with trained falcons.

Falconry is not without its undesirable aspects, but the same can be said about bird-watching or any other outdoor activity. Unfortunately, falconry attracts an unusual number of eccentrics, exhibitionists, and extremists of one variety or another to its ranks. These types almost never turn out to be skilled falconers, but they make a very bad scene – sometimes for years – in their attempts to be falconers; and what is even worse, they frequently abuse the birds that fall into their hands. Also, falconry provides a potential market for commercialism and illegal traffic in birds of prey. If a potential for profit exists, someone will be sure to take advantage of it, and illegal trade in wild falcons does occur. Proper laws and effective enforcement can deal adequately with these undesirable elements.

Responsible falconers recognize the problems that beset their sport, and they acknowledge the need for effective governmental regulations which protect the legitimate, bona fide falconers from radical and bizarre fringe elements, as well as satisfying the public's concern for the conservation of birds of prey. Much credit goes to organizations such as the British Falconers' Club, the North American Falconers' Association, and the International Association for Falconry and Conservation of Birds of Prey, for taking a positive approach to problems involving falconry by developing guidelines for laws and standards of ethics for the regulation of falconers' activities – proposals that have been favourably received by national and international conservation groups as well as by

54

various governmental agencies involved in the administration of wildlife regulations. Falconers on the whole are an articulate and informed group of sportsmen, and they are the natural allies of conservationists.

One final objection to falconry is the often stated belief that the demands of falconers for birds place an unacceptable burden on existing wild populations of raptors, particularly for highly desired, rare or endangered species, such as the peregrine and the gyrfalcon. This would be a serious indictment of falconers if it were true, and it remains a potential problem in the future as falconers increase in numbers and raptors decline in the wild. Until very recently, falconers have been solely dependent for their birds on the existence of healthy and viable *wild* populations of raptors, and falconers have long recognized the need for careful harvesting and husbanding of the breeding populations (Cade 1954). When certain populations have declined in the wild, it has been necessary to prohibit or severely limit the take for falconry, as has been the case with the peregrine in some parts of its breeding range. Many more such cases can be expected in the future.

Falconers have now solved this potential problem through their outstanding efforts over the past ten years to perfect the breeding of falcons and other raptors in captivity. Many people, including falconers, still do not appreciate the significance of this achievement, which to my thinking is the greatest innovation in the entire history of the sport. Some detractors have tried to diminish the role of falconers in this accomplishment by pointing out that the breeding of raptors in captivity is merely a branch of aviculture, not falconry. That is true; but let the record be clear: almost without exception, those who have succeeded in breeding raptors in captivity have been falconers or close associates of falconers, not aviculturists, not wildlife managers, and not preservationists. Only falconers have had the sustained motivation and the technical skills to succeed in a difficult task, and no one will ever be able to tally up the time, effort, and personal expense that all the private breeders in the world have put into what has become a truly global occupation (occupation in Ortega's sense).

Less than ten years ago, most people still thought that the practical breeding of birds of prey in captivity was a pipe-dream. Faith McNulty (1972) echoed the prevailing attitude when she characterized the captive breeding of peregrines as a feat "so difficult that it cannot repopulate the wild or provide birds for fanciers". At that time only American kestrels had been produced in large numbers in confinement, and fewer than a dozen peregrines had been raised; but since 1973 impressive numbers of peregrines, gyrfalcons, sakers, lanners, prairie falcons, merlins, and other species have been raised each year by an increasing number of establishments around the world. At least 17 species of *Falco* have now been bred in captivity: in addition to those mentioned above, the list includes the laggar, red-headed falcon, Eleonora's falcon, red-footed falcon, common kestrel, Australian kestrel, Mauritius kestrel, lesser kestrel, greater kestrel, and New Zealand falcon. It is probable that all species of falcons can be bred in captivity, not to mention many other kinds of hawks, eagles, and other raptors.

This remarkable conclusion means that no species of falcon *has* to become extinct. Some may eventually not be able to sustain themselves as populations in the wild, if their requirements for habitat are totally obliterated; but if man chooses they can kept as domestic populations. It also means that falconers can produce their own birds for training and hunting; they can now be free of any stigma that might attack to their continued use of wild birds. Already in North America more than half of the large falcons being flown in falconry are captive bred, and the percentage will no doubt continue to rise in all countries.

The future for the domestic production of falcons holds exciting possibilities for the artificial creation of new varieties of falcons and for the development of truly domesticated breeds. All species of falcons hybridize readily in captivity, and new forms have already been created by this technique, usually by means of artificial insemination; and as new mutants crop up in captive progeny it will be possible to breed selectively for special characteristics. As the homing pigeon stands in relation to the wild rock dove, so some distant breed of falcon may relate to the peregrine, and some future book will have to be written about the various breeds and races of domesticated falcons.

For now, we are still privileged to be able to observe, study, and write about the marvellous assortment of wild falcons that nature has arrayed on the all too fragile earth.

Part

II

Species Descriptions

Peregrine

(Great-footed Falcon, Duck Hawk)

Falco peregrinus

WHEN MOST PEOPLE think of a "falcon" they evoke an image of the peregrine, for this species has always had a special mystique and an involvement in the affairs of men unmatched by other birds. Indeed, the term "falcon" in the strict parlance of falconers refers specifically to the female peregrine, while the male is called a "tiercel" because he is about one third smaller than she. Because of its universality and familiarity, the peregrine falcon serves best as the standard of comparison for all other species in the genus *Falco*, especially as the peregrine is a sympatric breeding species with nearly every other species of falcon.

I have always been partial to Roger Tory Peterson's verbal portrait of the peregrine in his book *Birds Over America* (1948):

"Man has emerged from the shadows of antiquity with a Peregrine on his wrist. Its dispassionate brown eyes, more than those of any other bird, have been witness to the struggle for civilization, from the squalid tents on the steppes of Asia thousands of years ago, to the marble halls of European Kings in the seventeenth century."

His reference, of course, is to the fact that the peregrine has always been the *ne plus ultra* of falconry. A bird of the gauntlet and the mews just as much as it is a creature of wild river gorges and coastal palisades, the peregrine falcon has been admired by many devotees down through the centuries, such as falconers, naturalists and poets – but hated by gamekeepers, duck hunters and pigeon fanciers. In the last 20 years, the plight of the peregrine has served importantly to focus world attention on the problems of survival for endangered wildlife in the closing decades of the twentieth century, and the peregrine has become a prominent symbol of biological conservation.

The name peregrine means wanderer or migrator, and the falcon has, in fact, the most extensive natural distribution of any bird in the world, rivalled only by the osprey and the raven. Breeding populations occur on every continent except Antarctica and on many oceanic islands. It is not unusual for migrating peregrines to come aboard ships in the middle of the Atlantic Ocean, and I have seen migrants feeding on the wing and packing uneaten prey with them on passage at Fire Island, New York. One can safely conclude that there is no place on earth that peregrines have not been able to reach at one time or another, so great are their powers of flight.

Preferring landscapes of open expanse, nesting peregrines are found in such diverse regions and habitats as the circumpolar, arctic tundras, at least as far north as 76°N in western Greenland, and even farther north (in Novaya Zemlya, the Taimyr Peninsula, and on Stalinets Island) in the Russian Arctic, along major rivers in the taiga and temperate forest zones, in mountains, along sea-coasts or on islands wherever there are palisades and rocky crags, in the eucalyptus forests of Australia, and in the windswept plains of Patagonia south to the Falkland Islands and into Tierra del Fuego at 55°S. (Cade 1960.)

As breeding birds, peregrines are absent from high mountains such as the Himalayas and Andes, 3,960 m (13,000 ft) being the maximum recorded altitude, from the drier desert regions of Central Asia, Arabia, North Africa and Australia, and from the tropical forests of the Congo Basin, Central and South America, and southeastern Asia, although the black shaheen, a race of peregrine, breeds in the tropical forest of India, and peregrines on the South Pacific Islands nest in tropical forest.

Peregrines breed on New Caledonia, the New Hebrides, Solomon and Fiji islands of the Pacific but are curiously absent from New Zealand. They were formerly widespread and common on the Labrador coast but have never been known to nest on adjacent Newfoundland. They are also inexplicably absent from Iceland, the Faeroes, and all islands in the Bering Sea north of the Aleutians, places where nesting opportunities and an abundance of favoured prey seemingly create ideal conditions. (Cade 1960.)

As one might expect of such a wide-ranging species, peregrines vary geographically in body size, colour and pattern, breeding season, migratory behaviour, and other aspects of their biology. More than 22 different populations have been described as "subspecies" and given formal names by museum

R. David Digby

taxonomists, but only a few of these forms are distinct enough from their neighbours to be easily identified. The differences are mostly statistical, there being much gradation from one region to another, so that any given individual falcon cannot be assigned with much certainty to a particular population (or subspecies) unless its geographic origin is known. (Hickey 1969.)

Two of the most distinctive populations of peregrines also represent extremes in body size. The largest and most heavily marked peregrines on their underparts breed on the Aleutian and Komandorski islands in the Bering Sea. The usual buff ground colour of the ventral feathers in adults is replaced in these falcons by a bluish white, and the fleshy parts of the feet, cere and eye ring are pale lemon yellow instead of bright chrome yellow. Males are around 700–850 g ($24\frac{1}{2}$–30 oz) in body weight; females around 1,100–1,500 g ($38\frac{1}{2}$–53 oz). The resident Indian peregrine or black shaheen is one of the smallest forms, males weighing around 450–560 g (16–$19\frac{1}{2}$ oz) and females 600–750 g (21–$26\frac{1}{2}$ oz). (The still smaller Barbary falcon and red shaheen are provisionally considered here to constitute a separate species.) Black shaheens are very black on the back with equally black cheeks, bright rufous underparts, and very large feet for their body size. In 1933 the Russian falcon expert, G. P. Dementiev (1951), described a very small, dark peregrine (*F. p. pleskei*) from Sakhalin and the Shantar islands in the Sea of Okhotsk; those he identified as females average smaller even than red shaheens – one weighed only 500 g ($17\frac{1}{2}$ oz). It seems strange that such a small form would exist so far north in an area immediately adjacent to the region where the largest peregrines occur, and some authorities feel the specimens were incorrectly sexed.

African, Mediterranean, and western Pacific island peregrines also average rather small (slightly larger than black shaheens), while the peregrines native to Australia, South America and the American Arctic are medium-sized. Large peregrines occur in Great Britain, northern Europe, and the Russian and Siberian Arctic. Some of the largest peregrines ever measured used to breed in the eastern United States. One female trapped in Washington, DC, weighed over 1,500 g (53 oz), the size of a female gyrfalcon! (Alva G. Nye, Jr.).

Peregrines nesting in northern latitudes are highly migratory, while those nesting in northern maritime climates, at mid-latitudes, and in the Southern Hemisphere are much less so. The falcons that nest in the American Arctic and in Greenland migrate to Central and South America, some as far south as Argentina, while their counterparts in the Eurasian Arctic move south into Europe, Africa, the Middle East, India, China and South-East Asia. The peregrines nesting in the British Isles are largely resident there, as are the birds nesting on islands in the North Pacific. Falcons nesting in mountains at temperate latitudes move down into the plains or along coasts for the winter and shift southward to some extent, while birds nesting at lower latitudes in the Northern Hemisphere are essentially resident all year round on or near their nesting territories (e.g. southern California, Mexico, the Mediterranean region). Apparently no breeding population in the Southern Hemisphere – continental or insular – is migratory to any noticeable extent. (Hickey 1969, Cramp and Simmons 1980, Ratcliffe 1980.)

The peregrine is a bird hunter *par excellence*. It is one of the fastest and most aerial predators, and the functional design of the peregrine for pursuit and capture of flying quarry reaches a degree of perfection unmatched in other species. At least 132 bird species have been recorded in the diet of British peregrines (Ratcliffe 1980), 210 in central Europe (Cramp and Simmons 1980), 60 along the Yukon River in Alaska (Cade *et al.* 1968), more than 40 on the Arctic Slope of Alaska (White and Cade 1971), and for Victoria, Australia, 89 species (Pruett-Jones *et al.* 1981). Although no precise tally seems to have been published for North America, 200 species would not be out of order.

Peregrines tend to be opportunistic and catholic in their choice of birds, including in their diets species ranging in size from small passerines weighing less than 10 grams to large waterfowl (geese) and herons weighing 2,000 g (over 4 lbs). Within these extremes, however, certain sizes and types of birds are preyed upon more often than others. Male peregrines tend to catch birds most frequently in the size range from about 20 to 200 g ($\frac{3}{4}$ oz–7 oz) while females catch more birds in the 100 to 1,000 gram range ($3\frac{1}{2}$–35 oz).

In various parts of the world peregrines take certain species selectively and out of proportion to their relative numbers in the total available prey populations. Examples from North America include species with conspicuous "flash" patterns in flight – flickers, meadowlarks, red-winged blackbirds, blue jays; and those with special aerial courtship antics or patterns of flight – common snipe, rock and willow ptarmigan, mourning doves, teal, and shrikes. In Europe other examples include the cuckoo, various larks, various doves, jackdaw and hoopoe; in Australia, various parrots, especially the gallah, and, again, doves and pigeons.

Indeed, columbiform birds (doves and pigeons) are preferred wherever they occur throughout the worldwide range of the peregrine, and there can be no doubt that the feral rock dove and similar sized pigeons constitute the great bulk of the falcon's diet. Where they occur in numbers, feral and domestic pigeons typically make up from 20 to 60 per cent of the total individuals preyed upon during the breeding season. The size of a pigeon is optimal for most peregrines, and there is perhaps something about the way they fly that makes pigeons attractive targets, despite the fact that they are fast and shifty. Probably, the loose body feathers of pigeons and doves have evolved as an effective way to escape from the clutches of a falcon. Many times a stooping peregrine ends up with only a fist full of rump or tail feathers as the result of its efforts, while the slightly denuded pigeon or dove makes its escape to cover.

Young peregrines usually launch their first aerial attacks at flying insects such as dragonflies, cicadas, butterflies, and beetles, deftly snatching them up in their feet and eating them on the wing within a week after they first start flying. Adults occasionally catch insects too. There are cases on record of peregrines regularly visiting the mouths of bat caverns in the evening to catch bats as they swarm out for their nocturnal foraging, and flying foxes figure prominently in the diet of peregrines on tropical islands in the Pacific (Clunie 1972). In the tundra regions peregrines catch lemmings and voles in the "peak years" when these rodents are superabundant, but otherwise small terrestrial mammals constitute an insignificant fraction of the prey. Lizards and amphibians have been recorded a few times too, but perhaps the most unexpected prey to be taken are fish. I once saw a grayling snatched up by a peregrine as the fish broke water on the Colville River in Arctic Alaska, and Clayton White and I saw another peregrine make repeated attempts to catch fish from the same river.

Peregrines have an array of tactics for searching out, attacking, capturing, and killing their prey, and the precise combination of acts used in a given hunt will be determined in part by individual habits of the falcon and in part by the species of prey, the habitat, weather, season of the year, and other environmental variables.

Still-hunting is perhaps the most frequent method of searching. The peregrine perches atop some high vantage point, such as a cliff, tall tree, building or mountainside, from which it commands a wide view of open air space, and there watches for prey to move into a vulnerable position away from cover. The advantage of a high watch-point is that often the potential prey flies into the range of attack at an altitude lower than that of the waiting falcon, which can then more easily fly out and gain a position over the other bird. The pursuing falcon may gain additional altitude as it manoeuvres into position before delivering the final attack, which is a fast dive or "stoop" of tens to hundreds of metres and varying from a fully vertical plunge with closed wings to a shallow dive at a 45° angle with some wing-flapping. The stoop produces the speed by which the attacking falcon overhauls its intended victim, whose strategy for escape must be to shift and dodge the on-coming attacker at the last moment or to seek cover as quickly as possible.

Unless the attacked bird is small, 100 grams or less, a peregrine in full stoop always strikes the quarry with its feet rather than grabbing it ("binding"). The back talon frequently gashes into the prey, disabling it or killing it outright. Really severe strikes can result in the dismembering of a wing or severing of the head, and I have seen small birds literally torn into pieces by a stooping tiercel. More often, however, the strike serves only to stun the quarry, which may continue to fly, only to be attacked again, or which may give up and fall to the ground. The pursuing falcon then binds to the bird by grabbing it firmly in its feet and kills it by repeatedly biting into the neck until the nerve cord has been severed.

If the stooping falcon misses the bird on its first pass, it "throws up" over the fleeing bird and stoops again. A sequence of repeated stoops may ensue before the prey escapes or is finally caught, or the flight may end up in "tail-chasing". The falcon is more likely to grab the fleeing bird rather than to strike it after the first hard stoop, in which case it often shoots below the bird and rolls over to grab it from underneath. Apparently this mode of attack makes it more difficult for the prey to dodge away at the last moment.

An effective variation of the stooping attack occurs over open water, especially in heavily forested regions where the prey species are favoured by an abundance of cover. When a peregrine attacks a land bird over a river or lake it often stoops in such a way as to force the prey lower and lower on each pass, until it falls into the water. The peregrine then circles by and easily grabs the struggling bird from the surface. (Cade 1960.)

Still-hunting from a perch is also associated with another mode of attack called "ringing up" by falconers. Since these attacks are launched after high flying birds, the search takes the form of "sky-scanning." The falcon sits motionless with its head cocked to one side watching the upper air space. When it spots a bird in the air – often at altitudes and distances so great that a human observer cannot see it even with binoculars – the falcon evidently assesses the prospects carefully, for while every bird that passes over is watched, the falcon will actually pursue only the one out of thirty or fifty that appears to be vulnerable.

While the classic stoop from above the quarry is breath-taking in its reckless speed and adroit manoeuvring, the "ringing pursuit" to high altitude – the *haut vol* of French falconry – is truly spectacular, for it matches all the strength and special flying abilities of both the pursuer and the pursued in a contest that can last for many minutes, carry the contestants to 1,000 m (3,300 ft) or more in altitude, and traverse several kilometres of air space. The falcon usually begins by taking off into the wind so as to gain altitude as fast as possible and then continues to climb by flying in a wide helical pattern until it has mounted above the quarry. It can then execute a series of short stoops and tail-chases, until the quarry has been captured or until it dives for the ground, in which case the falcon follows in a stoop and usually takes the bird just as it is reaching the ground or on the ground if there is no deep cover.

In such an attack, the first strategy of the quarry is to stay above the falcon or to out-distance it by sustained flight. Powerful, fast flying birds such as pigeons, shorebirds or ducks typically rely on the latter, continuing to fly straight away while gaining altitude, but birds with light wing-loading such as owls, gulls, crows and herons ring up in tight spirals. Thus, while they cannot fly as fast as a peregrine, they can often gain altitude as fast or faster and so avoid capture. When the prey has been outflown by the peregrine at high altitude, it will try to dodge the falcon's stoops until it becomes exhausted or injured.

61

Its last recourse is then to fold its wings and drop straight to earth to seek cover, if it can escape the peregrine falling immediately behind it.

This ringing pursuit is also frequently used by peregrines living in forested country, for the prey is usually too high to make cover in time to avoid the attack. I have watched, to the limits of my vision with binoculars, as peregrines along the Yukon River in the Alaskan taiga fly up to catch snipe and sandpipers in this way. This method is also used with high success along coastlines or other "leading lines" where small, migratory birds pass over in large numbers in spring and autumn. High flying passerines are extremely vulnerable to this form of hunting, for they are quickly exhausted and cannot get down to cover fast enough to avoid capture.

An interesting variation of the ringing attack occurs when the prey is flying not so high and there is a good chance for it to escape into suitable ground cover. In this case, the attacking peregrine flies under the prey and forces it to flee by flying up and away from the ground. Once the prey has had to commit itself to escape by flight, then the typical ringing contest ensues. The Swedish ornithologist G. Rudebeck (1951), described this tactic from observations of migrant peregrines in Scania. (See, also, White *et al.* 1981.)

Peregrines also search for prey while circling or soaring high in the air, or "waiting on" in the falconer's language. From such positions they most often attack by stooping on prey below them, but they can go for higher birds by ringing up too. Sometimes males co-operate in hunting (Cade 1960, White *et al.* 1981).

Contour-hugging is occasionally used over land – along hedges, the edge of woods, or banks – but it reaches its most effective performance over the oceans. Maritime peregrines, such as those in the Aleutian Islands or in the islands of the Mediterranean, hunt by flying fast and low over the water, using waves to conceal their approach until they come suddenly upon surface-swimming water birds, which are panicked into flying or diving. A luckless member of the flock, responding a little too slowly, may be caught in a quick direct pursuit. Birds such as auklets or grebes, which are adept at sudden diving, can escape the initial onslaught, but some maritime peregrines learn to wait out the dives and return to attack again when the birds have surfaced and are exhausted for oxygen. During the breeding season some peregrines hunt almost exclusively over the sea, sometimes several kilometres from land, but unlike Eleonora's falcons, they go mostly for aquatic birds rather than for land birds migrating over the sea.

Sometimes peregrines will land on the ground after a bird has put into cover to escape, and they stalk around exploring with their feet in an attempt to flush the quarry out. They apparently also hunt this way for fledgling passerines and shorebirds on the tundra (S. K. Sherrod), and probably also for lemmings and voles. Young peregrines are more apt to hunt on the ground than older birds.

One of the commonest and apparently most effective anti-predator tactics of flocking birds, when a hunting peregrine or other diurnal raptor appears, is to mass up in a tight flying formation and to manoeuvre in a body so as to remain above the searching falcon or to stay out of its path. Sandpipers, gulls, terns, pigeons, crows, rooks, starlings, waxwings, and many other birds employ this tactic, which Niko Tinbergen and other naturalists have commented on. Peregrines often follow after these flocks, manoeuvre around them, and make exploratory stoops or feints in an apparent attempt to get an individual to break away from the formation, for a falcon will not stoop into a massed flock. If a single bird does break out, the peregrine will usually pursue it relentlessly. The dean of British falconers, Jack Mavrogordato (1966), calls this method of hunting "shepherding". He describes it extremely well in his account of rook-hawking, which he is perhaps the last person to have been able to practise to its full perfection on Salisbury Plain, now sadly ruined for this sport.

How fast do peregrines fly? This is one of the most frequently asked questions about the falcon and one of the most difficult to answer accurately. Though often said to be the fastest animal on earth, or the fastest flying bird, neither assertion is quite true, as Col R. Meinertzhagen (1959) was quick to point out. The peregrine's normal cruising speed is around 65 to 90 km per hour (40–55 mph), in the range with many other birds. While the peregrine is able to catch very fast flying birds such as swifts, pigeons, sandgrouse, and shorebirds, in level flight under its own muscle-power it can seldom catch up to a good homing pigeon, and its maximum speed in horizontal flapping flight probably does not exceed 105 to 110 km per hour (65–68 mph), nor would it be able to maintain that speed for long. Thus, the flapping peregrine is no faster than a cheetah running flat out.

The speed that a peregrine develops in a stoop is another matter. Most estimates vary from 160 to 440 km per hour (99–273 mph) according to Brown (1976), the latter figure being based on motion pictures of a falcon in full stoop at the Naval Research Laboratory in England during World War II. An aviator in a 1930 pursuit plane dived at a flock of flying ducks for practice, and, while travelling at 280 km per hour (173 mph), he observed a peregrine stoop past his aircraft at what he guessed was twice his speed (Lawson 1930). A peregrine that regularly stooped on feral pigeons from the tower of the Cologne Cathedral was calculated to dive at 252 to 324 km per hour (157–201 mph), but it is doubtful whether this bird could have been diving at maximum speed over the relatively short distances involved (Mebs 1972). Speed also varies with angle of descent: Hangte (1968) measured maximum speeds of 270 km per hour (167 mph) at a 30° angle of descent and 350 km per hour (217 mph) at 45°.

Theoretically a peregrine that stoops vertically with closed wings should achieve a terminal velocity

Parrott (1970) calculated the terminal velocity of a laggar falcon to be 360 km per hour (223 mph). The terminal speed of a falling peregrine should be somewhat faster, since it is a more compact and stream-lined bird; and the recent calculations of terminal speed by Orton (1975) place the rate of fall between 368 and 384 km per hour (228–238 mph).

The rate of success in hunting is another intriguing question often asked about peregrines. The popular notion that peregrines are so fast and skilful that they seldom miss their intended quarry is quite wrong, although some individual falcons – in the wild – do tally up very impressive scores in certain circumstances.

One problem in making observations of peregrine hunts is deciding which instances to count as bona fide hunts and which to exclude. If the observer counts every feint at a flock and every "playful" exploratory move toward another bird as an attempt to capture, he will obviously obtain a rather different estimate of "success" than the observer who has learned through long experience in the field how to tell when a peregrine is serious about her business. R. Treleaven (1980) has addressed this problem in an interesting discussion of "low intensity" versus "high intensity hunting". A peregrine intent on serious attack has a different wingbeat and attitude in the air than one that is just making exploratory or playful movements, although admittedly there is a gradation from exploratory feints to low intensity hunting to attack with strong motivation to kill, so that even a seasoned observer can be misled on occasion.

Rudebeck (1951) recorded 260 cases of migrant peregrines hunting in Scania in the autumn; only 7.3 per cent of these "hunts" ended in the capture of prey. Most of these falcons were no doubt inexperienced immatures, which are less effective than adults and which are noted for making frequent playful, mock attacks on other birds, and Rudebeck may not have distinguished this form of attack from true hunting. In Germany, Hangte (1968) observed 191 complete hunts between 1963 and 1967, 121 by the male and 69 by the female. The male was successful 13 times (11%); the female 12 times (17%). Clunie (1976) observed an immature peregrine hunting in an urban environment in the Fiji Islands; 6 out of 62 completely observed flights against pigeons were successful, and two other birds were caught but dropped and not retrieved, giving a success rate of about 10 per cent. A breeding female that fed on coots and grebes at a lake in Australia caught birds on 31 per cent of 41 recorded hunts (S. K. Sherrod). Various subadult peregrines feeding over coastal saltmarshes on the Atlantic Coast of the United States caught 10 birds in 25 attempts. Dick Treleaven watched breeding peregrines hunt along the Cornish Coast, where most attacks are on pigeons over water; they hunted with a success rate of 62 per cent (34 captures out of 55 attempts).

One of Cornell University's released peregrines, a tiercel we dubbed "The Red Baron", has provided impressive figures as an adult hunter. He has proved to be an especially favourable subject for observation, as he hunts mostly over very open coastal marshes and a majority of his hunts begin from a perched position after high flying migrant passerines or shorebirds. Also, he brings his prey back to the location from which he started, so that it is usually possible to see the entire hunt from beginning to end. In 1978, Marty Gilroy and Tom Allen recorded 81 of the Baron's hunts; 73 per cent resulted in capture. In 1979, the Baron caught 95 birds in 102 hunts (93% success); in May and June when many migrant land birds were overhead, he had one amazing run of 68 consecutive hunts in 44 days without missing. To my knowledge no other wild peregrine has matched this record, although capture rates of 90 per cent or better have been achieved by trained peregrines on Scottish grouse moors, where men and dogs give aid to the falcon waiting on above them.

These figures, though admittedly somewhat meagre, indicate that immature peregrines are much less successful hunters than the haggards, that there is probably continued improvement in hunting skill at least through the second year of life; and that the adult tiercels are more successful in catching prey than the females, though this may be true only during the breeding season.

Like other species of falcons, the peregrine is limited in its use of nesting sites by its inability to construct a nest, other than to make a shallow scrape in soil or similar loose materials. Even so, peregrines do place their eyries in a remarkably wide variety of locations.

Throughout its worldwide range, a ledge or hole on the sheer face of a rocky cliff or crag is the favoured type of nesting site. The sheer face can range from a few metres to hundreds of metres high, depending on geographical location, degree of safety from nest predators, and population pressure for nesting sites. Sometimes peregrines take over the old stick nests of other cliff-nesting species such as the raven, rough-legged buzzard, or golden eagle. Usually peregrine cliffs overlook a lake, river or sea.

Peregrines also nest on other formations that range from rocky cliffs through steep earthy slopes and cut banks along rivers to mounds on flat tundra, sand dunes (rarely), and low lying bog nests. The ground-nesting sites occur only in restricted parts of the total range. For example, peregrines occupy tundra mounds similar to those used by snowy owls rather frequently in the Siberian Arctic (e.g. Yamal Peninsula), but such eyries are unknown in Greenland and the American Arctic. Bog nests, located in small patches of heath within forested tracts and situated much like merlin nests, were once common in Estonia and Finland; but peregrines have rarely used similar habitats in other parts of the world, for example in Siberia, Alaska and Canada, where bogs abound in taiga. (Hickey 1969.)

Two types of arboreal nests have been reported, again in widely scattered parts of the total range: the

63

most frequent type involves use of the old stick nest of some other large bird – rook, raven, heron, buzzard, osprey or eagle. The other type is a large tree-hole or hollow, formed usually where a main branch has fallen away or where the top has broken off. This habit has allowed peregrines to establish breeding populations in some regions where there are no suitable cliffs, such as the north German plain, Poland, and the east coast of the Baltic Sea. In Finland and Sweden tree-nesting peregrines used to be interspersed with cliff-nesters and bog-nesters. Tree-nesting has also occurred sparingly in eastern Siberia and interior Alaska, and to some extent historically in the eastern United States (Hickey 1969). Recently a small tree-nesting population of six pairs was discovered on islands off the coast of British Columbia. Four pairs were using old bald eagle nests in large sitka spruces; the other two were apparently in hollows (Campbell *et al.* 1977). In parts of Australia tree nests (both types) are more common than cliff nests, and they occur frequently throughout the eastern two-thirds of the subcontinent (Pruett-Jones *et al.* 1981). There is one record for Ceylon, but none for Madagascar, Africa, South America or the Pacific islands.

One of the unsolved puzzles of peregrine ecology is why the tree-nesting habit has not become more widespread and common, especially since cliffs in forested regions are frequently occupied. If there is an adaptive advantage to nesting in trees in some forested regions, why not in all of them?

Peregrines also use man-made structures as nesting sites. This occasional and more or less sporadic habit has been recorded widely through the falcon's range but especially in Europe. The structures used include buildings of various sorts – churches and cathedrals, castles, metropolitan skyscrapers, and a barn in Finland – ruins and old towers, a water tower in Hungary, the stone pier of an unfinished bridge, and even a barrel in the San Francisco Bay marsh. (Rock quarries might also fall in this category.)

If man provides a suitable substrate, then buildings can become productive and long-used eyries, as demonstrated at the famous Sun Life Assurance Company building in Montreal. Here peregrines bred successfully for a period of 13 years after some enterprising ornithologists placed a nest-box with sand and gravel on the unyielding concrete ledge the falcons had used unsuccessfully as their eyrie in previous years. Recently peregrines have also accepted other artificial eyries constructed for them – woven willow basket nests in trees in northern Germany, specially constructed nest-boxes on cliffs in Norway (Tømmerass 1978), and nesting towers in coastal marshes of the eastern USA (Cade and Dague 1980). The adaptiveness of the peregrine in using such structures offers many potentialities for management to restore or to augment breeding populations. (See Hickey 1969 for further details.)

In the past peregrines typically occupied the same breeding territories and used certain specific nesting sites or eyries within these territories over many generations, often to the exclusion of other, suitable looking sites in the same general region. Hickey (1942) referred to this phenomenon of site tenacity as "ecological magnetism". Moreover, there was a rapid replacement of lost mates and pairs in the breeding populations. A lost mate was often replaced within a few days by another adult peregrine, and in Europe where peregrines were destroyed as vermin on game preserves, such as Scottish grouse moors, there are cases in which gamekeepers regularly shot both adults at the eyrie year after year. These two sets of facts have been documented over and over in every part of the peregrine's range. They indicate that, except where nest-sites are sparse, the breeding populations are limited through territoriality and other behavioural spacing mechanisms, which hold the density of nesting pairs below the environmental limits of food supply and nesting sites – although the average spacing of pairs does seem to be adjusted in some general way to the average richness of the available prey (Ratcliffe 1980).

Such a system of breeding dispersion leads to the production of "surplus" adults above the number that can find places in the rather fixed territorial social system, and these surplus birds account for the rapid replacements of lost breeders at the eyries. The number of such surplus adults in a given region will be determined in part by the production of offspring through time and by the dispersive tendencies of non-breeding falcons. There is growing evidence from ringed and marked birds to show that peregrines, despite their great dispersive powers, are highly philopatric and have strong tendencies to home back to their natal localities, rather than to explore far away for new nesting opportunities.

In any case, breeding populations have shown a high degree of numerical stability through time, until quite recently. The situation is best known in Great Britain, where the peregrine has been intensively studied for many years. A search of old literature and records revealed the location of 49 eyries that falconers had known in the sixteenth to nineteenth centuries; peregrines were still nesting at 41 of these locations (84%) in the 1930s (Ferguson-Lees 1951). Only 30 to 50 regularly used cliffs had been permanently deserted by peregrines in Great Britain before 1939 out of a known total exceeding 850, less than 6 per cent (Ratcliffe 1980). By the 1930s, 805 active peregrine nesting territories had been identified in Great Britain, of which 85 per cent on average were thought to be occupied in any given year, or some 680 breeding pairs. (D. A. Ratcliffe has now revised this estimate up to 800 occupied territories on average.)

During all these centuries, falconers, egg-collectors, gamekeepers and pigeon fanciers took a steady and sometimes heavy toll of eggs, young, and adult falcons, but the breeding populations held up despite heavy mortality, except in the western Highlands and Islands where long term deterioration in biotic productivity resulted in a permanent reduction in the number of pairs. Even a deliberate attempt by the

64

Air Ministry during World War II to eradicate the peregrine because it was a menace to RAF carrier pigeons was only partly successful. The control involved the systematic destruction of about 100 eyries in the south of England and Wales each year during the war and the shooting of some 600 adult and immature peregrines, and yet within 10 years after this carnage stopped peregrines were again breeding at about 80 per cent of these eyries. (Ratcliffe 1980.)

Similar though less detailed histories can be constructed for other peregrine populations. In 1972, as a guest of the late Felix Rodriguez de al Fuente – noted Spanish naturalist and falconer – I had the privilege of viewing the battlements of the fourteenth-century castle from which Don Juan Manuel, author of an early treatise on falconry, could look out over the lands around Penafiel and see four active peregrine eyries. It was a great thrill to find peregrines still nesting at three of these sites on our visit in 1972, and there is no doubt that 1,000 or more pairs of peregrines have existed under essentially stable conditions in Spain for centuries.

In North America east of the Rocky Mountains, J. J. Hickey (1942) obtained information on 408 known peregrine eyries. Only 17 of these nests had been definitely deserted by 1940, and he thought that eight others probably had been, or about 6 per cent of the total. More intensive studies on local breeding populations in Massachusetts (14 eyries), along the Hudson River in New York (10 eyries), and in Pennsylvania (21 eyries) revealed the same spatial and temporal stability in breeding pairs found in Britain and other parts of the world prior to the late 1940s (see Hickey, 1969).

Thus, breeding peregrine populations prior to World War II were characterized by a high degree of stability. There had been some decrease in the quality and use of eyries here and there, owing mainly to habitat destruction or deterioration caused by human occupation of the land, and there had been some changes in the density of regional populations owing to long term climatic or environmental changes that affected food supply independently of the quality of nest-sites. Otherwise, breeding peregrines existed as remarkably stable populations that showed a high degree of resilience to the more usual forms of direct mortality such as nest-robbing, shooting, and all the forms of natural loss from diseases, predators and accidents.

Suddenly in the 1950s something unprecedented began happening to peregrines simultaneously in Europe and in North America, although the initial events went virtually unnoticed in the latter. In Britain the dramatic recovery from the wartime persecution abruptly halted, as a high percentage of the breeding pairs failed to produce young. Fortunately, about this time Derek Ratcliffe began his detailed inquiry into the status of the peregrine in Britain, and the deteriorating situation there came under intensive study soon enough so that a plausible explanation began to emerge by 1963–64. Some of the early signs of trouble that Ratcliffe observed included an abnormally high incidence of egg loss during incubation and the eating of eggs by the adult falcons. Nesting failures and loss of adult falcons increased through the decade of the 1950s and into the early 1960s, followed by the disappearance of breeding adults from their traditional eyries.

In North America veteran falcon-watchers were observing the same phenomena locally and independently in places like Massachusetts, along the Hudson River, in Pennsylvania, and in southern California. G. Harper Hall (1955) saw the female peregrine eat one of her eggs at the Montreal Sun Life building in 1949, and many of her eggs disappeared from the nest in the last years of her reproductive history from 1948–52.

By 1963 breeding populations of the peregrine had been drastically reduced on both continents. In Great Britain and France peregrines were still present at less than half of the known eyries, and the situation was much worse over the rest of northern Europe, especially in Scandinavia, Finland and the Baltic regions where less than 10 per cent of the original populations remained. Numbers held relatively unchanged only in parts of the Mediterranean region, notably in Spain and on Sardinia and other islands of the Tyrrhenian Sea.

By 1964, in the United States, not a single breeding pair or even lone adult could be located east of the Mississippi River in a region where nearly 200 eyries had been occupied through the 1940s. Peregrines were also greatly reduced in the western states, particularly in California where probably not more than 10 to 20 per cent of the state's 100 known eyries still held peregrines, in Utah where all but two or three of the state's 40 known eyries had been abandoned, and similarly in other western states such as Oregon, Washington, Idaho and Montana. Less severe reductions had also occurred in Arizona, New Mexico and Colorado. The falcons were also gone from virtually all of their known eyries in Canada south of the boreal forest.

The loss of breeding pairs continued to spread through North America, eventually reaching into the Arctic, so that by the early 1970s many local breeding populations in the boreal forests and tundras of Alaska and Canada had been reduced to 50 per cent or less of their former numbers, but other populations in these northern regions were less affected (Cade and Fyfe 1970; Fyfe et al. 1976). Likewise, the maritime peregrines nesting in the Pacific Northwest coastal and insular regions for the most part remained unchanged in numbers.

The little information available from the Soviet Union suggests that a comparable decline in numbers had occurred first in temperate and then in Arctic populations there. Also, a drastic decline apparently occurred in Japan, where several hundred pairs once nested. Otherwise, peregrine populations in Africa south of the Sahara, in Australia, South America, and the western Pacific islands appear not to have changed significantly during the same period.

At first those who know about peregrines were perplexed to imagine how such a widespread, stable, and successful species could be brought to the verge of extinction over major portions of its range. It was mainly owing to the perceptive work of Ratcliffe and his co-workers in Britain that toxic chemicals began to be strongly suspected around 1962. In that year Moore and Ratcliffe reported on the high levels of chlorinated hydrocarbon residues in the first peregrine egg to undergo chemical analysis. Then, too, the correspondence in time and space between the decline of the peregrine in Britain and the use of DDT and dieldrin in agriculture was remarkably close (Ratcliffe, in Hickey 1969). By the time of the International Peregrine Conference held at the University of Wisconsin in 1965, most of the people who had been working with the species in the field were prepared to accept some causal relationship between the use of DDT and the decline.

Still, the peculiar reproductive failures of the breeding peregrine could not be understood in terms of any known influence of these toxic substances. At first pharmacologists thought that the reproductive effects might be the indirect consequence of detoxifying enzymes produced by the liver in response to the foreign organochlorine molecules in the falcons' systems. Such hydroxylating enzymes had already been demonstrated in laboratory animals and were known to alter the chemical structure of the steroid hormones as well as the organochlorine pesticides (Peakall 1967).

Ratcliffe was again the one to make the definitive observation which led to the final solution of the problem. He had continued to be curious about the high frequency of broken eggs he had found in falcon eyries beginning in the 1950s and by the egg-eating he had seen, and on handling some of the eggshells again they felt unusually weak and thin. This impression and the urging of colleagues led him to measure and weigh a large series of British peregrine eggshells preserved in museum and private collections from 1900 to 1967. Ratcliffe was able to show that over a very short period in 1945–47 there had been an abrupt 20 per cent decrease in the average shell thickness of peregrine eggs. Eggshells of sparrowhawks (*Accipiter nisus*) showed almost exactly the same pattern. These changes in thickness occurred precisely at the time when DDT and other organic insecticides began to be used on a massive scale in agriculture, and the implication was strong that one or more of these chemicals produce physiological changes that disrupt the normal formation of shells in affected females. (Ratcliffe 1967.)

Ratcliffe's exciting results were quickly confirmed by parallel findings on the eggshells of North American peregrines (Hickey and Anderson 1968). A series of eggs collected in Alaska in 1968–71 revealed a precise relationship between DDE residues in the contents of eggs (a reflection of levels in the female's body at the time of egg formation) and shell thickness (Cade *et al.* 1971).

It is now known that DDT and its breakdown products, notably DDE, are the causative agents. No other chemical pollutants are known to induce shell thinning at the concentrations in which they occur in the environment.

The mechanism by which DDE affects the eggshell is through its biochemical interference with enzyme systems involved in the movement of calcium and carbonate, the principal constituents of eggshell, from the maternal circulation in the shell gland to the shell membrane of the egg. Carbonic anhydrase is one, and calcium-ATP-ase is another (Miller *et al.* 1976). Moreover, in addition to thinning the shell, the DDE interference also decreases shell porosity, so that a thin shell actually loses water at a slower rate than a normal shell, a rather unexpected result (Cooke 1979).

Severe reproductive failure and decline in the breeding population occur when eggshells are 15 to 20 per cent thinner than normal. This degree of thinning occurs when the dietary intake of DDE is as little as 1 to 3 parts per million (wet weight) and is associated with a DDE residue in egg contents of about 20 ppm (Peakall *et al.* 1975). A recent global survey of peregrine eggshells (Peakall and Kiff 1979) has revealed post-World War II samples with this critical 15 to 20 per cent thinning from breeding populations in the British Isles, Sweden, Finland, Siberia, Alaska, southern California, eastern United States, Chile (probably), Cyprus, North Africa, Zimbabwe (Rhodesia), Zambia, and South Australia and Victoria.

The complex chain of events linking man's use of DDT to the concentration of persistent residues of DDE in living organisms, to the effects of DDE on eggshells, the consequent egg-breakage and reproductive failure, and the ultimate collapse of regional populations, has been verified in great detail for the peregrine and certain other predatory and fish-eating birds. The data gathered on the peregrine, in particular, served importantly in bolstering arguments to limit the use of DDT and dieldrin, first in Britain and later in the United States. The legal hearings to ban DDT in the United States brought the peregrine a degree of public notice and notoriety that none of us who had known the bird in a quiet, private way could possibly have imagined in those innocent years before chemical pesticides.

Although the peregrine falcon is widely recognized today as an "endangered species" – for example, the entire species is listed on Appendix I of the International Convention on Trade in Endangered Species of Wild Fauna and Flora – it has, in fact, been seriously threatened only in certain parts of its vast range, chiefly in the highly industrialized regions of the Northern Hemisphere. Moreover, there are encouraging indications that a recovery in the number of breeding pairs has begun in some seriously depleted populations since the use of DDT has been curtailed in these regions.

66

The situation is best known in Great Britain (Ratcliffe 1980) and in western Europe (Cramp and Simmons 1980). Peregrines began to make a slow recovery in Britain following the voluntary restrictions on use of DDT and dieldrin. By 1964 the decline had stopped; by 1971 there had been an obvious increase in the number of occupied territories (341 out of 726 examined), and by 1978 sample surveys indicated a total of at least 540 occupied territories. The national survey of 1981 revealed more than 600 occupied territories – more than had been known to be occupied at any time in the twentieth century!

On the British coasts, where the most severe reductions occurred during the pesticides era of the 1950s and early 1960s, historical sites have been reoccupied at a rapid rate in the last few years, while traditional eyries inland have all been taken over, and additional pairs have begun to nest at sites previously regarded as unsuitable. Some of these new eyries are on rocks little taller than a man. The recovery in Great Britain is truly astounding, as well as gratifying, for it augurs well for the future of the peregrine in those countries where men express their concern for threatened animals through corrective actions.

The situation is not so bright on the European Continent, where peregrines were much more severely devastated than in Britain, but even in Germany the residual population in Baden-Wurtemburg has increased some, Switzerland had gained about 20 pairs by 1980, and even the very severely reduced Finnish population had increased slightly (Marcus Wikman). In 1980 the European peregrine population probably numbered about 1,600 to 3,050 pairs as follows: Norway, 25 to 30; Sweden, 9; Finland, 30; Poland, perhaps 10; East Germany, apparently none; West Germany, 50; Denmark, none; Holland, none; Belgium, none; France, 150 +; Switzerland, 30; Spain, 1,000 to 2,000; Portugal, now rare; Italy, 170 +; Austria, 10 +; Hungary, 0 to 7; Czechoslovakia, 10 to 20; Romania, about 5; Bulgaria, rare; Yugoslavia, few pairs; Albania, rare; Greece, rare; Turkey, 100 to 500 pairs. (Cramp and Simmons 1980.)

The population figures for the Soviet Union are rather imprecise, but the peregrine appears to be extirpated from the Baltic states; there may be around 1,000 pairs in European Russia to the Caucasus region and eastward to the Volga River. It is really impossible to try to set any figure to the Siberian and Asiatic populations, but it is not unlikely that the tundra and taiga peregrines still number in the hundreds or low thousands of pairs.

In North America, the decline apparently stopped in the boreal regions in the mid-1970s, and by 1980 most long-studied populations had increased in numbers. For example, the Alaskan Yukon River population, which had dropped to about 75 per cent or less of the number of breeding pairs present in the 1950s, was back to full strength with a high yield of young in 1979 and 1980. In Arctic Alaska, the Colville River peregrines, which had been reduced to about one third of their earlier numbers, had come back up to two-thirds of the numbers present in the 1950s. The detailed histories of these and other sampled populations in North America have been recorded in a series of continental surveys carried out in 1970, 1975 and 1980 and published in the *Canadian Field-Naturalist* (see Cade and Fyfe 1970; Fyfe, Temple, and Cade 1976; White in press).

There has been much speculation and debate about the actual size of the breeding populations in the tundra and taiga regions of North America. While certain local breeding populations – mostly along rivers – are well known in this vast northern region, it is not easy to make extrapolations for the whole of the American Arctic and Subarctic. Certainly the number of autumn migrants observed in passage along the coasts of the Atlantic and Gulf of Mexico and down the Mississippi River valley bears some relation to the number of breeding pairs in the Far North. The data that F. Prescott Ward and his co-operators have accumulated on migrant peregrines – particularly in the last five years – show that this has to be a substantial movement of several thousand birds – perhaps 2,000 to 3,000 immature falcons, which in turn suggests an adult breeding population in Greenland, Canada, and Alaska of 2,000 to 3,000 pairs, somewhat more than half the maximum number I estimated to exist in the 1950s (Cade 1960).

In temperate regions of North America, more than 35 cliffs were occupied in California in 1980, clearly indicating an upswing in that state from a low of probably less than 20 occupied eyries in the early 1970s. Elsewhere, peregrines appear to be holding their own at reduced numbers in the Rocky Mountains, in part as a result of supplementing the poor natural production with fostered young from captivity, and they are doing well in New Mexico and Arizona, as well as in Mexico. At least four pairs of peregrines nested successfully east of the Mississippi River in 1980 for the first time in more than 20 years. At least three of these pairs involved captive produced birds that had been released for the purpose of restocking lost range (Barclay and Cade, in press; Cade and Dague 1980, 1981).

Overall in North America as the decade of the 1980s began, the numbers of pairs were approximately as follows: boreal regions, 2,000 to 3,000; Aleutian Islands, 500; southeastern Alaska and British Columbia coast, 200; Washington and Oregon, 10; California, 35 to 40; Baja California, 25; mainland Mexico, 20 to 30; Arizona, 15; New Mexico, 16; Texas, 6; Colorado, 10; Utah, 3 to 4; New Jersey, 3; Maryland, 1; Maine, 1; southern Quebec, 1 – giving a total North American population of some 2,846 to 3,862 breeding pairs.

Little concrete information exists on numbers in South America, and the known breeding distribution has recently been significantly extended northward along the Pacific Coast from Chile into Peru (Ellis and Glinski 1980) and even to a location north of Quito, Ecuador (Jenny and Ortiz 1981), so that we may expect additional surprises from this part of the peregrine's range. The peregrine apparently is a common raptor in the Falkland Islands (Cawkell and Hamilton 1961), and at least 10 to 15 eyries are known from southern Argentina (D. Ellis and T. Roundy). Perhaps a few hundred pairs occur in South America.

67

Our knowledge is only slightly better for Africa, where in the main the peregrine is a widely scattered, patchily distributed bird. It is probably most common in the southern third of the Continent on the Indian Ocean side; but there are also indications that it is rather common in the mountains of North Africa (where, however, its presence may often be confused with that of the smaller Barbary falcon). The late Leslie Brown knew of eight eyries in a 3,100 sq km (1,200 sq miles) region of Kenya (Cade 1969), and in Zimbabwe there are a total of 47 known eyries (R. Tompson). These figures suggest that in the whole of eastern and southern Africa from Kenya to the Cape there could be between 200 and 300 eyries.

Among land masses of the Southern Hemisphere, Australia stands out as the one with a large number of peregrines. Exact figures are just beginning to emerge from recent field studies, but it has long been known that the species is widespread and common there. N. Mooney estimates about 100 active eyries in Tasmania, and White *et al.* (1981) obtained information on no less than 217 nesting areas in Victoria; according to some estimates the total population is around 500 pairs there. Jerry and Penny Olsen (in press) have information on 200 occupied sites in South Australia and New South Wales. The estimate beginning to emerge for Australia will certainly be formulated in the thousands of pairs – perhaps between 3,000 and 5,000 pairs.

The peregrine also nests throughout the islands of the western Pacific as far east as the Fiji Islands (Clunie 1972). According to John DuPont just about every island with a headland or mountainside cliff overlooking forest has at least one pair of falcons, and Clunie's information suggests there could be around 50 pairs in the Fiji group alone. This Pacific island population, which is widely scattered from the Philippines south through the East Indies, New Guinea, and other islands of the southwest Pacific, must number a few hundred pairs at least. These are beautiful, dark peregrines, with a smoky suffusion in the breast feathers, rather small in body size but with the huge feet so often associated with falcons adapted to hunting in tropical forest.

In total, then, the world nesting population of peregrines can be conservatively placed at between 12,000 and 18,000 breeding pairs, with main centres of concentration in Australia, islands of the North Pacific and Bering Sea, Spain, and the British Isles.

Barbary Falcon

(Red-naped Shaheen)

Falco pelegrinoides

SINCE THE TRAVELS of Marco Polo, European falconers have recognized three small forms of peregrine-like falcons as distinctive – the Barbary falcon of North Africa, the red-naped shaheen of central and southwestern Asia, and the black shaheen of India. E. B. Michell (1900) describes them very well in his excellent book, *The Art and Practice of Hawking*. At one time taxonomists also considered them to be separate, but closely related, species – *Falco pelegrinoides*, *babylonicus*, and *peregrinator*. Until very recently, however, most modern authorities have included these three forms among the geographic races of the cosmopolitan peregrine.

Following an earlier lead by Swann (1936), Charles Vaurie (1961), an American authority on Palearctic birds, concluded that the Barbary falcons (*pelegrinoides*) and the red-naped shaheens (*babylonicus*) constitute a species, *Falco pelegrinoides*, distinct from the true peregrines. This separation has gained increasing acceptance in the last 20 years (Dementiev and Iljitschev 1961, Stepanyan 1969, Voous 1973, Cramp and Simmons 1980), and I am including the *pelegrinoides–babylonicus* complex here as a full species. Even so, it must be admitted that the information available for determining whether or not the Barbary falcon and red-naped shaheen are reproductively isolated from other peregrine populations is far from complete.

Whether there is today any gene exchange between the populations of *pelegrinoides* and *babylonicus* also remains in doubt. There is a geographic separation of some 1,000 km (620 miles) between the *known* eastern breeding limit of the Barbary falcon in Israel and the westernmost *known* breeding stations of the red-naped shaheen in Iran. To what extent this is a real separation remains to be determined by detailed studies in Iraq and Iran; but there is a fairly distinct morphological separation between the two forms, *babylonicus* being somewhat larger and paler in colour.

The Barbary falcon is said to replace the Mediterranean race of the peregrine, the so-called *brookei*, as the breeding form in Morocco from the Moyen Atlas southward, and right from the Mediterranean coast in Algeria and Tunisia south in widely scattered localities through the Sahara. However, the Barbary falcon has also been reported to breed in Tangier, within the North African range of *brookei* (Vaurie 1961), indicating that these two forms are reproductively isolated there. South of the Sahara, about from Cape Verde in Senegal and the southern Sudan in the east, the Barbary falcon is replaced by an African peregrine (*minor*), which is a medium-sized dark form, some individuals being quite black on the back. Whether or not there is any overlap in the breeding ranges of *minor* and *pelegrinoides* remains unknown, and as far as I am aware, there are no specimens from the sub-Saharan region that show intermediate physical characteristics between the two. The Barbary falcon, or some form close to it, also breeds in scattered locations in the Middle East – in Israel west of the Dead Sea and south to Elat, in eastern Sinai, in southwestern Arabia, and possibly in Iraq (Cramp and Simmons 1980).

The red-naped shaheen breeds from Iran eastward into Afghanistan, Pakistan, and probably Kashmir, and northward into the desertic regions of the Soviet Union in Turkmenia, Uzbekistan, Tadzhikistan, Kirgizia, Kazakhstan, and into the Mongolian Altai Mountains (Dementiev 1951). To what extent it meets the range of other peregrines to the north, for instance, in the Caucasus Mountains, remains unclear, but there are some old records (Rattray 1919) indicating that pairs of red-naped shaheens and black shaheens (*peregrinator*) were found breeding in the same habitat, but presumably reproductively isolated, "along the foot of the hills from Jhelum [vicinity of Kyber Pass] to Peshawar – on through Kobat to the borders of Afghanistan at Parachinar . . ." Another old record of interbreeding between these two forms (Dodsworth 1913) has been challenged by Stepanyan (1969). We need modern work to clarify these conflicting statements.

If the breeding range of the Barbary falcon does overlap with that of the peregrine in North Africa with no interbreeding, and if there is some intergradation between the Barbary falcon and the red-naped shaheen in the Middle East or some potential for the exchange of genes between them (and here the evidence is lacking), and if the red-naped shaheen is reproductively isolated from the black shaheen and other peregrines where they come together, then the *pelegrinoides–babylonicus* complex of populations

69

would meet all the biological criteria for a distinct species. It should be noted in passing that the black shaheens apparently do not make geographic contact with other peregrine populations to the north, east, or south of their *known* breeding range, and they therefore may represent another reproductively isolated population of falcons meeting the criteria for recognition as a full species.

The case for specific status of the *pelegrinoides–babylonicus* populations finds its strongest support, I believe, on the basis of morphological and ecological differences between these populations and adjacent races of true peregrines, as Dementiev and Iljitschev (1961) demonstrated in their detailed anatomical comparison of *babylonicus* with peregrines and other Palearctic falcons. The Barbary falcon and red-naped shaheen are small falcons, males weighing about 330–360 g ($11\frac{1}{2}$–$12\frac{1}{2}$ oz), females about 610–700 g ($21\frac{1}{2}$–$24\frac{1}{2}$ oz). A breeding female from southeast Uzbekistan reported by Stepanyan (1969) to weigh 850 g (30 oz) is atypical and may have been a true peregrine, as this weight falls well into the range for female peregrines from the forested zones of the Soviet Union to the north (Dementiev 1951). Thus, there is no overlap in weight with true peregrines when the sexes are compared. Sexual size dimorphism is even more pronounced than in typical peregrines, males averaging about 54 per cent of female weight, while the wing measurement is around 87 per cent.

These two small falcons have relatively longer wings and shorter tails than typical peregrines, and they are said to possess a massive pectoral girdle and sternum relative to the synsacrum and pelvic structures, features that should make them faster and more powerful fliers than peregrines (Dementiev and Iljitschev 1961); however, the wing-loading calculated for *babylonicus* (see Part I) is less than for the European peregrine. It is certainly true that in the experience of most falconers they fly full out when waiting on, almost constantly flapping and seldom setting their wings to soar, as peregrines often do, although Mavrogordato (1966) says that they are rather lazy birds. In all these respects they should be compared with the similar-sized orange-breasted falcon, which also has a massive pectoral structure and extreme sexual size dimorphism.

The plumage is decidedly paler than in peregrines, less barred, with much more rufous. The crown is always mixed with rusty red, and the nape is bright rufous chestnut, whereas these parts are black, slaty or bluish grey in peregrines. The Mediterranean peregrines do show some rusty red on the nape, but Vaurie maintains the two forms are always separable on the basis of other features.

The Barbary and red-naped shaheen are desert-adapted falcons, whereas adjacent and possibly partly sympatric populations of peregrines tend to be either coastal or montane in distribution. They nest on cliffs in more barren country than peregrines, favouring semi-desertic areas with rocky hills, desert foothills, and barren mountain slopes, up to about 2,500 m (8,200 ft) at least in the Soviet Union but probably also in North Africa and Arabia, although some pairs also nest along the coast in North Africa and along the Nile River (Cramp and Simmons 1980).

I think it is significant that nowhere else in its extensive range, which comes in contact with all the major deserts of the world, has the peregrine falcon evolved a distinctive desert form. As a whole, this species is not desert-adapted, and populations usually can exist in arid lands only where there are large bodies of water – rivers, lakes, or sea-coasts (e.g. Baja California and the Great Basin of western USA). The Barbary falcon and red-naped shaheen are biologically exceptional in this respect.

Otherwise their habits and behaviour are much the same as those of peregrines. They are primarily hunters of small to medium-sized birds, although they occasionally take pipistrelle bats. Males are especially fond of various species of larks, which are often common in Palearctic deserts, but birds up to the size of ducks and even geese have been recorded as prey (Dementiev 1957). As with peregrines, these small falcons have a special affinity for doves and pigeons, and they also take sandgrouse, which are very fast flying birds (Meinertzhagen 1954, Cramp and Simmons 1980). Dementiev (1957) says that the migratory shaheens in the northern part of the Asiatic breeding range follow the movements of pin-tailed and Pallas's sandgrouse, implying a special predator-prey relationship.

Not much is known about the numbers of Barbary falcons and red-naped shaheens, but they are generally reported to be widely scattered and rather uncommon or even rare. For example, the Russian ornithologist, Stepanyan (*fide* Cramp and Simmons 1980), has estimated that there are only 35 to 50 pairs in the entire central Asiatic range, and the red-naped shaheen has been placed on the official Soviet list of "endangered species" (Flint 1978). Both *babylonicus* and *pelegrinoides* are included on Appendix I of the Convention on International Trade in Endangered Species. Certainly if Stepanyan's estimate is correct, the central Asian shaheens constitute one of the most sparsely distributed falcon populations in the world; however, I suspect that friendly discussions with the Turkmenian and Kirghiz falconers would reveal the locations of many more eyries than are known to professional ornithologists.

The Barbary falcon is said to be common in the hills west of the Dead Sea in Israel, and 53 pairs were reported from Tunisia in 1975 (Cramp and Simmons 1980). The Arab falconers in Algeria and Morocco claim to know about many falcon eyries in the Atlas mountain ranges, but it is not always clear whether they refer to Barbary falcons or to peregrines (A. Ludlow Clark). The Barbary should be looked for on the arid, south-facing slopes of these mountains, while the peregrine may well reside on some of the better watered north slopes.

It seems likely that the breeding populations of *pelegrinoides* and *babylonicus* number several hundred pairs each, but much more fieldwork is needed to clarify the status of these falcons in terms of both distribution and density.

70

R. DAVID DIGBY.

Pallid Falcon

(Kleinschmidt's Falcon)

Falco kreyenborgi

THIS SOUTH AMERICAN form is certainly the least known falcon in the world. It occurs in Patagonia, and what we know about it is based on only five preserved museum specimens and less than a dozen recorded sightings and some photographs. Anderson and Ellis (1981) have nicely reviewed the history of our knowledge about this rare, pale-coloured falcon, which has been a great puzzle to ornithologists ever since the first example came to light in 1925; and they and their field associates (Ellis and Glinski 1980; Ellis, Anderson and Roundy 1981) have recently obtained additional, critical field data that go a long way toward answering the question posed by Stresemann and Amadon (1963), "What is *Falco kreyenborgi* Kleinschmidt?".

In 1925 some otter hunters captured a young falcon at an eyrie somewhere in southern Chile (the exact location is questionable), and this bird ended up in the hands of a German named M. Carlos Strauss, who lived in Punta Arenas. Eventually the live bird reached the zoological garden in Munster, Germany, where it died in 1932. At an unknown later date two other eyass falcons, said to be from the same eyrie as the first, also reached the zoo at Munster, attained adult plumage, and subsequently died there. These were the first three "pallid falcons" to be seen in Europe and to be preserved as specimens.

A German falconer, Herr-Doctor Kreyenborg, was intrigued by the distinctive appearance of the first bird brought to Munster and called it to the attention of Dr Otto Kleinschmidt, a leading authority on falcons. Kleinschmidt examined the falcon while it was still alive in the Munster Zoo and described it as a new species, *Falco kreyenborgi* (Kleinschmidt 1929), after having first mistaken it for a Barbary falcon.

Since Kleinschmidt's original description there has been much uncertainty as to how to treat the pallid falcon taxonomically. Indeed, for a time there was doubt as to whether the first three birds really came from South America, and there was speculation about an African origin; however, two subsequent specimens, one from the Argentine side of Isla Grande in 1940 (Olrog 1948), and another in 1961 from the environs of El Bolson, Rio Negro, Argentina, collected by K. Kovacs (Dementiev 1965), laid this argument to rest and firmly established the Patagonian region as the geographic range of this pale form.

Some taxonomists have considered *kreyenborgi* to be a subspecies of the peregrine falcon, others have suggested that it is a colour phase of the South American peregrine (*Falco peregrinus cassini*), but the tendency in recent years has been to recognize it as a full species. Stresemann and Amadon (1963) suggested that it might be a South American equivalent of the gyrfalcon group of species, although they were careful to point out that in all respects except coloration *kreyenborgi* has the characteristics of a peregrine and is indeed indistinguishable in measurements from specimens of *cassini*.

In December 1980, during field studies in Santa Cruz Province, Argentina, Ellis, Anderson and Roundy (1981) found a pair of South American peregrines with a brood of four recently fledged young. One of the young was darker than average for *cassini*, one was average, another was lighter than average, and a fourth was a pale-coloured pallid falcon! They were able to trap the latter, examine it in the hand, and photograph it before release, so that there is no question as to its form.

Thus, as some have suspected all along, it appears that specimens called *Falco kreyenborgi* are simply a rare (perhaps a recessive) colour morph of the peregrine falcon. The only other possibility, apart from some freak occurrence, such as a *kreyenborgi* egg being laid in a *cassini* nest, would seem to be that the parent falcons observed by Ellis *et al.* might both have been hybrids between *cassini* and *kreyenborgi*, which would then have to be considered populations (semi-species) that are not completely reproductively isolated from each other. But the fact that neither parent showed the intermediate characteristics that would be expected from hybrids between two species, and the fact that colour and pattern are the only characters that differ between individuals called *kreyenborgi* and *cassini*, argue strongly in favour of the first view.

This may be the last time for the name *Falco kreyenborgi* to appear at the head of a species account.

Gyrfalcon

(Gerfalcon, Jerfalcon)

Falco rusticolus

L<small>ARGEST AND MOST</small> majestic of the long-winged hawks, the gyrfalcon inhabits remote, circumpolar Arctic and Subarctic zones. In autumn and winter some individuals and populations move southward into north temperate regions, and only then do most birdwatchers have a chance for a rare glimpse of this great falcon, which the Emperor Frederick II of Hohenstaufen, in his thirteenth-century treatise, *De Arte Venandi cum Avibus*, extolled above all others as a hunter of cranes and similar large quarry. The Emperor wrote that the gyrfalcon "holds pride of place over even the peregrine in strength, speed, courage, and indifference to stormy weather".

The gyrfalcon is adapted to catch prey both in the air and on the ground. Though less manoeuvrable than the smaller peregrine, it is faster on the wing, more sustained in pursuit, and more powerful in striking its prey. It is more likely to hunt in direct pursuit low over the ground and is less prone to circling and soaring at a height from which to stoop down on quarry; but when it spots a vulnerable bird in the sky, the gyr can climb up "on its tail" and gain altitude remarkably fast without circling or "ringing up" to do so.

The difference in size between the sexes is marked, particularly in body weight. Males weigh 805–1,300 g ($28\frac{1}{2}$–46 oz) and average 53 cm (21 in) in body length; females are around 1,400–2,100 g ($49\frac{1}{2}$–74 oz) and 56 cm (22 in) in length, so that males are 62 to 68 per cent of female weights. Sexual differences in wing length and other dimensions are less pronounced (see Cramp and Simmons 1980), and one of the consequences of this fact is that males have a lighter wing-loading.

In flight the gyrfalcon reveals broad-based wings, relatively short and more rounded at the tips than a peregrine's. The longest primaries exceed the distal secondaries by less than half the wing length, and the tail is proportionately long – about 53 to 54 per cent of the wing length – and with a somewhat rounded tip. These features give *rusticolus* an accipitrine appearance in flight, and in the field grey gyrfalcons are sometimes confused with goshawks. The wingbeat of the gyr is usually slower, deeper, and more powerful than the peregrine's, and most of the movement appears to come from the shoulder joint. Cramp and Simmons (1980) provide other field characters.

The gyr's feet are heavy and strong, with toes rather thicker and decidedly shorter relative to the legs, than those of the peregrine, a difference that probably imparts a stronger grip but at some sacrifice to the area available for snatching birds in flight, but which may have an advantage in handling large mammals. The tarsus, which is longer than the middle toe, is stout and densely feathered on more than the upper half, often with a scattering of inconspicuous feathers lower down, a detail found in no other species of *Falco* and obviously associated with life in cold climates. The beak is large and powerful and capable of rendering a bite that can break the necks of the largest ducks and even geese.

The plumage of the gyrfalcon is less compact than the peregrine's. Body feathers in particular are softer, flight feathers not as stiff; down and other fluffy, insulative structures are highly developed. The gyrfalcon is the only species of *Falco* capable of entirely covering its toes while perched upright by fluffing out the feathers on its belly and flanks. Colour and pattern are extremely variable, ranging from

R. David Digby

white with dark streaks, spots, and bars on individual feathers to almost uniformly black with faint, lighter edgings and spots, but various grey intermediate plumages are most common. Adult plumages are similar, but males tend to be less heavily marked with streaks and bars on the ventral parts and head than females, some males being immaculate underneath.

In first year birds, the feathers are softer and more heavily streaked on the ventral surface than in adult plumages. The wings are broader with longer secondaries, and the tail is longer than in adults. (Descriptions from Brown and Amadon 1968, Cramp and Simmons 1980.)

In the old literature, naturalists wrote about white, grey and black "colour phases" of the gyrfalcon and even about different species of gyrs. In fact, the different plumage types grade imperceptibly into one another, with every kind of intermediate condition represented in different individuals. Generally, the high Arctic breeders in Greenland and the Canadian Arctic Islands are mostly all white (the *candicans* type), and white birds occur less frequently in the low Arctic regions, but they are not found at all as breeders in Iceland, where the resident population consists mostly of light grey individuals (the *islandus* type), nor in Scandinavia and the Russian Arctic, where the gyrs are mostly dark grey to bluish grey (the *gyrfalco* type). White falcons reappear in eastern Siberia, in the Bering Sea region, in western Alaska, to a limited extent on the Arctic Slope of Alaska, but not at all, so far as records show, in subarctic breeding populations. Black gyrs (the *labradorus* type described by Audubon) are most common in northern Quebec and Labrador and occasionally are encountered right across the American Arctic, even into western Alaska; but they do not occur in Eurasian populations. The Ungava region of northern Quebec is especially interesting, as the whitest and blackest varieties breed together in the same areas along with every kind of grey intermediate (Cade 1960).

The gyrfalcon breeds from 82°N in Greenland southward over the greater part of the circumpolar tundra regions of the world, including most arctic islands and the treeless foothills and barren grounds of continents. The breeding range extends south into partly timbered subarctic regions below 60°N, mostly in mountains or along sea-coasts, to about 55°N in limited parts of eastern Canada (Ungava and Labrador), northern British Columbia, southwestern Alaska (Alaska Peninsula and eastern Aleutian Islands), the Komandorski Islands, and probably Kamchatka.

Within this extensive northern range, gyrfalcons breed in a variety of habitats, which are basically determined by combinations of suitable nesting sites and abundance of prey. Since most gyrfalcons nest on cliffs, favourable rocky formations provide one of the key features of the nesting habitat, although tree-nesting pairs occur in parts of the Canadian and Eurasian taiga.

Three basic types of habitat can be recognized – maritime, riverine, and montane. Rocky sea-coasts and offshore islands are frequently used habitats, particularly where colonial seabirds or waterfowl concentrate to nest, as in Greenland, Iceland, the Canadian Arctic Islands, the Labrador Coast, Ungava Bay, Hudson Bay and the Bering Sea region (Cade 1960).

Where rivers drain down through mountains and foothills in tundra or at the edge of the taiga and cut river bluffs, or run past high rocky outcrops, gyrfalcons also find suitable nesting grounds. Rivers such as the Koksoak and the George in Ungava, the Horton and Anderson in the Canadian Northwest Territories, the Firth in Yukon Territory, the Colville and Utukok in northern Alaska, and the Anadyr, Kolyma, Indigirka, Lena, Yenisei and Pechora in Siberia provide this kind of habitat. To some extent lakes afford similar opportunities (e.g. Mývatn in Iceland; lakes in the Mackenzie District of Canada). Also, tree-nesting gyrs occur in river valleys and around lakes in some of these regions (around lakes in the Northwest Territories, in parts of Lapland, and in Eastern Siberia and Kamchatka).

Mountainous terrain above timberline, where cliffs and rocky crags abound, constitutes the third habitat for nesting gyrfalcons, at least up to 1,300 m (4,200 ft) in elevation. Well known regions include the Brooks Range and Alaska Range, the mountains of eastern Siberia, the Urals, and the fjelds of Norway and Sweden. (Summarized from Cade 1960, Cramp and Simmons 1980.)

Gyrfalcons overwinter as far north as they can find adequate numbers of prey to sustain them, and some are year-round residents in the same regions where they nest. The principal prey consists of willow and rock ptarmigan in winter, and gyrfalcons can be found wherever these grouse are common. Other gyrs winter in northern maritime regions where open leads in the sea ice provide habitat for hardy ducks such as old squaws, eiders and scoters and for alcids (northern Bering Sea region, Iceland, Greenland).

Arctic bird populations tend to fluctuate drastically in time and space, and ptarmigan populations in particular are "cyclic" in abundance and shift about from one region to another as feeding conditions change, while some willow ptarmigan populations perform migrations over considerable distances. These changes influence the movements of gyrfalcons, and there are regular migrations of *rusticolus* in some parts of the range, for example on both coasts of Greenland, some birds moving over water to Iceland and into the Canadian Arctic for the winter, and along the Alaska Peninsula at Cold Bay. It may be that most gyrfalcons regularly move out of the high arctic latitudes after breeding. (Salomonsen 1951, Cade 1960, Cramp and Simmons 1980.)

Some gyrfalcons do winter regularly as far south as the northern tier of the United States – the Puget Sound region, in particular, Idaho, Montana, the Dakotas, Great Lakes region, northern New York, and occasionally as far as New Jersey on the Atlantic coast and into eastern Colorado and western Nebraska in the Great Plains. In Eurasia they occasionally appear in Great Britain, Holland, Germany, and France, and in Russia as far as the Ukraine, along the middle Volga, and lower Don rivers. In most winters only a few individuals ever move much south of 55°N. These southern transients are most often found in habitats where there are wintering concentrations of waterfowl or upland game (chiefly grouse), or occasionally in the Soviet Union around towns where they feed on pigeons and crows.

Gyrfalcons feed mainly on other birds ranging in size from redpolls to geese (rarely, cranes), but they also catch some mammals, chiefly lemmings and voles, ground squirrels and Arctic hares. There is no question that ptarmigan (*Lagopus lagopus* and *L. mutus*) constitute the main prey species and over most of the upland and montane country which are the falcon's main habitats, ptarmigan make up 85 to 95 per cent of their diet by weight. Indeed, much of the gyr's life history has been modified by its dependence for food on these northern, essentially resident, grouse.

Even so, special feeding relationships develop locally. Coastal and insular breeding populations depend to a significant extent upon aquatic birds, especially colonial nesting auks and related species, gulls, and waterfowl; still, ptarmigan usually comprise 50 per cent or more of the total diet, even on islands some distance from mainland. In certain upland districts where waterfowl are unusually abundant, ducks make up as much as 50 per cent of the diet, and ptarmigan are less important.

In the Alaska Range ground squirrels may comprise as much as 50 per cent of the diet, and on some Canadian Arctic Islands, Arctic hares make up the bulk of the food. In northeast Greenland the varying lemming is heavily used during peak population years, especially by young gyrfalcons in the immediate post-nesting period; and when lemming and vole populations attract large numbers of rodent predators, gyrfalcons feed significantly on long-tailed and parasitic jaegers, short-eared owls, harriers and even on rough-legged buzzards. Gyrfalcons nesting in trees in the tundra-taiga habitat of the Canadian Northwest Territories depend less on ptarmigan than those nesting north of the treeline, and take large numbers of inland-dwelling gulls, terns, shorebirds and waterfowl (R. Fyfe). Immature gyrfalcons often shadow the large flocks of snow buntings and Lapland longspurs that leave Greenland in autumn, and the migratory populations of ptarmigan are also followed south by hungry gyrs. (Salomonsen 1951, Cade 1960, Cramp and Simmons 1980).

The gyrfalcon hunts in a variety of ways, but there are three main methods of search and attack. Perhaps the commonest tactic is to sit quietly on a mound or rocky outcrop commanding a long view down the side of a valley and to wait for vulnerable prey to appear on the ground or in the air below. If a displaying cock ptarmigan gets up and reveals himself, the gyrfalcon takes off low and fast, using features of the terrain to remain concealed from sight as much as possible, and attempts to catch the ptarmigan by surprise in a direct pursuit. Failing to achieve surprise, the attack develops into a tail-chase, usually down slope and downwind with the gyr gaining a few metres of altitude above the ptarmigan just before closing in a short, fast stoop. The prey is more likely to be knocked to the ground or driven into the ground than to be snatched in the air. Gyrfalcons also sometimes course low over the terrain employing contour-hugging, particularly along ridges where ptarmigan and ground squirrels are often caught by surprise when the gyr suddenly slips over the ridge from the opposite side. Especially in winter they hover over dense willow brush and attempt to flush ptarmigan into flight; in this situation escaping ptarmigan are sometimes hindered by snow cover and are caught as they flutter out of the snow (J. Platt).

Gyrfalcons also search from high up in the air by quartering back and forth over rather long tracks or by soaring, and then stoop down on fleeing quarry on the ground or fly low over the ground. Stooping is not their great forte, however, and gyrs catch most quarry only after a long chase, which can sometimes go several kilometres. They are excellent at chasing quarry up into the air and forcing the bird to remain aloft until it is exhausted and attempts to dive to cover. This is the method used to catch short-eared owls, jaegers, gulls, cranes and other birds with light wing-loadings and superior powers of rising rapidly in spirals. The gyr, however, does not "ring" but climbs straight up at a steep angle, often making only one turn before it has gained ascendency over its intended prey. This climbing ability, more than any other characteristic, made the gyrfalcon the favourite hunting hawk in times past for flights "out of the hood" – that is, directly off the falconer's fist – at large, high flying quarry such as herons, cranes and kites.

The breeding season begins early for gyrfalcons; indeed, among arctic nesting birds only the raven starts as early (White and Cade 1971). Until recently no investigators had been on the scene in winter to observe the establishment of territories and pairing. Thanks to the efforts of Nick Woodin (1980) in Iceland and especially Joe Platt (1976, 1977) in Yukon Territory we now know the essential details of this phase of the life history.

Many gyrfalcons (usually males) remain on territory around their eyries through much, if not all, of the winter (Cade 1960, J. Platt 1976). Males begin active defence of territories and start engaging in advertising displays in January or early February, utilizing a perch in an open location which commands a view of 180°–360° and is also a good station for still-hunting. Females arrive from mid-February to early March, and courtship and pair bonding occur over an extended period of six to eight weeks. Eggs are laid mostly towards the end of April, but with unusually bad weather can be delayed until May. The incubation period has usually been given as 28 to 29 days, but recent observations on both wild and captive gyrfalcons show quite clearly a period of about 35 days. Young hatch out from mid-May to mid-June, exceptionally even later, and the young fly from their nests at 7–8 weeks of age, in mid-July to early August, sometimes later. The young remain dependent on their parents for at least a month, longer in most cases.

Despite statements to the contrary, there is no evidence at all that gyrfalcons construct their own stick

77

nests. They either use a scrape, which they scratch out of the substrate on the ledge of a cliff, or more often the old stick nest of some other bird, most often a raven's nest but also old nests of rough-legged buzzards and golden eagles. The nest is most usually on a rocky crag or outcrop ranging in height from less than 10 metres to more than 100 metres; but gyrs also use stick nests in trees in parts of northwest Canada, in Lapland, and in eastern Siberia and Kamchatka. On Seward Peninsula, Alaska, they have been observed nesting on abandoned gold dredges and pile-drivers, but no other man-made structures apparently have been used. (Dementiev 1951, Cade 1960, Cramp and Simmons 1980.)

The actual nest-site is usually in a crevice or under an overhanging projection of rock on the cliff and quite well sheltered from wind, rain, and snow, though exposed sites are sometimes used. Some nests have great permanency and reveal their long use by the deep accumulation of excrement and prey remains from generation after generation of young. Such nests, which are on very hard rock, stand out in the general landscape and can be seen from several kilometres away; they have a magnetic attraction for gyrfalcons. Stick nests usually weather away and fall apart after a few years, and gyrfalcons cannot use the site again until they have been re-occupied by a species that builds anew. Also, ledges and other usable features on rocky cliffs are constantly eroding and changing, so that gyrfalcons have a marked dependence on other raptors and ravens for their nest-sites. Even so, the nesting territories have great constancy from year to year (Cade 1960, White and Cade 1971).

The clutch ranges from two to seven eggs, but these extremes are rare; four is the most frequent clutch, three next, and less often five. The average is nearly four eggs. There may be some adjustment of clutch size to food abundance, as in some owls and rough-legged buzzards, but the data are not numerous enough to make this conclusion certain.

The female does most of the incubation, but the male assumes a variable share during the day; he does not incubate at night. It has often been stated that incubation begins with the first egg and that the young hatch at staggered intervals of one or more days; however, careful observations of wild and captive gyrfalcons at the nest show that true incubation does not begin, usually, until the third egg has been laid, and clutches of four hatch out within a 24 to 36 hour span, as A. L. V. Manniche (1910), in fact, observed in northeast Greenland long ago.

The young are richly endowed with down and appear to regulate body temperature at a much earlier age than young of other large falcons. At any rate, the female stops brooding when the young are only 10 days old, and from that time on she joins the male in hunting, although she still spends more time near the eyrie than her tiercel and provides less food than he. Nevertheless, gyrfalcons appear to have adapted to the problem of rearing young under Arctic conditions rather differently from peregrines (which feed on a wider variety of mostly small, abundant avian prey, rely less on the female's participation in hunting, and brood their young for a longer period of time). The gyrfalcons have adapted by specializing on ptarmigan or on one or two other large prey species, by increasing the time both parents hunt, especially the female, and presumably by ranging farther away from the eyrie in search of food than peregrines do. The greater hunting range is made possible by the simultaneous hunting of both parents and by their larger size, heavier wing-loading, and faster and more enduring flight.

Gyrfalcons are not very demonstrative around their eyries when humans intrude. Often they slip away at the first sight of man's approach and circle about silently in the sky at some distance from the eyrie, exactly as golden eagles do. Some individuals are more aggressive and fly about overhead cackling, and a few will stoop aggressively. They are, however, strong defenders against other potential enemies, driving off other raptors, ravens, gulls and owls with great vigour. They are most aggressive in their attacks on golden eagles, the principal avian predator on young falcons in northern latitudes. They also effectively attack and drive off mammalian predators such as foxes, wolves, wolverines and even grizzly bears.

Like a number of arctic raptors and jaegers, gyrfalcons do not breed every year, and the number of breeding pairs in a given region and their reproductive success are strongly influenced by the availability of food, principally ptarmigan, which undergo well marked four-year or ten-year cycles in different parts of their ranges (willow ptarmigan show a four-year cycle in North America; rock ptarmigan have a ten-year cycle in Iceland). The average number of young per successful pair is about 2.5, and the regional production of young is determined mainly by the number of established breeding pairs in any year, to a lesser extent by adjustments of clutch size and brood size.

Over much of its range the gyrfalcon is an uncommon raptor, usually exceeded in numbers by sympatric peregrines and rough-legged buzzards, but it is not as rare as many have claimed. Because it breeds mainly in remote regions that have only been explored intensively in the last 30 years, the gyrfalcon has always been something of a mystery, as well as a rarity of extreme value, a truly royal gift.

In Alaska, gyrfalcons are relatively common breeders in the foothills and mountain valleys of the Arctic Slope and Brooks Range, on Seward Peninsula, and in the Goodnews Bay region of western Alaska. They are less common but widely distributed through all the mountainous districts of Alaska from the timberline up to about 1,300 m (4,200 ft). More than 50 eyries are now known in the Colville River drainage of northern Alaska, and the total breeding population of the Arctic Slope must fluctuate around 100 pairs, at a density of about one pair per 1,300 sq km (500 sq miles) – there were 40 occupied eyries in 51,200 sq km in 1975. On Seward Peninsula, D. Roseneau has catalogued more than 500 cliffs used by gyrfalcons and other raptors and ravens in a 44,000 sq km (17,000 sq miles) region from 1968 to 1972. Overall, gyrfalcons averaged about 48 nesting pairs in the first three years, but they dropped to 13 pairs in 1971, a poor year; they were back to 36 pairs in 1972. The average density in good years was one pair in a little less than 1,000 sq km (380 sq miles). He estimated that on average there are some 70 pairs of gyrfalcons on the entire Seward Peninsula. (Swartz *et al.* 1975.) In the Goodnews Bay region there are 12 nesting sites in about 2,600 sq km (1,000 sq miles), but it is not known how many of these nests have been occupied in any one year – perhaps 50 per cent, giving a density of one pair per 430 sq km (166 sq miles). In the Alaska Range, in Mount McKinley National Park with an inhabitable area of some 5,120 sq km (1,980 sq miles), there are five known eyries; but the maximum number known to have held pairs in one year is three, giving a density of one pair per 1,700 sq km (650 sq miles). Similar low densities occur throughout the Alaska Range and other mountains of southern Alaska. Given all these figures, and others contained in various survey reports since 1970 which bring the total known gyr eyries in Alaska to more than 150 (Cade and White 1976), it seems likely that 300 pairs for all of Alaska represent a minimum estimate, and it is more likely that the population fluctuates around 500 pairs.

Densities may be generally lower over the vast expanse of the Canadian barrens and Arctic islands, but in the well studied North Slope region of Yukon Territory they are similar (12 to 29 pairs in 19,500 sq km, an average density of one pair per 975 sq km or 375 sq miles). (J. Platt, Ph.D thesis.)

With an ice-free area of only 341,700 sq km (132,000 sq miles), Greenland nevertheless supports a sizeable population. F. Salomonsen refers to records of 200 to 300 white gyrfalcons passing through Scoresby Sound on the east coast in the first eighteen days of September and up to 250 being shot by the Danes in that area in a single migratory season. Forty pairs are said to breed in the interior fjord country of Scoresby Sound alone and another 25 pairs along the Liverpool coast. These figures indicate densities of one pair per 1,000 sq km (380 sq miles) or less. They are considered to be equally common all the way to Germania Land. Judging by the sample densities known for Scoresby Sound and the regions around Godthaab, Søndre Strømfjord, and Disko Island in western Greenland (W. Burnham and W. Mattox), it appears likely that in favourable food years an average density of one nesting pair per 500 sq km (190 sq miles) obtains on a regional basis and that the average number of gyrfalcons breeding in Greenland over many years is not less than 500 pairs but could be as high as 1,000 pairs (Cade 1960).

Iceland is another country with plenty of gyrfalcons (Brüll 1938, Vesey 1938, Wayre and Jolly 1958, Bengston 1971). Recently an Icelandic student, Olafur K. Nielsen, has tabulated information on more than 200 eyries, and in good ptarmigan years he believes that there are as many as 300 to 400 nesting pairs. In 1981, his study area of 5,200 sq km (2,000 sq miles) held at least 35 occupied cliffs, in which 24 pairs produced about 70 young, even though ptarmigan were not especially numerous. With an area of 87,000 sq km (33,500 sq miles), excluding glaciers, it would appear that Iceland has the densest regional population of gyrfalcons in the world, approximately one pair per 150 to 300 sq km (58–115 sq miles).

The bird is not common in Scandinavia, there being now only a few isolated pairs in the scattered fjelds of Norway and some island-nesting pairs along the north coast; but there are more in Finmark, and the Norwegian population overall is represented by about 65 active eyries (P. Tømmeraas 1978). Sweden hosts an estimated 30 to 50 pairs (Segnestam and Helander 1977), most strongly concentrated in Lapland. Pesticide residues are low in these gyrs, reproduction remains normal, the falcons are non-migratory, and there is no indication of recent decline in numbers (see Cramp and Simmons 1980).

Apparently there are no recent surveys for the great expanse of the Soviet Arctic, which, according to the old falconry records summarized by G. Dementiev in his book *Sokola Kretcheti* (1951), must have been home to many hundreds of pairs of gyrfalcons. Only five sources are cited for the official *Red Data Book of the USSR* (1978), the most recent in 1963. Nevertheless, the status is given as "rare", and the gyrfalcon is included on the official Soviet list of "endangered species". One source states that three pairs nest in an area of 1,500 sq km (580 sq miles) in the Murmansk region; otherwise, only the most general statements are made about numbers and densities. Dementiev indicates that gyrfalcons are more common in northeastern Siberia than in other parts of the Soviet range.

There has been some decline in numbers and even extirpation within historical time in the more southern parts of the original breeding range in Scandinavia and adjacent parts of Finland and Russia, possibly owing to unfavourable climatic changes, but more likely to human modifications of the environment (Cramp and Simmons 1980). Egg-collectors and falconers are often blamed for these local disappearances, but no one has ever produced convincing evidence that human depredations at eyries have resulted in permanent reductions in falcon populations.

The breeding range of the gyrfalcon extends over some 15 to 17 million sq km (5.7–6.5 million sq miles) of Arctic and Subarctic lands. If the overall breeding density is on the order of one pair per 1,000 sq km, then there are some 15,000 to 17,000 pairs of gyrfalcons in the world. If the average density is only half that figure, there are still 7,000 to 9,000 pairs. Even the latter estimate is far more than most people would surmise from the casual statements about its "rarity". While there are drastic local and regional fluctuations in the numbers of breeding pairs from year to year in relation to the unpredictable occurrence of prey in the Far North, there are no indications of a long term downward trend in numbers in most parts of the range in recent decades. If anything, numbers have increased over the last 30 years in Alaska and northwest Canada, and despite a thousand years of overgrazing by livestock, the heathlands of Iceland still support a phenomenal density of gyrfalcons.

Saker

Falco cherrug

FAVOURITE HUNTING BIRD of Arab falconers, the
saker is a rough-and-tumble version of the gyrfalcon. It nests in parklands and open forests at the edge
of the steppes from eastern Europe (possibly still in Austria, in Czechoslovakia, Hungary, Bulgaria,
Romania, Yugoslavia, Turkey, and the Soviet Union), throughout the semi-desertic steppes and forest-
steppes of central Asia, also in foothills, isolated crags, and montane plateaux up to about 4,000 m
(13,100 ft), as far eastward as Mongolia (Dementiev 1951). Migratory sakers move south into southern
parts of the Soviet Union, into China, Pakistan, the Middle East, parts of Mediterranean Europe and,
exceptionally, into North Africa. A sizeable number travel as far as northeastern Africa, passing down the
Nile to winter in the lands drained by its middle and upper reaches (Sudan, Ethiopia and northern Kenya).

Sakers average smaller than gyrfalcons, but there is some overlap – males are around 45 cm ($17\frac{1}{2}$ in)
in total length with a wingspan of 100–110 cm ($39\frac{1}{2}$–$43\frac{1}{2}$ in), and weigh from 730–990 g (26–35 oz); while
females average 55 cm ($21\frac{1}{2}$ in) in length with 120–130 cm (47–51 in) wingspans, and weigh from 970–
1,300 g (34–46 oz). Males weigh about 74 per cent as much as females and have wings that measure 90.7
per cent as much. Sakers are more rangy in appearance than gyrs, with somewhat narrower wing bases,
the tail averaging 55 to 56 per cent of wing length, and with less dense plumage, especially on the legs,
flanks and lower belly. Otherwise, *rusticolus* and *cherrug* are very close, and even in the hand some
individuals cannot be assigned easily to one or other species, in which case the geographic origin of the
bird has to be taken into account (Dementiev 1951, Cramp and Simmons 1980).

An example of this taxonomic difficulty is the so-called Altai falcon from the mountains of central
Asia. Given the name Turul by the Huns, it has been identified as the banner-bird of Attila; and after
him the sons of Genghis Khan hunted with these same birds on the plains near Samarkand. These Altai
falcons are darker and larger than most other sakers, and they have been considered to represent an
isolated population of gyrfalcons (Dementiev 1951), or to constitute a separate species (*Falco altaicus*),
but usually now they are included among the races of the saker falcon.

The saker obviously is phylogenetically very close to the gyrfalcon. As Dementiev (1951) pointed out,
in morphological aspects the western saker populations in Europe form a continuous series of colour and
size variations with the central Asian populations to the Arctic gyrfalcons (with the Altai falcons providing
an intermediate link). Their ecological characteristics, behaviour, and vocalizations are also extremely
similar, and as there is no overlap in breeding range between sakers and gyrfalcons, it is probable that
they are disjunct, allopatric populations of the same species, as several writers on the subject have noted
(Kleinschmidt 1958, Meinertzhagen 1954, Baumgart 1975). Some also include the laggar, lanner, and
prairie falcon as allopatric populations of one worldwide species, but it is perhaps best to consider all of
these forms as closely related species comprising a "superspecies". It is clear, however, that sakers and
gyrfalcons are more closely related to each other than either is to these other forms of "desert falcons".

Sakers are almost as variable in colour and pattern as gyrfalcons. Some are very pale cream or straw in

R. David Digby

ground colour with reduced brown bars or streaks on individual feathers and with very whitish heads and necks, while others give the appearance of a more uniformly chocolate brown all over. Brown-eyed albinos or partial albinos occur fairly often among the sakers kept by Arab falconers. Many sakers can be distinguished from their close relatives by the fact that their tails show white or pale spots on the inner webs of the rectrices rather than bars across both webs, by a translucent appearance of the pale underwing surfaces contrasting with dark primary tips and dark axillaries, and by their *gestalt* in flight. But none of these characteristics alone or in combination will distinguish all sakers from some gyrfalcons, laggers or lanners, and the immatures of all these species are particularly difficult to identify in the field.

In the western portion of their breeding range sakers nest mainly in tall trees, usually 15–20 m (50–65 ft) above ground, occupying the stick nest of some other species – various buzzards, eagles, vultures, raven and grey heron. The sakers are aggressive in their use of these nests and on occasion actually drive the owners away from an occupied nest. (Suggestions that they sometimes build their own stick nests have never been confirmed by actual observations.) In the steppes of Asia and in their mountain haunts they more often nest on the ledge or other suitable formation of a cliff at heights ranging from 8–50 m (25–160 ft) above the base. The same eyries are often used over and over, or the pair may have two or three alternative sites in the same territory. The nesting territories tend to be permanent in space but not necessarily occupied every year (Dementiev 1951, Cramp and Simmons 1980).

Dementiev says that sakers begin breeding in their first year, but such cases must be exceptional, and most individuals are probably two or three years old before they reproduce successfully. The clutches range from two to six eggs exceptionally, but three to five eggs are more typical, four being the mode. There is a strong indication that clutch size varies with the richness of the food supply from one territory to another, and from year to year, depending on population levels in the main prey species. Full incubation usually starts with the laying of the third egg and lasts for more than 30 days (old statements about 28 to 29 day incubation periods for large falcons are wrong).

The observed differences in stage of development among the young – particularly in large broods – result in part from asynchronous hatching and in part from difference in growth rates between males and females, as in other large, sexually dimorphic falcons. There is considerable variation in brood size (range from one to five), again suggesting that reproductive performance is sensitive to food supply. Young begin to fly around 45 to 50 days of age, but they remain dependent on their parents for food for another 30 to 45 days or longer, before dispersing from the nesting territory. The brood mates may remain together for a time or join others, especially if they encounter a localized source of food, such as a colony of ground squirrels.

Sakers feed mainly on small mammals, although they also take a variety of birds and other animals; but they catch most of their prey – regardless of type – on or near the ground and are generally less aerial than peregrines or even gyrfalcons. Typically sakers sit on rocks or stumps overlooking open habitat and watch intently for vulnerable prey moving on the ground. They launch a direct, low flying attack on the quarry, and if it is a large animal such as a hare they usually strike it with their feet in a series of shallow stoops before grabbing it. At other times they course about in the air 10–20 m (30–65 ft) above ground searching for prey below, and they often hover like great kestrels when some animal scurries about in cover and the falcon wants to fix its exact location for a pounce. Sakers often sit for hours on their favourite perches and give the impression of being rather more sluggish in their hunting than either gyrfalcons or prairie falcons; but when the occasion demands they can be bold and aggressive predators, pursuing their prey relentlessly and with a single-minded intensity surpassed only by goshawks (*Accipiter gentilis*), which they perhaps more nearly resemble in their hunting methods than do any of the other large falcons.

Ground squirrels or susliks of the genus *Spermophilus* occur throughout much of the breeding range of the saker, and these rodents comprise the bulk of the falcon's food wherever they are common. Depending on the local fauna, other rodents figure significantly in the diet – especially hamsters, jerboas, gerbils, various microtines (voles and lemmings), and in montane regions, marmots, mostly young ones. Lagomorphs such as hares and, in mountains, pikas, are also locally important. Small mammals usually make up from 60 to 90 per cent of all prey taken during the breeding season (Dementiev 1951, Cramp and Simmons 1980).

Next in importance are ground-dwelling birds, ranging from small species such as larks and wagtails to quail, sandgrouse, partridges, pheasants and bustards, although sakers also catch such aerial birds as ducks, herons, shorebirds, pigeons, corvids, and even other raptors (harriers, kestrels, and owls). Birds sometimes make up from 30 to 50 per cent of the diet of nesting pairs, particularly in the more forested parts of the breeding range (Cramp and Simmons 1980).

In addition, sakers feed on various lizards, principally the large forms in the genus *Uromastix*, and these reptiles may locally constitute a significant element of the diet, especially on the wintering grounds. (Arab falconers often resort to feeding lizards to their falcons when other food is unavailable.) Sakers also take insects on occasion, in particular large ground beetles. In Kazakhstan, Solomatin (1974) observed an adult feed its young with fungi (86 per cent water) during an extremely hot and dry period, a very unusual thing for a falcon to do.

No account of the saker or *Al Hur* would be complete without mention of the special place this bird occupies in the culture of the Arabs. Falconry has been an intimate part of Arab life for at least 2,000

82

years. In past times, the bedouin depended on their falcons to provide wild game as a supplement to their often meagre rations. Mounted on camels or horses, they traditionally hawked large, meaty quarry such as houbara bustards, stone curlews, desert hares, and even small gazelle, which the falcons were trained to harry about the head and to slow down until the saluki hounds could catch up and finish the job. Mostly the bedouin used passage sakers, which they trapped themselves or purchased in the markets at Damascus, Lahore and other places, trained in a remarkably short time, employed in the chase for several months in winter, and then released back to the wild at the end of the hunting season in spring, for it was impossible for them to feed the falcons and keep them in good health through the long, hot Arabian summer.

With its varied and indifferent taste for mammals, birds, or reptiles, its willingness to engage in tussles with large quarry on the ground, and its ability to hold up under severe treatment, the saker, among all falcons, has the attributes best suited to the Arab style of hawking. Perhaps it would be more correct to say that the peculiarities of Arab hawking represent centuries of accumulated trial-and-error adjustments of falconers to take advantage of the saker's special abilities to hunt under the limiting conditions of the desert.

The falcons are flown off the fist in direct pursuit like goshawks. They are never trained to wait on overhead as in western gamehawking or to ring up as in heron hawking, although sakers are quite capable of both. Indeed, the Arabs consider high flying a dangerous way to lose falcons, and the Kuwaiti falconers even tie the outer primaries together to prevent their falcons from going up. The Arabs want their birds to go straight to the mark and to take the quarry as quickly as possible, because the name of their game is to catch as many head as possible.

The Arabs also frown on the western practice of using dogs to point and flush game. Instead, they track the quarry for miles through the sand and use their falcons to spot game at a distance. Sometimes they employ a special bird just for this purpose. From time to time during a day's hunt the falconer holds his spotting falcon up high so that it has a good view of the surrounding terrain. If it sees even the slightest movement of a houbara or hare it will stare in the direction and bob its head vigorously. The falconer then hoods this bird and releases the hunting falcon.

This old way of life has been contrasted vividly with the new in an interesting book *Falconry in Arabia* by Mark Allen (1979). Now, hunting houbara with trained falcons has become the recreational pastime of many of the oil-rich shaikhs and princes of Saudi Arabia and the gulf states. Some of these men keep more than a hundred falcons under extravagant conditions reminiscent of Marco Polo's description of the Great Khan's hawking establishments. They make safari-like expeditions into the desert lasting for several weeks, with a train of specially equipped vehicles, retainers, falconers, and falcons. Increasingly now these hunting expeditions extend beyond the Arabian Peninsula to include places like the Cholistan Desert in Pakistan, Iran, Iraq, and North Africa – wherever some houbara are left to hunt.

Western conservationists have become increasingly concerned on two accounts about this modern phase of Arab hawking. First, there has been an alarming decrease in the numbers of houbara bustards in the last ten years, a fact which the Arab falconers fully recognize. In part this reduction appears to have been brought about by man-induced changes in habitat on the breeding grounds, but it is hard to escape the conclusion that these bustards have also been severely over-hunted in their winter quarters, particularly when automatic shotguns are used in conjunction with falcons. Shooting has recently been banned in several Arab countries, and there is growing interest in programmes to propagate houbara for release to the wild; but propagating bustards is even more difficult than propagating falcons. Real salvation for the houbara waits for a change in Arab attitudes and practices. They must learn to diversify their interests in quarry and develop an appreciation for the quality of the hunt as something more valuable than the amount of game taken. For example, sandgrouse are a numerous and challenging quarry, found throughout the Middle East. No falconer to my knowledge has mastered taking them with trained falcons, but I believe it could be done with the right birds and methods.

The other concern is about the number of falcons involved in contemporary Arab hawking. How many falcons are held captive in Arabia for falconry? I have questioned several western observers who have much firsthand information for making an estimate – men such as John Burchard, Gustl Eutermoser, Joseph Platt, and Roger Upton – and they agree that 3,000 trained falcons are about the right number for any given year. Among them they can count at least 112 men who keep approximately 2,700 falcons, and they estimate that at least 300 more are still being kept in the more traditional bedouin manner. Approximately 2,000 new falcons are being obtained each year during autumn migration to replace those lost during the hunt or released in the spring. As the price of falcons has gone up, more Arabs try to keep their birds permanently instead of releasing them at the end of the season. The majority of these falcons, around 90 per cent, are *female* sakers. (The Arabs have traditionally considered the larger birds to be males; they have had little experience with nesting falcons, so this misconception has carried on to present times.)

What effect does the taking of so many female sakers a year have on the wild population? One must remember that as most of these falcons are trapped as immatures in their first autumn, at least half of them would have died of natural causes before reaching one year of age if they had remained in the wild. Moreover, a fair number of the trained birds escape or are released under circumstances favourable to their survival and reversion to the wild – but one does not know what fraction are in this category nor

83

for sure whether they are capable of joining the breeding population. All one can say for certain is that the taking of 2,000 immature sakers a year is not equivalent to a total loss of that many birds from the wild population, but the potential impact of the preferential removal of females on replacements in the breeding population is greater than would be the case if both sexes were taken equally.

The crux of the matter depends on the size of the species population in the wild. Unfortunately, much of the saker's breeding range lies in regions that have been little studied. The breeding range is very large, in the order of 10 million sq km (3.9 million sq miles). There are also indications that the breeding range is expanding northward in the Soviet Union (V. M. Galushin, according to Cramp and Simmons 1980).

Population data for European countries have been summarized by Cramp and Simmons (1980). In the periphery of the range west of Russia, numbers of nesting pairs are low, and declines have occurred in most areas in the last 20 to 30 years. The total population in this region appears to be on the order of only 100 to 150 pairs, while Turkey has an isolated population estimated at 10 to 100 pairs.

Dementiev (1951) considered the saker to be "actually abundant in various places" in the European part of the Soviet Union and also in parts of its Asiatic range, but the dispersion of pairs is not uniform over large regions, and pairs tend to be clumped in areas where food is especially plentiful, as around suslik colonies. Thus, estimates of density range from an extreme of 3 to 4 pairs in 1.2 ha (3 acres) to more typical spacings of 4 to 6 km ($2\frac{1}{2}$–$3\frac{1}{2}$ miles) between pairs, to highly dispersed pairs spaced 10 km (6 miles) or more apart – more typical of the desertic steppes and mountains of central Asia (Dementiev 1951, Cramp and Simmons 1980). Brown and Amadon (1968) give 312 sq km (120 sq miles) as the maximum size of a breeding territory, but the available information indicates that in many parts of the range territories average only 100 sq km (39 sq miles) or less, for example in the forested districts around Tula, south of Moscow (Flint 1978).

The saker has been placed on the list of "rare species" in the official *Red Data Book USSR* (Flint 1978). The section on numbers in nature states that there is no precise information, but there appears to be a tendency toward a reduction in numbers. For example, in a comparison of the period from the late 1930s to the 1960s, the number of sakers at the edge of the forest-steppes in Kazakhstan is said to have been reduced "5 times", while in the true steppes they have decreased "8 to 10 times". The Naursum Reserve, where Dementiev (1951) found 21 nests in 1938, is mentioned as an area where sakers are almost not breeding at all at the present time. This undocumented statement is difficult to reconcile with Solomatin's (1974) finding that pairs sometimes nest only 500 m (1,600 ft) apart in this reserve.

If one makes the assumption that sakers are distributed at an overall average density of only one pair per 500 sq km (190 sq miles) there would be about 20,000 nesting pairs. If, as seems not too far-fetched, the dispersion averages about one nest per 100 sq km (39 sq miles) then there are around 100,000 pairs of sakers in the world. These are only speculative figures, but they are interesting to think about, especially as there has been a tendency among ornithologists in the past to underestimate the numbers of raptors. If the true population size falls between these limits, as I believe it does, then the 2,000 sakers trapped each year for falconry are inconsequential to population stability of the species, even if none of them returns to the wild to breed.

Lanner

Falco biarmicus

Throughout much of Africa the bright and colourful lanner is the commonest large falcon. Its main centre of distribution and abundance lies south of the Sahara in the semi-desertic regions and drier savannahs and woodlands of the Sahel, East Africa, and southern Africa, from sea-level to more than 2,000 m (6,600 ft) in elevation. Lanners are seldom found in habitats with more than 625 mm ($24\frac{1}{2}$ in) of rain per year, and are usually replaced by the much rarer peregrines in higher rainfall areas, although the habitat separation is not complete and pairs of *biarmicus* and *peregrinus* may nest in the same countryside, occupying mutually exclusive territories (Brown 1970).

The range also extends northward in scattered, disjunct regions of true desert and desertic mountains in the Sahara, Egypt, Arabia, Sinai, and limited parts of the Middle East, to the Mediterranean coast at various places in North Africa. Peripheral and now largely relict populations of lanners also exist in Mediterranean Europe (historically in Sicily, Italy, Yugoslavia, Albania, Greece and Turkey), and it has been known to nest once near the Caspian Sea, USSR in 1949 (Cramp and Simmons 1980). Thus, among the "desert falcons", the lanner is the African counterpart of the Eurasian saker, the Indian laggar, and the American prairie falcon, but it is most similar to the laggar, with which it may be conspecific.

Lanners are medium to large falcons with long bodies and tails, and long, expansive wings giving them a lighter wing-loading and a more buoyant flight than either peregrines or gyrfalcons. The tail averages 51 to 53 per cent of the wing length. Lanners are larger than African peregrines but smaller than European ones. Males are about 35–40 cm ($13\frac{1}{2}$–$15\frac{1}{2}$ in) in total length, with a wingspan of 90–100 cm ($35\frac{1}{2}$–$39\frac{1}{2}$ in), and weigh 500–600 g ($17\frac{1}{2}$–21 oz); females average larger, around 45–50 cm (18–$19\frac{1}{2}$ in) in length, with a wingspan of 100–110 cm ($39\frac{1}{2}$–$43\frac{1}{2}$ in), and weigh 700–900 g ($24\frac{1}{2}$–$31\frac{1}{2}$ oz), so that males average about 69 per cent of the weight of females. Lanners from North Africa and the Middle East average somewhat larger than those from southern Africa and from Europe; some of the former approaching small sakers in size.

The North African and Middle East lanners are also close to sakers in coloration, tending toward rather uniform light brown or sandy and lacking the rich, highly contrasting colours of European and southern African lanners. The South African lanners are particularly striking in adult plumage, which features a black forehead and line along the upper cheeks and a thin, blackish moustachial streak contrasting with white cheeks and throat, a bright rufous crown and nape, bluish upper surfaces like a peregrine, and unmarked, creamy buff underparts. The immatures are browner with less conspicuous facial features than adults and are rather like young peregrines in general aspect, while the North African immatures look more like young sakers, with which they are not infrequently confused.

Lanners are rather sedentary falcons, and the members of a pair are often together throughout the year, sometimes hunting co-operatively even in the non-breeding period. There are some shifts in local populations from season to season – such as vertical movements from highlands to plains or post-breeding summer movements out of severe desert haunts into more mesic areas – but no long distance migrations occur.

Nesting begins in winter or early spring in temperate zone latitudes, and in the bleak Sahara it is closely correlated with the beginning of the spring migration of Palearctic birds, which provide the nesting falcons with a predictable, if transient, food supply, while in tropical latitudes laying corresponds mainly with the dry season. Thus, actual laying dates vary widely with latitude and environment: in South Africa, June to August; Zimbabwe, May to November but mainly August; Kenya, July; Somalia, March to April; northern Nigeria, February and March; Sudan, January to March; Egypt, March to April; Sahara, late March; and in Sicily, late February to mid-March (Brown and Amadon 1968).

Lanners most often nest on rocky cliffs or earth bluffs, but they also occupy old stick nests of other birds (mostly crows) in trees and, increasingly in recent years, on electricity pylons and telegraph poles. In addition, they sometimes use buildings or other man-made structures in urban districts (A. C. Kemp).

The clutches typically consist of three to four eggs, and two or three young usually fledge from successful eyries. The pairs are regular breeders, and productivity does not appear to vary from year to year as much as it does in the case of the saker, because the prey populations exploited by lanners are more stable than those of the Palearctic steppes. However, this generalization needs verification for those lanners nesting in severe desert.

Like the other desert falcons, lanners have rather catholic diets consisting of a variety of birds, small mammals, reptiles and insects; but they are more aerial in their hunting than either sakers or laggars, and small to medium-sized birds make up the bulk of prey in most places. Avian prey consists of a variety of passerines, quail, doves and pigeons, sandgrouse, and exceptionally birds as large as bustards and guineafowls. Many of these birds are taken in surprise attacks on or near the ground, for lanners are easily outdistanced by most birds in prolonged flights. Lanners also stoop from height like peregrines but less successfully, owing to their lighter build and greater flight surfaces relative to body weight.

Lanners feed on various species of rodents, and they take a surprising number of bats, including fruit-eating Megachiroptera. In some places lizards are the main food, especially where the large *Uromastix* species is abundant. Lanners also take advantage of temporary swarms of beetles, locusts, grasshoppers, and flying termites, and like many other raptors they learn to follow grass-fires to exploit disturbed or injured prey.

Over most of its arid to semi-arid range in Africa and the Middle East, the lanner shows a special affinity for isolated waterholes, where many birds congregate daily to drink (Cade 1965, Willoughby and Cade 1967, Maclean 1968, George 1970). Hundreds to thousands of doves and sandgrouse, in particular, flock to waterholes at certain times of day, and even though they have learned to approach the water cautiously and to drink rapidly once at the water (Cade 1965), their sheer numbers and concentration make it possible for several falcons (up to a dozen or more) to obtain prey on a routine basis. Typically the hunting lanner perches some distance away in a concealed position in a tree or on a hillside and watches the water. Once a flock of birds moves to the water's edge and begins drinking, the falcon suddenly drops down from its perch and flies very low over the ground in an effort to remain hidden from view. It attempts to strike into the flock while the birds are still on the ground or to take one just as it lifts up, before it has developed speed. If the water is actually down in a hole or pit, then the falcon can often get on top of the drinkers before they realize they have been attacked. Also, sandgrouse frequently drink standing or floating in the middle of the water, or a parent sandgrouse may be deeply soaking its belly feathers in preparation for delivering water to its young. Such birds and others with slight disabilities must be especially vulnerable to an attacking falcon. I have also seen a lanner strike through a group of "frozen" laughing doves perched in an open acacia tree at a well in the Namib Desert and carry a bird away.

The lanner is a rather common falcon through most of its African range, but it has declined drastically in Europe in the last 25 to 30 years and is said to be near extermination there (Bijleveld 1974, Cramp and Simmons 1980). The total number of pairs in Europe in the 1970s may not have exceeded 50 (Hudson 1975). The causes of this decline are not known, but it seems likely they are the same ones that have affected the peregrine so severely in Europe – deterioration or loss of nesting habitat owing to human land-uses and, especially, contamination of avian prey with pesticides. In Israel lanners, along with other raptors, were wiped out by thallium sulphate used to poison rodents (Mendelssohn 1971).

Lanners are evidently common raptors in widely scattered, disjunct regions of North Africa, but there is no way to estimate their total numbers. On the high, arid plateaux in Morocco nesting territories have been reported (Brosset 1961) to average 300–400 sq km (120–150 sq miles).

South of the Sahara, the known breeding range encompasses some 15 to 20 million sq km (5.8–7.7 million sq miles), and the numerical strength of the species obviously lies in this vast region. For example, 84 eyries have now been catalogued in Zimbabwe (W. R. Thomson), but they represent only a small fraction of the total thought to be present. Alan Kemp has estimated the nesting population of the Transvaal Province (282,750 sq km; 109,170 sq miles) to be about 1,400 pairs (one pair per 202 sq km; 78 sq miles), and the bird is also a widespread and common breeder throughout the Republic of South Africa and Namibia (South-West Africa). It would not be overstating the situation to suggest that in the whole of southern Africa south of the Okovango and Zambezi rivers (an area of about 3.5 million sq km; 1.3 million sq miles) there are between 9,000 and 18,000 pairs of lanners. When one stops to consider that there is an additional breeding range of about 15 million sq km (5.7 million sq miles) south of the Sahara, even at a population density averaging as low as one pair per 1,000 sq km (390 sq miles) there should be at least another 15,000 pairs. Certainly the total African breeding population of lanners must number in the tens of thousands of pairs.

R. DAVID DIGBY

Laggar

(Lugger, Luggar, Luggur)

Falco jugger

STRUCTURALLY AND BEHAVIOURALLY the laggar is very like the lanner, and is the latter's ecological and geographic replacement on the Indian Subcontinent south of the Himalayas, from Afghanistan and Baluchistan in the west to Assam and central Burma in the east. It is not, however, as restricted to dry environments as the lanner and occurs in regions of moderately high rainfall as well as in arid zones, although it does avoid really humid forests (Ali 1968). The rufous crown and nape of the adult are reminiscent of the lanner, as well as the pale fulvous to pinkish underparts; but the immature plumage is distinctive in having solid, chocolate brown underparts contrasting with a white throat and is so similar to the Australian black falcon as to indicate a close relationship. The two (*biarmicus* and *laggar*) also overlap completely in body size and all linear measurements, although the laggar gives the impression of being even more lightly wing-loaded and kite-like in flight than the lanner.

Like lanners, laggars frequently stay paired throughout the year, and the mates hunt together, one startling the prey while the other waits in a favourable position to make the kill or working in concert by alternately stooping at flying birds (Ali 1968). For the most part, pairs remain resident in one area and do not migrate.

Laggars mainly inhabit open country – semi-desertic scrublands, cultivated plains with scattered trees, and open forests up to about 1,000 m (3,300 ft) (Ali and Ripley 1978). They are not birds of mountainous terrain. Laggars are not shy of human habitations, and frequently nest in and around towns and villages.

They nest on rocky outcrops, earth banks along rivers, in old stick nests of other birds (usually crows or kites) at heights of 10–15 m (30–50 ft) in tall trees such as peepul, banyan and mango, or lower down in acacias in the more arid western parts of the range. Other birds commonly nest in the same tree with a pair of laggars – potential prey such as rollers, doves and pigeons, which are not molested by the falcons and are not even disturbed by their comings and goings (Ali and Ripley 1978). This commensalism parallels the situation sometimes found at peregrine eyries in the Arctic, where nesting geese and shorebirds cluster around the falcon's nest (Cade 1960). The advantage for the non-raptors appears to be the incidental protection they receive from the aggressive behaviour of the falcons toward other predators, both avian and mammalian, that intrude close to the eyrie.

Usually three to four eggs are laid in January, in southern India, to as late as May in the northwestern extremity of the breeding range. Two to three young fledge from successful nests (Brown and Amadon 1968).

The types of prey are much the same as for the lanner – small mammals, birds, reptiles, and insects, with birds predominating in most areas – but *Uromastix* lizards are very important in some localities (Dementiev 1951). Around towns and villages feral pigeons are the main food items (Ali 1968). In the wild, laggars are known to seize birds wounded by hunters and will also pick up the carcasses of skinned birds that have been discarded by museum collectors (Brown and Amadon 1968), suggesting that they may be scavengers to some extent.

Both laggars and lanners are trained for falconry, but the laggar does not have a good reputation as a hunting hawk. Mavrogordato (1966) sums up the prevailing western opinion by saying that he regards the laggar "as an inferior alternative to the lanner, which it superficially resembles in size and build, though not in colour. Luggars stoop quite prettily to the lure, but lack courage and drive. Even one that had been given the 'salt treatment' [purged with sal ammoniac] in Pakistan for my benefit seemed none the better for it". Judging from the reported behaviour of wild laggars, falconers might achieve better performance from trained birds by flying two of them together in a cast.

In India and Pakistan the laggar has been used mainly as a decoy or *barak* to trap sakers and peregrines. The trapper ties a bundle of feathers and nooses to the falcon's feet and also ties its wings so that it cannot fly too far away. When a saker or peregrine appears, the trapper tosses the *barak* up into the air, and the wild falcon, seeing the laggar flying heavily with what appears to be prey in its feet, will attack and attempt to snatch the bundle away, whereupon it is likely to become ensnared by the nooses.

Naturalists familiar with the Indian fauna consider the laggar to be a common falcon throughout its range, which covers about 4.8 million sq km (1.9 million sq miles). Ali and Ripley (1978) characterize it as "the commonest and most easily identified of all our falcons", but unfortunately there seem to be no published data on density or spacing of pairs with which to make estimates of total population size. If densities are comparable to those of lanners in Africa or sakers in Eurasia, then there probably are 10,000 to 25,000 pairs, or more.

PLATE VII
Laggar
Falco jugger
Adult female,
above right
Immature male,
below left
Map page 185

88

R. DAVID DIGBY.

Prairie Falcon

Falco mexicanus

Although the prairie falcon has the most restricted breeding distribution among the North American species of *Falco* and also among its close relatives in the worldwide "desert falcon group", it is often common where it does occur in the arid and semi-arid deserts and steppes of western North America. It also breeds less commonly in timbered mountains up to 3,700 m (12,100 ft) in the same habitat occupied by the peregrine, and sometimes the two species are found together at the same cliff (if it is big enough) or more often, occupying the same eyrie in different years.

Less variable in physical appearance than its close relatives, the prairie falcon is generally rather uniformly brownish on the back, some old males tending towards a silvery blue cast, with a thin, dark malar streak, light cheeks, and creamy white underparts barred (in the adult) or streaked (in the juvenile) with brown. In flight it reveals dark under primary-coverts and dark brown axillaries contrasting with a generally whitish underwing surface. Averaging somewhat smaller than the peregrine, males are about 37–38 cm ($14\frac{1}{2}$–15 in) in length with a wingspan around 95 cm ($37\frac{1}{2}$ in), and they weigh 500–635 g ($17\frac{1}{2}$–$22\frac{1}{2}$ oz). Females are around 45 cm ($17\frac{1}{2}$ in) in length with a wingspan of 105 cm ($41\frac{1}{2}$ in) and weigh 760–975 g ($26\frac{1}{2}$–$34\frac{1}{2}$ oz), so that males are about 64 per cent of the female weight (Enderson 1964). The tail is 55 to 57 per cent of the wing measurement.

Two of the most distinctive traits of the falcon, when viewed close up, are its large, "blocky" head and its big, owlish eyes. No other falcon has eyes as large in proportion to its body as the prairie falcon, but their adaptive significance is not known.

While sharing with other desert falcons a relish for small mammals and reptiles as well as birds, the prairie falcon is a far more dashing and spirited bird with a heavier wing-loading than either the laggar or the lanner, or even the saker for that matter. Indeed, in aerial performance it is a match for the peregrine in most respects, and its rather aggressive and highly-strung temperament produces an altogether capable and determined hunter, which will often attempt quarry under circumstances that most peregrines would find inhibiting.

The prairie falcon is by far the best of the desert falcons for training, and American falconers frequently use *mexicanus* in place of peregrines for fine flights at a variety of waterfowl and upland gamebirds, as well as at crows and other quarry, including jackrabbits (*Lepus* spp). How well I remember a 780-gram female that used to be flown in the 1950s by a member of the old Southern California Falconers' Association at the Sepulveda Reservoir in San Fernando Valley. One day she utterly demolished a 3.5-kilogram (7 lb 8 oz) jackrabbit by repeatedly stooping at its head as it tried to run for cover. Her aggressive frenzy rose to such a pitch that even after the hare had fallen she kept on stooping and striking at the head for perhaps 5 minutes before finally settling down on the quarry. She had literally ripped the jackrabbit's long ears to shreds with the repeated gashing of her sharp, rear talons. This hunt was probably the closest thing to hawking gazelle ever witnessed in North America.

Wild prairie falcons no doubt sometimes take on prey the size of adult jackrabbits and marmots, but their preference is for any of the smaller species of diurnal ground squirrels (*Spermophilus* spp) that occur throughout the falcon's western haunts – animals ranging in size from the spotted spermophile weighing less than 100 g ($3\frac{1}{2}$ oz) to the large California ground squirrel at 1,000 g (35 oz) and also prairie dogs (*Cynomys* spp) up to 1,500 g (52 oz). Other rodents are also taken as opportunities arise, and one naturally wonders whether the very large eye of the prairie falcon is in some sense a "desert adaptation" allowing the falcon to hunt more effectively at dusk when the first of the numerous nocturnal desert rodents become active above ground, although no naturalist has reported prairie falcons to be especially crepuscular.

In the more severe deserts, such as parts of the Mojave and Colorado deserts of southern California, where bird life and even diurnally active rodents may be scarce, prairie falcons catch many large lizards, the principal species being the very large chuckwalla (*Sauromalus obesus*), adults weighing 1,000 g (35 oz) and more; and the smaller collared lizard, leopard lizard and desert iguana which weigh from 50 to 60 grams ($1\frac{1}{2}$–2 oz). I have even found shells of desert tortoises (*Gopherus agassizi*) at eyries in the Mojave Desert. Large insects are also taken, especially by young prairie falcons.

PLATE VIII
Prairie Falcon
Falco mexicanus
Immature male
Map page 185

R. DAVID DIGBY

Prairie falcons also catch a wide variety of birds, particularly those that tend to be ground-dwelling – various species of western quail and grouse, doves, meadowlarks, horned larks, lark buntings and longspurs – by flying fast and low and taking most individuals by surprise as they rise to escape. In the breeding season, birds, including forest species, are a more important part of the diet of prairie falcons nesting in the mountains than mammals are; and birds are also the main prey in the post-breeding season after the ground squirrels have become dormant, and in winter when the falcons concentrate in the Great Plains and lower desert valleys of the Great Basin and California. In winter prairie falcons are usually found around concentrations of birds – winter flocks of horned larks in particular (Enderson 1964), but also meadowlarks and other flocking passerines, where ducks mass on open water, and around the feeding grounds for flocks of sharp-tailed grouse and prairie chickens (Bent 1938).

Except for one unsuccessful attempt to use a building in Calgary, Alberta (R. W. Nelson), and two cases of successful nesting in subterranean situations (Haak and Denton 1979), prairie falcons apparently nest only on rocky cliffs or steep earth embankments. They are not known to use trees (apart from one old record) as their close relatives in the Old World do. They prefer a pot-hole or well sheltered ledge positioned anywhere from less than 10 m (33 ft) to more than 100 m (330 ft) above the base. Richard Fyfe has demonstrated in Alberta that prairie falcons will readily accept man-made excavations on otherwise unsuitable cliff faces and that a considerable increase in local nesting density can thus be effected (Fyfe and Armbruster 1977). Prairie falcons also frequently use old stick nests of other species on cliffs, golden eagles, red-tailed hawks, and ravens in particular. Many field workers have commented on the close symbiosis between the raven and the prairie falcon: old raven nests increase the number of sites available to the falcons, and the falcon's prey caches are no doubt raided by the stealthy ravens. Pairs of ravens and prairie falcons usually exist peacefully together on the same cliff (Bent 1938), more so, apparently, than pairs of ravens and peregrines.

Clutch size averages around 4.5 eggs in most populations, 5 being the most usual, but clutches of 6 are less frequent than clutches of 3 and 4. Broods of 5 are not uncommon either, but even so the average number of successfully reared young varies considerably from region to region and year to year – from 1.2 to 3.4 per starting pair (Enderson 1964, Olendorff and Stoddart 1974). Variation in the numbers and biomass of prey probably accounts for regional and temporal differences in productivity, as indicated by the intensive, co-operative study organized by the US Bureau of Land Management (BLM Report 1979) in the Snake River Canyon of southern Idaho.

Here, along a magnificent stretch of cliffs and canyon walls running for 130 km (80 miles), there exists the largest concentration of nesting raptors in the world – more than 600 pairs representing 15 species. In some years more than 200 pairs of prairie falcons are packed into this canyon at a density of one pair per 0.65 km (2,100 ft) or less. Where the canyon is deep and there are multiple tiers of rock, two to three pairs may actually be positioned vertically one above the other, and intermixed along the river with pairs of golden eagles, red-tailed hawks, ravens and other species.

According to my old friend and field companion, Morley Nelson, who first drew public attention to this unique aggregation of raptors, in late February and March when all these pairs have come into the canyon to take up their nesting territories and start their courtship, the aerial acrobatics and mating calls of so many displaying hawks, eagles, and falcons produce an emotion in the beholder that can only be likened to the effect of great symphony – the 1812 Overture comes to mind – or the ringing poetry of Tennyson's "Ulysses".

Largely through Nelson's initial efforts, the US Department of the Interior set aside 10,522 ha (40 sq miles) of the canyon as "The Snake River Birds of Prey Natural Area" in 1971; and since then most of the rest of the canyon and some 245,000 ha (962 sq miles) of adjacent sagebrush and grasslands, mainly to the north of the river, have been under intensive study by the Bureau of Land Management and its contractors as a potential "Snake River Birds of Prey National Conservation Area". As a consequence of these studies a great deal has been learned about the prairie falcons and their prey in this region.

The principal prey species is usually Townsend's ground squirrel, an animal weighing around 150–200 g (5–7 oz) and making up from 40 to 80 per cent of the total biomass consumed by the nesting prairie falcons and their young, depending on the year. The prairie falcons' entire nesting schedule is closely tied to the life cycle of these diurnally active rodents, whose burrowing habits and food requirements are particularly favoured by the grasses growing on deep, well drained soils formed by loamy deposits to the north of the Snake River.

The prairie falcons arrive at their eyries in the Snake River Canyon in January, just as the ground squirrels begin emerging from six months of underground dormancy. The falcons lay their eggs at the time when the juvenile ground squirrels become active above ground, and the young falcons hatch out when the numbers of ground squirrels are at a maximum. The departure of the young falcons from their eyries and their development into independent hunters occur in May to July, as the ground squirrels gradually disappear underground to begin aestivation. By the time all the squirrels have gone underground, the prairie falcons have dispersed out of the canyon to remain away until the next January. Some move up into higher rangelands, but most apparently shift eastward into the western edge of the Great Plains, judging from ringing returns.

The Bureau of Land Management studies between 1974 and 1978 reveal how the numbers of ground squirrels influence the breeding density and dispersion of the prairie falcons and their reproduction. The density of squirrels was highest in 1975 and 1976. A severe drought occurred in the winter of 1976 and spring 1977. The density of squirrels in March 1977 was slightly reduced, but the April figures were substantially lower than the previous two years owing to the fact that the squirrels did not reproduce at all in 1977. Consequently, the March 1978 squirrel densities were 50 per cent lower than in 1975–76, while April densities were only 25 per cent of the 1975–76 numbers.

The prairie falcons were to some extent able to adjust by switching to alternate prey, mainly feral pigeons and jackrabbits. Even so the influence on reproductive output, particularly in 1978, was dramatic with only 289 young fledged in the canyon population compared to 526 and 631 in 1975 and 1976. This difference does not reflect a significant change in the number of pairs settling to breed or a reduction in clutch size, but rather a dramatic decrease in the percentage of successfully reproducing pairs and a decrease in the number of young reared by those pairs that were successful.

Thus, changes in clutch size, as seen in some lemming and microtine predators (snowy owl, rough-legged buzzard) or breeding density (pomarine jaeger, rough-legged buzzard) in relation to prey density do not appear to be a part of the prairie falcon's immediate reproductive adjustment to food supply (see Newton 1979 for general discussion). Possibly the reason is because the irregularities in prey numbers produced by drought are unpredictable and less severe than the cyclical changes associated with lemming and microtine populations. It is also likely that the close relationship between sakers and susliks in Eurasia is very parallel to the situation outlined here between the prairie falcons and Townsend's ground squirrels – while Arctic gyrfalcons that depend on ptarmigan populations, which cycle drastically over a long period of years, show an intermediate response to changing food supply, including adjustment of breeding density in addition to changes in reproductive output of successful pairs, but not change in clutch size.

While continued drought over several years might well lead to such a severe reduction in numbers of squirrels and other prey that the number of breeding prairie falcons would also drop significantly, a more serious possibility relates to the long term prospects for preservation of the sagebrush-grasslands that the ground squirrels depend upon for their habitat. The use of these lands for grazing livestock is not detrimental to the squirrels or falcons (or other wildlife of the area), but intensive agriculture and irrigation are, as revealed by the acreage already ploughed under and planted along the Snake River. It is not enough to protect the nesting habitat in the canyon, for the 600 and more pairs of raptors nesting there are largely dependent for their food supply on the animals living in the adjacent rangelands. As the then Secretary of the Interior, Cecil Andrus, wrote in 1979, "We were well aware then [1971] that the 26,000 acres [105 square kilometres] set aside would protect only a portion of the nesting area – a small 'bedroom' for some of the many birds of prey along the Snake River. To assure survival, the birds would need not only additional 'bedroom' space, but an adequate 'dining' area as well." Studies involving radio-telemetry tracking of hunting prairie falcons reveal that some birds fly as far as 26 km (16 miles) away from the canyon for food, and the hunting ranges, which overlap broadly, vary from 92–162 sq km (36–62 sq miles) for six pairs and from 26–141 sq km (10–54 sq miles) for 16 individuals. These large hunting ranges indicate that the existing prairie falcon population of some 200 pairs nesting in the Snake River Canyon depends for its food supply on about 3,000 sq km (1,160 sq miles) of adjacent range. Based on calculated reproductive requirements for a stable falcon population and on computer simulations of changes in the biomass of ground squirrels assuming additional increments of land brought under agriculture, it has been predicted that an additional conversion of no more than 15 per cent of the land to crops could reduce the available prey to a level that would be too low to allow the falcons to produce enough young to maintain the current breeding population.

Although the prairie falcon is not known to reach densities comparable to that of the Snake River population in any other part of its range, it is nonetheless rather common for a raptor of its size in many places. Locally prairie falcons have encountered some problems with man and have declined in numbers. This seems to have been particularly true in the Central Valley of California, where R. L. Gerrett and D. J. Mitchell found only one of 33 historical eyries still occupied by a nesting pair; they suggested that extensive conversion of native range to cropland was an important factor in the demise of this population. Housing developments around isolated buttes in the Mojave Desert have caused prairie falcons to abandon some eyries, and at least one Canadian population of prairie falcons has suffered temporary decline as a result of toxic chemicals used in agriculture, showing the same reproductive problems as the peregrine (Fyfe et al. 1969, 1976).

Otherwise, the status of the prairie falcon is secure, despite the fact that it is on the "blue list" of the National Audubon Society. Most western states and Canadian provinces now keep inventories of prairie falcon eyries, as do a number of private researchers (BLM Report 1979). These sources indicate that the total population of the species is in the range of 5,000 to 6,000 pairs with a breeding distribution covering some 4 to 4.5 million sq km (1.5–1.7 million sq miles).

Black Falcon

Falco subniger

STRIKINGLY BEAUTIFUL, THIS Australian falcon is uniformly sooty black to very dark brown in adult plumage, except for some pale mottlings on the inner webs of primaries, pale tip to tail, whitish chin and ear-coverts, and white, unexposed bases to feathers of the legs, abdomen and breast. Immatures show more white, particularly on the throat, ear-coverts, tail, webs of primaries, and additional white spots on breast, under tail-coverts, and some under wing-coverts. The greyish blue bloom to the feathers on the back is the result, no doubt, of copious powder-down (some other falcons have this bloom well developed, and it may function as a waterproof coating). The fleshy parts are bluish to bluish white, even in the adult, an unusual deviation from the typical yellow to orangish adult colour in other falcon species.

Black falcons are rather large in appearance: males are around 45–48 cm ($17\frac{1}{2}$–19 in) in length with an estimated wingspan of more than 100 cm ($39\frac{1}{2}$ in); females up to 54 cm (21 in) in body length with longer wings (though sexual dimorphism in size is not pronounced in this species). The wing length averages 368 mm ($14\frac{1}{2}$ in) for males and 402 mm (16 in) for females (Brown and Amadon 1968), or about the same as for the gyrfalcon; but *subniger* weighs less than half as much as *rusticolus*. Brown and Amadon give weights for two males as 597 and 607 g (21–$21\frac{1}{2}$ oz), and for one female as 670 g ($23\frac{1}{2}$ oz). Thus, the wing-loading of the black falcon compares closely with that of the grey falcon, and both species are very buoyant, kite-like fliers.

This powerful falcon inhabits mostly the less well watered inland areas of interior Australia, the total distribution covering about 4 million sq km (1.5 million sq miles). It is usually rather rare, but at times can be locally common. Populations are nomadic and shift about in association with movements and concentrations of prey, especially quail for which the falcon has a special affinity (see Bedggood 1979).

It appears likely that the black falcon is one of the Australian species whose reproduction is influenced by the irregular occurrence of rainfall in the outback, as egg dates range from June to December, though September and October are the months in which most clutches have been found. The falcon adopts the unused nest of some other large, arboreal species (crow, kite, eagle) usually at a considerable height above the ground. Some pairs, however, take a nest in a low bush if there are no tall trees, possibly in response to a high density of prey in the area. This species has been said to build its own nest, but detailed, firsthand reports have not been published. Apparently the nests are not lined.

Two to four eggs are laid, usually three. There is little recorded about the nesting cycle or development of the young, which hatch with a grey down that is hair-like on the head and neck (Serventy and Whittell 1967). Adults have been reported not to defend the nest and young against human intruders, but Olsen and Olsen (1980) report that six pairs with young all attacked a person who climbed up the nest trees, although when the tree was first approached, the birds flew away and stayed very high in the air. No vocalizations accompanied the attacks, as happens with attacking peregrines and Australian hobbies at their eyries.

While taking some of its prey on the ground, the black falcon is typically an aerial hunter and feeds mainly on birds caught in the air. Its normal flight is a characteristic undulation at low altitude with alternating periods of slow flapping and gliding; but it can fly very fast when attacking. The black falcon is an aggressive hunter. It may launch an attack from a perched position or stoop from height in the air, where it sometimes soars high up. It is very persistent in tail-chasing and typically utters loud screams as it attacks, as though attempting to intimidate the prey. A bird that takes refuge in a bush is often frightened into flight by the falcon, which dives rapidly and repeatedly at the bush screaming constantly (Frith 1969). This rather unusual technique is somewhat akin to the attack of aplomado falcons on birds that seek cover in bushes. The black falcon also pirates prey away from other raptors, including the peregrine falcon, and it has even been reported to feed on carrion. Quails and starlings are common prey, but it also catches strong quarry such as galahs, pigeons and ducks. The latter are stooped at and struck repeatedly until they fall to the ground, where the black falcon binds to the prey and kills it by biting into the neck in typical falcon fashion. It also sometimes catches rabbits and other small mammals on the run, as they bolt for cover or a burrow. Bedggood (1979) has described several other hunting tactics, including low contour-hugging along the banks of irrigation ditches.

There is much more to be learned about the hunting habits, breeding behaviour, and nesting ecology of this interesting species. Its relationship to other species of *Falco* is not clear either.

PLATE IX
Black Falcon
Falco subniger
Adult female
Map page 185

R. David Digby

Grey Falcon

Falco hypoleucos

THE GREY FALCON is evidently the rarest and least known of the six species of *Falco* in Australia, where it is endemic to the mainland. It occurs widely in scattered pairs through the more arid and open forests of the interior and avoids the heavily timbered regions of the north, east and south, although typically perching and nesting in trees. In no part of its range, which covers some 4 million sq km (1.5 million sq miles), has it been reported to be other than rare. As an example, two photographers (Jack and Linsay Cupper 1980) spent six years searching for a nest of grey falcons, during which time they saw pairs on six occasions and finally located one nest after a concentrated effort involving 12,000 km (7,500 miles) of travel in 1979.

As its name suggests, this is a very pale coloured falcon, and some individuals appear almost white at a distance in bright sun. In the field the grey falcon is easily distinguished from all other Australian hawks by the black wing tips, bright orangish eye rings, cere and legs, which contrast with the general whitish appearance, and by the short tail, which gives the medium-build bird a rather thick-set appearance. Males have body lengths of around 30–35 cm (12–14 in), with a wingspan of 75–85 cm ($29\frac{1}{2}$–$33\frac{1}{2}$ in); females are about 41–43 cm (16–17 in) long with a wingspan of 95–100 cm ($37\frac{1}{2}$–$39\frac{1}{2}$ in). Serventy and Whittell (1967) give the weight of the male as 336 g (12 oz); by estimation the weight of the female should be around 500 g ($17\frac{1}{2}$ oz). These are very light weights compared with the body lengths and wingspans and indicate an unusually light wing-loading for grey falcons.

Observers do, in fact, characterize the flight as rather slow and flapping, although the falcon is said to fly fairly rapidly when pursuing prey. Its short tail is frequently flicked from side to side in flight, as though these movements are somehow necessary to maintain equilibrium (Frith 1969). The grey falcon is rather sluggish, spending much of the day quietly perched in a tree, or at times soaring to heights of several hundred metres. It is a rather tame species and often allows humans to approach closely in the field.

Its hunting behaviour and, indeed, most of its habits are like those of the "desert falcons", and it remains an open question whether it is an Australian member of this "superspecies" or is only convergently similar. The grey falcon takes most of its prey on or near the ground, and it hunts either by flying close to the ground or above small shrubs, snatching most prey in a sudden surprise attack, or by perching motionless in a tree and waiting for vulnerable prey to appear within striking range.

The prey consists of small mammals, including juvenile rabbits, and birds, reptiles and insects. Flying grasshoppers and other flying insects are sometimes hawked out of the air and eaten on the wing in hobby-like fashion, but most insects apparently are caught on the ground. Small birds are also taken on the wing.

Grey falcons use the old stick nests of other arboreal nesting birds such as crows, kites, hawks and eagles for their eyries, which are usually at heights of 20 m (65 ft) or more above ground (Serventy and Whittell 1967, Macdonald 1973, Frith 1969). They are said to line these old nests with soft materials such as animal hair or strips of bark and sometimes to build their own nests. It is interesting to note that all six of the Australian falcons use stick nests in trees to some extent, and all have been reported to build their own nests on occasion; but since nest-building is such exceptional behaviour for falcons, we really need some careful descriptions of falcons in the act of constructing nests.

The clutch ranges from two to four eggs, but three is the most frequent number. Eggs are laid from July to October and even November in Western Australia, September being the main month. Very little has been recorded about the nesting cycle, but apparently females do most or all of the incubating, which lasts about 35 days (Cupper and Cupper 1980). According to some accounts, adult grey falcons do not defend their nests against human intruders, but Olsen and Olsen (1980) have recently cited two instances in which pairs did defend. It may be that such behaviour is weak or absent if only the base of the nesting tree is approached, whereas the birds become aggressive if the intruder climbs the tree and threatens the nest at close range. Defensive behaviour may also vary, as in other species, with the stage of the breeding cycle, that is, whether eggs or young are present.

Orange-breasted Falcon

Falco deiroleucus

THE MEDIUM-SIZED but powerful orange-breasted falcon is something of a mystery. It is resident in most of the New World tropical forests from southeastern Mexico through Central America south to Peru, Bolivia, Paraguay, and northern Argentina, but it is decidedly rare, even for a falcon, throughout this vast range of some 10 to 12 million sq km (3.9–4.6 million sq miles). It may be entirely absent from the central Amazon basin, as it appears to prefer forests with some elevation or slope up to about 2,200 m (7,200 ft), and, also, drier regions such as the Chaco of northern Argentina (Short 1975, see also Boyce 1980).

The species is known from about 50 museum specimens and scattered field observations. Fewer than 10 nesting sites have been recorded, and the closest known eyries are 50 km (30 miles) apart. The orange-breasted falcon may be the most sparsely distributed falcon in the world, and one wonders why the bird should be so rare, especially as it encounters no other species with which it could be in sharp competition for food or nest-sites. Its much commoner, look-alike congener, the bat falcon, is too small to be a serious competitor, although Boyce's (1980) account of the falcons at Tikal indicates some aggressive interactions between the two.

The orange-breasted falcon typically perches in an exposed position and makes itself readily visible, and it also frequently attracts attention by its loud, high-pitched, rapid screams, "ke-ke-ke-ke". It is a conspicuously marked bird with a black head, cheeks, and back, whitish throat blending into an orangish upper breast and ruff-like crescent extending around the sides of the head, a feature which contrasts prominently with the black face. It also has a broad band of black feathers slightly tipped with buff in the mid-ventral region, and a second area of chestnut on the belly, thighs, and under tail-coverts, the latter with some black barring even in adult plumage.

Its head appears unusually large in proportion to body owing to an elongation of the black ear-coverts and the feathers producing the orange crescent on the sides. When these latter feathers are flared out in aggressive display they produce a ruff around the black face and give the head a somewhat owl-like aspect.

Rather comparable in size and build to the Barbary falcon, the orange-breasted falcon also has evolved extreme sexual dimorphism in size. Males are around 35–36 cm ($13\frac{1}{2}$–14 in) in length and weigh between 330–360 g ($11\frac{1}{2}$–$12\frac{1}{2}$ oz); females are 38–40 cm (15–$15\frac{1}{2}$ in) and weigh 550–650 g ($19\frac{1}{2}$–23 oz). Thus, the largest females weigh twice as much as the smallest males. There is also a marked sexual difference in the relative size and shape of the head, more so than in other falcons. Females have big, narrow heads with long, accipitrine faces, whereas males have a "blockier", more typical falcon-shaped head. (Friedmann 1950, Brown and Amadon 1968.)

This species is also the most powerfully armed of all falcons relative to body size, with huge feet and long, grasping toes with accipiter-like talons. The toes compare in absolute size with those of many peregrines. The beak is also massive, laterally compressed, deepened, and keeled on its dorsal surface, features which produce an extremely powerful bite. These special features are developed to some degree in other forest-dwelling, bird-eating falcons such as the black shaheen in India; the Australian, New Guinea, and Fiji peregrines; and the New Zealand falcon. The large feet appear to be associated with the greater need to snatch birds out of the air and hold on to them over closed canopy rather than striking them first in a stoop and then grabbing them as they fall to ground. The large beak may be an adaptation to bite and kill struggling quarry quickly, and Clayton White has suggested to me that such a beak may be particularly advantageous for dispatching vigorous and difficult prey such as parrots, which are frequently taken by both orange-breasted falcons and Australian peregrines.

In addition, observations on captive birds reveal that the orange-breasted falcons use their powerful beaks to break up the leg bones and wing bones of their prey. They seem to eat more bone than most falcons do – particularly the ends of leg bones of birds as large as pigeons and half-grown chickens. Furthermore, the bone is usually completely digested, as the regurgitated pellets consist only of feathers and horny parts, except that the denser bones of mammals are cast up.

Some authorities (Otto Kleinschmidt; Erwin Stresemann) have considered the orange-breasted falcon to be a Neotropical form of the peregrine, or a very closely allied semi-species. It can be considered an ecological substitute for the peregrine, but it is not a true peregrine, nor, I believe, is it even closely related. Its closest relative is the bat falcon (see page 101).

The orange-breasted falcon has all the morphological features associated with very fast, flapping flight – long, pointed, blade-like wings, stiff primaries and tail feathers, short tail, compact body feathers,

PLATE XI
Orange-breasted
Falcon
Falco deiroleucus
Adult male,
above right
Immature female,
below left
Map page 186

98

R. David Digby.

and enlarged pectoral muscles. It has a rapid wingbeat and appears to rely on power more than gravity to gain speed in pursuit of prey. It is capable of catching very fast birds such as doves and pigeons, small to medium-sized parrots, swifts and swallows in direct flight. It also feeds on other medium-sized to large passerines and forest birds, including jays and caciques, and at Tikal in Guatemala, on a surprising number of migratory shorebirds such as killdeer, pectoral sandpipers and lesser yellowlegs (Peter Jenny). It also commonly catches bats and insects in the air and shows a decidedly crepuscular pattern of activity.

Orange-breasted falcons apparently hunt mainly in the air over continuous tropical forest, but they must also hunt to some extent along rivers and around lakes, and Boyce (1980) has suggested that they hunt mainly at the edges of forests around clearings. According to the observations of my associate, Peter Jenny, in Guatemala and Ecuador, orange-breasted falcons often hunt from a perched position in a tall tree overlooking the forest canopy or from a hillside looking down on forest below. They make direct, merlin-like chases from the perch after passing birds – either in a climbing pursuit terminating in a short stoop or simply in a very fast tail-chase. Some of the chases go up into the air and become long contests of endurance, with the two birds often disappearing from sight through binoculars. The perched falcon will also sky-scan for high flying birds such as swifts and go up to meet them in the air. On two occasions Jenny also saw a male stoop from a soar in excess of 400 m (1,300 ft); and Boyce (1980) mentions one stoop in which the bird disappeared below the canopy, but apparently fast, direct pursuit is this bird's main forte.

Little is known about the falcon's breeding habits. In two seasons of field work in Guatemala and Ecuador in 1979 and 1980 Jenny obtained more information from observations on six pairs than had previously been reported in the literature all the way back to Latham's "orange-breasted hobby" from Surinam in his *Synopsis of Birds* (1781).

Evidently in most parts of its range, territorial establishment at the eyrie and mating begin at the end of the rainy season (January in Guatemala), two to three eggs are laid during the dry period (March), and the young are on the wing and flying with their parents at the beginning of the next rainy period (late May). The whole cycle was about two months earlier in eastern Ecuador, where February is the driest month and heavy rains usually begin in April or May.

Orange-breasted falcons nest in cavities in large, emergent trees, such as a silk cotton tree, or in holes on the faces of rocky cliffs, exceptionally on a man-made substitute such as a Mayan temple at Tikal. Ludlow Griscom's statement that they nest in church towers and belfries in Central American cities needs confirmation but seems plausible in view of the falcons at Tikal (Boyce 1980). All of the eyries Jenny observed, whether on a cliff, temple, or in a tall tree, looked out over vast stretches of unbroken, climax forest.

Early in the breeding season both adults are extremely vocal around the eyrie, uttering their fast, rattling, high-pitched "ke-ke-ke-ke" scream which penetrates through dense forest most effectively; and they spend much time chasing other large birds – other raptors but also large parrots and toucans – away from the vicinity of the nest cavity. It may be that the falcons are competitive with other hole-nesting species for sites. Courtship displays, food transferring, copulation, and all close interactions between male and female are accompanied by soft, slowly repeated piping notes, virtually identical to notes uttered by bat falcons in the same situations. Apparently only the female incubates and broods, and the male calls the female out of the nest cavity by piping to provision her with food. He never feeds the young directly in the nest. If the female does not answer his call for food, the male caches the prey in some convenient clump of epiphytes in a nearby tree.

Once out of the nest, the young falcons are quiet and unobtrusive most of the time. They do not give the loud food-begging calls so characteristic of most other falcons, even when one young is being fed and the other is not, unusual behaviour that may have evolved as an adaptation to avoid detection by horned owls or other forest-lurking predators. They do, however, give the defensive "ke-ke-ke-ke" scream at an early age.

How many orange-breasted falcons are there? perhaps a few hundred to a few thousand at most. It could well be that there are more peregrines nesting in the British Isles than there are orange-breasted falcons in the whole of the Neotropics. One gains some idea about how difficult this species is to find by considering Jenny's effort: from January to May of 1979 he and his companions travelled 5,415 km (3,300 miles) by road, 2,160 km (1,300 miles) in a low-flying aircraft at 100 m (330 ft) above the canopy, and 297 km (180 miles) by motor canoe on four rivers – all in prime habitat for the falcons in Guatemala, Belize, Ecuador and Peru – and they knew where orange-breasted falcons had previously been collected or found nesting. They observed a total of 15 orange-breasted falcons at four nest-sites and obtained information about two other nests (compared to 95 bat falcons), only one eyrie being at a known location. With this one exception, Jenny found that localities where specimens had been collected in the past are today without tropical forest and without orange-breasted falcons.

What is the future of such a rare, sparsely distributed species with an apparent affinity for climax tropical forests, which are being destroyed and fragmented at a staggering rate? It could become extinct without notice. Fortunately, the orange-breasted falcon appears to prefer mid-level forests, such as occur on the rugged lower slopes on the eastern side of the Andes, and so far these forests have been less disturbed than those in the lowlands or those at higher elevations. A few dozen pairs of orange-breasted falcons might be able to hold on indefinitely in such a region.

Bat Falcon

Falco rufigularis

HIGHLY ACTIVE AND common, the bat falcon is a smaller rendition of the rare orange-breasted falcon. and occupies much the same Neotropical range as the larger species. The two species are remarkably similar in plumage coloration and pattern, the principal differences being the larger area of chestnut on the belly of the orange-breasted and the completely unbarred chestnut under tail-coverts of the adult bat falcon. The little bat falcon averages less than half the weight of the larger species and has more conventionally proportioned feet and beak, its beak being somewhat laterally compressed and slightly keeled.

There has been some question about whether the close similarities in plumage are convergent – possibly the result of some form of mimicry or the evolution of similar visual signals associated with interspecific aggressiveness and territoriality (Cody 1969) – or simply indicate close common ancestry. The vocalizations and behaviour patterns of the two falcons are also very similar, and I believe that Ridgway and Friedmann (Friedmann 1950) were correct in concluding that these species are more closely related to each other than either is to other species of *Falco*. They appear to represent a divergence in body size from a common ancestor resulting in exploitation of a different set of prey species (based primarily on size), a difference in ecology and niche that has allowed them to occupy co-extensive distributions throughout the Neotropics.

The bat falcon's total historic range was somewhat greater than that of the orange-breasted falcon, extending from southern Sonora and Tamaulipas in Mexico southward throughout the lowland sub-tropical and tropical forests of Central America up to about 1,500 m (4,600 ft), and thence south to eastern Ecuador, Peru, Bolivia, Paraguay, northern Argentina, all of Brazil, and the island of Trinidad. Now that the extensive, continuing modifications of habitat in the Neotropics have begun to influence the distribution and local numbers of *rufigularis*, it is impossible to give a precise, current assessment of its distribution and abundance.

Bat falcons are essentially resident throughout the year in the same areas, and many adults remain paired all year round. Their favoured haunts are usually where an opening of some sort creates an edge with the closed forest – along major rivers, roads, around agricultural clearings, burned areas or second-growth pastures.

As with the orange-breasted falcon, male and female bat falcons are extremely dimorphic in size, being among the most dimorphic falcons in this respect (males average 61 per cent of female body weight and 86 per cent of wing length). There is also a difference in the shape of their heads, but it is not so pronounced as in the orange-breasted falcon. The sexes are virtually identical in colour and pattern, the juveniles differing from adults mainly in having black bars on the under tail-coverts and a more orangish throat. The body plumage is very compact, and the wing and tail feathers are stiff and swift-like in texture, anatomical correlations of fast flight. The insides of the legs are very thinly feathered – a trait held in common with the orange-breasted falcon and probably a heat-dissipating adaptation to the hot tropical climate.

The facial pattern and features are even more pronounced than in *deiroleucus*. The light throat and continuous crescent on the sides of the neck contrast sharply with the black head and cheeks. The feathers on the upper neck and cheeks are proportionately longer than in other species of falcons, and when these feathers are flared, the head has an enlarged, highly conspicuous, almost cobra-like appearance, which is used as an aggressive signal in close encounters with other bat falcons. It may also function in distant territorial advertisement, as I have seen bat falcons perched conspicuously atop dead trees in Chiapas, Mexico with their necks and cheeks flared out, producing a visual sign that even a human being could see from 50 m (160 ft) away.

Males range between 22.5–24 cm (9–9½ in) in total length with wingspans of 56–58 cm (22–23 in), and weigh from 108–148 g (4–5 oz) (Haverschmidt 1962). The comparable figures for females are: 25–27.5 cm (10–11 in) in length, wingspans of 65–67 cm (25½–26½ in) extrapolated from data on males, and weights from 177–242 g (6–8½ oz). Thus the species averages a little larger than the American kestrel, a little smaller than the merlin.

Bat falcons are rather vocal and assertive birds. The common alarm or aggressive call is a high pitched "ke-ke-ke-ke" very similar to that of kestrels but more rapidly repeated. The male's call is higher pitched than the female's. The falcons utter these calls when the nest is threatened, when driving off other predatory birds, and sometimes when attacking prey. Courting females and young also utter a whining food call, and the mated males and females give a low intensity "chit" when they approach each other closely on a perch and particularly in or around the nest-hole. It is apparently some kind of contact or recognition call, perhaps signalling submissiveness.

Bat falcons are extremely agile and active hunters, catching a variety of small birds, bats and flying insects on the wing. They are among the most aerial of falcons and almost never descend to the ground for prey, although they will occasionally snatch sitting birds or insects from bushes or branches of trees. They have three main methods for searching and attacking, as I had an opportunity to observe in Chiapas, Mexico, where I spent part of the 1978 field season with Gary Falxa, Devora Ukrain and Dave Whitacre, who have amassed a great amount of data on this species.

Most often bat falcons perch in the tops of tall trees – often dead ones – from which they can command a good view of surrounding open or semi-open habitat. In this respect they are very like kestrels, except that whereas kestrels mostly search the ground for prey, bat falcons watch intently for prey to fly into a vulnerable position in the air remote from cover. From these perched positions, the falcons usually launch their attacks on prey that is flying low by diving down off the perch and approaching rapidly from behind, dropping down below the quarry before delivering the strike, which is executed by shooting up at the last instant and making a high reaching grab with extended legs and feet. This manoeuvre is similar to many attacks on dragonflies. Bat falcons have extremely fast wingbeats and give the appearance of generating a great deal of thrust with the upstroke as well as with the downstroke of their wings, as swifts do. By dropping low and using bushes or other vegetation for concealment, they can catch up to a small bird or dragonfly in seconds and often snatch the prey before it realizes it is under attack. Most such strikes are executed at distances under 100 m (330 ft) from the perch.

Perched falcons also watch the upper sky for prey (sky-scanning), and when a vulnerable prey appears, they will fly up on their tails like miniature gyrfalcons to intercept the quarry at heights of several hundred metres. I saw several of these high flights in southern Mexico in 1978, and watched these small, compact falcons with their massive pectoral muscles and rapid wing strokes covering a kilometre of air space in an astonishingly short time. When it becomes possible to make comparable measurements under standardized conditions, I believe the bat falcon and orange-breasted falcon will prove to be the fastest members of the genus in level, flapping flight.

Alternatively, in the second main method of hunting, bat falcons will sometimes course about in fast flight very low over tree-tops or bushes in apparent attempts to flush prey into flight ahead of them, in which case they tail-chase the escaping prey and snatch it out of the air. This mode of hunting may follow after an unsuccessful attack from a perch.

When wind or thermal conditions are right, bat falcons will also hunt by flying about and soaring at heights of 100 or more metres above ground and striking at flying insects or birds. Dragonflies and other insects are frequently hawked out of the air in this way and eaten on the wing in hobby-style. They also occasionally stoop from height with folded wings like a peregrine waiting on.

Bat falcons do most of their hunting in the early morning or late evening, and they are decidedly crepuscular, often hunting well after sunset. Bats are often caught around the entrances of their caves or colony-trees, or around culverts under roads. During the middle hours of the day they are usually to be seen perched quietly on look-out in their territories, occasionally sallying out to catch a passing insect.

Until recently most of what we know about the food habits of the bat falcon came from Will Beebe's (1950) classic observations on a pair that nested within view of his office window in the National Park of Aragua, Venezuela at an elevation of 1,100 m (3,600 ft) in montane rain forest. During a period of 164 days from 20 February to 1 August, in which the pair fledged two young, Beebe catalogued a total of 33 mammals, including four species of bats and one terrestrial jungle mouse (*Heteromys anomalus*); 163 birds drawn from 56 species, including 26 swifts, 34 hummingbirds, 17 swallows, 10 warblers, 19 tanagers, and 12 fringillid finches; 2 arboreal lizards; one tree frog; and 19 insects representing 14 species, mostly lepidopterans. Many of the birds were lowland species that Beebe reckoned had to have been caught several kilometres from the nest. Moreover, the avian prey divided out in a revealing way with respect to four major parameters of their niches:

PLATE XII
Bat Falcon
Falco rufigularis
Adult male,
above (sunning)
Adult female,
below centre
Map page 186

Aerial – 23 species, 87 individuals. Tree-top – 19 species, 37 individuals. Open country – 10 species, 17 individuals. Jungle (below canopy) – 4 species, 5 individuals.

Beebe also estimated that the pair and their dependent young must have consumed not less than 600 birds and bats during their breeding season.

The more recent, extensive study by Falxa, Ukrain and Whitacre (in press) of nesting bat falcons in southern Mexico in 1977 and 1978, based on 462 prey items, showed that 35 species of birds drawn from

R. DAVID DIGBY

18 families totalled around 65 per cent of the consumed biomass. These birds included 13 species of North American migrants. Insects, especially dragonflies, were second in importance (18 per cent), while bats made up about 14 per cent of the biomass. Moreover, these workers found important seasonal differences: birds made up most of the diet early in the breeding season (March), but insects comprised 40 to 45 per cent of the biomass consumed in late May and June, with the onset of the rainy season and a dramatic increase in the population of dragonflies.

As one would expect, bat falcons have a higher success rate in capturing individual insects than in capturing birds. Falxa *et al.* observed that about 60 per cent of attacks on dragonflies resulted in capture, whereas bat falcons were successful in catching birds only 10 to 25 per cent of the times. It would be most worthwhile to learn how energy expended per unit of energy captured compares for bird and insect prey. A 10-gram bird is equivalent in weight to 20 dragonflies, but since it is unlikely that to catch a small bird, a falcon expends more than 5 to 10 times the energy required to catch an insect, it would seem that hawking insects is a relatively inefficient way for bat falcons to forage, except when dragonflies are extremely abundant. This problem needs quantitative study in general for falcons, and bat falcons would make excellent subjects because of the ease with which their hunts can be recorded.

Bat falcons nest mainly in hollows of trees, occupying natural cavities and, probably, holes excavated by parrots and woodpeckers (not unlike kestrels). They nest in both live and dead trees at heights of 10–50 m (30–160 ft) above ground in habitat ranging from undisturbed tropical forest to large pastures with a single, remnant tree several kilometres from any continuous forest. They also sometimes nest on a rocky cliff-face, and occasionally on man-made structures. One unusual nest was placed in a pocket in the crown of an oil palm (Falxa *et al.*).

Nests are often close to human habitation, and the bat falcons show little concern for humans moving about on the ground. They are, however, vigorous defenders of their nests against intruders in the tree, human or otherwise, and they attack and drive away other birds of prey entering their territories. Falxa *et al.* recorded bat falcons chasing no less than 14 different species of raptors, some such as the grey hawk (*Buteo nitidus*) up to nearly a kilometre away from the nest.

Bat falcons usually lay 2 or 3 eggs, sometimes 4, but most often 3; and the average for 25 Mexican clutches is 2.9 (Falxa *et al.*). Laying apparently occurs mainly during the dry season (February, March, April in southern Mexico) but varies considerably from pair to pair and from season to season. In southeastern Mexico 14 successful pairs fledged an average of 2.5 young (range 1 to 4) indicating that about 86 per cent of eggs laid result in successfully reared young, a high success rate similar to that of American kestrels and other hole-nesting species. A number of non-nesting pairs were present in this population; however, it is not known why some pairs do not breed in a particular year.

Historically the bat falcon has occupied a large area essentially including all of the lowland Neotropical forests of Mexico, Central and South America up to elevations of 1,500 m (4,900 ft) locally, a total distribution approximating 13 million sq km (5 million sq miles). Within this vast range the bat falcon is often the commonest falcon, with densities of the order of one pair per 100 sq km (39 sq miles) or less (nearest neighbour distance can be no more than 1.3 km); but in other regions, particularly at higher elevations, it is much less common, perhaps no more than a pair per 1,000 sq km (390 sq miles). The total bat falcon population must number in the several tens of thousands of pairs, but data are too few for any precise estimate.

The numbers are certain to be changing in any case. In 1977 and 1978 Falxa, Ukrain and Whitacre were unable to locate any nesting bat falcons at historically known collecting sites in the eastern coastal plain of Mexico north of Veracruz. The whole area is now under intensive agriculture, virtually all of the lowland tropical forests having been cut for wood or to create fields; and DDT has been used extensively on cotton and other crops. Significantly, eggshells collected in this region between 1954 and 1967 show 18 per cent thinning compared to a pre-DDT sample (Kiff, Peakall and Hector 1981), a degree of thinning associated with population declines in peregrines and other species.

In the less disturbed forests of the nearby Sierra Madre Oriental, Falxa *et al.* found four pairs and several individual falcons; but it was not until they travelled east of the Isthmus of Tehuantepec that they found bat falcons nesting commonly. They located more than 30 pairs in southeastern Mexico, where mechanised agricultural practices are not yet extensive, and those that were observed closely showed good reproduction, as described above.

The rapid clearing of the lowland tropical forests in all of Latin America will have lasting effects on many species living in these complex ecosystems, including all of the native falcons and raptors. The bat falcon probably benefits temporarily from forest-cutting and burning, because the clearings, when not too extensive, produce optimum hunting areas, and the isolated giant trees left standing in fields seem to be preferred nesting places. Thus, depending on the recentness and extent of clearings, bat falcons may increase density locally; but isolated tropical forest trees do not regenerate, and so they represent a temporary habitat at best.

In the long run, the distribution and numbers of bat falcons in the Neotropics will depend upon how many tracts of native forest are left standing and what their geographic and topographic configurations are. There seems little doubt that the species will undergo further, serious decline before the end of the twentieth century. We can only hope that the situation now existing on the eastern coast of Mexico north of Veracruz will not be repeated too many times in other parts of the bat falcon's range.

Aplomado Falcon

Falco femoralis

T HE APLOMADO FALCON differs in form and habits from its close relatives, the orange-breasted and bat falcons, although it does show some similarities to them in the pattern and colour of its plumage. It is decidedly accipitrine in shape, with a relatively long, somewhat graduated tail (65 to 70 per cent of the standard wing measurement, compared with 48 to 51 per cent for the other two species), and long legs. Although it has a long falcon wing, the tip is less pointed, the number 8 primary being longest and P10 being shorter than P7. Males are about 37–38 cm ($14\frac{1}{2}$–15 in) in length, females about 43–45 cm (17–$17\frac{1}{2}$ in). Wingspan has not been recorded. Of small to medium build, males from eastern Mexico weigh 260 g (9 oz) on average, females 407 g ($14\frac{1}{2}$ oz). Data from Dean Hector (in press).

The body plumage is rather soft, and the flight feathers are not as stiff as those of the peregrine or orange-breasted falcon, the texture of the feathers being comparable to that of the prairie falcon or gyrfalcon. The markings and colours follow the general pattern seen in the bat falcon and orange-breasted: there is a whitish to buffy or rufescent throat and upper breast followed by a black mid-ventral and flank region, with narrow white tips to the individual feathers, and rufescent lower belly, thighs and under tail-coverts. The distinctive head has a thin black malar strip, whitish to rufescent cheeks, with another thin black line running posteriorly from the eye and dorsal to the light cheek patch. This line is separated from the bluish grey crown by a crescentric pattern of whitish to rufescent feathers running from the dorsal, posterior margin of one eye around the hindneck to the other eye. The back and upper wing surfaces generally match the bluish grey of the crown, while the tail is distinctively marked with alternating bars of black and white. The sexes are similar, and first year birds are much like adults, except that they have brownish edgings on the feathers where the adults are black or greyish and the ventral area is heavily streaked instead of barred.

This colourful falcon has a New World distribution that historically extended from the southwestern United States (southern and western Texas, southern New Mexico and Arizona) in suitable areas through all of Mexico and Central America south throughout South America, including Trinidad, to Tierra del Fuego, covering a total area of nearly 22 million sq km (8.4 million sq miles). Since the beginning of the twentieth century the aplomado falcon has become increasingly scarce in the northern portions of its range, and it was last reported nesting in Texas and New Mexico in the 1950s, although there have been several more recent sightings of individuals (Hector 1980). It is also now extremely uncommon in northern Mexico, becoming regular in occurrence only from Veracruz southward. No one knows why the bird has become so rare in the United States, but deterioration of habitat from agriculture and stock-raising may have had something to do with it. In northern and eastern Mexico, intensive agriculture and use of DDT appear to be current problems, as eggshells collected in the last 25 years show marked thinning like those of bat falcons from the same region (Kiff, Peakall and Hector 1981). The current situation in South America is not well known, but in many, perhaps most, parts of its range there, the aplomado falcon probably remains as common as ever, particularly so in the tablelands of Patagonia, one of its chief strongholds.

The aplomado falcon is a bird of open grasslands and savannahs where tall cacti, tree yuccas, or trees such as mesquite, Nothofagus, and occasionally taller pines and oaks grow in open stands. The bird shows a wide bioclimatic tolerance, occurring in summer-rainfall deserts of North America, arid tropical zones, humid tropical coastal plains, montane grasslands (altiplano and puna zones of the Andes) at elevations of 4,000 m (13,100 ft), to the cold, wind-swept tableland of Tierra del Fuego. It is migratory to some extent in the northern and southern extremities of its range, perhaps also at high altitudes, and it has been stated to occur in Central America only as a migrant (Brown and Amadon 1968), although there is now evidence to indicate nesting in Nicaragua (Howell 1972).

Aplomado falcons use the old stick nests of other birds as their eyries, occasionally also bromeliads. In the Chihuahuan desert region of Texas, New Mexico and northern Mexico, the falcons usually choose old nests of the white-necked raven located at heights of 2.5–8 m (8–25 ft) in yuccas or mesquites, or sometimes those of Swainson's hawks. They no doubt also use the nests of hawks such as Harris's hawk, white-tailed hawk, caracara, and other species which share the same range and habitat with the aplomado falcon, but few details have been recorded from South America.

Two or three, rarely four, eggs are laid at different times of the year, depending on locality. In the Chihuahuan region they are laid from March to June; in eastern tropical Mexico from February to June (D. Hector); in southern Chile laying occurs in November; while in northern South America (Caribbean region) the season is around April. Both parents incubate, but little is known about care and development of the young (Brown and Amadon 1968).

The food consists of birds, small mammals, reptiles and insects caught in the air or on the ground (most birds and insects are taken in flight). Aplomado falcons sometimes hawk flying insects out of the air and eat them on the wing in a hobby-like manner, and they also learn to sweep back and forth in front of grass-fires to catch locusts and other disturbed animals.

The aplomado falcon has often been characterized as a rather sluggish bird, more prone to capturing easily taken prey such as grasshoppers, lizards and mice, rather than as an active pursuer of birds. This false impression may come from the fact that like many hot climate birds aplomado falcons are not very active in the middle hours of the day, when they are more likely to be seen quietly perched on a telegraph pole, fence post or dead tree, occasionally taking a snack on an easily caught insect.

Recent observations in Mexico by Dean Hector (in press) agree more with the early characterization of Col H. J. Grayson (Lawrence 1874) and most South American naturalists that aplomado falcons are very capable bird predators. They are decidedly crepuscular in hunting habits, often catching quarry after sunset. Members of a pair often hunt together and apparently co-operate in catching birds. Hector has gathered statistics on hunting performance to make two important points: pairs are more successful in catching birds than singles are; pairs, on average, catch larger prey than singles do.

Grayson likened the aplomado falcon to the sharp-shinned hawk (*Accipiter striatus*) in its "stealthy manner of hunting for its prey beneath the thick foliage of the woods, flying near the ground, or perching in secluded places, from whence it watched, cat-like, for quails, ground doves, etc.". At other times he saw it acting in a more falcon-like manner, boldly chasing its prey in open country. Apparently its most usual method of attacking birds is direct pursuit and tail-chasing. Hector noted, however, that when doves and other birds tried to escape by seeking cover in dense trees or bushes, the aplomado falcon would plunge right into the foliage and often catch the bird off its perch before it could fly out, again revealing its accipiter-like traits; or the female would flush the bird out, and the male waiting in the air above would strike at it in the open. The fact that it regularly catches doves, pigeons, parrots and even snipe in direct flight attests to its considerable speed, but in many instances these birds are apparently driven down into cover before they are actually taken. To what extent the aplomado falcon attacks by stooping from height has not been reported, but it probably occasionally does stoop. In many respects it appears to parallel the red-headed falcon and the New Zealand falcon in its hunting habits.

Except for some loss of breeding range in the Chihuahuan Desert and adjacent parts of northern Mexico, the status of the aplomado falcon seems to be secure for the immediate future. Indeed, it may actually benefit from deforestation for agriculture and pasturelands in Latin America. The grasslands and scrublands that follow after cessation of agriculture in the Neotropics, and the rangelands created by cutting climax forest, are exactly the sorts of habitat best suited to the aplomado falcon's life style, and it is likely that the distribution and abundance of this species will increase rather than decrease in the years ahead.

PLATE XIII
Aplomado Falcon
Falco femoralis
Immature male,
above right
Adult male,
below left
Map page 186

106

R. DAVID DIGBY

New Zealand Falcon

Falco novaeseelandiae

ENDEMIC TO NEW ZEALAND, this falcon occurs widely over both the main North and South islands, as well as on many of the smaller outlying islands, south to the Aukland Islands, but it is absent from the semi-tropical North Aukland peninsula. It occurs in mountains up to about 1,300 m (4,200 ft) down to sea-level. While largely resident in the same localities all year round, some individuals move north after the breeding season, and there probably are some altitudinal shifts as well.

The New Zealand falcon shares its environment with only one other, regularly occurring diurnal raptor, the Australasian harrier (*Circus approximans*). Consequently, the falcon has a rather wide ecological range and is a rather generalized raptor in many respects.

Nick Fox, an English biologist and falconer, has greatly increased our knowledge about the New Zealand falcon in a 4-year field study centred in the northeastern sector of South Island. Most of the information that follows has been summarised from his excellent doctoral dissertation presented to the University of Canterbury (1977).

The New Zealand falcon is medium-sized; but there is considerable variation in size and coloration, so much so that for many years there was argument about whether one or two species were present in New Zealand. Males from different populations average between 37–44 cm ($14\frac{1}{2}$–$17\frac{1}{2}$ in) in length and have extreme weights varying from 252–342 g (9–12 oz), while females average from 44–47 cm ($17\frac{1}{2}$–$18\frac{1}{2}$ in) in different populations and have weights ranging from 420–594 g (15–21 oz). Males vary from 56–62 per cent of female body weight.

The New Zealand falcon is rather dark in general aspect with a variable number of narrow whitish bars, sometimes entirely absent, on an otherwise blackish brown tail and with dark wing feathers barred and spotted with whitish. In adults the upperparts are plain blackish to brownish black, usually darkest on the crown, or the individual feathers may be barred with paler brown marks. The chin and throat are whitish with narrow brown streaks. There is a pale supercillary line with a dark streak below, running through the eye and continuous with the dark malar stripe. The underparts are pale buff to white but heavily streaked or barred with brown on the chest and belly, with somewhat ocellated markings on the flanks. The thighs and under tail-coverts are rufous with dark shaft-streaks. First year birds are browner than adults, and the lighter coloured individuals also have rufous occipital patches. The fleshy parts are bluish grey to bluish white, whereas they are bright yellow in adults. Adult males also tend to be a little brighter in general aspect than females with more bluish tones in their dorsal feathers.

The New Zealand falcon's relationship to other members of the genus *Falco* has long intrigued ornithologists, especially the Russians. Suschkin (1905) considered *novaeseelandiae* to possess many "primitive" traits in common with the kestrels (*Tinnunculus* subgenus) but ended up placing it closer to the merlins (*Aesalon* subgenus) on his phylogenetic tree than to any other group of falcons. On the basis of geography, one would expect to find the closest congener in Australia; indeed, Brown and Amadon (1968) suggested that the New Zealand falcon and the brown falcon (*berigora*) of Australia are both

R. DAVID DIGBY

aberrant hobbies (*Hypotriorchis* subgenus) and therefore are related to the Australian hobby (*longipennis*), but there are no morphological or behavioural traits that tie these three species more closely together than to any other species of falcons.

Another Russian, Boris Stegmann (1933), first pointed out that the New Zealand falcon has a laterally compressed bill with a distinct dorsal keel, features that it shares in common with the orange-breasted falcon and less dramatically, also, with the aplomado and bat falcons. From this observation, Fox has developed the concept of a "Gondwanaland group" of falcons. He derives all four from a common ancestral population that split up as the present continents began to drift apart in the late Cretaceous. However, the timing of these events seems much too early in the course of avian evolution for the common ancestor of the four to have been in existence. As *Falco* itself is defined, it could hardly have been present before the Miocene, when the southern continental land masses were already well separated. Still, if an ancestral population of these four species existed on one of the southern land masses in the Pliocene, dispersal across the relatively narrow stretches of water existing then would have been easier than now.

I do, however, agree with Fox that there are sufficient morphological and behavioural similarities among these four species to make a close phylogenetic relationship plausible, as discussed in Part I.

Even more than the aplomado, the New Zealand falcon has decidedly accipitrine features. The wings are relatively shorter in proportion to body length and rounder at the tips than in most falcons. The tail length averages 68 to 70 per cent of wing length. The number 8 primary is longest, followed in adults by P9, P7, P6, and P10 in that order. Interestingly, P10 is as long as or slightly longer than P6 in first year birds, owing to the fact that P10 in adults is some 10 to 12 mm shorter than in juveniles. The aerodynamic or adaptive significance of this difference is not known. The tarsus is also rather long and thick, but the toes and talons are not markedly different from those of a conventional bird-catching falcon. The body plumage is rather soft and lax, and the flight feathers are more flexible than in highly aerial falcons such as the peregrine or orange-breasted falcon, traits which one sees in accipiter hawks and other forest-dwelling falcons.

The physical characteristics and behaviour of the New Zealand falcon give the impression that this species has been strongly influenced by selection pressures associated with a forested environment, and New Zealand was originally mostly covered by forests and brushy habitats. Today much of the forest is gone, and open agricultural areas and pasturelands are extensive, especially in the eastern half of South Island, where tussock grasslands predominate and where sheep and cattle raising are the main industries.

New Zealand falcons occur in both forested and open country, but there are some interesting differences between the populations in the two kinds of habitat, as Nick Fox has shown. The "bush falcons" of wooded environs average smaller and darker than the "quail hawks" or "eastern falcons", which are mostly associated with grasslands and pasturelands. Male "bush falcons" average 264 g ($9\frac{1}{2}$ oz) in weight with a standard wing measurement of 236 mm (9 in), while male "eastern falcons" average 330 g ($11\frac{1}{2}$ oz) with wing lengths of 255 mm (10 in). Comparable figures for females are: "bush", 474 g ($16\frac{1}{2}$ oz) and 273 mm ($10\frac{1}{2}$ in); "eastern", 531 g ($18\frac{1}{2}$ oz) and 297 mm ($11\frac{1}{2}$ in). Although there is an intermediate-sized "southern" population occupying a small area in southwestern South Island the differences between the "bush falcons" and the "eastern falcons" are pretty much independent of latitude and correlate best with habitat – small, dark falcons in the timbered regions, larger, lighter coloured forms in open, unforested areas or slightly brushy habitats.

It would be interesting to know to what extent recent historical changes in the fauna and flora, brought about by man's intensive occupation of these islands, have influenced these morphological and behavioural characteristics of falcons in different parts of New Zealand, or have favoured the numbers of one form relative to the other.

Fox has shown that there are some important differences in the diets of the forest-inhabiting and open country falcons. Generally speaking New Zealand falcons feed on a wide variety of native and exotic birds ranging in size from 1,000 g (35 oz) to less than 10 g ($\frac{1}{3}$ oz); on mammals, all introduced, ranging from nearly 3,000 g in weight to 20 g or less; to a limited extent on lizards; exceptionally on fish; and to some degree on insects such as locusts, dragonflies and beetles. The falcons in Fox's study area in northeastern South Island fed mostly on exotic prey. Of the 22 avian species he recorded in the diet, no fewer than 14 are introduced forms, mostly European passerines such as yellowhammer, greenfinch, skylark, blackbird and chaffinch. All birds constituted 80 per cent of all individual prey items and 62 per cent of total biomass consumed, but introduced birds made up about 58 per cent of all prey and 45 per cent of the biomass. Exotic quadrupeds, including rabbit, hare, house mouse, brown rat, black rat and stoat made up only 3.2 per cent of all individual prey, but owing to the large size of the rabbits, hares and stoats, these mammals provided 38 per cent of the total biomass. Fox has made the intriguing suggestion that the larger size of the "eastern falcons" pre-adapted them to feeding on these mammals, a source of food that has become available to *novaeseelandiae* only in the last 200 years or so.

Fewer data exist on the food habits of falcons in the forested parts of New Zealand, but what there are suggest that native birds are far more important, particularly active and flocking species such as parakeets (five species), pigeons, and the tui or parson bird (*Prosthemadena novaeseelandiae*), but probably also cuckoos and kingfishers. The more secretive indigenous birds, the New Zealand wrens, flycatchers and warblers have probably never been staple prey.

New Zealand falcons are extremely versatile and aggressive hunters. Of the eight or so basic searching techniques used by diurnal raptors – still-hunting, fast contour-hugging flight, soaring and prospecting, hovering, slow quartering at low level, stalking on the ground, listening and flushing from cover – Fox has recorded *novaeseelandiae* doing all but hovering and slow quartering. Still-hunting from a perch is by far the most common method (65 to 70 per cent of all searches), and soaring and prospecting from high in the air is second (10 to 25 per cent).

Of the five basic techniques for attacking – direct flying attack, tail-chasing, ringing, glide attack and stooping – New Zealand falcons use the first two far more frequently than the latter three, in conformity with their accipitrine morphology. Stooping constitutes only 5 to 15 per cent of all attacks. New Zealand falcons pursue birds into thick cover and plunge into the foliage of trees and bushes to catch the prey or drive it out. According to Nick Fox, they sometimes attack large mammals such as rabbits and hares by binding into them like goshawks, rather than stooping and stunning or killing the quarry with blows before landing on it, a remarkable feat considering that some of these animals weigh six times as much as the falcon.

New Zealand falcons are also highly aggressive defenders of their nests and hunting areas. Human intruders are so frequently attacked and struck in the head by parent falcons at the nest that Fox was able to take advantage of their unusual degree of boldness by rigging nooses on his hat and catching numbers of falcons for ringing, colour-marking, and physical examination by this unusual method! The falcons also attack many other large birds and mammals which intrude on to their areas or approach their nests closely: harriers, gulls, shags, herons, dogs, cats and chamois; but they generally do not attack grazing sheep. Some of these attacks, particularly on harriers and other New Zealand falcons, occur as much as 0.5 to 1 kilometre from the nest.

The territories or home ranges, which vary considerably in size depending on terrain, vegetation, and prey densities, tend to be occupied year round, and some aggressive defence of the areas occurs even in the non-breeding season. Ranges in the open grasslands are smaller, on the order of 15 sq km (6 sq miles) and breeding populations are denser than in forested habitats, where occupied areas seem to average around 150 to 200 sq km (58–77 sq miles). This difference may be related to the fact that less of the forested habitat is optimal for the falcon's hunting methods, despite its accipitrine habits, or to a lower density of prey, or to both factors working in concert to reduce the availability of prey to the falcons.

New Zealand falcons nest in a wide variety of situations, but Fox was able to group them into four main types: ledges on the faces of cliffs or rocky outcrops varying from 6–30 m (20–100 ft) in height and mostly accessible to humans without a climbing rope; at the base of large rocks on steep hillsides; on the ground under logs or dense bushes; and sites located in epiphytes on dead or dying trees or, rarely, in hollow tree trunks. The scrapes are always made in grassy soil, humus, or similar organic debris and never on gravel or other rocky materials, and they are usually well screened by overhanging projections of rock or vegetation. Falcons nesting in open country use the first two types primarily, while falcons in forested habitat use mainly the latter two. (Although sea-cliffs occur in many parts of New Zealand, falcons are not known to nest on them or in any other habitat overlooking bodies of water, a curious difference from the peregrine, which prefers to have water located nearby its eyrie.)

From 2 to 4 eggs are laid from September to December; Fox found an average of 2.7 eggs in 25 nests, the mode being 3. The young hatch out after 30 or more days of incubation, and they begin flying at 32 to 35 days of age but are not hard-penned until the males are more than 50 days old and the females more than 60 days. Like other falcons, the young are dependent on their parents for food for several weeks after they leave the nest.

Although one often reads that the New Zealand falcon has been greatly reduced in numbers since European settlement, Nick Fox (1978) found the species surprisingly well represented on both North and South islands, particularly on the latter. The falcon has certainly lost nesting habitat where intensive agriculture is practised and, of course, around major urban centres; but it seems to thrive in the presence of grazing livestock and has adjusted well to the open pasturelands. More significantly, these falcons have switched over to exotic prey, which include not only several bird species that are well adapted to man-dominated environments but also several species of mammals that represent an entirely new class of prey for the falcons. It may well be that the prey densities and biomass available to falcons are greater in some parts of New Zealand now than before European settlement; if so, falcon densities may be greater in these parts too. Consequently, there may have been no net decrease in falcon numbers over New Zealand as a whole; and there could even have been an overall increase.

In any case, the current situation is most encouraging for the continued survival of this unique species, despite some local problems in the recent past with habitat deterioration and pesticides (DDT). Nick Fox (1978) has estimated the total breeding range of the bush falcons to be some 40,000–45,000 sq km (16,000 sq miles), and the range of the eastern falcons to be some 55,000–56,000 sq km (21,000 sq miles), while the intermediate southern falcons occupy about 13,000 sq km (5,000 sq miles). Based on sampled densities for different parts of the breeding range, Fox has estimated that there are 3,700 to 4,400 breeding pairs of New Zealand falcons, of which 3,100 to 3,200 are eastern, 450 to 850 are bush, and 140 to 270 are southern.

The bush falcons are most vulnerable to further changes in land use and to continued destruction of native forest. Most of the southern falcons are protected in the Fiordland National Park, while the eastern falcons have adjusted well to man-dominated lands and to introduced prey species.

Merlin

(Pigeon Hawk)

Falco columbarius

"**I** LIKE IT WELL that men flee with a cast of Merlins at once at the Lark or Linnet. For over and besides that they of themselves love company and to flee together they do also give greater pleasure or delight to the lookers on. For now that one (at the stooping) strikes the bird and then the other at her down come: And when that one climbeth to her mountee above the Lark, then that other lieth low for her best advantage, which is most delectable to behold." So wrote the Elizabethan gentleman and poet, George Turberville, in *The Booke of Faulconrie or Hawking* published in 1575.

In the heyday of falconry in the Middle Ages, the merlin was recognized in the social hierarchy of the times as "Milady's Falcon", but this doughty little hunter was far more than an heraldic object to be carried to court on a bejewelled glove. Through the centuries the merlin has been one of the most frequently trained falcons for a special branch of falconry, lark-hawking. Catherine the Great was an ardent follower of the merlin and the lark, as were many other royal personalities. Mary Queen of Scots loved hawking too, and she may well have seen merlins flown in the environs of Tutbury Castle, where Elizabeth I held her prisoner under the watchful eyes of Her Majesty's Falconer, Sir Ralph Sadler, who allowed Mary out of the castle on short hawking excursions, much to the displeasure of his English sovereign.

Lark-hawking with merlins has flourished nowhere more expertly and continually than in Great Britain, where it is still a legal form of sport to this very day, thanks to a benign provision for special licensing that has been continued under the Wildlife and Countryside Act, 1981. In 1979 the British Falconers' Club devoted a section of its journal, *The Falconer*, to the merlin and its quarry. While some of the methods and some of the gear are different today, and suitable ground is much more reduced than in Elizabethan times, it is clear from the accounts of men such as Bill Ruttledge, whose experiences reach back towards Michell (1900), and Robbie Wilson, who hawks now and looks to the future, that lark-hawking with merlins has lost none of those qualities that Turberville and many others after him have found so pleasurable.

The classic hunt for skylarks with a merlin, or cast of two, is a ringing flight, in which the falcon starts from the fist as the lark rises from the ground. In such a circumstance, if the ground is free of protective cover, the lark is forced to escape by flying. Since a skylark is not as fast as a merlin in level flight, its tactic is to gain altitude rapidly and attempt to outclimb its pursuer. The merlin gains less altitude per linear distance than the lark. Thus, a contest of endurance develops between the lightly wing-loaded, slower, but steeply rising lark, and the more heavily wing-loaded, faster, less steeply rising merlin. This flight is a miniature version of heron-hawking with a large falcon.

In early season young larks and moulting adults are rather easily caught, but later on a full-summed skylark is a formidable challenge to even the best trained merlin. A really good ringing flight, in which the contestants are well matched, will go several hundred metres up and a kilometre or more in ground distance before the lark succumbs to a short stoop from the victorious merlin, or the merlin becomes winded and gives up, spreading her tail and stretching her wings in a tell-tale glide back to earth.

Merlins are small, compact, dashing and fearless falcons, which appear rather uniformly dark at a distance in the field. They range from about 25–30 cm (10–12 in) in length, with wingspans of 50–62 cm ($19\frac{1}{2}$–$24\frac{1}{2}$ in). Males average about 92 per cent of females in linear dimensions: the wing length of males from Europe averages 199 mm (8 in), females average 217 mm ($8\frac{1}{2}$ in) (Cramp and Simmons 1980). The tail is longish, about 60 per cent of wing length, and is somewhat rounded at the tip, as in the gyrfalcon, with which the merlin shares many structural similarities on a smaller scale. European males weigh 162 g ($5\frac{1}{2}$ oz) on average; females 212 g ($7\frac{1}{2}$ oz); North American males average 159 g ($5\frac{1}{2}$ oz) in autumn, 169 g (6 oz) in spring, females 218 g ($7\frac{1}{2}$ oz) and 244 g ($8\frac{1}{2}$ oz) respectively (William Clark).

Sexual dimorphism in size is not so marked in merlins as in most other bird-eating falcons, but adult males and females differ in the colour and pattern of their plumages to a degree equalled or exceeded only by some of the kestrels. The male appears much brighter, with more contrasting marks than the rather uniformly brownish female. He is generally slaty blue on his dorsal surfaces, with a dark head, weakly expressed facial pattern, whitish throat, pale rufous to buffy undersides with dark streaks and bars, and his tail has a pale grey tip, broad, blackish subterminal band, and a series of less distinct, blackish bars set against a slate grey background. The first year males and females are similar to the adult female but lack her grey rump and upper tail-coverts.

There is some geographic variation in size and coloration in the different populations of merlins. A very dark, blackish merlin occurs in the humid coastal district of British Columbia, and two large, pale forms occur in ecologically similar but disjunct ranges, one in the prairie parkland of Saskatchewan, Alberta, southwestern Manitoba, Montana, the Dakotas and Wyoming, the other in the forest-steppes of Kazakhstan and southwestern Siberia. A rather distinct form, larger and darker than the Eurasian merlins, also breeds on Iceland.

The merlin is a breeding bird of northern, Holarctic distribution, nesting in America from northern California (*ca.* 42°N) rarely; Oregon, Idaho, Montana, Wyoming (*ca.* 45°N); the Dakotas, northern parts of Minnesota, Wisconsin, Michigan; through Ontario and Quebec to the Maritimes and Maine; and thence northward to the limit of trees in northern Canada and Alaska. In the Old World, it breeds from Iceland, the Faeroes, northern British Isles, Scandinavia, Finland, and from the treeline in Russia and Siberia to Kamchatka, southward through most of the taiga from Sakhalin Island westward through Mongolia, southern Siberia, and the forest-steppes of Kazakhstan about to 49°N, west to the Baltic states.

Throughout this vast range, merlins nest wherever forests and scrublands are extensively broken by expanses of open country. In the boreal regions they favour habitats at or near the latitudinal and altitudinal limits of coniferous forest, but they are also found around bogs and lakes, old forest burns in mid-successional stages of recovery, along major rivers, and in prairie parklands and forest-steppes. Recently merlins have moved into the suburban environs of Saskatoon in the Canadian prairie, where they now have a well established breeding population of some 12 pairs (L. Oliphant); they also nest in Edmonton and several other urban areas in central Canada.

In North America, the most frequently used nest-site is an old stick nest built by a crow, magpie or other bird in a tree. But in other parts of its range it also nests on high cliffs (Iceland, Newfoundland), on the ground among herbaceous or shrubby vegetation or under dense, low hanging tree branches (much of Eurasia, parts of North America), occasionally in tree cavities (North America), exceptionally on an old haystack (Kazakhstan; Dementiev 1951), while Swann (1936) says it sometimes nests under the roof of an abandoned building although precise records seem to be lacking.

Merlins use the same nesting areas but not necessarily the same sites year after year, and in Britain some of these places are known to have been occupied for up to 100 years, paralleling the fidelity that peregrines and many other falcons have for their eyries (Newton 1979). Some of these locations are so attractive to merlins that even when both members of the pair are shot, another pair replaces them the following year: Wm. Rowan (1921) described a patch of old heather in which merlins nested for 19 consecutive years despite the fact that every year a gamekeeper shot the pair and not a single egg hatched. There were many other patches of heather on the moor where merlins seemingly could have nested, but there was evidently something special about this one place. J. J. Hickey (1942) calls this phenomenon "ecological magnetism".

While the merlins readily recognize these special places for nesting and find them, biologists have a difficult time identifying suitable breeding habitat, and merlin nests are notoriously hard to locate owing to this difficulty. Generally, in open, upland country nesting areas are in small valleys, near the head-waters of a stream, or on hillsides strewn with boulders and small crags (Newton 1979). Such places command a wide view over surrounding terrain, and the merlins have certain perches where they sit conspicuously and possibly advertise their presence to other merlins. These perches also frequently become splashed with white droppings, and when a territory becomes vacant, these "splash marks" may in part serve as identifying signs of a suitable territory to prospecting merlins.

Depending on latitude and on the climatic conditions of the particular region, male merlins return to their nesting areas in late winter or early spring (end of February to end of April) and establish their territories. Usually the females join them some days to weeks later; but in some cases the female remains on territory all year round, and the returning male joins her (Lynn Oliphant). Laying begins in May and extends into June, depending on latitude, three to five eggs being laid approximately every other day. Incubation, which is mainly by the female, begins with the next to last or last egg, and hatching occurs in about 30 days. The whole breeding season is timed so that the young merlins are raised when there is an abundant and highly vulnerable supply of food in the form of fledgling passerines. The male merlin does all of the hunting during courtship, laying and incubation, and depending on the situation he may continue to provide all or nearly all the food right through the nestling period. The young often leave the nest before they can do more than flutter about, at 25 to 27 days of age. They remain in the vicinity of the nest, dependent on their parents for food, for a further two to four weeks before dispersing.

The newly independent young are rather social at first and often keep together as a sibling group after they leave the nesting area, and I suspect that they may even start migration together, as merlins are often seen in loose groups during the autumn passage. In late August and September, along the Yukon River in Alaska and along the old Richardson Highway in the Alaska Range, I have seen as many as six to eight juvenile merlins together in loose foraging flocks, suggesting that broods sometimes merge. They fed mainly on flying insects, and in one instance I saw them mobbing a magpie.

Even more curious are the mixed hunting associations of juvenile merlins and sharp-shinned hawks (*Accipiter striatus*) which I saw along the banks of the Yukon River at the end of summer. Members of the two species appeared perfectly at ease with one another, making hunting flights from the same tree and returning to it to perch close by; and I have often wondered whether the very similar size and physical appearance of these birds (the juvenile plumages of the two are remarkably convergent) have something to do with their interspecific sociability at this time. Juvenile merlins and sharp-shinned hawks often migrate in loose aggregations too, as Stanley Temple and I had a chance to observe one spectacular September at Cape Ray, Newfoundland, where many of these birds leave the island together to make their overwater flight to Nova Scotia and thence down the mainland coast. At Fire Island, New York, during the height of autumn migration in October, I have also seen perched merlins gaze up into the sky and then take off to join groups of soaring sharp-shinned hawks, which were drifting south along the coast.

Merlins are migratory for the most part, although some remain more or less resident in the general region where they breed (some in Iceland, Britain, Central Asian mountains such as Ala Tau, Tien Shan, Kirghiz, Altais, and others; and western British Columbia; and urban areas in the Canadian prairies). None of the Eurasian populations makes a trans-equatorial movement, although some do move across the Mediterranean to winter in the Nile River Valley and in western North Africa. Others move into China as far south as Haninan and spottily along the coast of Vietnam, but the majority of the Eurasian merlins winter a few degrees of latitude south of the breeding range in southern Europe, Russia, the Middle East, and into India. American birds winter from southern British Columbia south through Mexico and Central America into northwestern South America as far south as northern Peru across the equator. On the East Coast merlins winter regularly from Florida all along the coast of the Gulf of Mexico south, but sometimes they occur farther north in winter along the Atlantic Coast as well. They also occur on islands through the Caribbean. Merlins nesting in the northern prairie parklands shift southward into the western Great Plains and semi-desertic areas of the Southwest or into cities. The main movements of merlins out of the boreal forests of Canada and Alaska follow either the Mississippi River watershed south or the Atlantic Coast. (Bent 1938, Cramp and Simmons 1980, Dementiev 1951).

In winter merlins tend to be found in open habitats, especially coastal flats and salt-marshes where sandpipers and other small shorebirds concentrate, in treeless plains and agricultural lands where larks, pipits, and other small land birds occur in large winter flocks, or in urban areas where house sparrows and Bohemian waxwings are numerous (L. Oliphant).

Merlins feed on a wide variety of small to medium-sized birds up to the size of golden plover, pigeons and even small ducks, but the majority of the species taken weigh less than 50 grams. In Northumberland, Ian Newton and his colleagues (1978) found that 82 per cent of the prey taken in the breeding season consisted of species weighing less than 50 g ($1\frac{1}{2}$ oz), and 67 per cent were of species less than 30 g (1 oz). The fieldfare weighing 140 g (5 oz) was the heaviest commonly taken species, and female merlins presumably caught most of them. In the breeding season there is no doubt that open country, ground-nesting birds comprise the bulk of food, particularly larks and pipits of several species. On migration and in winter most merlins shift over to small sandpipers, the dunlin being commonly taken, plovers, and related shorebirds, although merlins migrating along the Atlantic Coast of North America show a special fondness for flickers (*Colaptes auratus*) which are migrating in large numbers at the same time. Merlins wintering on plains or steppes continue to pursue flocking, ground-dwelling passerines right through the year and probably follow them in spring and autumn migrations.

Merlins also catch a variety of small rodents, some shrews, and occasionally lizards and other vertebrates. They delight in snatching large flying insects in the air – day-flying moths, butterflies, dragonflies, grasshoppers and beetles – usually hawking them from a perch rather than in continual flight like a hobby. Young merlins take a higher proportion of rodents and insects than adults, and when they first become independent they often feed mainly on insects and rodents, until their bird-catching skills become perfected.

Being small and active, merlins have high metabolic rates and voracious appetites. Page and Whitacre (1975) kept detailed records on the hunting habits of an adult female merlin wintering on Bolinas Lagoon, California from October to February 1972–73. She killed an average of 2.2 birds per day (20 day sample) and consumed an estimated 71 g ($2\frac{1}{2}$ oz) of food per day, approximately one-third of her body weight per day. 'They actually saw the merlin eat 140 birds of 15 different species and estimated the totals as shown in the following table:

Species	Observed	Estimated
Least sandpiper (*Calidris minutilla*)	51	112
Dunlin (*Calidris alpina*)	49	108
Western sandpiper (*Calidris mauri*)	12	26
Sanderling (*Calidris alba*)	8	18
Yellow-rumped warbler (*Dendroica coronata*)	4	9
Water pipit (*Anthus spinoletta*)	3	7
Savannah sparrow (*Passerculus sandwichensis*)	3	7
Northern phalarope (*Lobipes lobatus*)	2	4
Red-winged blackbird (*Agelaius phoeniceus*)	2	4

During the season, the merlin caught 5.6 per cent of the dunlins, 7.1 per cent of the least sandpipers, 7.5 per cent of the western sandpipers, and 13.5 per cent of the sanderlings that wintered on Bolinas

Lagoon. A single merlin probably consumes on the order of 800 to 900 birds a year.

Leslie Brown (1976) calculated that a pair of merlins with three young consumed the equivalent of about 450 small birds during the breeding season, but this figure is probably an under-estimate because he assumed an adult ration of only 35 to 50 g per day. If one assumes a breeding season of 100 days from pairing to independence of the young, the pair of adults alone would consume more than 400 small birds averaging 30 g each. In their first 60 days of life, three young might well require an additional 300 small birds, so that the total impact of a family of merlins on the local avifauna is considerable. Lynn Oliphant and his colleagues have calculated that a pair raising four young to independence over 120 days require 800 house sparrows.

While wild merlins sometimes hunt like trained ones by ringing birds up into the air (exhaustion hunting) or stooping from height (Rudebeck 1951, Bengtson 1975), the more usual attack is a low, fast, horizontal flight less than a metre above ground, in which the prey is often taken by surprise as it flushes, or in wooded areas at tree-top level, in which case the prey may be snatched directly off its perch. The attack may be launched from a perch (still-hunting) or from fast exploratory or migratory flight. When tail-chasing, merlins attempt to climb up above the quarry for a short, final stoop just as gyrfalcons do, and they are more comparable to gyrfalcons in their methods of searching and attacking than to any other falcon. The prey is often taken in the air close to the ground or on the ground: the wintering female that Page and Whitacre (1975) observed directed 278 out of 343 attacks at quarry on the ground, 49 at flying birds, and 16 at birds perched off the ground.

Hunting success is generally considered to be low, but it no doubt varies considerably from individual to individual and depends on method of attack as well as environmental circumstances. Rudebeck (1951) recorded a success rate of only 5 per cent for 139 hunts during autumn migration in Scannia, but most of his records probably pertain to young merlins. The adult female at the Bolinas Lagoon captured birds on 12.8 per cent of her 343 recorded hunts (Page and Whitacre 1975). It would be interesting to know the capture rate of adult males during the breeding season, when they must be catching 8 to 10 birds a day. Also, judging from trained merlins, hunts involving two falcons are more successful than hunts with one, and several observers have reported that wild merlins often do hunt together usually as pairs (Cramp and Simmons 1980), up to 30 per cent of the time according to Bengtson (1975).

The merlin occupies a very large breeding range, exceeded in size only by that of the peregrine, American kestrel, and common kestrel; but it is rather sparsely distributed throughout. Among the small Holarctic diurnal raptors, its overall numbers rank far below those of congeners such as *sparverius* and *tinnunculus* and sympatric, bird-eating hawks such as *Accipiter nisus* and *A. striatus*. It is not at all clear why this should be so.

In areas of good habitat in Britain, Newton (1979) estimates densities around 5 to 10 pairs per 100 sq km (39 sq miles), and the total population of the British Isles certainly exceeds 800 pairs. Other recent estimates for European countries include: 2,000 pairs in Sweden, 1,600 pairs in Finland, and 1,600 pairs in Estonia (Cramp and Simmons 1980). Galushin (1981) mentions densities of 5 to 6 pairs per 10 sq km (4 sq miles) in northeastern Komi A.S.S.R. No good estimates exist for North America. There are some 200 known nesting localities in the prairie parkland of Alberta (R. Fyfe), but they do not represent the total population by any means. Even data on locally sampled densities are few. Oliphant and Thompson (1978) found merlins nesting an average of 3 km (2 miles) apart in Saskatoon in 1976 and a minimum distance between pairs of 2.5 km ($1\frac{1}{2}$ miles) along the North Saskatchewan River. Twenty-seven pairs pairs were known to be breeding in southern Saskatchewan in 1977, but many suitable areas were not surveyed, and Oliphant tells me he thinks the total population in Saskatchewan is not less than 2,000 pairs. Counts of merlins at autumn migration observatories such as Cape May, New Jersey, indicate that several thousand pairs must be present in North America, but the species may not be nesting at the same densities generally encountered in the Eurasian range, where a few tens of thousands of pairs must be present.

The merlin has suffered some long term decline in numbers owing to alteration of habitat – particularly in Europe – and in some parts of its breeding range it fell victim to the same DDT-induced eggshell thinning that reduced other populations of raptors, for example in Britain (Newton 1973) and in Alberta, Canada (Fyfe *et al.* 1976). With restrictions on use of DDT and other chlorinated hydrocarbon pesticides, the downward trends noted in the mid to late 1960s have been reversed, and merlins now appear to be on the increase, for example in the Canadian prairies (Oliphant and Thompson 1978).

The main potential threat to merlins in the future is habitat modification by man. Some changes in habitat are probably beneficial to merlins – forest fires for example – but afforestation in the open uplands of Britain is not beneficial, as historical records of individual eyries in Northumberland have shown (Newton *et al.* 1978).

Red-headed Falcon

(Red-headed Merlin, Tūrūmti)

Falco chicquera

O FTEN REFERRED TO as a "merlin" (although not really closely related to *columbarius*), the turumti or red-headed falcon of India and Africa is a dashing and spirited bird rather slimmer in build and with proportionately shorter wings than either the red-naped shaheen or the northern merlins, with which it is often compared. It is roughly the size of a pigeon with a body length of 31–36 cm (12–14 in), and a standard wing length ranging from 190–207 mm (7½–8 in) for males and from 220–232 mm (8½–9 in) for females, males averaging 88 per cent of the female measurement (Indian birds, Ali and Ripley 1978). African birds average slightly larger than those from India. The tail length is 66 to 67 per cent of wing length. Weights of 240 g (8½ oz) and 257 g (9 oz) are known for two females from Africa (Kalahari Desert, Tom Cade; Brown and Amadon 1968). Males probably weigh about 160–180 g (5½–6½ oz).

As the English name denotes, this falcon is distinctively marked with a deep chestnut coloured head, including crown, nape, sides, and cheek stripes, a feature which readily distinguishes it from all other falcons. Otherwise, it has a whitish cheek and throat, which merges into chestnut on the upper breast. The rest of the underparts are whitish, more or less heavily barred with black. The upperparts are ashy to bluish grey with some darker barring. The darkest and most heavily barred birds come from the equatorial regions of Africa.

The red-headed falcon has a disjunct distribution with one population resident and breeding on the Indian Subcontinent from Baluchistan, Sind and the Northwest Frontier of Pakistan eastward through Rajasthan and the Gangetic Plain into the Himalayan foothills, the Nepal Valley, to Assam and Bangladesh. It is common on the Deccan Plateau but avoids dense tropical forest and is entirely absent from Ceylon (Ali and Ripley 1978). The other population occurs in Africa in the equatorial belt south of the Saharan region from the west coast to the east coast and throughout East Africa and southern

Africa, from coast to coast, into the Cape Province. The red-headed falcon appears to be largely resident throughout its range, and the adult mates keep together in permanent pairs all year round.

On the Indian Subcontinent red-headed falcons are usually found in the drier parts, preferring open plains, semi-desertic areas of scrub, open deciduous forests, cultivated fields interspersed with small groves of trees, and the environs of villages (Ali 1977, Ali and Ripley 1978). In most of East Africa and in southern Africa they are also found in dry areas, but are locally distributed and seldom common. Nor do they associate with human habitation in Africa. In equatorial Africa, red-headed falcons are most often seen in low-lying and swampy savannahs of fairly high rainfall, and they seem most often to be associated with Borassus palms, which serve as well protected nest-sites and hunting perches (Brown and Amadon 1968, Brown 1970, Colebrook-Robjent and Osborne 1974, Osborne 1981).

Leslie Brown (1970) particularly emphasized the close association of the red-headed falcon with Borassus palms and related species such as the doum palm and the Indian palmyra palm. These tall palms, 20–30 m (65–100 ft) high with swollen trunks at the top just below the tuft of broad, fan-like leaves, are virtually unclimbable, thus serving as secure nest-sites. The falcons lay their eggs in the concavity at the base of a living frond next to the heart of the palm (Colebrook-Robjent 1974). In India other trees are apparently used according to Ali and Ripley (1978) and Dharmakumarsinhji (undated): mango, peepul, *Fiscus* spp., and the "neem", and in Zambia Colebrook-Robjent found them using pied crows' nests in *Acacia albida*.

In the Kalahari Desert of southern Africa red-headed falcons occur widely but sparsely in semi-desertic, open acacia scrub hundreds of kilometres from any palm tree, but where they nest in this vast region remains a mystery. I looked diligently for nests in the open camelthorn woods in the dry beds of both the Auob and Nossop rivers in the Kalahari Gemsbok National Park on several trips in 1964–66 and found none, although pairs were seen hunting at waterholes. My associate, Gordon Maclean (1970) conducted an even more intensive study from October 1964 to April 1966: he never found a nest either, and considered the species "very rare". In August 1964, E. J. Willoughby, L. I. Greenwald, and I encountered at least three pairs regularly at the boreholes immediately south of Mata Mata along the Auob at the northern end of the Park. They always flew off east and disappeared on the horizon over the fixed sand dunes between the Auob and Nossop. I suspect they may have had their eyries in the small, isolated groves of *Boscia albitrunca*, which grow in protected swales within the extensive red sand-dunes of the Kalahari, or in the occasional camelthorn acacia found away from the river beds.

Except for Colebrook-Robjent's observations in Zambia, very little has actually been recorded about the nesting habits of *chicquera* in either Africa or India, and the species needs study. In India, the breeding season is from January to May with most eggs being laid in March. Laying dates vary greatly in different parts of Africa: September in South Africa and Zambia; March to May in Sudan; February in Nigeria (Brown and Amadon 1968). When not in a palm, the eyrie is always an old stick nest. Three to five eggs are laid, most often four. Incubation requires 33 days, and the young are in the nest for 37 days before they fly (Colebrook-Robjent and Osborne 1974).

Although feeding to some extent on rodents and lizards and occasionally on large insects, red-headed falcons are primarily bird hunters and catch most of their quarry in the air. They also take bats in the late evening. Most of the birds normally caught are small, weighing 100 grams ($3\frac{1}{2}$ oz) or less: various larks, pipits, wagtails, swallows, bulbuls, babblers, rosy pastors, starlings, sparrows, weaverbirds, cuckoos, swifts, plovers and sandpipers, quails, and doves. Falconers have, however, trained red-headed falcons to catch more spectacular quarry – rollers, hoopoes and nightjars in high, ringing flights, and even birds as large as cattle egrets and white egrets, as they are aggressive little falcons with relatively larger feet and talons than those possessed by the true merlins (Ali and Ripley 1978, Dharmakumarsinhji undated).

Red-headed falcons nearly always hunt together as a pair, one bird tail-chasing the quarry closely over the ground at full speed while the other comes in at a different direction; and they are decidedly crepuscular in their hunting activities. In 1964 I saw pairs of red-headed falcons hunting sociable weavers and other small birds daily at waterholes in the Kalahari but only at dawn and at sunset. They were never seen at any other time and must have been able to satisfy their food requirements in no more than one or two hours of hunting in a day. The attack is usually direct and arrowlike, speed being attained by rapid, deep wingbeats, which are produced by a powerful pectoral musculature (the sternum is deep-keeled), very different from the more undulating flight of the merlin. Red-headed falcons seldom glide or soar. They launch their attacks either from a perched position, often concealed by foliage, or in a fast, flushing flight in which the falcon attempts to beat out prey from shrubbery or dense canopy by suddenly darting through an opening or hedge-hopping at speed, thus stampeding sheltered birds into flight ahead of the predator. Like other short-winged, long-tailed, "accipitrine" falcons, red-headed falcons do not hesitate to fly into foliage to attack their prey.

The turumti has a fairly large total distribution, some 11 to 12 million sq km (4.4 million sq miles) in Africa and about 4 million sq km (1.5 million sq miles) in India, but it appears to be decidedly rare and local throughout most of its African range, although Colebrook-Robjent found eight pairs nesting in the flood plain of the Kafue River in Zambia with an average distance of only about 2 km (6,700 ft) between nearest neighbours. It numbers perhaps a few thousand pairs at most in Africa. In India it seems to be somewhat commoner, or at least more conspicuous, and certainly numbers in the several thousands of pairs there.

118

R. David Digby

Teita Falcon

Falco fasciinucha

SLIGHTLY LARGER THAN the merlin, this small version of the peregrine is another widely distributed but generally rare species about which little is known, although some interesting bits of information have been accumulated in the last 20 years (Benson and Smithers 1958, Holliday 1965, Ripley and Heinrich 1966, Colebrook-Robjent 1977, Hunter *et al.* 1977, Dowsett 1980). Apparently resident throughout its range, the Teita (or Taita) falcon has been recorded in widely scattered localities from the mountains of southern Ethiopia and Kenya south to the Zambezi River gorges on the border between Zambia and Zimbabwe, a north to south distribution of some 3,000 km (1,850 miles). It occurs most often in drier woodlands with less than 100 cm (39 in) annual rainfall and is usually found in association with precipitous, rocky habitats, craters, river gorges, inselbergs, and crags at elevations of 600 m (2,000 ft) or less (Zambezi River) to 3,600 m (11,800 ft) in Ethiopia. Curiously *fasciinucha* has not been reported in recent years from localities where it was first discovered in Kenya (Teita Hills) or in Ethiopia (Brown 1970).

In coloration the Teita falcon is somewhat like the African hobby, but differs by having a whitish throat and cheeks and a chestnut patch at the back of the head. The male is somewhat more brightly coloured than the female, while the first year bird is generally more brownish than the adult, with blackish brown shafts on the cinnamon feathers of the chest and abdomen.

The Teita falcon represents the extreme expression of those trends seen in the body forms of the hobbies (subgenus *Hypotriorchis*). It is a robust little falcon with a very short tail and relatively very long wings, which reach to the tip of the tail when they are folded at rest. Brown and Amadon (1968) give the wing length as ranging from 203–237 mm (8–9½ in), while the tail is only about 80 mm (3 in), 40 per cent or less of the wing length. A weight of 212 g (7½ oz) is given for one captive male (Holliday 1965), and of 306 g (10½ oz) for one female (Ripley and Heinrich 1966), suggesting that the Teita falcon falls in the weight class of the Eurasian hobby; yet the hobby has a wing averaging 30 to 40 mm longer and a proportionally longer tail, averaging 50 to 51 per cent of wing length. The foot of the Teita falcon is more hobby-like than peregrine-like as the toes are not disproportionately long relative to the tarsus.

The Teita falcon is a hunter of small birds, but it also catches some flying insects such as big butterflies and probably also dragonflies and flying ants. It is said to catch doves weighing 100 or more grams; but species that have actually been recorded are smaller: yellow-vented bulbul, rock martin, rock pratincole, and red-billed quelea.

Hunter, Douglas, Stead, Taylor, Alder and Carter (1979) describe the flight as fast and heavy, with shallow, stiff, and rapid wingbeats, rather like that of a parrot, but interspersed with gliding. This characterization fits with an indicated wing-loading of 0.38–0.4 g per sq cm, very heavy indeed for so small a bird. According to Dowsett (in press), the Teita falcon catches most prey from a high circling position in a full stoop, and Hunter *et al.* say that the wings and tail are held completely closed in the stoop. Occasionally the falcon dives below the prey and then rises up to grab it from underneath. Some insects are de-winged and eaten while the falcon continues to fly. It seems likely that the Teita falcon to some extent employs all the aerial hunting tactics used by other bird-catching falcons. Its speed may rival or exceed that of *deiroleucus* and *rufigularis*.

The best known nesting locality for Teita falcons is the Zambezi River gorge immediately below Victoria Falls, where the first pair was discovered by an American falcon enthusiast, the late R. A. Herbert, during the Pan African Ornithological Congress in 1957. Since then three eyries have been located within a distance of 5 km (3 miles) along the river. According to W. R. Thomson (unpublished report to ICBP) three other eyries are known in Zimbabwe.

The only other recorded nest site is on an inselberg west of the Shire Valley in Malawi (Hunter *et al.* 1979). Two young had already flown at this eyrie on 11 November 1976, but the actual nest site appeared to be a wide, deep slit (122 × 38 × 46 cm) located three-quarters of the way up a sheer rock face about 30 m (100 ft) high. In the Zambezi gorge, all the eyries are wind-holes in basaltic cliff-faces and situated more than half way up vertical faces exceeding 100 m (330 ft) in height.

In this southern part of the range, Teita falcons sometimes lay eggs as early as July, but more usually in August or as late as September. The clutch is usually three eggs, sometimes two or four (Colebrook-Robjent 1977). R. J. Dowsett gives the incubation time for one egg as 26 days; if normal for the species, it has the shortest incubation time of any falcon by two days. Young are in the nest in September to November and are dependent on their parents for a further period of time before dispersing.

The Teita falcon is certainly one of the rarest species of *Falco* in the world, with a total population that may well number only a few hundred birds. Its main centre of distribution is especially in the several hundred kilometres of inaccessible gorges of the Zambezi from Victoria Falls to Lake Kariba, where several dozen pairs may well reside. The region would repay intensive study.

R. DAVID DIGBY.

Hobby
(Eurasian Hobby)

Falco subbuteo

THE PALEARCTIC HOBBY is one of the most aerobatic of falcons, challenging even the swifts for mastery of the air, although perhaps not as fast as it is often reputed to be. It is a rather slim, long-winged, long-tailed falcon not much larger than the common kestrel, light and buoyant on the wing compared to the peregrine or merlin. Hobbies range from 30–36 cm (12–14 in) in body length with wingspans of 82–92 cm (32–36 in). Adult males average only about 5 per cent smaller than females in linear dimensions, and the difference between first year males and females is even less. The standard wing measurement of adult males from the western Palearctic averages·256 mm (237–279 mm; $9\frac{1}{2}$–11 in), and of adult females, 268 mm (248–282 mm; $9\frac{1}{2}$–11 in). The tail averages 50.5 to 51.0 per cent of wing length, but this proportion is deceptive because both the tail and the wings are long relative to body size. At rest the tips of the primaries reach well beyond the end of the tail. Males weigh about 180 g (131–232 g; $4\frac{1}{2}$–8 oz), females, about 225 g (141–340 g; 5–12 oz), indicating that hobbies are rather more lightly wing-loaded than either peregrines or merlins. (Data from Brown and Amadon 1968, Cramp and Simmons 1980). Males are 80 per cent of female weights.

The whole plumage is compact, and the flight feathers are stiff as befits a highly aerial bird – about comparable to the peregrine in these features – but the feathers are not as stiff as those of the orange-breasted falcon, bat falcon, Teita falcon, oriental hobby and African hobby, all of which I suspect are faster flying than the true hobby. Adults are dark slate on their upperparts with a somewhat paler, unbarred tail; the underparts are heavily streaked with black on buff; the combination of pale cream throat and cheeks, which are emphasized by the black head and moustachial stripes, with the rufous thighs and under tail-coverts distinguishes the hobby from all other species of *Falco*. Males are somewhat more richly coloured than females, and first year birds appear browner than adults and less rufous on legs and under the tail. There is not much geographic variation either, hobbies from the drier parts of the range in North Africa and Central Asia being paler than those from the northern forests, and the birds nesting in China being slightly smaller than hobbies nesting elsewhere. (Dementiev 1951, Brown and Amadon 1968, Cramp and Simmons 1980.)

The hobby breeds throughout most of the Palearctic region – excluding the tundra and northernmost part of the taiga, the dry steppes and deserts of Asia, and high mountains – from 67°N south through most of China, to the Middle East, and into northwestern Africa, and from Kamchatka and Japan in the east to Spain and Portugal in the west. It occurs from sea-level up to about 3;050 m (9,000 ft) in some mountainous parts of Asia. (Dementiev 1951, Cramp and Simmons 1980.)

The breeding populations are highly migratory in all parts of the range except in southern China, where some or all of the nesting hobbies are resident. Their numbers there are considerably augmented in winter by northern birds which move down from the boreal forests and forest-steppe regions to winter in South China, Burma, and the Indian Subcontinent south of the Himalayas and west to the Valley of the Indus. Hobbies from the western Palearctic perform a trans-equatorial migration and spend the non-breeding season in the austral spring and summer months in the southern third of Africa from Kenya south but principally above 10°S, although they are often common in Zambia, Zimbabwe and adjacent countries, much less so into South Africa and the Cape Province. (Dementiev 1951, Cramp and Simmons 1980.)

The hobby's African distribution seems to be determined partly by the occurrence of an abundant food supply in the form of flying insects, especially termites, which swarm during the warm, wet season

PLATE XVIII
Hobby
Falco subbuteo
Adult female
Map page 187

122

R. DAVID DIGBY

from November to April in southern Africa, and in part by the numbers and distribution of congeners which use the same food sources and possibly compete for them. The latter include the highly social lesser kestrel, the western red-footed falcon, and the eastern red-footed falcon. These are all flocking species that feed on flying termites and flying ants, as do the hobbies, which tend to be somewhat gregarious in the non-breeding season too; members of two to three of these species can be found in mixed foraging aggregations where termites or ants are swarming.

Food-partitioning and avoidance of competition among species with preferences for the same prey could come about in several ways. For one thing, there is an interesting scaling in size among these four falcons: hobby > lesser kestrel > western red-footed > eastern red-footed, suggesting that each species may have a somewhat different capability for catching flying insects. There also seems to be some partitioning of the total potential foraging range in Africa among these four species, as Rudebeck (1963) noted. The hobby is rare in South Africa but common from Zambia north into Kenya; the eastern red-footed falcon is common in Malawi, Zambia, Zimbabwe and south into the Transvaal and eastern Cape; but it is not as common in the latter areas as the lesser kestrel, which is also widespread and very common on the high-veld of South Africa (Transvaal and Orange Free State). The main concentration of western red-footed falcons occurs to the north and west of the centre of abundance of its close relative *amurensis*; for example, *vespertinus* is much less common than *amurensis* in South Africa, but the reverse is true in Namibia. Thus, while these four species of small, gregarious feeders on flying insects overlap broadly in their African distributions, each has a geographic area of main abundance distinct from the others (Cade 1969).

The spring passage of hobbies through Kenya coincides with the beginning of the rainy season, when termites are swarming, and according to the observations of Meinertzhagen (1954) the falcons move north in the hundreds at that time, gorging on the insects as they migrate. Hobbies arrive rather late on their breeding grounds, not until late April in the south or sometime in May in the more northern areas, and their whole schedule of activities in the breeding season may also be significantly timed to take optimum advantage of abundant food sources to feed their young in the form of fledgling birds and insect "blooms" which appear in mid-summer (July peaks). (See Newton 1969 for a general review of reproductive timing in raptors in relation to abundance of food.)

While the hobby is almost exclusively a tree-nesting species, which has been recorded rarely nesting atop cliffs in the mountains of Central Asia (Dementiev 1951), it avoids dense, continuous tracts of forest. Nor do the breeding pairs frequent coastlines or islands, extensive wetlands, rainy or fog-bound moorlands, steppes, deserts, or any kind of completely treeless country. Rather, they prefer habitats which are warm and rich in flying insect life and small birds, with open expanses of low herbaceous or grassy vegetation interspersed with small groves of tall trees or fringed by mature woods.

Hobbies usually use the old stick nest of another bird, perhaps most often in a pine but also in spruces, larches, oaks, poplars, elms, and even willows (Dementiev 1951). The nest usually commands an un-obstructed view of open countryside. In England 90 per cent of 208 eyries were in old nests of the crow; the rest were divided among those of rook, magpie, red squirrel, sparrowhawk, jay, and grey heron. Hobbies have also been recorded using the nests of raven, common buzzard and black kite in other parts of Eurasia. The height of nests above ground ranges from less than 6 m up to 32 m (19–100 ft); the average for 140 nests in England is 13.7 m (44 ft). (Data from Cramp and Simmons 1980.)

Hobbies often reuse nests in successive years, as long as they remain in good repair, but most pairs have alternate sites that range from 100–3,000 m (330–9,800 ft) apart. The nesting territories are even more permanent than the specific sites, and traditions of use spanning several decades are known; however, hobbies appear not to be as historically fixed to particular breeding areas as peregrines and merlins are. Perhaps this is because they are more dependent on the ephemeral nests of other species or because their particular habitat requirements, which depend upon the "edge effect" of juxtaposed woodland and open country, shift geographically as woodlands expand or retract from either natural or man-induced causes. In Britain, for example, clearance of the original forests had become significant by Roman times and continued to accelerate through the Middle Ages; Ratcliffe (1980) has made the point that this deforestation provided good peregrine habitat in plenty, and it seems likely that the same may have been true for the hobby.

Hobbies are wonderfully aerial and acrobatic in courtship, although breeding birds can be remarkably unobtrusive during much of the season. Early in the season, however, the male advertises by performing circling flights over tree-tops around the nesting area or by high soaring, sometimes with prey conspicuously dangling in his feet, possibly as an attraction to females. Later the male and female soar together over their area, sometimes diving together towards the ground or dashing down over trees. The male also performs a courtship flight consisting of a long, shallow, fast glide with wings angled up, followed by a series of rapid fluttering beats with the body rolling alternately from side to side, and terminating in a dive from height, either to the nest, where much interaction with the female takes place, or over the head of the perched female. In some of these aerial displays the wings produce a drumming sound similar to that of woodcock or snipe. (See Cramp and Simmons 1980 for further details of courtship.)

The commonest vocalization is the so-called wryneck-call, "kew-kew-kew-kew" or "tyu-tyu-tyu-tyu", used as announcement and in greetings between mates; also, sometimes during copulation.

Copulation takes place on the branch of a tree or on the rim of a stick nest; it is said to be attempted sometimes in flight (see Cramp and Simmons 1980), but this interpretation of aerial contact between mates needs careful study. (Swifts copulate in the air by locking their feet together, but it would be a very difficult feat for a male falcon to mount the back of a female in flight.)

The usual clutch is 3 eggs, sometimes only 2, exceptionally 4, with an average of about 2.9. Incubation, mostly by the female, requires about 30 days; the young, which remain in the nest for 28 to 34 days, are cared for and fed by the female, while the male provides all or most of the food. The young remain dependent on their parents for food for a further 3 to 4 weeks, exceptionally even longer.

Parents transfer food to the fledged young in the air, often dropping prey for the young to catch. The young indulge in a great deal of playful chasing after their parents and each other, and other large species (crows, honey buzzards) often become the objects of playful attacks and stoops. Local broods of common kestrels sometimes join with the hobbies in these frolics. The young begin to catch insects after a few days of flight, starting with slow flying forms such as beetles and progressing quickly to dragonflies and other rapidly moving species; only much later do they attempt hunting birds or bats, often in co-operation with a parent or sibling. (Cramp and Simmons 1980.)

The hobby feeds mainly on flying insects and small birds, to some extent on bats, and exceptionally on small ground mammals and reptiles. It hunts chiefly in the open sky high above vegetative cover and feeds opportunistically on whichever species of flying insects and birds happen to be locally abundant. Particularly on its wintering grounds the hobby is often attracted to prey disturbed by bush-fires, but its usual targets are swarming insects (flying ants, termites) and flocks of foraging birds (swallows, swifts) or birds that flock to roosts in evening. It is decidedly crepuscular and even hunts by moonlight; hence, bats are often encountered and taken. According to Dharmakumarsinhji (undated), the little pipistrelle bat is the most commonly taken prey on the wintering grounds in western India. The hobbies generally eat them on the wing, just as they do insects.

Hobbies snatch high flying prey in their feet during a fast attack in level flight, or in a downward stoop, but perhaps most often in an abrupt upward swoop or pull-out following a dive. Particularly at twilight, the latter tactic has the advantage of placing the hobby below the quarry in a position where the falcon is not so easily seen against the ground, while the prey is fully silhouetted against the sky. Hobbies frequently catch swallows and swifts, which are among the fastest of birds, but it seems likely that the hobbies catch most of these birds by surprise rather than by out-flying them in a tail-chase.

The ornithological accounts I have read are vague as to whether the hobby rings flying birds to exhaustion the way merlins do. Dharmakumarsinhji says that the hobby will not continue to pursue prey for a very long time, and falconers have generally despaired of producing such flights with trained hobbies (see Michell 1900, for example). One is naturally led to think that such an aerial falcon would adopt this tactic, unless, as Michell maintained, the hobby is not really a powerful flier. Its calculated wing-loading of 0.21–0.25 g per sq cm suggests buoyancy rather than power.

More than 70 species of birds have been catalogued as prey in Europe. In addition to swallows and swifts, hobbies often take larks, pipits and wagtails, especially males when engaged in their aerial song-flights. In Britain and West Germany escaped parakeets figure regularly in the hobby's diet. Hobbies also occasionally catch insects and other animals on the ground, dropping down from a perch or while quartering low over the ground, or from a hovering position. Hobbies pirate small mammals from kestrels and feed them to their young. (See Cramp and Simmons 1980 for additional information on food and feeding.)

While nesting hobbies reach fairly high densities locally, they tend to be patchily distributed through the total breeding range, which comprises some 35 million sq km (13.5 million sq miles). The closest nests can be no more than 100 m (330 ft) apart, and in such situations the falcons might almost be considered semi-colonial nesters, although no more than three to four pairs usually are involved in these clumps. More usual distances between nests are around 3–5 km (2½ miles) in good habitat (Cramp and Simmons 1980), and Fiuczynski (1978) reported breeding densities around West Berlin of one pair per 2.4–8.4 sq km (about 1–3 sq miles).

Hobbies remain in good numbers in most parts of their breeding range. There has been some historical decline in Europe, but not much change in the twentieth century, compared to some other raptors. Recent decreases have been noted in France (from an estimated 1,000–2,000 pairs prior to the 1960s to fewer than 1,000 pairs in the late 1960s), in Denmark (decreased since 1880 down to 10–20 pairs in early 1950s to 5–10 pairs in 1970s), and in Finland (from estimated 2,700 pairs in the 1950s to perhaps half that number in the 1970s). The population in England has remained stable since 1900 at around 100 pairs, following a decrease in the nineteenth century, and the same is true in Austria. An increase has been noted in the Netherlands (from around 20 pairs in the 1950s to 500–800 pairs in the 1970s) and possibly in the Soviet Union, where Galushin (1977, 1981) has estimated 2,500 pairs in 270,000 sq km (104,000 sq miles) of the central European region. The summary of populations provided by Cramp and Simmons (1980) indicates that the total European breeding population, including Russia, numbers not less than 10,000 pairs and is probably considerably larger. According to Dementiev (1951), hobbies are not as common in the eastern parts of the Soviet Union as in the west, nor is the current status of the species known in China; but it seems likely that the total breeding population of the species falls somewhere between 30,000 and 60,000 pairs.

African Hobby

Falco cuvieri

Slightly smaller than its Eurasian cousin, *subbuteo*, the African hobby is another species which has a rather extensive distribution – most of the wetter savannah areas south of the Sahara and including some dry thornbush country – but which is nowhere very common. Even so indefatigable a field observer as Leslie Brown (1970) admitted he was lucky to see as many as six African hobbies a year in Kenya, although he did indicate that the species is more common in well-watered savannahs elsewhere in Africa. During more than 15 months of field work in southern Africa in 1964–66, I never saw one; Thiollay (1976), on the other hand, found 14 pairs in a 2,700 ha (6,600 acre) area of savannah and forest in the Ivory Coast.

The African hobby occurs in a narrow equatorial zone approximately delimited by 5–10°N from the Ivory Coast east into Ethiopia and thence south throughout most of East Africa and the eastern half of southern Africa into the Cape Province. It is absent from the tropical forests of the Congo Basin and from the drier regions in the western parts of southern Africa. Open woodlands with a luxuriant growth of grasses and an abundance of flying insects and small birds constitute its preferred habitat.

Although it does not appear to be migratory in any regular way, some individuals do move about from one locality to another, when not breeding. These local shifts may relate to weather patterns, which in turn produce local abundances of insects.

In the field, the African hobby reveals itself as a darkish, long-winged, very fast-flying little falcon. At rest the tips of the wings reach to the end of the tail. It can be told from the Eurasian hobby by its rich red undersides and thighs, and from the Teita falcon by the lack of grey upper tail-coverts and rump and unpatterned nape. The plumage of adults is very compact with a gloss to the dorsal areas. The flight feathers are stiff, like those of swifts.

African hobbies are about 27–30 cm ($10\frac{1}{2}$–12 in) in length. The standard wing measurement is from 208–243 mm (8–$9\frac{1}{2}$ in) for males; 230–254 mm (9–10 in) for females (McLachlan and Liversidge 1957). Sexual size dimorphism is somewhat less pronounced than in *subbuteo*, males averaging 10 per cent smaller than females in linear dimensions, but weighing about 80 per cent as much as females. The tail is more than 50 per cent of the wing length, and the tip is decidedly rounded. Thiollay (1976) gives weights of males from the Ivory Coast from 150–178 g (5–6 oz); of females, 186–224 g ($6\frac{1}{2}$–8 oz).

According to Brown (1970), the African hobby is "incredibly swift and graceful in the hunt". It is often seen flying at great speed close to the ground or just over the tree-tops, and like other hobbies it is noticeably crepuscular in its hunting activities. Little seems to be known about its actual hunting tactics, but it probably most often hunts from a perch and flies its prey down in direct pursuit, much like a bat falcon. Its wings and tail, however, are proportioned enough like the Eurasian hobby so that it probably also flies about searching for insects on the wing (see Thiollay 1977).

Numerically the prey consists mostly of insects, especially flying termites, but also of many small birds, and probably bats as well. On limited observations it appears that the young are fed mainly, if not exclusively, on small birds caught and delivered to the female by the male. The adult female stays close to the nest and feeds herself to some extent on termites and other insects.

Brown (1970) suggested that a regular supply of flying termites may be the key to the distribution of the African hobby. For example, in higher rainfall areas, such as western Kenya, termites are available in numbers for five or six months, and to a lesser extent in almost any month, so that African hobbies have their preferred food available to them over a much greater portion of the annual cycle than in arid areas. The density of small birds is probably also much greater in these same regions.

The nest is in a tall tree from 15–30 m (50–100 ft) above ground. It is usually, if not always, the old nest of some other bird, probably crow, kite, buzzard, or eagle. The usual clutch is three eggs, which are laid in October in South Africa, September in Zimbabwe, November in Zambia and Tanzania, October in Congo, December and March in Uganda, December and April in Kenya (Brown and Amadon 1968), and late February to early April in the Ivory Coast (Thiollay 1976). Generally, the laying dates correspond with the end of the dry season or the beginning of the rains, so that the young are fledged about two months later at a time when flying insects and small fledgling birds are at peak numbers (Thiollay 1976).

PLATE XIX
African Hobby
Falco cuvieri
Adult male
Map page 187

Why is the African hobby so uncommon in most of its range of some 7 million sq km (2.7 million sq miles)? There is no apparent reason, and Thiollay's (1975, 1976, 1977) important 5-year study suggests that it may, in fact, be more common than generally thought, at least in the broad savannah-forest ecotone extending across the middle of Africa north of the equator. It appears to be more numerous than the Teita falcon, red-headed falcon, Dickinson's kestrel and grey kestrel. If the density Thiollay found in the Ivory Coast applies widely, then there could be several thousand pairs altogether; however, he has cautioned that deforestation for agriculture is inimical to *cuvieri*.

R. DAVID DIGBY

Oriental Hobby

Falco severus

Although the oriental hobby is very similar to the African hobby and obviously closely related to it, there are some subtle differences in build that may have behavioural and ecological significance. They are close to the same body size – oriental hobbies also range from 27–30 cm ($10\frac{1}{2}$–12 in) in length; and males have wing measurements ranging from 211–220 mm ($8\frac{1}{2}$ in), females from 221–248 mm ($8\frac{1}{2}$–$9\frac{1}{2}$ in) according to Ali and Ripley (1978) – but the tail of *severus* is decidedly shorter than that of *cuvieri*, averaging only 44 to 45 per cent of wing length. The end of the tail is squarish or even slightly notched; at rest the tips of the wings extend to the end of the tail or beyond. These morphological differences must reflect somewhat different aerodynamic characteristics and suggest that *severus* may be a more powerful and faster flier than *cuvieri*. Brown and Amadon (1968) give the weights of two males as 168 and 183 g (6–$6\frac{1}{2}$ oz), of four females as 192, 225, 249 and 249 g ($6\frac{1}{2}$–$8\frac{1}{2}$ oz). These weights fall in the range of the Eurasian hobby, and suggest that *severus* averages slightly heavier than *cuvieri* and that sexual size dimorphism is also greater.

The colour is blackish on the head, including cheeks and sides, nape, and upperparts generally – the darkest birds coming from islands (Celebes to Solomons), the lightest from India and Pakistan. The sides of neck, chin and throat are whitish tinged with rufous; the rest of the underparts are dark brick red with some black shaft-streaks on the sides of the breast. Young in first plumage are dark brown above, rufous below streaked with black from breast to under tail-coverts.

The oriental hobby is distributed in the tropics of continental Asia from the lower Himalayas (1,800–2,500 m; 5,900–8,200 ft) in Pakistan eastward through Nepal, Bangladesh and into Assam, and from there to Indo-China, but not into the Malay Peninsula or on to the larger islands of Indonesia. It does occur, however, on the Sunda Islands, Philippines, Celebes, Moluccas, New Guinea, Japen, New Britain and Solomon Islands (Ali and Ripley 1978, Brown and Amadon 1968).

It is primarily a bird of well-forested foothills, though ranging from sea-level to more than 2,500 m (8,200 ft) in elevation. Unlike *cuvieri* of Africa, it is not found in more open, lightly wooded country, although it usually is near clearings or breaks in the forest, where it prefers to perch in tall trees and alights on the topmost branches.

Although apparently resident in its insular range and in southeastern Asia, according to Dharmakumarsinhji (undated) there is a regular migration of oriental hobbies into Gujerat and Saurashtra (west coast of India), where they arrive in September to November and depart in March to April. At this season they may often be seen sitting on the beach or on sand dunes, much like peregrines.

Like the Eurasian hobby, *severus* is often seen in loose flocks of ten to a dozen birds, hawking flying insects much as swallows or swifts do – darting at high speed, wheeling and flipping up to snatch the prey in their feet. In fact, they are often attracted to foraging flocks of wood-swallows (*Artamus* spp), which they join in insect-catching. At other times they perch in the tops of trees at the edge of clearings, sallying forth to pursue flying prey. Apparently they hunt mostly at some height in the air – like Eurasian hobbies – and are not often seen coursing fast and low over the ground like *cuvieri*.

They hunt chiefly in the twilight hours at dawn and at sunset, often remaining active well into darkness. The most frequently caught prey are flying insects – locusts, cicadas, large beetles, dragonflies, flying ants and termites – which they usually eat on the wing, but they also take many small birds and pipistrelle bats, and occasionally mice and lizards. It is likely that small birds and bats are the main foods brought to the young.

Oriental hobbies nest in tall trees (pines, among others) in the old stick nests of other birds such as crows, magpies and other raptors. They often choose a dominant tree on the slope of a steep hill or one growing out of a cliff-face. Three to four eggs are laid, usually in May or June in India, March to May in the Assam hills. Incubation probably requires about 28 to 30 days – 26 days given by Baker (*fide* Ali and Ripley 1978) is probably too short – and the young are in the nest for another month or longer.

The oriental hobby occupies a moderately extensive, mainly insular range of some 3.5 million sq km (1.3 million sq miles). It appears to be more common in many parts of its range than its African counterpart, *cuvieri*. In this regard, the oriental hobby compares with the red-headed falcon, which is more common in India than in Africa (and with the laggar, which is more common in India than is the lanner in Africa). It is not easy to understand why these differences exist between the two regions, unless it is because these African species encounter a larger number of congeneric and other raptorial competitors in their ranges, for Africa does have a much richer raptor fauna than India.

128

Australian Hobby

(Little Falcon)

Falco longipennis

THE AUSTRALIAN HOBBY is third in the series of closely related, allopatric species which replace each other in Africa, tropical Asia and adjacent islands, and in Australia. It is larger than *cuvieri* and *severus*; males are around 30–31 cm (12 in) in length; females 33–35 cm ($13-13\frac{1}{2}$ in). The wing measurement of males averages about 242 mm ($9\frac{1}{2}$ in); of females 266 mm ($10\frac{1}{2}$ in) (Brown and Amadon 1968). Females weigh around 300–310 g ($10\frac{1}{2}$–11 oz), while males are probably about 220–230 g ($7\frac{1}{2}$–8 oz) (no exact data). Sexual size dimorphism is about the same as in the African and oriental hobbies; males have wings averaging 91 per cent of female wing length. The tail is moderately long, 50.5 per cent of the wing measurement, similar in this respect to *cuvieri*.

In general aspect this hobby appears dark on all dorsal surfaces, with crown, hind neck, cheeks, ear-coverts and malar area sooty black. The rest of the back and upper wing-coverts are dark slate grey, becoming lighter on the rump, tail-coverts, and tail. The lores, chin and throat are buffy white, merging into a rufous half collar around the neck. The upper breast is buffy with heavy blackish streaks, but the ground colour becomes rufous brown on the lower breast and belly, which are blotched and barred with black, especially on the flanks. Hobbies in the northern, drier parts of Australia are paler than individuals from the wetter regions. Also, the immature plumage is more distinct from the adult than in the other species of hobbies. Like *cuvieri* and *severus*, the adult plumage is compact, the flight feathers stiff, but not quite to the degree seen in the oriental hobby or bat falcon; also there is less sheen to the dorsal feathers in *longipennis*. (The compactness and glossiness of the dorsal feathers, so well developed in tropical falcons, may be adaptations to shed rain.)

This falcon is generally distributed throughout Australia, including Tasmania and the Lesser Sundas, and non-breeding birds move in winter to New Guinea and some adjacent islands. It is usually found in wooded country and prefers well watered areas, but it can also be found in semi-desert scrub, being absent only from treeless regions.

The Australian hobby is a noisy falcon, frequently uttering a shrill, harsh chatter when it attacks other birds, much the same as the black falcon. It has most of the habits of other hobbies, dashing about rapidly with quick wingbeats, soaring, occasionally hovering briefly and somewhat awkwardly by comparison with kestrels, and flying about in the air, catching insects and eating them on the wing. It appears to be less crepuscular than other hobbies, although Frith (1969) says it catches early flying bats towards dusk.

This hobby feeds mainly on birds, some of them considerably larger than it is (pigeons, galahs, ducks) but mostly smaller species such as starlings, grass finches and other passerines; on large insects such as grasshoppers, dragonflies and winged ants; and on bats. It is an aggressive hunter, exceptionally bold in pursuit of birds, often making a kill close to humans and has even been reported to snatch prey from a man's hand (Brown and Amadon 1968). It apparently searches for prey either from an elevated perch or from a flying position at some height in the air and attacks in a swift stoop, often striking the prey very low over the ground.

The Australian hobby lays its eggs in the stick nest of some other bird – raven, Australian magpie, little crow – usually positioned in a big tree 15–25 m (50–80 ft) above ground. Authors of bird books have repeatedly stated that it sometimes builds its own nest, but I have yet to hear from a field naturalist who has actually seen it done. Pairs do, apparently, line old nests with materials such as green leaves and strips of bark. Two to three eggs, rarely four, are laid from September to December, depending on the region.

Not much has been recorded on the nest life of this falcon. It is known to be highly aggressive and defensive around its nest towards other birds of prey, potential mammal predators, and man. Serventy and Whittell (1967) state that the male calls the female off the nest to accept food from him in the air. It is likely that, as with other falcons, the female does most of the incubating and guarding of the nest and young, while the male provides most of the food for the entire family.

Naturalists in Australia agree that this hobby is a rather common falcon, ranking third in abundance among the six breeding species, below the Australian kestrel and the brown falcon. No population studies have been made, but it seems likely that 10,000 pairs would be the right order of magnitude for this species.

R. DAVID DIGBY

Eleonora's Falcon

Falco eleonorae

ACH YEAR AN estimated 5,000 million migratory birds leave their nesting grounds in Europe and make an autumnal crossing of the Mediterranean Sea and the adjacent area of the Atlantic Ocean to winter in Africa. Most of these are small land birds, 75 g ($2\frac{1}{2}$ oz) or less, which migrate mainly at night and seek a landfall at daybreak. Strategically located and biologically timed to exploit this rich but transitory source of food are some 10,000 Eleonora's falcons, which nest on islands and coastal sea-cliffs from Cyprus to the Canary Islands.

This specialized hobby is the only breeding bird in the Palearctic that nests so late in the year, well after the summer solstice when daylength is decreasing. Hartmut Walter's detailed ecological study of this falcon provides many insights into how its morphological, behavioural and physiological traits have been modified by natural selection to fit this species into a unique breeding season niche, and much of the following account is a summary of his interesting book, *Eleonora's Falcon* (1979), to which I enthusiastically refer the reader for the full particulars.

Eleonora's falcon is a larger hobby than *subbuteo* with a body length of 36–40 cm ($14–15\frac{1}{2}$ in) and wingspan of 110–130 cm (43–51 in), a proportionally longer tail (54 to 54.5 per cent of the wing), and longer, narrower wings. The wing of adult males measures 312 mm (300–323 mm; $12–12\frac{1}{2}$ in); of adult females, 327 mm (312–347 mm; $12–13\frac{1}{2}$ in). Adult males weigh about 350 g ($12\frac{1}{2}$ oz); females, 390 g ($13\frac{1}{2}$ oz); but fledglings weigh much more, 470–510 g ($16\frac{1}{2}–18$ oz), owing to fat deposits. Sexual size dimorphism is only weakly expressed: males average about 95 per cent of females in linear measurements, and first year birds show even less difference. (Walter 1979, Cramp and Simmons 1980.)

The plumage is quite variable in Eleonora's falcon. Most observers have concluded that there are two distinct colour phases, a "normal" form (pale morph) and a melanistic form (dark morph) – see for example, Wink *et al.* (1978), Walter (1979), Cramp and Simmons (1980). In actual fact, as my former student A. L. Clark has shown (unpublished Ph.D. thesis), there are three distinct phenotypes, including an intermediate "dusky morph". Clark refers to these plumages as the light, dark and black phases. About 75 per cent of the adult population consists of light phase individuals, and about 25 per cent are either dark or black. Clark observed that light phase parents produce only light phase offspring, whereas pairs consisting of one light phase and one dark phase mate produce offspring that are either light phase or dark phase. The mating of dark phase individuals together produces offspring that are light, dark or black. His observations are consistent with the action of a single, allelic pair of genes with incomplete dominance: the dark phase should be heterozygous; the light and black phases, homozygous. The black phase is rare, and occurs at a frequency of about 1.8 per cent in accord with the Hardy–Weinberg theory.

The light morph looks much like the Eurasian hobby in general pattern, but the facial features are not so striking, and Eleonora's falcon lacks the rufous coloured thighs and vent of *subbuteo*. It also has much darker under wing-coverts than the hobby. The dark morph is patterned like the light morph but has a deep, smoky suffusion in the ground colour of all areas, while the black morph appears somewhat glossy and uniformly melanistic at a distance, although on close inspection it shows some faint barring in the feathers. The immatures of the three phases are much like their respective adults but are somewhat more heavily barred or edged with rufous on the individual feathers.

Eleonora's falcon is highly migratory, and the breeding populations leave their nesting areas in the latter part of October or early November, passing eastward through the Mediterranean region and thence south through Suez and down the Red Sea to spend the nonbreeding season mainly in the environs of Madagascar, but also in the Mascarene Islands and along the coastal areas of Tanzania and Kenya, up to 400 km (250 miles) inland. Evidently even the falcons nesting in the Canary Islands make this same migration, rather than moving down the west coast of Africa, so that some falcons perform a one-way movement of 8,000 km (5,000 miles) or more. Eleonora's falcons often fly with hobbies and sooty falcons, and they return to their breeding grounds in spring, with the peak of arrival in May, long before they are ready to begin breeding.

During its long migrations and on its "wintering" grounds, Eleonora's falcon feeds mainly on flying insects in typical hobby fashion, doing most of its hunting at dawn and dusk and eating on the wing. It continues to feed on insects when it first arrives back on its Mediterranean breeding grounds; but as the laying season approaches in late July, the males especially become hunters of small land birds, which they capture when the prey are at greatest risk over open water. Thus, the Eleonora's falcon appears to be primarily an insectivorous species which has become secondarily adapted, mainly through behavioural and ecological adjustments, to feed on small land birds under the special conditions existing during their

PLATE XXII
Eleonora's Falcon
Falco eleonorae
Adult male, above
(dark phase)
Adult female, centre
Immature female,
below
Map page 187

132

R. DAVID DIGBY.

autumn migration in large numbers over water. Eleonora's falcon shows little development of the morphological adaptations seen in the true bird-catching specialists (large feet, long talons, high degree of sexual size dimorphism, and heavy wing-loading), although its beak is rather large for its size.

Walter (1979) analysed more than 5,000 remains of prey from the nesting grounds and identified 90 species of birds, but three species of shrikes (*Lanius* spp) and half a dozen species of warblers (*Sylvia* spp) and related species, all weighing less than 50 grams ($1\frac{1}{2}$ oz), made up most of the prey. Quite a few swifts have been recorded at Essaouira, off the coast of Morocco, early in the season, and birds up to the size of hoopoes, small rails and cuckoos are caught. The hoopoe is actually a significant item at some nesting colonies (A. L. Clark).

Walter (1979) has estimated that the total breeding population of Eleonora's falcon annually consumes about 1,600,000 to 2,000,000 birds. The impact of this predation on the total number of migrants crossing into Africa is certainly negligible, but its influence on the numbers of some preferred species, such as shrikes, is less clear. Nor do we know what selective influences the predation may be exerting through the culling of weak or otherwise less fit individuals.

The basic reproductive adaptations of Eleonora's falcon to its food supply have to do with timing and spacing. It breeds later in the year than any other Palearctic nesting species, and it would be interesting to know something about its photoperiodic response or other factors involved in this late timing. Females lay in late July and August, and hatching coincides with the start of large-scale migratory movements of small birds in late August and early September. The young falcons are reared during the peak of autumn migration, when small land birds are most abundant. It is significant that no other Northern Hemisphere bird of prey has evolved such a late breeding season, although the related African species, *concolor*, produces young at the season when the trans-Saharan migration of Palearctic birds is in full swing.

Eleonora's falcon nests in colonies, a habit that has become well developed in only two other, small, mainly insectivorous species – the lesser kestrel, and western red-footed falcon – and to a lesser degree in some populations of the common kestrel. (The sooty falcon and occasionally other species of *Falco* nest in dispersed "colonies" or groups, but there is no group defence of a common area as there is in *naumanni* and *vespertinus*.) The nesting colonies range in size from 2 to 200 pairs, and the defended nesting territories of each pair are very small, ranging from one to 200 square metres (Walter 1979). Colonial nesting allows the members of a colony to benefit from group defence of the nesting area against enemies and competitors, but its main significance probably lies in the fact that the entire breeding population can be accommodated in the limited nesting habitat on the cliffs and islets that are optimally located to intercept the autumn passage of migrants over open water.

There is just enough time for the young falcons to mature and leave the nest before the number of migrants has dwindled to an unexploitable level. According to Walter (1979) the young leave their nest areas within 15 days after they begin to fly. If they are then independent of parental care, they have a remarkably short period of post-nestling dependency. Possibly the heavy fat deposits laid on by the young falcons while they are being fed by their parents compensates for a shortened period of parental care and tides them over until they have developed the skill to catch insects.

Young Eleonora's falcons have long been sought throughout the Mediterranean region as human food because of their fat, succulent, squab-like flesh. A fledgling with a fat-free weight of 350 g (12 oz) may accumulate more than 100 g ($3\frac{1}{2}$ oz) of fat while being fed birds by its parents. This is a considerable energy reserve, for even with the additional work required to fly several hours a day in migration, it provides enough energy to last the young falcon for a week or more at an expenditure of calories equivalent to three times its basal metabolic rate per day.

Walter (1979) made a detailed comparison of the Eleonora's colony on Paximada in the Dionysian Islands northeast of Crete with the colony on the Isles of Essaouira in the Atlantic off the coast of Morocco. He found significant behavioural and ecological adjustments of the falcons to local conditions that influence the availability of migrant birds. The falcons at Essaouira began nesting about a week earlier than those on Paximada, and they laid an average of 2.98 eggs (mode 3), compared to an average of around 2.1 (mode 2) on Paximada. The number of young surviving to fly from nests as Essaouira averaged about 2.5 (excluding human depredations); on Paximada, about 1.5. At Essaouira the adult falcons hunted all day long and even at night, delivering an average of more than 3 birds per day to their nests, whereas those on Paximada hunted for only a few hours in the morning and brought in an average of less than 1.5 birds a day. These differences can be explained by the following facts: the autumn migration begins earlier in the region of Essaouira than in the eastern Mediterranean; larger numbers of Palearctic migrants pass over into Africa in the western sector than in the eastern; and the location of Essaouira in relation to points of departure from Europe is such that many migrants continue to pass over those islands all day long and into the night, while Paximada is located so that migrants are likely to pass over only in the early morning hours.

Since Eleonora's falcon is not highly adapted morphologically to catch birds, its methods of hunting migrants over water are especially interesting to the student of falcon behaviour, and both Walter (1979), and Lud Clark, who studied Eleonora's falcons for three seasons in Morocco, have devoted much attention to this subject. The falcons have four main methods of searching for migrant land birds, which are mainly pursued and caught over water, where they have no cover into which they can escape.

At Paximada and other colonies where the migrants pass over high and where strong winds prevail, the falcons fly up to about 1,000 m (3,300 ft) or less and hang facing into the wind in a standing glide (stationary hunting), watching ahead and below for oncoming migrants. Many hunting falcons join in this search, creating a kind of phalanyx past which the migrating prey must move. The initial attack is usually a stoop at a bird flying below the waiting falcon, followed by short tail-chases and repeated stoops as the quarry drops lower in the air space to evade capture. Usually other falcons (up to ten or more) join in the attack, and continue to harry the prey until it becomes exhausted over the water and is caught, not necessarily by the first attacker. These group hunts are not really co-operative or organized efforts, as each falcon hunts strictly for itself; but the result is exhaustion of the prey leading to a high probability that some falcon will catch it.

At Essaouira and other colonies where different conditions prevail and where migrants often approach at much lower elevations – even right over the water – the falcons adopt other methods of search. Probably the commonest and most effective method, according to Clark's observations, is for the falcon to fly straight out from the island into the wind and against the oncoming traffic of migrants until a vulnerable target is contacted and can be attacked either by stooping, tail-chasing, or a combination of both. Curiously Eleonora's falcons seldom snatch these little birds out of the water, where they eventually fall if pursued long enough, in contrast to peregrines which often use this tactic over rivers or lakes.

On calm days the falcons search mainly by flying in broad, sweeping circles or figure-of-eight patterns at moderate heights over the open water a few hundred metres or so out from the colony site and more or less at right angles to the path of migration. Apparently this pattern of search optimizes the possibilities for contacting prey under calm or nearly calm conditions, and it may be the most efficient mode of hunting in some circumstances.

Some falcons, mostly females and non-breeding immatures, search from a perched position at the colony site and launch direct attacks at birds observed in the surrounding air-space. While it is the least expensive method of hunting in terms of energy expended, it is apparently not highly successful.

Variations of these basic modes have been described, but the essential elements in the successful hunting of birds by Eleonora's falcon are, first, to encounter a land bird over water and far enough from cover so that it can be attacked repeatedly and, if necessary, flown to exhaustion and, secondly, the group attack, which greatly increases the likelihood that the prey will make a mistake in evasive manoeuvre, become confused, or eventually fatigued.

How successful are Eleonora's falcons in catching birds? Walter (1979) did not keep detailed records on a large sample of observed hunts, but he reckoned that more than 50 per cent of pursued birds escaped, even including multiple attacks by more than one falcon. He estimated that only about 11 per cent of attacks by single falcons ended in capture, whereas group attacks resulted in a much higher capture rate around 44 per cent; however, the rate per individual falcon in a group was not much, if any, better than when a falcon hunts alone. A. L. Clark, who kept detailed records on more than 200 hunts by Eleonora's falcons at Essaouira, got a rather different impression of their efficiency. Of 114 pursuits by single falcons, 77, or 68 per cent resulted in captures, while 62 or 71 per cent of 87 pursuits by two or more falcons were successful. Successful group pursuits required an average of 53 seconds and 11.6 stoops per kill, while successful attacks by individuals required on average only 36 seconds and 5.8 stoops per kill. Thus, group pursuits are not more efficient than single pursuits, and Clark reached the interesting conclusion that the group pursuits should actually be considered competitive rather than co-operative. The only advantage of the group pursuit is that it reduces searching time for those individuals that join the pursuit later.

It used to be thought that the population of Eleonora's falcon was rather small. Vaughan (1961), who first attempted to estimate the total species population, was in fact criticized for "optimistically" suggesting that "the total world population of Eleonora's falcon is under 4,000 birds, about half of which breed in the Aegean and Crete". Walter (1979) catalogued information on 148 different breeding locations that have been mentioned; of the 108 "confirmed" sites, two became extinct before 1850, 11 discovered between 1850 and 1950 have ceased to exist or have not been surveyed since 1950, and 95 are known to have been reproductively active since 1950. Estimates for the size of these colonies give a mean total breeding population estimate of 4,400 pairs (range of 1,930 to 7,000), and Walter feels there probably are an additional 3,000 nonbreeding immature and adult falcons in the summer population. Moreover, some previously unrecorded colonies are still becoming known to ornithologists, so that 10,000 returning birds each spring appears to be the right order of magnitude for Eleonora's falcon.

Thus, the status of this species looks secure for the time being. Unlike the peregrine and some other bird-eating raptors, Eleonora's falcon has not been significantly influenced by DDT or other pesticide residues (Clark and Peakall 1977), probably because it feeds on birds for less than four months out of the year. Direct human disturbances seem to be the main causes of egg and nestling losses, careless activities of tourists, boaters and fishermen around colonies, and hunting and killing by boys and young men armed with sling-shot or rifles (A. L. Clark). Even so, the colonies are often protected by bad weather and rough seas, which make landings or close approach by boat difficult, particularly in the Aegean Sea, which is the centre of abundance for the species. Of greater long-term significance may be slow changes in the numbers of migrating birds crossing the Mediterranean – there already appears to have been a historical decrease in clutch size of Eleonora's falcon on Paximada Island, possibly in response to reduced food supplies – and the potential for really serious changes in habitat and insect populations on the non-breeding grounds in Madagascar, where the native forests are disappearing at a distressing rate.

135

Sooty Falcon

Falco concolor

ALTHOUGH SOMEWHAT SMALLER, the sooty falcon of Africa and Arabia is closely related to Eleonora's falcon, and can be confused with the melanistic phase of the latter. As both the common and scientific names suggest, this is a uniformly dark species which, interestingly, has a melanistic phase as well as a "pale" phase. The latter is uniformly slate grey with dark shaft-streaks to the individual feathers. The primaries are unbarred black and contrast with the rest of the plumage; there is also a small black spot below each eye and a small buffy area on the throat. The melanistic phase is uniformly dark slate to blackish brown with no contrast between the wings and body. First year birds are browner than adults with buff-edged feathers, while some have prominent facial patterns and a general appearance very similar to immature Eleonora's falcons, from which they are not easily distinguished in the field.

Sooty falcons have much the same habits as Eleonora's falcons, and according to Walter (1979) the two are derived from a recent, common ancestral species since the retreat of the last glacial ice sheet in Europe, perhaps no more than 15,000 years ago. Nevertheless, there are some curious structural differences between the two, suggesting a greater degree of niche differentiation than one might expect of recently separated species which also occupy allopatric breeding ranges. The sooty falcon is larger than the Eurasian hobby, with a length of 33–36 cm (13–14 in) and a wingspan of 85–110 cm ($33\frac{1}{2}$–$43\frac{1}{2}$ in) but averages about 10 per cent smaller than *eleonorae* in linear dimensions. In particular, it has a relatively shorter tail (47.5 to 48 per cent of wing length), which is slightly wedge-shaped at the tip, the central pair of rectrices averaging about 6 mm longer than adjacent pairs and 13 mm longer than the outer pair. Sexual size dimorphism is no more pronounced than in *eleonorae*: the wing length of adult males averages 274 mm (264–283 mm; $10\frac{1}{2}$–11 in) or 96.1 per cent of the female wing average, 285 mm (273–297 mm; $10\frac{1}{2}$–$11\frac{1}{2}$ in). At rest the wing tips extend beyond the end of the tail. (Data from Cramp and Simmons 1980.) Apparently adult body weights have not been recorded, but in view of the prey taken by the sooty falcon it would not be surprising to find that its weight is very close to that of Eleonora's falcon. Recently Walter (in press) recorded juvenile weights of 300–340 g ($10\frac{1}{2}$–12 oz) at 30 days of age.

These structural comparisons suggest that sooty falcons may be less heavily wing-loaded than Eleonora's, but the short tail may make them less buoyant overall and faster in direct pursuit. They apparently do not hover, and in most flight attitudes the primaries are faired backward relative to the inner wings and body more than is usually the case with *eleonorae* (Cramp and Simmons 1980), again suggesting a design for power and speed.

The sooty falcon breeds in some of the most inhospitable environments in the world – at scattered localities in the Libyan desert and adjacent parts of Egypt, eastward into Sinai and rarely Israel, and south into the Red Sea and Gulf of Aden, where it nests on islands, especially in the Dahlak Archipelago. Recently it has been confirmed that the sooty falcon also nests in some numbers in Arabia, on islands in

136

R. DAVID DIGBY.

the Gulf of Oman and on the Howar Islands south of Bahrain in the Arabian Gulf (Cramp and Simmons 1980; Walter, in press). There may be other, as yet unknown breeding populations in this region, including some in the Arabian desert.

On islands, the sooty falcon nests inside holes in outcroppings of coral or rock, in shaded clefts on low cliffs, or on the ground under dense Euphorbia bushes (Clapham 1964). A nest of eggs was once found far out on the open, unvegetated gravel plain of the Libyan desert under a cairn of sandstones marking a camel route; the temperature around the eggs was 42.2°C (108°F), far above the normal incubation temperature of birds (Booth 1961). Elsewhere in the desert it is likely that the falcon nests in pot-holes on small rocky outcrops or in steep eroded banks of wadis, but no details have been recorded. Deep shade must be an absolutely critical factor for any successful nesting site within the known breeding range.

Sooty falcons are not colonial nesters to the degree that Eleonora's falcons are – indeed, in the desert they are very widely scattered – but on islands pairs do aggregate, as many as 100 nests having been found on one island (Clapham 1964). Minimum distances between nests are, however, 40–50 m (130–160 ft), and there apparently is no group defence of a colony area, as there is with Eleonora's falcons (Walter 1979).

The nesting habitat is too impoverished in locally produced animal life to support falcons, and like Eleonora's falcon, *concolor* has shifted its breeding season to the autumn to correspond with the trans-Saharan and trans-Arabian migrations of Palearctic birds from Eurasia into Africa. Such birds are almost as vulnerable to falcon attacks over the vast, unvegetated tracts of desert as they are over water, and depending on where their nests are located, sooty falcons take advantage of both situations.

During their breeding season, sooty falcons feed on a variety of these migrants – mostly on small passerines such as willow warblers and shrikes – but also on a surprising number of larger birds such as bee-eaters, golden orioles and hoopoes (Cramp and Simmons 1980), waders and marine birds (Walter, in press), and even on sandgrouse according to Meinertzhagen (1954). Occasionally they also take prey, including rodents, on the ground. While group hunting of birds as described for Eleonora's falcon does occur (Walter, in press), mates tend to hunt together more, and one pair may contend with another in chasing the same bird.

Sooty falcons migrate at the end of their nesting season to spend the off-breeding season mainly in the environs of Madagascar and adjacent African coast, some birds straggling to Mauritius and south as far as Natal, South Africa. During this period and on migration, they often occur in groups of up to 15 birds, frequently in the company of Eleonora's falcons, and feed mainly on flying insects but also on bats. They are quite crepuscular in activity and also hunt at night, often roosting together in giant baobabs (Walter 1979). From late December on, many appear to be paired – well before spring migration, which begins in April.

The sooty falcon remains something of a puzzle, for it is much more common on Madagascar than Eleonora's falcon, in the ratio of about 10:1 where Walter (1979) made his observations. An earlier comparison of these relative numbers led Moreau (1969) to estimate that the total population of *concolor* was more than 10,000 birds, based on Vaughan's (1961) figure of 2,000 breeding pairs of Eleonora's falcons. Walter (1979) estimated that there were 5,000 sooty falcons in a 1,000 sq km (390 sq miles) sector of Madagascar around Morondova in late December, and this figure together with the revised estimate of 4,400 pairs of Eleonora's falcons suggests that the number of sooty falcons is at least double Moreau's estimate, more than 20,000 birds. The known breeding populations cannot account for more than a small fraction of the wintering birds. Where do the rest of these sooty falcons nest? The recent "discoveries" of nesting falcons in the Gulf of Oman and in the Arabian Gulf suggest that the whole Arabian region may yield more nesting localities (Walter, in press).

Western Red-footed Falcon

(Red-footed Kestrel)

Falco vespertinus

O<small>FTEN CONSIDERED TO</small> be an aberrant or specialized kestrel, this distinctive species with bright red fleshy feet, cere, and eye-ring, is, I believe, more closely allied to the hobbies. It does hover to some extent like the kestrels – so do many other species of *Falco* – but it is proportioned more like a hobby. Moreover, the female and immature plumages bear a closer resemblance to that of the Eurasian hobby than to any of the kestrels, and its common alarm call is like the "kew" cry of *subbuteo*.

The red-footed falcon is a small species about the size of the male *subbuteo* but with a slightly longer-appearing tail, which is also more rounded at the tip than in hobbies. The body length is 29–31 cm ($11\frac{1}{2}$–12 in) with a wingspan of 66–78 cm (26–$30\frac{1}{2}$ in). Although the female is somewhat bulkier than the male, sexual size dimorphism is not pronounced. The wing measurement of males averages 244 mm, of females, 246 mm ($9\frac{1}{2}$ in), so that males have wings 99.2 per cent as long as females. Males weigh around 150 g (5 oz) or 89 to 90 per cent of females, which average 167 g (6 oz). The tail length is about 52.5 per cent (males) and 53.7 per cent (females) of the wing measurement, a ratio that falls in the range of hobby species and is far lower than the range for kestrels (60 to 75 per cent). (Data from Cramp and Simmons 1980.)

Sexual dichromatism is marked in the adult plumage. The male appears dark sooty grey, darkest on rump, tail and under wing-coverts, and lightest on the underparts. The flight feathers appear greyer than the wing-coverts and in certain lights produce a silvery or pearly sheen. His thighs, lower belly and under tail-coverts are a rich chestnut, another hobby-like character.

The adult female is blue grey barred with black on her upperparts, while her underbody and under wing-coverts are orange-buff with some streaks on the flanks and, in flight, conspicuous barring on the flight feathers and under tail. She has distinctive head features with an orange-buff crown and nape, fading to yellowish white on forehead and cheeks, which emphasize a dark brown eye patch and short moustache.

To a remarkable degree the ecology and life history of the red-footed falcon parallel those of the lesser kestrel (*naumanni*), although there is little morphological similarity. Both species are highly gregarious throughout the year and nest, usually, in colonies of closely spaced pairs; both are mainly insectivorous in diet; and both are highly migratory between the Palearctic and Africa.

The red-footed falcon is a long-distance, trans-equatorial migrant with completely separate areas for breeding and for sojourning during the non-reproductive period. Its breeding range, which generally lies northward of the lesser kestrel's, extends across the broad band of steppe, forest-steppe and cultivated north temperate areas from eastern Europe, where it now occurs patchily, through the Soviet Union from the region of the Black and Caspian seas north into the Baltic states and northern Russia about to 63–64°N; and thence eastward in a narrowing latitudinal range from about 45–50°N to 60–62°N to the eastern tributaries of the Yenisei and the upper Lena River in Siberia.

After a migration of 6,000 to 11,000 km (3,700–6,800 miles) from October or November to March or April, red-footed falcons are found in the semi-arid grasslands and savannahs of Angola, Namibia, Botswana, Zimbabwe, and to a lesser extent in neighbouring parts of Zambia and South Africa, where they feed on swarms of locusts and flying insects, often in company with lesser kestrels and other falcons.

On its breeding range in the Palearctic *vespertinus* can be found nesting in all kinds of open terrain fringed with trees or interspersed with small, isolated groves, or where riparian woodland transects open country. It avoids deserts, mountains and completely closed forests, not commonly occurring in Europe above 300 m (980 ft), although in Asia it breeds up to 1,100 m (3,600 ft) and exceptionally to 1,500 m (4,900 ft). Nesting pairs are most often found in glades, scattered coppices, orchards, parks, marshes, and cut or burned areas within forests. (Dementiev 1951, Cramp and Simmons 1980.)

Usually a few to a few dozen pairs take over the old or unused stick nests of rooks and sometimes crows or kites. Raven and magpie nests are taken over by single pairs. Colonies of several hundred pairs also occur: the pairs sometimes evict magpies, rooks and even hooded crows from their nests, and there is some indication that neighbours may join with the prospecting pair in mobbing the corvid owners (Horváth 1975).

L. Horváth (1955, 1956) found in Hungary that red-footed falcons generally select the higher nests among those available, 13–20 m (40–65 ft) above ground and within a few metres of the crown. In the northern parts of the breeding range, they also use holes in trees, in southwestern Siberia nests on shrubby pea-trees and willows, and occasionally they occupy holes on cliffs or embankments and even nest on the ground under dwarf shrubs like some merlins (Dementiev 1951).

As with the lesser kestrel, there is little or no intraspecific defence of nest-sites against other members of the colony, and during communal displays individuals can settle near another's nest without provoking conflict. Horváth (1955) observed, however, that when nests are abundant in a particular place, those occupied by the falcons comprise a rather constant proportion of the total rookery: from 11.9 per cent for a rookery of 84 nests, to 13.5 per cent for one with 334 nests, suggesting some kind of behavioural spacing mechanism. Even more interestingly, he has found (Horváth 1975) that red-footed falcons practise group territoriality; all the pairs in one isolated colony defend not only their nests but also a foraging area from members of other nearby colonies.

Red-footed falcons seem to require gregarious, social organization right through the year. For example, communal, aerial activities continue throughout the breeding season. Between morning and evening feeding periods, adults gather in flocks and soar on motionless wings high above the colony and then gradually descend lower towards late afternoon and fly together in wave-like motion among the trees and just above the ground, turning sharply at fixed points with flashing wings, constantly uttering loud calls. This behaviour has no parallel in other species of falcons. In view of Horváth's observations, one is led to speculate that these aerial evolutions represent some kind of territorial display.

The breeding season is rather late for the latitudes at which red-footed falcons nest and appears to be timed so that young hatch when the mid-summer flush of insects and young rodents takes place. Horváth (1956) examined 65 clutches in Hungary, which ranged from 2 to 5 eggs. He considered the mean of 3.48 lower than usual owing to a high percentage of young females in the population at the time. Dementiev (1951) suggested that clutches vary from year to year depending on food supply.

Cramp and Simmons (1980) give the incubation period as 22 to 23 days, exceptionally 27, based on Horváth (1955, 1956); but as no other small falcon has such a short incubation Dementiev's (1951) figure of about 28 days is probably more accurate. Both sexes incubate in roughly equal proportions during the day, but only the female at night. She broods the young for their first 7 to 10 days of life; then she joins the male in feeding the young, which leave the nest at 25 to 26 days and begin flying at 27 to 30 days. They are said to be independent hunters in another 7 to 10 days, a remarkably short time.

Adults feed almost exclusively on insects the year round, but they feed their young mainly on small vertebrates, an interesting difference from *naumanni*. They are opportunistic feeders, exploiting local abundances and seasonally variable populations of prey. Orthopterans are the principal prey, especially field-crickets, mole-crickets and bush-crickets, while grasshoppers and locusts are usually less important in the Palearctic, although they are sometimes heavily used in Africa – where, however, flying ants and termites are the main·prey. Many other ground-dwelling and flying insects have been recorded as food (see Cramp and Simmons 1980).

In Hungary the chicks are first fed on frogs (*Pelobates fuscus*), fledglings of small birds, sand lizards and orthopterans in decreasing order of importance (Horváth 1955), but after they leave the nest the young are fed almost exclusively on insects. No doubt annual and regional variations in diet occur; for example small mammals, especially voles, are important items for both young and adults in parts of the Soviet Union. Dementiev (1951) also lists house mice and several other small mammals, including shrews.

Red-footed falcons hunt by hovering and dropping down on ground prey or landing near by and then pouncing. They can run quite adeptly after prey over the ground, and they also hawk flying insects (rarely birds) out of the air like hobbies. They still-hunt from exposed perches, and drop down suddenly to ground level and approach the intended quarry in low, fast flight. Thus, their hunting behaviour combines both kestrel-like and hobby-like tactics. Like hobbies they are also decidedly crepuscular in their foraging time.

The red-footed falcon has declined somewhat in Europe west of the Soviet Union in the last 20 years. For example, in Hungary the numbers have changed from an estimated 2,000 to 3,000 pairs in 1957, to 500 to 600 pairs in the 1970s, following a decrease west of the Danube. As the numbers and distribution of breeding pairs tend to vary from year to year depending on food sources, it is not easy to assess the significance of short term regional changes.

V. M. Galushin has estimated that there are about 400 pairs in 270,000 sq km (104,200 sq miles) of central European Russia, stating that the species is generally more abundant in the southern sector of its range than in the north, where a higher proportion of isolated nesting pairs are encountered. The total Palearctic breeding range approximates 7 million sq km (2.7 million sq miles). If Galushin's figures represent an average density, then there would only be around 10,000 breeding pairs; but it is likely that numbers are higher in the steppes and forest-steppes of the central Soviet Union, and it seems reasonable to think that the total population is above 20,000 pairs.

PLATE XXIV
Western Red-footed
Falcon
Falco vespertinus
Adult female,
above left
Adult male,
below right
Map page 187

R. DAVID DIGBY

Eastern Red-footed Falcon

(Amur Red-footed Falcon)

Falco amurensis

THIS FORM IS sometimes considered to be only a well differentiated, disjunct allopatric "subspecies" of the western red-footed falcon; however, it is morphologically and behaviourally so distinct from *vespertinus* that were the two to come into contact across the narrow geographical gap that now separates them in the Lake Baikal region of Siberia, it seems most likely that they would remain reproductively isolated populations. For that reason it is appropriate to consider them as separate species. (See also Cramp and Simmons 1980.)

The plumage of the adult male generally resembles that of *vespertinus*, except that the axillaries and under wing-coverts are immaculate white, instead of black, a distinctive feature which almost certainly has significance in intraspecific communication, possibly in sexual display – further strengthening the probability of behavioural reproductive isolation from *vespertinus*. In addition, the adult female is notably unlike the female of *vespertinus* and shows a much closer resemblance to the female hobby.

Moreover, *amurensis* is a smaller bird than *vespertinus*. The wing measurement of males averages 232 mm (218–245 mm; $8\frac{1}{2}$–$9\frac{1}{2}$ in); of females, 234 mm (225–242 mm; 9–$9\frac{1}{2}$ in), some 10 mm less on average than *vespertinus*. Males weigh around 136 g (97–155 g; $3\frac{1}{2}$–$5\frac{1}{2}$ oz), while females weigh around 148 g (111–188 g; $4\frac{1}{2}$–$6\frac{1}{2}$ oz). (Data from Brown and Amadon 1968.) Thus, sexual differences in size are small: males average 99 per cent of females in wing length and 92 per cent in body weight.

The Amur red-footed falcon occupies a limited breeding distribution of some 2 to 3 million sq km (0.7–1.1 million sq miles) in the southeastern Trans-Baikal region of Siberia, northwestern Mongolia, Manchuria, Korea, and northern China, south to the Chin Ling Shan Range and Kiangsu Province. Individual nests have also been reported from middle Asia (at Tengyuanyin) and Burma (Dementiev 1951).

The species winters in small numbers in southern China, Burma and India, but the vast majority of birds apparently fly all the way into southern Africa, probably passing eastward of the Himalayas for the most part, through Burma, Assam and India, and across the Indian Ocean to a first landfall on the coast of southern Arabia or the Horn of Africa, and thence south through East Africa. The details are not well documented, but it is known that *amurensis* occupies a region in southern Africa that is mainly to the south and east of the region occupied at the same season by *vespertinus* (Cade 1969), and it arrives on average later than *vespertinus* – in December, having travelled some 10,000 to 12,000 km (6,200–7,400 miles).

Little is known about the life history and ecology of this species, but what information there is suggests that there are important differences from *vespertinus*. For one thing, while *amurensis* migrates in large flocks, roosts in large aggregations, and forages in flocks during its African sojourn, it is not known to form large nesting colonies, and indeed the majority of pairs may nest in relative isolation from others. It would be most interesting to know whether the pairs maintain individual territories around their nests.

The nesting habitat consists of forest-steppe, riparian woods, and moist, marshy localities in broad-leaved forest. It avoids treeless country and dense forest.

These falcons usually arrive on their breeding grounds in May, but they do not lay until early June. They nest in a variety of deciduous and coniferous trees, usually in the nest of some other bird, particularly raven and magpie, but it has been suggested that they build their own nests on occasion. As with other species of *Falco*, this suggestion requires confirmation.

Clutches usually range from three to five eggs, exceptionally up to six. Incubation is probably about 28 to 30 days, as clutches are completed around mid-June and hatchlings first appear around mid-July.

Dementiev (1951) recorded no information on food habits from the breeding range. In southern Africa, the falcons feed like *vespertinus*, *naumanni* and *subbuteo* on flying termites and ants, as I once had a chance to observe in the low veld of the Kruger National Park, and on local outbreaks of locusts.

There is no information on which to base an estimate of the numerical strength of the eastern red-footed falcon. Nothing is known about densities on the breeding grounds, and it seems likely that the best possibility for gaining some understanding of its population would be for the South African ornithologists to undertake systematic censuses of roosts as they did for the lesser kestrel (Siegfried and Skead 1971).

PLATE XXV
Eastern Red-footed
Falcon
Falco amurensis
Adult male,
above left
Adult female,
below right
Map page 187

142

R. DAVID DIGBY

Common Kestrel

(Eurasian Kestrel)

Falco tinnunculus

With the common kestrel we come to a group of nine or ten closely related and mostly allopatric species, all called kestrels or "wind-hovers" because one of their common methods of searching for prey on the ground is to hover in a stationary position in the air looking down. This species is the commonest diurnal raptor over most of the Palearctic and much of Africa, and it is probably the most numerous species of *Falco* in the world. Its success as a species can be attributed to its adaptability to a wide range of habitats, including the ability to adjust to the agricultural and urban environments of man; to the use of many different kinds of nesting places; wide choice of abundant, mostly ground-dwelling and relatively easily caught prey; propensity to adjust breeding density to abundance of prey and to the clumped distribution of favoured nesting sites; and versatility in hunting, including the use of hovering to a degree unmatched by other sympatric and potentially competitive raptors. In short, *tinnunculus* is generalized in most of its habits and quite plastic in response to local conditions.

It is a small to medium-sized falcon, 32–35 cm ($12\frac{1}{2}$–$13\frac{1}{2}$ in) in length with a wingspan of 71–80 cm (28–$31\frac{1}{2}$ in). The wings are long relative to the body, but so is the rather graduated tail, so that the tips of the wings at rest do not come close to the end of the tail. The wing of adult males from the western Palearctic averages 246 mm (233–258 mm; 9–10 in); of adult females, 256 mm (229–272 mm; 9–$10\frac{1}{2}$ in). The tail is 66.3 to 66.8 per cent of the wing measurement. In summer males weigh around 156 g ($5\frac{1}{2}$ oz), but in winter they are somewhat heavier, around 167 g (6 oz). Summer females weigh 193 g (7 oz) on average, winter ones 201 g (7 oz). Sexual size dimorphism is not pronounced: the male's wing is 96.1 per cent of the female's, and males weigh 80.8 to 83.1 per cent of female weight. (Data from Cramp and Simmons 1980.)

Most species of kestrels show marked differences in plumage between adult males and females, and *tinnunculus* is no exception. The male is a brightly coloured and contrastingly marked bird with a grey head and tail, which contrast with a chestnut, black-spotted back and upper wing-coverts and blackish brown primaries, forming a striking pattern at rest or in flight. The tail also has a broad, black subterminal band and a narrow, whitish tip. The underparts are generally buffy to whitish with rows of darker spots or bars. A black moustachial stripe below the eye contrasts with a whitish throat and cheek. The female is a less strikingly marked, more uniformly brownish to chestnut coloured bird. She has heavy barring on back and upper wings, and a brown and black barred tail with a somewhat narrower subterminal band than the male and with a buffy tip. Her underparts are darker and more streaked than on the male. She also has a thin moustache below the eye, contrasting with a light throat and cheek. The first year bird (male and female) is similar to the adult female but usually somewhat lighter appearing with whitish edges to the dark bars on the upperparts and broader streakings on the breast and belly.

As one would expect of such a wide-ranging species, there is some geographic variation among the different breeding populations, which vary mainly in the shade of chestnut and in the amount of blackish spotting and barring, also in size. Generally kestrels from moist tropical areas (India, West Africa) are darker than temperate zone birds, while those from semi-desertic areas (North Africa, Middle East, Central Asian steppes) are redder or paler. Insular forms in the Canaries and Cape Verde Islands average smaller than continental birds. Brown and Amadon (1968) provide summary descriptions of the named subspecies.

PLATE XXVI
Common Kestrel
Falco tinnunculus
Adult male, above
Adult female, below
Map page 188

144

R. DAVID DIGBY

The kestrels in southern Africa show a curious trend toward masculinization of the female plumage, which has quite a bit of blue in the tail and head, although males and females are still quite distinct in other respects. While strong sexual dimorphism in plumage characterizes most kestrels in the subgenus *Tinnunculus*, various populations or species have secondarily evolved towards sexually monomorphic plumage. As we shall see in subsequent accounts, in some cases both sexes have a masculine plumage, while in others both have a feminine plumage. There is no obvious adaptive or evolutionary consistency to these deviations from sexual dichromatism. Why, for instance, should the male and female Seychelles kestrel both have a bright masculine plumage, while the male and female Mauritius kestrel, not very far away on another island, both have a brown, feminine plumage?

The common kestrel breeds over the greater part of the Eurasian land mass from 70°N in Scandinavia, 68°N in Finland, and commonly from 65°N throughout the Palearctic, southward, being absent only from the higher mountains above 4,500 m (14,200 ft), from severe deserts such as the Gobi, Sahara and Arabian, from southern China and southeastern Asia, and most of the Indian Subcontinent south of the Himalayas, except for a population in southwestern India and Ceylon. It also nests coastally and in mountainous parts of Arabia, in northwestern Africa and other scattered semi-desertic localities throughout the Saharan region, and throughout most of Africa south of the Sahara, except for the Congo Basin and some coastal districts.

Kestrels nesting in the northern and eastern parts of the Palearctic are migratory and move south to winter mainly in the southern zones of the breeding range in China, the Middle East and Africa, but also in some otherwise unoccupied areas of India and in the Philippines. There is a major trans-Saharan migration. Some kestrels winter as far north as southern Fenno-Scandia, and most of the nesting kestrels in the British Isles remain throughout the year, a few moving across the Channel as far as Iberia. The Indian and African breeding populations are mainly resident, as are insular populations in the Atlantic. (From Cramp and Simmons 1980.)

Within this vast range common kestrels occupy habitats ranging from moorlands, heaths, grasslands from high fjells to prairies and steppes, semi-desertic scrub, meadows and salt-marshes, tropical savannahs, parklands, the edges of forest, coastal dunes and cliffs, all kinds of agricultural lands with scattered groves, hedgerows, windbreaks, and other man-made habitats such as airfields, railway rights of way, highways and motorways, canals, and human settlements, even the largest cities where they include some open space for hunting. They are not regularly found in tundra, forest-tundra, extensive taiga, barren mountains, dense woodlands, treeless wetlands or true deserts.

Common kestrels use a wide variety of nesting sites. A hollow or fork in a tree, up to 22 m (70 ft) above ground, is the most frequent, and the old stick nest of some other bird is often taken over. Holes or ledges on a cliff or building, up to 50 m (160 ft) high, are also common sites. Pylons and other poles are sometimes used, and kestrels readily accept nest-boxes in some regions, particularly in Holland. They also sometimes nest on the ground, on low banks, or down rabbit burrows, especially on islands where mammal predators are absent (e.g. Orkneys).

Rockenbauch (1968) examined 122 nests in Germany and found 37 in trees, 22 on church towers, 28 on other tall buildings, 25 on crags, 9 in barns, and one on a pylon. Leslie Brown (1976) compiled data on 291 nests in southern England and found that 177 were in holes or forks of trees, 53 in old nests in trees, 27 on buildings or bridges, 26 on cliff ledges, and 4 in nest-boxes. But 354 nests in northern England and Scotland gave a different distribution: only 62 were in holes or forks of trees; 76 in old tree nests, 60 on buildings or bridges, 153 on cliffs, and 3 in nest-boxes, reflecting no doubt the availability of the different sites in the two regions.

The common kestrel is a spring breeder in both the Northern and Southern Hemispheres with the tendency for laying to become later as latitude increases away from the equator to the north or to the south, although seasonal rains may modify this tendency in some regions (compare below, south India, Sudan, and Cape Verde Islands, all between 10–20°N). The laying period in Europe and Asia north of the Himalayas ranges from late March in the south to early June, with most eggs laid in April and May; Korea, late April and May; in North Africa, April and May; Egypt, March and April; northern India, April to May, to early July at high altitudes; south India, February to March; Canaries, April; Cape Verde Islands, October; Sudan, May and June; Somalia, late April or early May; West Africa, February and March; Kenya, August to September; southern Tanzania, September; Zimbabwe and Malawi, July to October but mainly August and September; and South Africa, September and October. (From Brown and Amadon 1968.)

The clutch usually ranges between 3 and 6 eggs, exceptionally 1 to 9, with an average of 4.6 to 4.7 in many parts of the Palearctic breeding range. Later clutches average smaller than early clutches, and at least in parts of the range (e.g. Norway) the number of eggs varies with the food supply, chiefly voles, from year to year. In years when vole numbers were high, Yngvar Hagen (1969) found that 25 pairs of kestrels laid a mean of 5.1 eggs, of which 85 per cent hatched and 72 per cent produced fledged young, but in poor vole years 10 pairs laid an average of only 4.3 eggs, of which 65 per cent hatched and only 44 per cent produced fledged young.

It is probable that this sort of reproductive adjustment to food supply is more frequent in kestrel populations than present records indicate. Professor Rudolf Drent and his students have some extremely interesting studies under way in Holland to show that artificial feeding of pairs of kestrels around their

146

nest-boxes can significantly increase clutch size, hatch rate, and brood survival to fledgling. The mechanism by which the female assesses the quality of the feeding situation and becomes physiologically prepared to lay a large clutch or a small clutch is unknown, but it probably has to do with her plane of nutrition during the rather prolonged courtship period and may be determined by the rate at which the male delivers prey to her. In another Dutch study, Cavé (1968) showed that he could experimentally accelerate or slow ovarian development in captive kestrels by the amount of food he fed them in late winter and early spring. Ian Newton (1979) has nicely summarized what little is known about the influence of food on the timing of laying and on clutch size in raptors.

The list of prey compiled by Cramp and Simmons (1980) is extremely varied and reveals the kestrel as an adaptable and opportunistic feeder. The kinds of animals kestrels eat range from earthworms and snails to large insects of many sorts, lizards and small snakes, small terrestrial mammals, bats, and many kinds of birds, including some as large and fast as plovers, turnstones, lapwings, partridges and young pigeons. There is no doubt, however, that over most of its Palearctic range voles (principally *Microtus arvalis* and *M. agrestis*) and related microtines are staple and important foods, the abundance of which partly controls such significant population parameters as breeding density, clutch size and fledging success. In Africa other small, abundant mammals such as the multimammate mice (*Mastomys* spp) replace microtines in the diet. Small birds, especially fledgling passerines, are important items during the breeding season, and according to the observations of Thiede and Thiede (1973, *fide* Cramp and Simmons 1980) the kestrels inhabiting Nepal specialize on birds, as do some pairs nesting in cities where small mammals are unavailable. Other local or regional differences in diet occur, depending on the relative abundances of different kinds of prey; for example, in southern Europe viviparous lizards are heavily used, and orthopteran insects (especially crickets and grasshoppers) replace the more available coleopterans so frequently taken in northern Europe.

Kestrels focus most of their attention for hunting on the ground, and they search for prey principally in two ways, either from a high, exposed perch such as a tall pole, dead tree, cliffside or building – where they can command an unobstructed view of the surrounding ground – or by the characteristic, active hovering flight, which allows them to scan the ground below in open areas where there are no suitable observation posts. On spotting vulnerable prey, kestrels usually descend in a series of alternating gentle swoops and hoverings, checking on the prey as they close, before finally dropping sharply to the ground to catch the prey in their feet. Kestrels also hunt by direct attack, snatching prey from trees, bushes or tall grass, and sometimes in the air. They usually eat their quarry on the ground, especially if it is large, or on a perch, but they also sometimes eat insects and very small mammals on the wing.

Breeding pairs of kestrels show a wide range of densities and patterns of dispersal. They defend only the immediate environs of the nest, no more than a 25–30 m (80–100 ft) radius around nest-boxes in Holland (Cavé 1968), but even so the pairs typically are spaced some distance apart and breed as solitary units with large but overlapping hunting ranges of 100–400 ha (250–1,000 acres) and breeding densities ranging from one pair per 80–2,500 ha (200–6,000 acres), averaging around 500 hectares in Europe. (See Newton 1979, Walter 1979.) The low degree of territorial intolerance around nests allows deviations from this typical dispersed pattern to occur when food is locally superabundant or where highly favourable nesting sites are clumped – for example, certain woodlands with an abundance of nest-sites or cliffs with numerous pot-holes and ledges. Under these circumstances nests may be placed very close together – as many as 32 in a 20-ha (50-acre) wood in Europe – or the kestrels may become "colonial" as in Japan, where Fennell (1954) found about 40 pairs nesting together on a 1-kilometre stretch of cliff along the Yamese River, with nests spaced from 1–95 m (3–310 ft) apart. Kestrels also sometimes join in a mixed breeding colony with lesser kestrels and red-footed falcons, as Ferguson-Lees (1972) observed in the Ukraine.

Kestrel populations fluctuate naturally in some regions owing to changes in food supply (rodent cyles) or to the effects of severe winters, so that the influence of other factors on numbers through time is difficult to assess. In Europe, though, there is no doubt that kestrels suffered severe declines resulting from the use of pesticides of various sorts in the 1950s, but the species has since recovered well in those regions where use of chemical poisons has been controlled. Clear cases of decline and recovery are known for England, where dieldrin was a particular problem (Prestt 1965), in Sweden where methyl mercury killed many birds (Segnestam and Helander 1977), and in Israel where the rodenticide, thallium sulphate, wreaked great havoc on raptor populations (Mendelssohn 1972).

The population status had improved generally in Europe by the late 1970s, and the country by country estimates of numbers summarized by Cramp and Simmons (1980) indicate that for Europe as a whole, excluding the Soviet Union and Turkey, there must be on the average not less than 200,000 pairs of kestrels nesting in an area of some 3.8 million sq km (1.4 million sq miles). Vladimir Galushin (1981) has estimated 3,500 pairs in 270,000 sq km (104,200 sq miles) in the central European part of Russia. If we take the range of possibilities for the whole of the Palearctic breeding range, some 34 to 35 million sq km (13–13.5 million sq miles), to lie between one pair per 20 sq km and one per 50 sq km, then there would be between 680,000 and 1,750,000 pairs of kestrels in that part of the range, not including the population in southern India or the breeding kestrels in some 13 million sq km (5 million sq miles) of Africa south of the Sahara. The world breeding population of kestrels must lie in the range of 1 and 2 million pairs.

147

Moluccan Kestrel
(Spotted Kestrel)

Falco moluccensis

THE MOLUCCAN KESTREL has a limited distribution in the East Indies from Java and Bali in the southwest, east through the Lesser Sundas to Timor, and north to Celebes and the Moluccas, where it is a permanent resident throughout. It is a geographically isolated representative of the Eurasian kestrel, and is doubtfully distinct as a species from the latter. Were the two forms in geographic contact, it is probable that there would be no reproductive isolating mechanisms to prevent the free exchange of genes between the two populations. One wonders, in fact, about the extent of the geographic separation and why one or the other of these two falcons does not occur on Sumatra, in Malaysia, and in South-East Asia, especially as Sri Lanka (where *tinnunculus* occurs) lies in the same latitudes.

The Moluccan kestrel is a darker, more richly coloured version of the common kestrel but with less marked sexual dichromatism. The adult male is dark chestnut above, narrowly streaked with dark marks on crown and nape and spotted on back and upper wing-coverts with black. The upper tail-coverts and tail are grey, the latter tipped with white and bearing a broad black subterminal band. The primaries are blackish with chestnut spots on the inner webs, and the secondaries are chestnut with four or five black bars. The sides of face and neck are chestnut, streaked with black. The throat, chin and thighs are plain chestnut or nearly so, while the rest of the underbody is rich chestnut streaked and spotted with black. The under wing-coverts are white with black spots.

The adult female differs from the male in having her crown and nape more heavily streaked and her back more heavily barred with black; but her upper tail-coverts and tail are also grey. Her tail is tipped with black (worn feathers) and has eight to ten black bars. Her undersides are much like the male's but more heavily streaked and barred with black, and her thighs are paler. Again, one sees much the same trend toward masculinization of the female plumage as in the *tinnunculus* population of southern Africa. The immature bird resembles the female but is even darker with heavier black bars and streaks, and with a more broadly tipped black tail band.

The wing length of males ranges from 205–233 mm (8–9 in); of females, from 221–234 mm ($8\frac{1}{2}$–9 in), so that sexual size dimorphism is not pronounced (Brown and Amadon 1968). The male wing averages about 96.3 per cent of female wing length. Body weights apparently have not been recorded but probably do not differ significantly from those of *tinnunculus*.

The only species of kestrel in most of the East Indian region, *moluccensis* can be recognized at a distance in the field by its kestrel mannerisms and especially by the typical hovering flight. The Australian kestrel may occur with it in the Lesser Sundas and Java during the austral winter months, but it is a much paler coloured bird with greatly reduced black marks.

The Moluccan kestrel is said to be very common in suitable localities (Brown and Amadon 1968), but not much is known about the biology of this species. It frequents open country, including cultivated areas, entering towns readily, and is known to occur up to 1,525 m (5,000 ft) in elevation. Like other kestrels it perches on exposed branches of trees much of the time, searching the ground below for prey; or it flies out and hovers over open country.

The food consists of small mammals, lizards and probably small snakes, small passerine birds and large insects. These kestrels catch most of their food on the ground, but they also hawk some insects and small birds out of the air.

Virtually nothing is known about the breeding habits of *moluccensis*, except that it usually lays four eggs in nests in trees, and it sometimes nests in towns. The laying season is rather protracted, as one might expect for islands so close to the equator, from April to August in Java and from March to August in Celebes. These months generally correspond with the drier part of the year.

The distribution is entirely insular and occupies about 460,000 sq km (178,000 sq miles) of land area. Most of the islands are mountainous and originally were heavily forested, so that open habitats suitable for kestrels must have been limited in former times. It is quite likely that agriculture and forest-cutting have created additional usable habitat for this species, but even so there could hardly be more than a few thousand to a few tens of thousands of pairs. Someone should do a proper study of this species, especially since it is one of the few falcons to have occupied equatorial islands extensively.

R. DAVID DIGBY.

Australian Kestrel

(Nankeen Kestrel)

Falco cenchroides

Another geographically separate population, the Australian kestrel is a pale version of the common kestrel and is probably not really a distinct species from either *tinnunculus* or *moluccensis*. It is widely distributed and common throughout Australia, including Tasmania and smaller offshore islands, and also breeds in the highlands of New Guinea. It occurs to some extent in all habitats except dense forest, but reaches its greatest density in open forests and savannahs. Like other kestrels it seeks cultivated lands and does not shun urban environments.

The Australian or nankeen kestrel is resident over most of its range all year, but falcons nesting in the southern temperate latitudes of Australia are partly migratory. It would be interesting to know where the individuals that appear in the austral winter on Aru, Celebes, Lesser Sundas and Java come from. Australian kestrels also shift about some in response to local abundances of food, such as mouse plagues.

Sexual differences in plumage are as pronounced as in the Eurasian populations of *tinnunculus*. The adult male has a pale grey crown and nape with faint blackish shaft streaks. The back and upper wing-coverts are pale chestnut with very sparse, subterminal blackish marks on some feathers. The tail is plain, pale grey, tipped with white and with the usual black subterminal band. A faint, dark grey moustachial streak below the eye stands out from a greyish white cheek and whitish throat. The rest of the underparts are whitish with faintly darker shaft-streaks to some feathers. The adult female is a generally darker bird with a chestnut head, nape, back and tail. The dorsal feathers are more heavily streaked and barred with black. The tail has a buffy tip (in fresh plumage), black subterminal band, and nine to ten rows of narrow, indistinct black bars. She is more rufous below and more heavily streaked than the male.

This is a large kestrel, about the same size as the Eurasian species, and the kestrels on New Guinea average even larger (and darker) than those in Australia. It ranges from 30–36 cm (12–14 in) in body length with an approximate wingspan of 70–76 cm ($27\frac{1}{2}$–30 in). The wing measurement of adult males from Australia ranges from 237–255 mm ($9\frac{1}{2}$–10 in); from New Guinea, 254–262 mm ($9\frac{1}{2}$–$10\frac{1}{2}$ in); and the wing of females from Australia ranges from 255–275 mm (10–11 in): data from Brown and Amadon (1968). Penny and Jerry Olsen (1980) give the weights of three wild males as 162, 162, and 170 g ($5\frac{1}{2}$, 6 oz), and of one hatched and reared in captivity as 190 g ($6\frac{1}{2}$ oz). Three wild adult females had weights of 160, 190, and 192 g ($5\frac{1}{2}$, $6\frac{1}{2}$ oz); one reared in captivity was 200 g (7 oz). These data indicate little difference in weight between males and females; however, Brown and Amadon (1968) record a weight of 273 g ($9\frac{1}{2}$ oz) for one adult female.

Nankeen kestrels have much the same predatory habits as their Eurasian counterparts. They hunt mostly ground-dwelling prey, either from a stationary perch or by flying over open country and repeatedly turning into the wind to hover. The only other Australian raptor that hunts frequently the same way is the far less numerous black-shouldered kite (*Elanus notatus*).

Only recently have some quantitative studies on diet been made by Olsen, Vestjens and Olsen (1979). They found that while arthropods were the most frequently taken prey, vertebrates constituted the bulk of the food, about 69 per cent of the consumed biomass. Grasshoppers and other orthopterans were the most important arthropod prey, followed by beetles, spiders, moths and other lepidopterans, centipedes and ants. The occurrence of considerable numbers of arachnids in the diet of Australian kestrels is a difference from the recorded food habits of common and American kestrels. Birds, particularly starlings, make up a major part of the diet in settled districts; and in areas where mice reach plague proportions, kestrels feed almost exclusively on these rodents.

Where available, a tree cavity is the preferred nest-site, but the kestrels also use old nests of other birds. When tree sites are not available, they will nest in crevices on cliffs, on buildings, in caves, and on the Nullabar Plain they have been found inside blow-holes, one nest being 4.6 m (15 ft) below the surface (Serventy and Whittell 1967). Brown and Amadon (1968) also record the use of broken-out tops of tall ant-hills.

Over much of Australia laying occurs from July to December, but mainly in September and October; but in Western Australia September is the peak month. The clutch size is usually 3 to 5 eggs (mean of 99 clutches, 3.85 eggs); but the range is evidently from 1 to 7 eggs, and there is some indication that clutches vary in size in different years depending on seasonal feeding conditions. The mean brood size for 171 nests is 2.97 young, indicating that on average only about one egg is lost per nest, so that productivity is generally high as in other kestrels. (Data summarized from Olsen and Olsen 1980.)

The Australian kestrel occupies a total range in excess of 7.5 million sq km (2.9 million sq miles). Apparently no density figures or population estimates exist, but it is considered to be one of the two commonest raptors in Australia. If its nesting densities are comparable to those of *tinnunculus* in Eurasia – say one pair per 10 to 100 sq km – then there should be some 75,000 to 750,000 pairs in existence.

PLATE XXVIII
Australian Kestrel
Falco cenchroides
Adult male,
above left
Adult female,
below right
Map page 188

150

R. David Digby

American Kestrel
(Sparrow Hawk)

Falco sparverius

IGNORANTLY CALLED "SPARROW HAWK" by the European colonists of the New World, this brightly coloured little falcon is the American counterpart of the common kestrel, although it is about 25 per cent smaller than the Old World species. Indeed, except for the Seychelles kestrel, it is the smallest species in the genus *Falco*.

Paralleling the distribution of *tinnunculus* in Eurasia and Africa, *sparverius* has a very widespread range throughout the Western Hemisphere, breeding from above the Arctic Circle in Alaska and northwestern Canada (about to 67°N), south through most of Canada and the United States into Mexico, parts of Central America, and most of South America (excluding the Amazon Basin) to Tierra del Fuego at 55°S. It also occurs on most of the islands in the West Indies, and on Guadalupe Island (Mexico) and the Juan Fernandez Islands (Chile) in the Pacific Ocean.

The American kestrel occurs in a great variety of habitats from sea-level or below up to about 3,700 m (12,000 ft) in the Rockies and to 4,300 m (14,000 ft) in the Andes, but it requires open ground for hunting, and so it is most often found in habitats such as mountain meadows, burned or logged forest in early succession, marshlands, grasslands and savannahs of all sorts, deserts, open pine forests, and any kind of mixed woods and grasslands, agricultural lands, vacant building sites in cities and towns, airfields, athletic fields, cemetaries, highway and railway rights of way, electricity transmission lines, lake shores, and sea-coasts, especially in migration.

Males differ strikingly from females in plumage, and the American kestrel is the only species of *Falco* in which the juvenile male and female differ from each other as much as the adults do. Evidently there has been a strong selection for sexual dichromatism in most kestrels, but why sex differences should include the juvenile plumage in only this one species is puzzling. American kestrels do breed in their first year, so that sexual recognition becomes important before the first annual moult; but many other falcons are capable of breeding the first year in immature plumage, and, indeed, most male and female falcons recognize each other without strongly dimorphic plumage. Juvenile American kestrels are also peculiar in that they undergo a partial body moult in the first autumn of life (Parkes 1955).

There is a great deal of individual variability in the male plumage, but North American birds usually have a slate coloured crown with a central rufous patch (reduced or even absent in some) and distinctive facial features consisting of a whitish area around the beak, continuous with a white throat, white cheeks contrasting with a black moustachial streak below the eye, and a second black stripe running dorsoventrally along the posterior edge of the ear-coverts. The nape and sides of the neck are buffy apricot with a black "oscellus" on each side. The back is bright rufous with a few transverse black flecks. The wing coverts are grey with scattered black streaks, and the primaries and secondaries are black to greyish with white spots on the inner webs. The underparts are mostly buffy apricot to rufous with a variable amount of black spotting. The under wing-coverts are whitish, and the under tail-coverts are plain creamy buff. The tail is highly variable; generally it is rufous with a whitish tip and a broad subterminal black band, but the outer pair of rectrices have both webs white with four broad, black bars on the inner web anterior to the subterminal band. The adjacent pair also have a variable amount of white. (Friedmann 1950.)

The female is a less variable, more uniformly rufous brown bird with black barring on the upper surfaces. Her head and facial features are much like the male's but more subdued in colouring. Her underparts are buffy with brownish streaks. The tail is coloured like the back with a subterminal black band and 9 to 11 narrower black bands.

There is also much geographic variation in colour and pattern, particularly in the males. For example, in Cuba, the Isle of Pines and southern Bahamas, the kestrels occur in two distinct colour morphs: a rich, rufous phase, and a pale phase. In Puerto Rico, Virgin Islands and Lesser Antilles, the plumage is dark and richly coloured, and the tail feathers of the males have black shafts. In the lowland pine savannah of northeastern Nicaragua, the chestnut crown patch is greatly reduced or absent in both males and females, and the females have developed some masculine traits – grey upper wing-coverts and reduced barring on the back and scapulars (Howell 1965).

The size is also quite variable. Generally American kestrels are around 19–21 cm ($7\frac{1}{2}$–8 in) in length with wingspans of 50–60 cm ($19\frac{1}{2}$–$23\frac{1}{2}$ in), and have relatively shorter tails than in *tinnunculus* (about 64 to 67 per cent of wing length in different populations). Birds from the more northern and southern parts of the breeding range are, however, considerably larger than those from subtropical and tropical latitudes. The wing of North American males averages about 183 mm (174–198 mm; 7–8 in), of females, 195 mm (178–207 mm; 7–8 in); the wing of males from the southern half of South America (southern Peru to Tierra del Fuego) ranges from 183–200 mm (7–8 in); and sub-samples from Alaska and Tierra del

152

R. David Digby.

Fuego would probably average even larger. Males from Florida have wings measuring 165–180 mm (6½–7 in), females, 175–186 mm (7–7½ in); males from Puerto Rico, Virgin Islands and Lesser Antilles, 160–172 mm (6½ in), and females, 160–178 mm (6½–7 in) (Data from Brown and Amadon 1968). In Nicaragua, male wings average about 167.5 mm (160–179 mm; 6½–7 in), females, about 173 mm (167.5–177 mm; 6½–7 in). (Data from Howell 1965.)

Body weights vary geographically, too, and also seasonally, birds generally being heavier in winter. Craighead and Craighead (1956) give an average of 109 g (4 oz) for 50 North American males, and 119 g (4 oz) for 67 females. In my experience these figures are on the light side, and I believe that the weights Porter and Wiemeyer (1970) reported for captive yearlings are closer to norms for wild birds: males averaged 112 g (103–120 g; 3½–4 oz), and females averaged 141 g (126–166 g; 4½–6 oz). By comparison, the very small kestrels that Tom Howell (1965) found in the lowland pine savannah of northeastern Nicaragua weigh hardly more than large shrikes: five males averaged 73.4 g (63–78 g; 2–2½ oz), and five females, 81.0 g (75–87.6 g; 2½–4 oz). These kestrels and the ones on Puerto Rico and the Lesser Antilles are among the smallest representatives of the genus *Falco*. While these small forms of *sparverius* have predictably light wing-loadings (0.19 g per sq cm), the similar-sized *araea* of the Seychelles has a significantly heavier loading (0.24–0.27 g per sq cm).

Sexual size dimorphism is not very pronounced in American kestrels and varies in degree among different populations. The wing of males averages about 93.9 per cent of the female wing in North American populations, 92.1 per cent in Ecuador, Peru and northern Chile, but as much as 98.2 per cent in Puerto Rico, Virgin Islands and Lesser Antilles, and about 96.8 per cent in Nicaragua. The weight of males is around 90 to 91 per cent of female weight.

American kestrels in the northern parts of the breeding range – north of about 45°N – are highly migratory, while other populations are less so, and those in latitudes south of about 35°N are mostly year-round residents. The movements are not well understood, but apparently the northernmost breeders winter the farthest south; at any rate, typical northern kestrels are locally common in winter throughout Central America into Panama. In New York State and the northern half of the contiguous United States generally, some kestrels remain in the vicinity of their nesting territories through the year, while most leave and in some cases are replaced by other kestrels which move in from the north. Resident populations in states such as Florida, Texas and California are greatly augmented in winter by migrants from the north and from montane breeding habitats (Bent 1938, Brown and Amadon 1968, Cramp and Simmons 1980). To some extent the density and distribution of wintering populations are influenced by the availability of prey, especially by the numbers of microtine rodents, and by weather, snow cover, temperature and winds.

Males and females have somewhat different patterns of distribution in the winter. Males predominate in the northern parts of the winter range, while females are more common in the south (Roest 1957, Willoughby and Cade 1964). Moreover, males occupy habitats that are more wooded or otherwise covered, while females more often occur in open habitats away from trees, windbreaks, farmsteads and similar cover (Koplin 1973, Mills 1976, Stinson *et al.* 1981). These differences probably have evolved as a way to mitigate intraspecific competition for food, but it would be interesting to know why females occur in the more open habitats. Are they in some way better adapted to hunting in the open than males are, or vice versa? Why are males the ones to stay farther north?

The feeding habits are much like those of *tinnunculus*: the American kestrel is also a generalized predator of invertebrates and small vertebrates. Invertebrates include mainly insects, especially grasshoppers, but also scorpions and earthworms, the latter being taken on walking forays after rains when the worms are crawling above ground. In suburban areas of southern California I have seen kestrels land and walk about feeding on earthworms that have exposed themselves by crawling out of lawns on to wet sidewalks or pavements. Kestrels also feed on a variety of small reptiles (lizards and snakes), birds, and mammals including bats.

In his study of 47 nesting pairs of kestrels in a montane habitat at Sagehen Creek in the Sierra Nevadas, Tom Balgooyen (1976) found that the prey ranged in size from insects weighing 0.05 g or less to birds weighing 89 g (3 oz). Insects as a group constituted 31.7 per cent of the diet by weight of this breeding population, reptiles made up 26 per cent, mammals 25.7 per cent, and birds 16.6 per cent. Vertebrates made up nearly 70 per cent of the total biomass consumed, again showing the similarity between American kestrels and common kestrels. Data on the diet of kestrels in Chile also confirm the importance of vertebrates (Yanez *et al.* 1980).

Balgooyen observed 813 attacks on prey: 70 per cent resulted in capture, and there was no difference in success between males and females or in the types of prey they hunted. Earlier in the season when the kestrels hunted mostly birds and mammals, the rate of capture was only 40 per cent, but later on when insects, especially grasshoppers, became abundant, the rate of capture increased to 90 per cent. The kestrels launched attacks at prey by still-hunting from a perch 97.2 per cent of the times; they attacked from a hovering position only 1.8 per cent of the times, and 1.0 per cent of the times they made hawking flights in the air. These kestrels hovered only when the wind was moving at 5 km per hour (3 mph) or faster. The maximum range of hunting flights from a perch was 275 m (900 ft), but the average was only 34 m (112 ft).

Mated kestrels engage in a rather prolonged period of pre-laying activities. After the males establish their nesting territories, which tend to be all-purpose in nature (Balgooyen 1976), the females join them. At first the females are only loosely bonded to particular males, and they may move about among two or more territorial males before settling down with a particular one. Promiscuous matings occur rather frequently during this initial phase (Cade 1955, Balgooyen 1976). Eventually monogamous pairs are formed, copulations become frequent between mates for several weeks before the first eggs (Balgooyen recorded five acts of copulation in 10.5 minutes), and the male keeps busy bringing food to the sedentary female, which eats to repletion and then caches any extra food the male brings to her.

Nest-site inspections and eventual selection take place at this time too. American kestrels are much more fixed on tree cavities as nest-sites than *tinnunculus*, although they sometimes nest in a pot-hole or other cranny on a cliff, particularly in the western United States (also on Guadalupe Island), in holes of earth banks, not infrequently in some kind of enclosed space on a building, and exceptionally in an old stick nest of some other bird, especially the enclosed nests of magpies. They readily accept nest-boxes as substitutes for tree cavities and even seem to prefer them to natural sites.

There are several indications that the availability of suitable tree cavities may be the chief density limiting factor on breeding populations of kestrels. For one thing, kestrels engage in a great deal of conflict with other hole-nesting species. Since they do not excavate their own holes, kestrels depend on natural cavities or on holes drilled by large woodpeckers such as flickers, red-headed woodpeckers, pileated woodpeckers and others. Not only do the kestrels have to compete with woodpeckers for their holes, they also have to contend with such possessive hole-nesters as starlings, screech owls and squirrels. Kestrels are not always the winners of these contests.

More convincing evidence comes, however, from the use of nest-boxes. Nesting densities of kestrels have been considerably increased by putting out suitably located boxes in places where natural cavities are scarce or absent. Alex Nagy (1963), former curator of the Hawk Mountain Sanctuary in Pennsylvania, erected half a dozen nest-boxes on his 130-ha (320-acre) farm, and for a period of 8 years prior to 1961 he always had one or two pairs breeding in the boxes. In 1961 he increased the number of boxes to 9, and owing to a favourable food year he had six pairs nesting in the boxes and one pair under the eaves of a building. The nearest distance between two pairs was only 33.5 m (110 ft). The seven pairs produced 31 young from 32 eggs! In Wisconsin, Hamerstrom *et al.* (1973) put up 48 boxes on a 20,243-ha (50,000-acre) study area in 1968, after two had been used before, and they studied the occupants through 1972 for a total of 252 nest-box years. They noted activity by kestrels in 77 cases, and 204 young kestrels fledged from 51 successful nests; during the same period there were only two natural nests, which produced five young. These and other North American examples parallel the case in Holland, where Cavé (1968) introduced 246 nest-boxes into an area recently reclaimed from the sea. The very next year, 109 pairs of common kestrels nested in the area. These examples show how responsive kestrels are to new nesting opportunities, and this simple technique offers great potential for significantly increasing populations.

American kestrels lay from 3 to 7 eggs but typically 4 or 5. Balgooyen (1976) found that 42 clutches in his study area averaged 4 eggs. The hatching rate of these 168 eggs was 89.3 per cent, and 98 per cent of the hatchlings survived to leave the nest, for an overall success of 87.5 per cent of eggs laid. This high productive output is typical of kestrel populations and is no doubt related in part to the security provided by nesting in tree cavities, as in the case of other hole-nesting birds. Also, though not widely recognized, some pairs of kestrels in more southern latitudes are double-brooded; cases have been reported in Florida, Tennessee and southern California. The incidence of two broods per year is likely to be even higher in tropical environments, as Johnson (1965) states that in Chile and adjacent parts of Peru, Bolivia, and Argentina, after raising a first brood in October, kestrels frequently produce a second in December or January.

The density of nesting kestrels varies greatly in different parts of the breeding range. In the Sierra Nevada Mountains where Balgooyen (1976) found a population apparently spaced out in all purpose territories, the average size of 32 territories was 109.4 ha (270 acres), but the total study area of 18,100 ha held 18 pairs one year and 25 pairs the other, giving overall densities of one pair per 1,006 ha (2,480 acres) to one pair per 724 ha (1,780 acres). In a 3,072-ha area of Jackson Hole, Wyoming, Craighead and Craighead (1956) found 11 pairs nesting in 1947 and 10 pairs in 1948, or an average of one pair per 307 ha (760 acres), although the actual defended territories averaged only 129.6 ha. In a 9,472-ha region of southern Michigan where nest-sites apparently were limiting, Craighead and Craighead found only 2 pairs nesting in 1942, 4 pairs in 1948, and 5 pairs in 1949 (range of one pair per 1,894 to 4,736 ha; 4,680–11,700 acres). Two other similar sized study plots in southern Michigan (9,216 ha each) had no nesting kestrels. It appears that local densities in North America range from approximately one pair per sq km to one pair per 100 sq km (39 sq miles) or more.

If one assumes that breeding densities north of 45°N (in an area of some 7.39 million sq km; 2.8 million sq miles), are on the order of one pair per 100 sq km, and densities in the rest of the North American breeding range to the south (some 5.76 million sq km; 2.2 million sq miles), are about one pair per 5 sq km (2 sq miles), then the North American breeding population must number more than 1.2 million pairs. The Central and South American population may well be equally as large, so that the total population of *sparverius* could be larger than that of *tinnunculus*, even though the former occupies a smaller total distribution. It is also likely that the distribution and density of kestrel populations are increasing in the tropics as a result of human land uses, especially from deforestation in Amazionia.

155

Madagascar Kestrel

Falco newtoni

ANOTHER GEOGRAPHIC COUNTERPART of the common kestrel, *newtoni* is endemic to Madagascar and the atoll of Aldabra in the Indian Ocean, with a few individuals straying rarely to the Comoro Islands. It is about the same size as the American kestrel. Like most other kestrels it occurs in open country, and it ranges from sea-level up to 1,830 m (6,000 ft).

There are two colour phases. The "normal" adult male has a greyish rufous crown and nape with black streaks and chestnut upperparts with black spots. His upper tail-coverts are grey with black spots, his tail grey with a broad subterminal black band and six to seven narrower black bars and a whitish tip. The primaries are blackish brown with white to chestnut blotches on the inner webs, while the secondaries are chestnut with black bars. The underparts are whitish, unmarked on throat, thighs and under tail-coverts, but streaked on the breast and spotted on the belly and under wing-coverts with black. The adult female is very similar, but she has more chestnut in the crown and less grey.

In the dark rufous colour phase the crown and nape are nearly black, contrasting with a dark chestnut back and upper wings. The underparts are dark chestnut with black streaks and spots, including the under wing-coverts which are chestnut and black and contrast sharply with the pale wing quills. The fleshy parts are bright orange instead of the usual yellow.

Falcons resident on Aldabra average smaller in size and are lighter in colour, particularly females, some of which have unmarked whitish underparts. This population is sometimes referred to as the Aldabra kestrel and is given the subspecific designation, *F. newtoni aldabranus*. (Summarized from Brown and Amadon 1968.)

First year birds look like females but are more heavily streaked on their crowns and undersides. Also, their wing and tail feathers are edged and tipped with buff.

Sexual size dimorphism is more pronounced in this species than in some kestrels. According to Siegfried and Frost (1970), the wing length of males from Madagascar averages about 193 mm (191–201 mm; $7\frac{1}{2}$–8 in), or 91.5 per cent of the female wing, which averages 211 mm (198–220 mm; 8–$8\frac{1}{2}$ in), while the weight of seven females averaged 144 g (131–153 g; $4\frac{1}{2}$–$5\frac{1}{2}$ oz) and the weight of four males, 105 g (90–117 g; 3–4 oz), or 72.9 per cent of female weight. The tail is also relatively short for a kestrel, 64 to 65 per cent of wing length.

In Madagascar this kestrel is common and very tame, frequenting towns, villages and roadsides, as well as open country – natural grasslands and agricultural lands. Individuals often roost under the eaves of buildings and return to the same places nightly, so that the walls become marked with droppings (Rand 1936).

This species hunts like other kestrels but may hover less frequently, although Siegfried and Frost (1970) observed that it often hunts from a low hovering position. Usually it still-hunts by sitting on ant-hills, trees, electricity poles or similar perches and watching for prey on the ground. It takes small mammals, occasional birds, reptiles and frogs, but mainly insects, which make up about 75 per cent of all items caught. Most prey is taken from the ground, except for some insects which are hawked in the air. Milon, Petter and Randrianasolo (1973) noted that the Madagascar kestrel tends to be crepuscular in habits, and they observed it hunting around Tananarive in company with Eleonora's falcons.

The breeding season in Madagascar begins in September. This falcon nests in buildings, on rocky ledges, in tree cavities, and sometimes on epiphytes growing on tree trunks. Apparently only the female incubates, and the male calls her from the nest to be fed.

Numbers on Madagascar have not been estimated, but it seems likely that cultivation, deforestation and the growth of towns and villages have favoured this species. For example, Siegfried and Frost (1970) counted 195 kestrels along 798 km (495 miles) of road in the deforested central highlands (4.1 km per bird), whereas along 572 km (355 miles) in the forested eastern lowlands, they only found 12 birds (one per 47.7 km). The species tends to be replaced by the barred kestrel in the humid eastern forests.

If *newtoni* occurs in densities comparable to other kestrels, then Madagascar with an area of 585,188 sq km (225,940 sq miles) might have in the order of 30,000 to 60,000 pairs. It is far less abundant on Aldabra, and the population there is listed as "rare" in the IUCN/ICBP *Red Data Book* (King 1977). Apparently this isolated population is more or less stable at about 100 individuals, which may be as many as the habitat can support. Benson and Penny (1971) suggested that this kestrel may have colonized Aldabra only after the arrival of man, for it seems to be very dependent for nest-sites on buildings, introduced palms, and old nests of the pied crow, which also probably did not take up residence in the atoll until human activities had created conditions favourable to its survival. The distribution of nest-boxes in suitable areas might well result in some increase in the numbers of this small, isolated population of kestrels.

PLATE XXX
Madagascar Kestrel
Falco newtoni
Adult male
Map page 188

Mauritius Kestrel

Falco punctatus

THE MAURITIUS KESTREL is the rarest species in the genus *Falco* and one of the rarest and most endangered of all birds. My interest was first drawn to this species with the publication in 1966 of the Aves section of the IUCN *Red Data Book*. The Mauritius kestrel was listed as a "critically endangered species" with a relict population then estimated to number only 20 to 25 birds. These survived in the remnants of native forest that had managed to withstand the massive destruction by the human population, one of the densest in the world, only because it had to be left growing in the rugged gorges and escarpment in the southwestern corner of Mauritius. Little known even from former times when the kestrel was more common and widely distributed over Mauritius, it seemed likely that this unique species might quickly pass into oblivion before anything significant and rewarding became known about its habits and ecology.

One of my graduate students, E. J. Willoughby, and I (1964) had recently completed some experiments on breeding American kestrels in captivity, and it seemed to me that captive propagation might be an appropriate procedure to use to save the Mauritius kestrel from extinction. This would be done in conjunction with some detailed field studies to determine the critical factors in the life history and ecology of the species, factors that might be manipulated in some way to increase its chances for survival.

I began to explore these ideas slowly with various authorities, and finally in the early 1970s the International Council for Bird Preservation, the World Wildlife Fund (US), and the New York Zoological Society became interested in the plight of the kestrel and other endangered birds on Mauritius. As a consequence, one of my associates, Dr Stanley A. Temple, was able to go over to Mauritius for two years to begin a programme of research and conservation that has continued under the sponsorship of these three organizations and in co-operation with the government of Mauritius. The work has been carried on by a series of project leaders including (besides Temple) W. Newlands, P. Trefrey, D. S. McKelvey, F. N. Steele and C. G. Jones. All have contributed in some way to our recent knowledge about this falcon, which continues to survive, as Jones (1980) says, "despite our conservation efforts".

Slightly smaller in linear dimensions than the common kestrel, the Mauritius kestrel is a heavy-bodied, little falcon which actually weighs more, on average, than *tinnunculus*. It is also proportioned differently and has a decidedly accipitrine shape and habits, as befits a forest-dwelling raptor. Brown and Amadon (1968) give the range for the wing measurement of males as 168–182 mm ($6\frac{1}{2}$–7 in); for females, 183–186 mm(7–$7\frac{1}{2}$ in), although Temple (in press) found the average to lie close to the lower figures in both cases. The tail length is around 74 to 75 per cent of the wing measurement, an even more extreme divergence from "typical" falcon proportions than shown by the New Zealand falcon. Temple weighed three adult males which averaged 178 g (6 oz) and five adult females which averaged 231 g (8 oz). Thus, sexual size dimorphism is rather pronounced in this kestrel, males averaging 92 to 94 per cent of the female's linear measurements and only 77 per cent of female body weight, a great sexual difference comparable to that of *newtoni*.

The plumage is remarkable for a kestrel in that there is no difference between male and female; both wear a hen-like plumage similar to that of the female common kestrel. The crown, nape and upperparts are chestnut, streaked on the crown and barred on the back, upper tail- and wing-coverts and secondaries with black. The tail is also chestnut with a subterminal and six to seven narrower black bands. The underparts are whitish with large, distinct black spots and heart-shaped marks on individual feathers.

No one knows how many kestrels there were on Mauritius before man began to destroy the falcon's habitat, but they apparently were never abundant, although widely distributed from sea-level into the mountains in the native evergreen forests, which once covered most of the island and which are estimated to have extended over 1,644 sq km (630 sq miles) in 1753. If we allow a generous average of one pair of kestrels per 5 to 10 sq km, there could have been between 164 and 328 pairs on average, so that the total species population has probably never numbered more than a few hundred birds in the best of times.

When Stan Temple arrived on the island in 1973 he was only able to locate six or seven kestrels, although subsequent events proved that at least nine must have been present (Temple 1974, 1975, 1977). The kestrels failed to produce any young in the 1973 breeding season, and one pair of adults disappeared from their area under suspicious circumstances during the deer hunting season in the forest. It was then decided to take a mated pair of adults into captivity for propagation, and the birds were trapped in December 1973. Unfortunately, the female soon died, and she was replaced by another, unmated female trapped in March 1974 – leaving, as it turned out, two pairs in the wild to begin the 1974 breeding season. A total of six known birds represented the entire species *punctatus*.

One of the wild pairs nested in a tree cavity, which seems to have been the usual kind of site chosen

158

R. DAVID DIGBY

by the kestrels in recent years. Their nest was depredated by the introduced macaque monkeys that have become a great menace to all arboreal nesting birds on the island. The other pair nested in a pot-hole on the sheer face of a tall cliff where no monkey could climb; three young fledged from that nest in 1974, marking the first time in several years that the kestrel population had increased – to a total of nine birds.

Fortunately the progeny from this pair continued the habit of nesting in inaccessible places on cliffs, so that by 1976 the wild population had increased to 12 birds, including three known pairs – two productive pairs nesting on cliffs and the tree-nesting pair which continued to be unsuccessful. Since 1976 the wild population has remained stable at around 15 birds and has not continued to grow at the initial rapid rate following the successful cliff-nesting in 1974 (Jones 1980). However, in November 1980, Carl Jones found a fourth pair of kestrels nesting in a new or previously unknown location, so that the situation in the field continues to show some improvement, especially in view of the fact that during the years 1973–78 five adults and three nestlings were removed from the wild for captive breeding.

The Mauritius kestrel is a rather confiding species, and recent field workers have often been able to approach within a few metres of a sitting bird. At the same time, owing to the rugged terrain and dense forest it inhabits, the kestrel can be quite elusive and difficult to observe, often remaining hidden like a hawk within the crown of a tree or perched motionless on some sheltered vantage point.

This kestrel is adept at hunting below the forest canopy and uses several techniques for searching and pursuing. Most often it searches from a perch, often a concealed one, but it also sometimes hovers over open scrub in typical kestrel fashion and then drops into the undergrowth for prey. Its short, rounded wings are not well suited to hovering, however, and this tactic is not frequently used (see Jones 1980 for some examples). It also quarters slowly back and forth just over the canopy and dives through the cover for prey. Sometimes it hawks flying insects out of the air, and it has even been noted hopping on the ground after locusts along the seashore. Inside the forest, under the canopy, it employs the accipitrine tactic of flying from tree to tree, stopping in a concealed position to watch, and stalking after arboreal prey such as geckos by hopping rapidly along branches after them. Most prey is actually caught in a quick surprise attack or by tail-chasing.

The Mauritius kestrel feeds on insects, especially aerial forms such as dragonflies but also on terrestrial cockroaches and crickets; on lizards, especially arboreal geckos; on small birds; and occasionally on mice and shrews. Lizards and small birds appear to be the most important items in terms of biomass; and the kestrel consumes large numbers of the iridescent green tree geckos of the genus *Phelsuma*. The native white-eye (*Zosterops bourbonica*) is probably the most important prey species according to Jones (1980), and it also feeds on other passerines such as the introduced common waxbill. It is interesting to recall that sexual size dimorphism in this kestrel is rather pronounced, as it is in other bird-eating falcons.

So far as is known, most of the breeding biology follows pretty much the usual kestrel pattern. The breeding season is protracted, though, and one suspects that at least some of the females can be double-brooded, as demonstrated in one case in captivity (Jones 1980). Courtship usually begins in September, and eggs can be laid any time from October to January, but (on limited data) October and November appear to be the peak months. The known nest-sites, all recorded since 1973, have been either in a tree cavity or a pot-hole on a sheer cliff. It would be interesting to know whether these kestrels once nested in epiphytes, as the barred kestrel has recently been reported to do on Madagascar, before the introduced monkeys made such locations impossible to use.

The clutch is usually three eggs but sometimes fewer. Incubation requires about 30 days, and the young remain in the nest for 38 to 39 days. One interesting difference from other species of kestrel is that the young remain with their parents in the vicinity of the nest-site until the next breeding season, a very long period of association between parents and offspring.

Today the few remaining, no doubt highly inbred Mauritius kestrels survive in a remnant, degraded forests of some 3,035 ha (7,500 acres) in area in the Black River Gorges and similar environs. Habitat destruction and alteration have no doubt been the overriding causes for the reduction of this species to extreme rarity, although human persecution of the so-called "mangeur de poules" and nest depredations by introduced monkeys have been contributing factors. The latter may well be the most important factor limiting the population within its present restricted range (Temple 1977). It is also quite possible that genetic deterioration from inbreeding among the few remaining individuals has resulted in a lessened reproductive capacity, or to greater susceptibility to diseases or other stresses.

Unlike the Seychelles kestrel and most other species in the *Tinnunculus* subgenus, the Mauritius kestrel has shown no adaptability to the altered environments created by man. It has not adapted to man-made structures as nest-sites or even established itself in stands of exotic trees. For reasons that are not entirely clear it seems to be ecologically tied to the native evergreen forest as its habitat. This fact means that there are limited possibilities for preserving this species on the island of Mauritius. The available native habitat might well be saturated with 10 pairs of kestrels; moreover, there is uncertainty as to whether even the present 3,035 hectares will remain intact much longer.

The only long range future for such a species in nature lies in the possibility of a successful translocation of kestrels on to some other island, such as Réunion, where a sizeable native evergreen forest still exists. The political and philosophical barriers against such a move are so horrendous, the only way I can envisage that it could ever happen would be for the government of New Zealand to annex the Mascarene Islands.

160

Seychelles Kestrel

Falco araea

$\mathbf{N}$OW RESTRICTED TO three or four small islands of the Seychelles group in the Indian Ocean, this kestrel is the smallest species in the genus *Falco*. The wing measurement of males (from museum skins) averages 148.5 mm (146–151 mm; $5\frac{1}{2}$–6 in); of females, 154 mm (152–156 mm; 6 in). The tail is relatively long, even for a kestrel, being 71 to 72 per cent of wing length. There is little sexual size dimorphism; the linear measurements of males average 96 to 98 per cent of female measurements. Three males average 73 g (62–74 g; 2–$2\frac{1}{2}$ oz), and five females 87 g (84–90 g; 3 oz) (S.A. Temple), placing these falcons in the same class as the small representatives of *sparverius* in Nicaragua (Howell 1976).

The adult male's plumage is a brightly coloured, contrasting dress that is clearly allied to the cock plumage of such sexually dichromatic species as the common kestrel and lesser kestrel. The crown and nape are slate grey, contrasting with a dark chestnut back spotted with black. The upper tail-coverts and tail are grey, and the tail is further tipped with white and bears a broad subterminal and three to four narrower black bars. The upper wing-coverts and secondaries are chestnut with black spots and bars. The sides of the head and neck are greyish, the throat pale rufous white. There is a faint moustachial streak. The rest of the underparts are rufous buff, paling to whitish on the under tail-coverts and to pinkish buff on the under wing-coverts. (From Brown and Amadon 1968.)

This species is also singular in the degree to which the adult female's plumage has become masculinized. The female differs from the male only in being slightly paler above and below, but she wears none of the usual brownish feathering so characteristic of the "hen" plumage of most female kestrels.

As recently as 1939 this species occurred on most of the granitic islands of the Seychelles, but although it is known to have experienced a contraction of its range since then, its status as a species remained unclear until the studies by C. J. Feare, S. A. Temple and J. Proctor (1974) in the early 1970s. By 1965, Gaymer *et al.* (1969) thought that *araea* was restricted to Mahé and numbered no more than 30 birds. The first edition of the IUCN *Red Data Book* listed the Seychelles kestrel as a "critically endangered" species (Vincent 1966).

The species is now known to be well distributed all over Mahé and some small adjacent islets (*ca.* 140 sq km; 54 sq miles), on Silhouette (12 sq km; $4\frac{1}{2}$ sq miles), and to a restricted extent on Praslin (67 sq km; 26 sq miles). Roadside surveys on Mahé, mostly below the 250 metre contour, yielded a minimum of 49 pairs rather regularly spaced apart. Close observations of five pairs revealed that the size of home ranges, which probably remain stable the year round, varied from 103.2 ha (255 acres) to 49.8 ha (123 acres); average 82.8 ha. On the basis of this small size of home ranges and the widespread distribution over the island, Feare, Temple and Proctor estimated that there could be 100 pairs on Mahé alone. They also estimated at least 10 pairs on Silhouette but found only a couple of birds on Praslin and none at all on La Digue, Frigate, Felicité, Cousin, Cousine, Curieuse or Aride, although Penny (1974) included La Digue as a place where kestrels are seen rarely. The population now appears to be holding stable at 100 to 120 pairs, and the species has been re-classified as "rare" in the revised *Red Data Book* (King 1977).

This kestrel occurs both in open country and in dense forest. Indeed, the latter was probably its original habitat, when one considers the fact that the Seychelles were largely covered with forest before the islands were settled by man in the eighteenth century. Also, its long tail and short wings appear to be adaptations associated with flight in wooded habitat, and it has often been observed hunting in dense forest. It apparently hunts mainly, if not exclusively, from a perch and has never been reported to hover, traits which further indicate a primary affinity for forest.

The principal prey seem to be lizards, especially skinks (*Mabuya seychellensis*) but also geckos, which presumably are snatched from the trunks and branches of trees; large insects are also important items of food; occasionally a small bird such as a fody or white-eye is caught; and sometimes, mice. The local name, "manguer des poules", is surely a misnomer, for the most this tiny falcon might do is to catch recently hatched chicks.

According to M. Penny (1974), who has spent much time in the Seychelles, these kestrels probably originally nested in holes among the rocks on mountain-sides, although it is not clear why they should not also have used tree cavities. In any case, the introduced barn owls have taken over the rocks and the church towers, which were also favoured by the kestrels. Now the falcons nest mainly in the open, thatched roofs of houses or in the bowl-shaped base of fronds of the coconut palms, which have largely replaced native forest in the lowlands.

The clutch is remarkably small for a falcon – usually one or two eggs, although Penny mentions finding one brood of three young in a palm tree. The breeding season extends from September to March and suggests the possibility that the females may be double-brooded. If so, the small clutch size becomes easier to understand.

Conservation education in the Seychelles apparently has brought about some change in local attitude toward the kestrel, and it is no longer persecuted as much as it used to be (King 1977). The species has shown considerable ability to adapt to altered habitats created by human occupancy, and to adjust to competition for nest-sites from barn owls. Its numbers, which remain small for a total species population, might well be further increased by providing nest-boxes in suitable vacant areas on Mahé and on other islands where the kestrel presently does not occur at all.

PLATE XXXII
Seychelles Kestrel
Falco araea
Adult female
Map page 188

Lesser Kestrel

Falco naumanni

Judging from their many similarities in plumage, the lesser kestrel must be closely related to the common kestrel, although its habits are quite different, being a highly social and essentially flocking species on its breeding grounds, in migration, and during its non-breeding sojourn mostly south of the equator in Africa where roosting aggregations of 6,000 to 10,000 kestrels have been observed. As its name implies, the lesser kestrel is a somewhat smaller and slimmer bird, with a body length of 29–32 cm ($11\frac{1}{2}$–$12\frac{1}{2}$ in) and a wingspan of 58–72 cm (23–$28\frac{1}{2}$ in).

There is little difference between males and females in linear measurements but a surprising difference in body weights. For example, the wing measurement for adult males from the western Palearctic averages 239 mm, for females 240 mm ($9\frac{1}{2}$ in); and of the six standard measurements given in Cramp and Simmons (1980) only those for tail length and length of toe are significantly different between the sexes. The tail length averages 60 per cent of the wing measurement in males and 62 per cent in females; both sexes are relatively shorter tailed and longer winged than the common kestrel. Thus, based on standard linear measurements, one naturally concludes that sexual size dimorphism is virtually non-existent in this species, and some theorists have made a special point about this apparent lack of difference in relation to the lesser kestrel's highly insectivorous diet and weak intraspecific aggressiveness (Newton 1979, Walter 1979).

On the other hand, the recorded adult body weights (summarized by Cramp and Simmons 1980) – while extremely variable, males ranging from 90–172 g (3–6 oz) and females from 138–208 g (5–$7\frac{1}{2}$ oz) – indicate that on average males weigh only about 76 per cent as much as females do. This is a very marked dimorphism for a kestrel and represents the same degree of difference found in some of the bird-hunting falcons, such as the merlin. Obviously the female has a much heavier wing-loading than the male: she consequently performs differently in the air and should have different prey-catching abilities from the more buoyant male. (It would be interesting for someone to record the difference in frequency and characteristics of hovering in males and females; females should hover less, and flap more during hovering, than males.)

Why are the body weights so variable in this species? The lightest male is only 52 per cent of the heaviest; the lightest female, 66 per cent. Do these ranges reflect true individual differences in size (mass), or do they indicate wide fluctuations in nutritional state (fat accumulation) based on seasonal or other differences in food intake? The latter seems most likely, but the existing studies on this species do not enlighten us.

The plumage of the adult male resembles that of the common kestrel, except that it has no dark spots on the chestnut back, and the inner wing is mostly blue-grey in the lesser kestrel rather than chestnut. No dark moustache or other prominent facial features are present. The underparts are lighter and less marked than in the common kestrel, and the whiteness of the underwing is especially prominent, presenting a shiny, flashing appearance when the male turns suddenly into the light, as he does in flight display.

The adult female is even more similar in plumage to *tinnunculus* than the male, and correct identification of the two females in the field is difficult on details of plumage alone. Generally the female lesser kestrel has paler and less streaked underparts, especially the underwings and under tail-coverts. The juveniles of both sexes are like the adult female. Some immature males, after a partial post-juvenile moult, have noticeably grey heads and some grey in the tail, but most are indistinguishable from females before the first complete moult.

The talons of the lesser kestrel are unusual in colour, ranging from yellowish white to pale brown. The only other falcons with such pale talons are the red-footed falcons and the white gyrfalcons.

The lesser kestrel has a breeding distribution in the Palearctic that is almost totally separated from areas in Africa, Arabia, and the Indian Subcontinent where it spends the non-breeding period of its annual cycle. The breeding range consists of several disjunct areas and isolated nesting colonies, so that it is not easy to summarize or quantify in area. There are about 20 isolated breeding populations – mostly single colonies – in North Africa from northern Morocco to the Libyan coast, and a few nesting localities, still, in Israel, Lebanon and Syria. In Europe there is an extensive breeding distribution through most of Spain and eastern Portugal; small, isolated patches of breeding range occur in southern France, Sardinia, Sicily, southeastern Italy, Austria, Romania and elsewhere in eastern Europe; and a large part of Greece and Turkey fall within the regular breeding range. The latter is continuous with a large breeding area around the Black and Caspian seas in the Soviet Union. Lesser kestrels also breed extensively throughout much of the Soviet steppe and forest-steppe regions north to about 56° 15′N around Kukmov and to 55°N

164

in the Trans-Ural region. There have been isolated colonies nesting in the Trans-Baikal region, and there is one other, fairly extensive, isolated breeding area in eastern Mongolia, Manchuria and North China, about which little is known. (Summarized from Dementiev 1951, Cramp and Simmons 1980.)

A few lesser kestrels overwinter in southern Spain, southern Turkey and in northwestern Africa, but the great bulk of the breeding population migrates out of the Palearctic to spend the months of October to March in Africa south of the Sahara, excluding the Congo Basin. They are not nearly as abundant in western Africa and southwestern Africa as they are in eastern and southeastern Africa, nor are they as common north of the equator as they are south. The bulk of the population occurs from Zambia and Zimbabwe south into Botswana and, especially, South Africa, where it outnumbers all other migratory and resident species of *Falco*. Apparently even most of the eastern Asiatic kestrels migrate into Africa, although ringing records are not numerous; but some birds move into southern Arabia, and into the Indian Subcontinent as far south as the Godavari River valley. (From Dementiev 1951 and Cramp and Simmons 1980.)

Both on its breeding grounds and in its southern quarters, the lesser kestrel is a highly insectivorous falcon which inhabits open arid or semi-arid landscapes wherever ground-dwelling or aerial insects are abundant. These insects are usually most accessible on and over warm or hot, lightly vegetated, partly bare ground. Lesser kestrels depend on a *high* density of insect prey, and both annual and seasonal variations in density and distribution result from local or regional scarcities and abundances of insects, especially orthopterans (see Moreau 1972). In the Palearctic breeding range these kestrels occur primarily in association with the Mediterranean vegetational zone, with continental steppes and forest-steppes, and semi-desertic lands, penetrating slightly into temperate and boreal zones at the extreme northern limits of the range. The lesser kestrel is mainly a lowland species, not nesting regularly above 500 m (1,600 ft), and usually lower, in Europe, although in Asia it nests regularly up to 1,500 m (4,900 ft) and exceptionally up to 3,000 m (9,800 ft) in the Tien Shan Mountains (Dementiev 1951).

In migration lesser kestrels can be found flying over a wide range of habitats, but they seek out savannahs, grass veld, open scrub, croplands, or similar open habitats where insects are abundant and vulnerable, to spend the non-breeding season. The high veld of the Transvaal and Orange Free State in South Africa is prime habitat at this season.

This kestrel is an opportunistic feeder, exploiting a wide range of small aerial and terrestrial animals. Thus, the food includes, besides insects, various other invertebrates, particularly scorpions and centipedes, and small vertebrates, particularly lizards. Insects predominate, however, and include chiefly the larger Orthoptera such as field crickets, grasshoppers, bush-crickets and mole-crickets; Coleoptera, especially chafers and dung-beetles, and ground-beetles; flying ants; flying termites; and dragonflies; but many other groups and species have also been recorded.

Franco and Andrada (1977) analyzed 23,960 prey items from pellets collected throughout the year in southwestern Spain: 94 per cent consisted of invertebrates; 6 per cent were vertebrates (64 per cent and 36 per cent by weight of items). Orthopterans made up 60 per cent of the individuals; coleopterans, 22 per cent. Vertebrates consisted of 1,078 small mammals, 271 reptiles, 52 birds, and one parsley frog (*Pelodytes punctatus*).

A somewhat different picture emerged from an analysis of 25,097 items obtained from pellets in Austria (Glutz *et al.* 1971). Again, orthopterans predominated at 67 per cent of all items with coleopterans second at 29 per cent; however, grasshoppers and vertebrates were almost absent, the latter forming only 0.4 per cent of the total, which was mostly small mammals. (See Cramp and Simmons 1980.)

It is interesting to note that the male lesser kestrel seldom offers small insects to his female during food transfer ceremonies prior to incubation. These items are much more likely to be small mammals, birds or especially lizards, or large invertebrates such as centipedes. (The kestrels bite off the centipedes' heads and cast them away before eating the remainder.) These carcasses dangle conspicuously in the male's feet during display flights and presumably serve to attract and stimulate the female. They are also relatively large, nutritious packages of food and may aid in rapidly building up the female's condition to allow for the development of her eggs, which constitute a significant energy demand on her system.

It has also been noted that as the nestlings grow older, a higher percentage of vertebrates is brought to the nest (Franco and Andrada 1977). Could this change reflect activity by the larger female, which stops brooding around the fourteenth day of the nestlings' lives and starts hunting again? Possibly she catches and brings back larger-sized prey, on average, than the small male. It is tempting to think so, but much more carefully collected data are needed to test this hypothesis.

In keeping with their social nature, lesser kestrels usually hunt in small parties or large, disorganized flocks flying 10–15 m (30–50 ft) above the ground and continually turning into the wind to hover and check the ground before moving on to make another sweep. They typically hover for shorter periods and with less wing-flapping than common kestrels, more often hanging motionless in the wind in a standing glide, before swooping down to pounce on prey on the ground. They also commonly hawk flying insects out of the air much like hobbies, taking them in downward swoops and quick throw-ups from below with the feet up. They follow grass-fires and also descend to the ground and catch locust hoppers by stalking on foot. According to Meinertzhagen (1959), they can become so gorged on these abundant and easily caught prey as to make flight difficult. They also sometimes take insects attracted to street lamps or floodlights at night. Particularly in the non-breeding season where insects are swarming in great numbers, lesser kestrels often hunt in mixed flocks with common kestrels, red-footed falcons, and hobbies.

One of the most gregarious of all falcons, lesser kestrels nearly always nest in colonies, though solitary pairs have been found, and the social organization and behaviour of this species deviates considerably from that typical of most falcons. The colonies vary in size from 2 to more than 500 pairs, but a common number is 15 to 25 pairs. Territorial defence, if any, is limited to the immediate nest-site and its ledge or entrance, so that the spacing of pairs in a colony appears to be determined by the physical geometry of available sites and not by intraspecific aggressiveness, although this subject needs more study.

The nest-sites are holes or recesses in tall buildings, typically a church or cathedral, or in an old wall or ruin; sometimes on a natural cliff or earth bank, including burrows of other species such as rollers; less often, in cavities in trees – a pollard willow (once), and smooth-leaved elms (Dementiev 1951, Cramp and Simmons 1980). According to G. P. Dementiev, lesser kestrels sometimes nest in mixed colonies with common kestrels, and in such situations some hybridization occurs (hybrid specimens are in the Zoological Museum, University of Moscow). The habit of nesting on buildings is so much commoner today than the use of natural sites that one wonders what influences man-made structures have had on the long term numbers and distribution of this species over the centuries, and whether these kestrels exercised a wider choice of natural nest-sites in pristine times.

While not very aggressive among themselves and even rather timid and passive when threatened by powerful enemies, lesser kestrels will join together to attack and drive off some intruders around their nesting colonies – ravens, vultures, jackdaws, and even some other raptors on occasion. Peregrines, lanners or eagles cause widespread panic among the kestrels, which leave the colony and circle up high in the air to avoid them. On the other hand, adult birds show little fear of human intruders – especially at colonies in towns – and incubating birds seldom leave their eggs unless the nest is approached directly for close inspection.

The pairs are monogamous and remain together for the breeding season and probably longer, if both members survive. Also, young males of the previous year sometimes help feed nestlings, as is the case with many other colonial nesting birds. Males and females take an equal share in diurnal incubation (clutch sizes range from two to eight, usually three to five), and the female catches her own food during this time; but she alone incubates at night. She does all the brooding of the newly hatched young, until they are about 14 days old. During this time the male provides all the food for the young and for her. Later she joins the male in actively hunting and providing food for the young, which begin to fly at 28 days of age. The young leave on migration with their parents some six to eight weeks later. How long they are actually dependent on their parents for food is not known.

The numbers of lesser kestrels were not well documented historically, but there is some indication for central Europe that fluctuations in population characterized the period from 1850 to 1955 (Glutz et al. 1971). Massive declines and loss of entire colonies have occurred in recent years in most of the European range, except in France where a small population of less than 100 pairs has remained more or less stable over the last 20 years. In Spain there are still an estimated 50,000 pairs, but this number represents a marked decrease from a population that probably numbered more than 100,000 pairs in the 1960s. In Austria the kestrels dropped from 280 pairs in 1960 to between 4 and 7 pairs in 1978. Similar situations have been reported for most European countries to the west of the Soviet Union. Greece and Turkey still have widespread and generally numerous colonies, although local declines have occurred there too. (Summarized from Cramp and Simmons 1980.) The species was reported to be still common in the Ukraine, Crimea, Caucasus, and Central Asia as of the 1950s (Dementiev 1951), but there is little recent information on the Asiatic populations.

It is not known for sure why lesser kestrels have declined so severely in Europe, especially as they have such great affinity for man-made structures and benefit from deforestation and other human land-uses. It could be that insect populations have been so drastically reduced by pesticides and other controls employed in agriculture that a sufficient food base is no longer available to support the kestrels in their former numbers, especially as *naumanni* appears to require prey in *super*abundance around colony sites. In Israel excessive use of the rodenticide, thallium sulphate, was responsible for reducing a population of 2,400 to 3,000 pairs to a remnant of a few pairs (Mendelssohn 1972).

According to the information summarized by Cramp and Simmons (1980), the numbers now breeding in Europe, excluding the Soviet Union, should be on the order of 150,000 pairs. Based on the extent of the total breeding range, the entire breeding population might be roughly four to five times that size – that is, 650,000 to 800,000 pairs.

The lesser kestrel is one of the few species that occupies a larger area in the non-breeding period than during the breeding season, and censuses of "winter" roosts are one way to obtain information on the population status of this species. Siegfried and Skead (1971) organized such a census for South Africa in 1967: 155 regularly occupied roosts yielded an estimate of 154,000 kestrels. If similar roosting aggregations occur in Zambia, Zimbabwe, Mozambique, Botswana and Namibia, then there could easily be 400,000 to 500,000 or more kestrels sojourning in Africa south of 10°S latitude.

167

Fox Kestrel

Falco alopex

A RATHER UNCOMMON, locally occurring species, the fox kestrel has a narrow equatorial range in Africa extending from Ghana to the Sudan and Red Sea coast, southern Ethiopia, and Kenya, but not east of the Rift Valley. It occurs up to 2,150 m (7,000 ft) in Eritrea. It occupies a distribution that is largely allopatric to that of its nearest congener, the greater kestrel, and as Leslie Brown (1970) puzzled, it is difficult to understand this distributional separation, as the two species are ecologically quite different and should be able to share a much larger common range without competing for resources.

As the common name suggests, the plumage is a foxy red colour all over, with narrow black shaft-streaks on the head and broader streaks on the back and wing-coverts. The tail is narrowly barred with about 15 black bands, which vary from very faint in some individuals to well developed in others. The primaries are black on their outer webs, and the inner webs are also tipped with black; otherwise the wing quills are whitish with black bars across their inner webs. The underparts are somewhat paler than the upper with narrow black streaks on the breast but not on the throat, belly or thighs. The first year bird is much like the adult but has more distinctive black markings on the wing-coverts and scapulars and broader bars on the tail.

A medium-sized, long-winged, and long-tailed falcon, the fox kestrel ranges from 33.5–37.5 cm (13–14$\frac{1}{2}$ in) in length, being somewhat larger than *rupicoloides*. There is little difference in size between males and females: the wing measurement of males ranges from 266–293 mm (10$\frac{1}{2}$–11$\frac{1}{2}$ in), about 97 per cent of the female wing, which ranges from 269–308 mm (10$\frac{1}{2}$–12 in). The tail, which is long and conspicuously graduated at the end, averages about 70 per cent of the wing measurement in males and about 68 per cent in females. (Data from Brown and Amadon 1968.) Body weights apparently have not been recorded but probably average 250–300 g (9–10$\frac{1}{2}$ oz).

Not much is known about the life history of the fox kestrel. It inhabits rocky hills and gorges in open country, mainly in dry savannahs and semi-desertic to desertic environments. It migrates during the dry season into the better watered savannahs of West Africa, where it nests on isolated rocky hills, arriving from the north in October and departing again in May or June.

The nest is located in a cranny or pot-hole on the sheer face of a rock and the falcon often uses the same site year after year, as other cliff-nesting raptors typically do. As far as known, it does not use the nests of other species or nest in any other situation than on rocky formations.

The fox kestrel catches large insects and small mammals on the ground. It apparently does not take birds. In open country it perches on trees or rocks and watches for prey moving in the grass, and according to Brown and Amadon (1968) it does not hover. The wings and tail suggest a buoyant, slow flier, and certainly more observations are needed before one can be sure about all of its hunting and flying characteristics. Like other raptors of the savannah the fox kestrel is readily attracted to grass-fires, catching insects and other prey disturbed or injured by these conflagrations.

There is no basis for forming a conception of the numerical status of *alopex* at present. It occupies a moderately large total range of more than 5 million sq km (1.9 million sq miles), but the dispersal of nesting pairs within this range appears to be determined by the occurrence of its preferred nesting habitats, and these rocky hills and cliffs are not uniformly or abundantly distributed. The numbers could be only in the tens of thousands of pairs, or they could be in the hundreds of thousands. Some work in Nigeria, Chad or the Sudan is badly needed to bring our knowledge about this species up to date.

R. DAVID DIGBY

Greater Kestrel
(White-eyed Kestrel)

Falco rupicoloides

A PECULIARITY OF THIS medium-sized falcon is that it is the only species in the genus *Falco* with a white iris: all other falcons have brown eyes. The adaptive significance of the eye colour in *rupicoloides* is undetermined, but it may have something to do with species recognition, as the greater kestrel otherwise wears a rather nondescript, bleached-out version of the generalized female plumage pattern seen in several other species of the subgenus *Tinnunculus*. Leslie Brown (1970) questioned whether *rupicoloides* should be considered a true kestrel, but I believe he had no solid basis for his doubts, as both the plumage and the behaviour of this species fit best into the complex of characters which define kestrels.

The greater kestrel is a resident African species with a curious and unexplained bipartite distribution. It occurs in open grasslands, savannahs and semi-desertic scrub, habitats which are widespread and more or less continuous throughout East Africa and southern Africa. One population occupies a disjunct area in Somalia and northern Kenya south into Tanzania. Then there is a gap in distribution from Tanzania to Zimbabwe, and the species is encountered again over very wide areas of southern Africa, including Namibia, Botswana, Zimbabwe, and South Africa. It occurs up to 2,150 m (7,000 ft) in elevation.

Males and females are alike in plumage, which in comparison with the array of plumages in other species of kestrels represents the feminized type. The head and nape are pale rufous with longitudinal black stripes running along the feather shafts. The back, shoulders and scapulars are rufous with black bars, while the rump, upper tail-coverts, and tail are pale bluish grey, the latter with six transverse black bars and a whitish tip. The primaries are dusky, the inner webs banded with pale rufous. The underparts are pale fawn with brown stripes on the breast and belly. The first year birds are like adults, except for having flight feathers broadly tipped with buff.

Greater kestrels average about 35 cm ($13\frac{1}{2}$ in) in body length, and the wing length of males from southern Africa averages 274 mm ($10\frac{1}{2}$ in) – or 97 per cent of the female wing, which averages 282 mm (McLachlan and Liversidge 1961). The length of tail is around 60 per cent of wing length (not precisely determined). Kemp (1978) gives the range of weights for males and females from southern Africa as 240–300 g ($8\frac{1}{2}$–$10\frac{1}{2}$ oz), the lightest (male) being 80 per cent of the heaviest (female).

There is some geographical variation in colour and size. The birds in southern Africa are larger and darker than those from Kenya and Somalia, particularly those north and east of Lake Rudolf. Four males from the northern part of the range averaged 178 g (6 oz), and two females weighed 193 and 207 g (7 oz), the males being about 89 per cent of the females' weight (Brown and Amadon 1968).

The greater kestrel is rather sparsely distributed in grasslands with widely spaced thorn trees, the high veld of South Africa being typical habitat. These kestrels are usually seen in pairs, which occupy the same territory year round, according to the observation of Alan Kemp (1978) in South Africa. One territory which he carefully mapped out was 569 ha (1,400 acres) in area, and four other adjacent pairs appeared to be occupying territories of similar size.

Only the male defends the entire territory, while the female defends the area immediately around the nest. The kestrels seldom engage in overtly aggressive actions such as chasing and fighting, but rely instead on various territorial advertising displays, for example perching prominently on high structures in various parts of the territory, or high hovering 50 m (160 ft) above ground, or soaring. They act aggressively within their territories towards birds such as crows, kites, buzzards, other falcons and

PLATE XXV
Greater Kestrel
Falco rupicoloides
Adult female
Map page 188

herons, as well as towards other members of their own species. Hunting tends to be concentrated in areas around the nest during the breeding season, but there is more use of the entire territory at other times of the year.

During much of the day the greater kestrel gives the appearance of being a rather sluggish and inactive bird, spending much time perched quietly on trees, bushes, fence posts and electricity pylons. But it also soars and hovers over open grasslands like other kestrels, and it can speed along close to the ground quite rapidly when pursuing quarry – at such times behaving more like a large falcon than a kestrel.

It feeds on insects, mainly orthopterans, and on small mammals, lizards and small snakes, all of which are caught on the ground; but it can also take insects and some small birds in flight. Once as O. P. M. Prozesky of the Transvaal Museum and I were travelling along a dusty road in the high veld, we spotted a greater kestrel perched on a telegraph pole along the road. The falcon was facing into a strong wind and looking intently down at the ground. Suddenly it flew down in a long diagonal swoop parallel to the road and struck at something in the short grass but missed. Instead of flying off, it sat on a mound of earth near by. A small bird which appeared to be a cisticola warbler flew up about one metre from the kestrel and was immediately blown away downwind and up into the air. The kestrel jumped into the air in quick pursuit and within 20 m (65 ft) had caught up to the little bird. The chase developed into a ringing flight, but the little bird had to struggle in the strong wind, and the kestrel was able to snatch it out of the air on its second pass.

The greater kestrel nests in trees in the old stick nests of other birds, frequently those of the pied crow (*Corvus capensis*), but it has also been found in the old nests of the secretary bird (*Sagittarius serpentarius*) and in other nests located in the tops of dense-crowned acacia trees. Like the lanner, it has been found nesting with increasing frequency in recent years in stick nests located on pylons and electric utility poles.

The three to five eggs are laid at various times of the year depending on geographic location: in South Africa, from August to November, or even as late as February; in Kenya, in various months, January, May, June, October; in Tanzania, in May; and in Somalia, from late April to mid-June (Brown and Amadon 1968).

While not as numerous as some other kestrels, *rupicoloides* appears to have a secure future. It has been able to adjust, at least in part, to man's agricultural modifications of its original habitat, and it has benefited from the construction of roads, fences, and pylons, which provide perching places from which to hunt and display and new nesting opportunities.

If we assume an average density of one pair per 10 sq km (4 sq miles) and allow for an overall range of 3 million sq km (1.1 million sq miles) in southern Africa, then there should be around 300,000 pairs resident in Africa south of the Okovango and Zambezi rivers; however, this figure is probably too high, as the species is not uniformly dispersed over its entire range, and we are left with an order of magnitude estimate of 100,000 pairs. The East African range is smaller, and the greater kestrel is less common there, except in Somalia. The total species population probably falls between 100,000 and 200,000 pairs.

Grey Kestrel

Falco ardosiaceus

ANOTHER AFRICAN SPECIES occupying the wetter savannahs south of the Sahara, the grey kestrel occurs in a broad equatorial belt from Senegal to Eritrea and thence south through East Africa into southern Tanzania and Mozambique, and thence westward through Zambia, southern Zaire and Angola, avoiding the coast of East Africa and the Congo Basin. It seems to share a relationship with Dickinson's kestrel similar to that between the fox kestrel and the greater kestrel, and *ardosiaceus* and *dickinsoni* are probably derived from a common ancestral species.

This is essentially a slate coloured bird, similar in many respects to the light phase of the sooty falcon – but quite different in proportions and habits. The adult is uniformly slate grey above and below but palest on the throat, the individual feathers having dark shaft-streaks, especially on the head and neck. The primaries are blackish with indistinct splotches of white on the inner webs. The tail is grey, the central pair of rectrices uniformly so, the others with lighter grey marks on their inner webs. Males and females are the same; the immature bird is like the adult but paler on the abdomen (Brown and Amadon 1968).

The grey kestrel is a small to medium-sized falcon, from 27.5–32.5 cm (11–13 in) in length. There is a moderate difference in size between males and females, although two samples give somewhat different results. Brown and Amadon provide figures indicating that the wing measurement of males (205–232 mm; 8–9 in) is about 90 per cent of that for females (235–251 mm; 9–10 in), whereas Thiollay's (1977) more restricted sample from the Ivory Coast suggests less difference – males average 226 mm or 96 per cent of the female average, 235 mm. Males from the Ivory Coast weigh 222 g (8 oz) on average, 90 per cent of the female average, 247 g ($8\frac{1}{2}$ oz). The tail is long relative to the wing and averages 64 to 65 per cent of the wing measurement, providing a clear distinction in the field from the proportionally shorter-tailed sooty falcon.

The grey kestrel is a bird of the more mesic savannah regions of Africa, apparently more common in West African savannahs than elsewhere. It appears to be resident throughout its range and is usually seen in pairs, which probably remain permanently bonded throughout the year.

Except for Jean Marc Thiollay's (1975–77) extensive studies of the raptor fauna in a zone of contact between the savannah and forest in the Ivory Coast, there is not much recent information about this species. In this region Thiollay found that grey kestrels occurred most often in open savannah (58 per cent of all records), secondarily in wooded savannah (24 per cent) and cleared forest areas for agriculture or other human occupance (15 per cent), and to a very limited extent in dense savannah and riparian woods.

This kestrel is said to use old stick nests of other birds, or occasionally to nest in a hollow tree; but the domed nests of the hammerkop (*Scopus umbretta*) are most commonly used, and Brown (1970) suggested that the grey kestrel only uses hammerkop nests. On occasion the falcons have been known to drive the hammerkops away from active nests and to usurp them. Some nests are as high as 18 m (60 ft) above ground (Brown and Amadon 1968).

Three to five eggs are laid in various months depending on locale: January in Ghana, April in Nigeria, March to April in Sudan, April in Uganda, October in Tanzania. Apparently only the female incubates – at least she incubates most of the time – and the male provisions her with food. When he arrives near the nest with food, he calls to her, and she emerges from the nest to take the prey from him. At first she remains with the newly hatched young, but while they are still downy (perhaps *ca*. 2 weeks), she begins to assist the male in bringing prey to the nest. In response to a special call given by the parents, the young come to the entrance of the hammerkop nest to receive the food. The young leave the nest about one month after hatching and do not return to it once they have flown. The parents continue to feed them in

173

adjacent trees in their territory for an undetermined period (Serle 1943, Loosemore 1963 *fide* Brown and Amadon 1968).

The grey kestrel is a diurnally active hunter – not markedly crepuscular like the sooty falcon or Dickinson's kestrel – and is most often seen perched on a tree watching for prey on the ground. In fact, still-hunting from a perch was the only tactic Thiollay (1977) observed the grey kestrel to use in his study. When hunting over open country where there are no high perches, it flies rather slowly and hovers like other kestrels at 3–15 m (10–50 ft) above ground, according to Brown and Amadon (1968). Although appearing rather sluggish much of the time, like the fox kestrel it is capable of flying very fast with quick wingbeats. It also has the habit of hawking flying termites and locusts out of the air and is most likely to be confused with the sooty falcon at such times.

The food habits have not been studied in great detail, but the principal prey consists of insects, worms and lizards, with frogs, bats and other small mammals as occasional items (Brown and Amadon 1968). In Thiollay's (1977) study area in the Ivory Coast, grey kestrels were most often seen hunting on lands cleared for agriculture or around industrialized areas (52 per cent of all records), around plantations in the savannah (30 per cent), on degraded savannah (9 per cent), on natural, open savannah (8 per cent), and rarely around thickets or the borders of forest.

The grey kestrel occupies a rather large range in Africa – some 10 million sq km (3.9 million sq miles) or more – but is nowhere very common. Is it limited by its special reliance on hammerkop nests? In Thiollay's (1975) study area of 2,700 ha (6,670 acres), where there were ten regularly occurring species of breeding raptors, there were only three pairs of *ardosiaceus* – far fewer than the number of African hobbies, which are not known for their abundance either. If Thiollay's data are representative and the bird occurs on average at a density of one pair per 100 sq km (39 sq miles), then the species-population would be around 100,000 pairs. Apparently the grey kestrel has benefited from human land-use in the Ivory Coast, and there is no reason to be concerned about its status for the foreseeable future.

PLATE XXXVI
Grey Kestrel
Falco ardosiaceus
Adult female
Map page 188

174

R. David Digby.

Dickinson's Kestrel

Falco dickinsoni

Dickinson's kestrel is another greyish, African falcon, which occurs from Tanzania south to Mozambique and northeastern Transvaal and thence westward through Zambia and Zimbabwe to Angola. It is found most often in wet, somewhat marshy savannahs at low elevation and has a special affinity for Borassus palms, as does the red-headed falcon. Consequently, it is locally distributed and nowhere very common, although it has been reported to be more numerous in Zimbabwe (where it is associated with drier habitats) than elsewhere (McLachlan and Liversidge 1962; A. R. Thomson). A resident, non-migratory species, it is usually seen in pairs.

Males and females are alike in plumage. The head and nape of the adult are whitish grey, tinged with brown and with fine, black shaft-streaks, merging into blackish slate on the upper wing-coverts and back. The upper tail-coverts and tail are pale grey, the latter with a broad subterminal and several narrower black bands. The wings are blackish with some whitish barring. The underparts vary from pale grey on the throat to brownish grey on breast and belly with more or less distinct, dark shaft-streaks. The first year bird is similar to the adult but browner, especially on the underparts (Brown and Amadon 1968).

The Dickinson's kestrel is about the same size as the grey kestrel, with a slightly shorter tail and less difference between males and females. It is about 27–28 cm ($10\frac{1}{2}$–11 in) in body length, and the wing measurement of males and females ranges from 210–236 mm (8–9 in). The tail length is about 63 per cent of the wing measurement. Body weights apparently have not been recorded, but most likely fall in the 200–250 g (7–9 oz) range.

Dickinson's kestrel is rather robust-looking for its size. It sits upright in a constantly alert posture and is an active falcon. It is probably a more capable hunter than most writers have credited it to be (see Brown 1970, for example). As it is also a rather tame species, it should not be difficult for someone to make detailed observations on its ecology and behaviour.

Its food appears to consist mainly of insects such as orthopterans, but it also takes crabs, frogs, lizards, small birds and small mammals; and vertebrates may figure more importantly in its diet than present records suggest. It apparently hunts mainly from a perch in a tree – often a dead one – from which it can survey the surrounding open ground, and it takes most of its prey on the ground, though it will pursue birds in flight.

One I saw perched in a tree at a waterhole in northern Kruger National Park in July 1966 launched an attack at a small bird (perhaps a black tit, *Parus nigrescens*), which it chased into the tree-tops, through the branches of two trees, and then out over a grassy area, where the bird escaped by dropping into tall grass just as the kestrel was about to close on it. Brooke and Howells (1971) saw one fly to its nest carrying a newly fledged black-eyed bulbul (*Pycnonotus barbatus*) in its feet.

Also, O. P. M. Prozesky told me that he had seen these kestrels at the Gorongosa crater in Mozambique hawking bats at dusk. Dickinson's kestrel may have well developed crepuscular habits, for it has rather large eyes for the size of its head, proportionally larger, in fact, than all other falcons except the prairie falcon. It is also said to hover occasionally, and is attracted to grass-fires, as are many other savannah-dwelling raptors.

Dickinson's kestrel usually nests in the crowns of Borassus palms or in the broken, hollow tops of these or coconut palms (White 1945, Brown 1970). Where palms are not available, however, it has been known to use an old stick nest atop an acacia in Zambia (B. L. Mitchell *fide* Brooke and Howells 1971), a hammerkop's nest in Zimbabwe (Masterson 1951), and the "inspection hole" on a girder of the Birchenough Bridge across the Sabi River in Zimbabwe (Brooke and Howells 1971).

Two to three eggs are laid at various times depending on the region: September to December in South Africa; September to October in Zimbabwe; October to November in Malawi; July to October on the island of Pemba off the northern coast of Tanzania (White 1945, Brown and Amadon 1968). Not much else is known about the breeding biology.

There is no way at present to assess the numerical status, for Dickinson's kestrels are too scattered and local to allow for any kind of estimate of regional densities. It is fairly widely distributed over more than 4 million sq km (1.5 million sq miles), and there is no reason to suspect that its numbers have diminished in recent years owing to changes wrought on the land by an expanding human population.

The four African "kestrels" – *rupicoloides*, *alopex*, *ardosiaceus*, and *dickinsoni* – have to some degree overlapping ecological requirements and partially sympatric distributions. To what extent do they replace each other ecologically and to what degree can they adjust to each other's presence in the same community? There is need for a comparative study.

Barred Kestrel

(Banded Kestrel)

Falco zoniventris

APECULIAR AND LITTLE studied falcon, the barred kestrel is endemic to Madagascar, where it occurs mainly in tropical forests of the humid eastern part of the island. According to the information obtained by members of the French-English-American zoological expedition to Madagascar at the beginning of the 1930s (Rand 1936), the species was then rather common around Maroantsetra and Anadapa in the northeastern part of Madagascar, occurring from sea-level up to 1,000 m (3,300 ft), but was rare elsewhere. Not much else had been learned about its natural history until the recent report by J. F. R. Colebrook-Robjent (1973).

This is another small falcon, averaging slightly larger than the sympatric Madagascar kestrel, which has adapted to life within the forest by converging towards the accipitrine shape and mode of hunting. The wings are relatively short and broad and the tail long; the plumage is quite soft and lax.

The wing measurement of males averages 217 mm ($8\frac{1}{2}$ in); of females, 227 mm (9 in); and the tail is about 65 per cent of the wing measurement. Body weights apparently have not been recorded but probably range from 180–240 g ($6\frac{1}{2}$–$8\frac{1}{2}$ oz) for males and females. Sexual size dimorphism is not very pronounced, male wings averaging 95.6 per cent of the length of female wings.

The adult male has a whitish forehead and indistinct eyebrow, narrowly streaked with brown. His head, neck and interscapular region are grey to dark grey with black shaft-streaks. His lower back, rump, and upper tail-coverts are bluish grey, lightest on the coverts, and all with black shaft-streaks and dark and light bars. The tail is blackish tipped with white, the central pair of feathers unbarred, the others more or less barred with greyish white. The upper wing-coverts and scapulars are grey with blackish bars. The sides of the face are grey with dusky streaks; the throat is white with some brown streaks towards the breast. The rest of the underparts are whitish with greyish brown bars. The adult female is very similar in pattern to the male but generally darker in colour. (From Brown and Amadon 1968.)

According to Brown and Amadon, Madagascar barred kestrels feed on insects, small reptiles, including chameleons, and occasionally on small birds, and take food both on the ground and in vegetation; but the recent observations of Colebrook-Robjent (1973) suggest a rather different kind of predator. He only saw these kestrels hunting and catching chameleons in the trees. The falcons took most of their prey rather high up on the bare branches of large *Albizzia* trees or other leafy trees. However, his observations were made only over a two week period just prior to egg-laying, and it could be that the male falcons were selecting the chameleons specially for feeding to females. If this species is something of a specialist on arboreal lizards, it would be most interesting to learn whether these kestrels also feed their young heavily on chameleons. Three of seven stomachs from specimens examined by Rand (1936) contained chameleons.

Colebrook-Robjent (1973) never saw barred kestrels hover, although they are said to do so rarely (Brown and Amadon 1968). Apparently the typical manner of hunting is for the kestrel to take a stand on the dead branch of a tree and to remain motionless while keeping an acute watch on the surrounding trees for a chameleon to reveal itself by some motion. Colebrook-Robjent saw the falcons take off suddenly in rapid flight and swoop up into the foliage of trees 200 or more metres (650 ft) away and return with prey. Frequently they launched attacks into dense vegetation.

The barred kestrel is the last species of *Falco* to reveal the location of its nest-site to ornithologists. Since *zoniventris* is sometimes said to be closely related to Dickinson's kestrel and the grey kestrel, some have speculated that it might have similar nesting habits, especially as both of the latter sometimes use the domed stick nests of the hammerkop, which is common in Madagascar. However, Colebrook-Robjent (1973), between 5 and 26 September 1972, observed three pairs that were investigating large, basin-shaped epiphytes on the lateral branches or trunks of large native forest trees. He saw food transfers take place there and found well made scrapes in the epiphytes. On 23 October his Malgashe guide climbed to one of the epiphytes and found three heavily incubated eggs.

Colebrook-Robjent considered barred kestrels to be "fairly common" in the area where he worked along the Manantenina River system in the Prefecture of Sambava, Province of Diego Suarez. More significantly, he found that they were not wholly dependent on uncut, virgin forest but were managing to survive and breed in situations where the bottomlands were being cultivated with vanilla, coffee, rice, bananas and coconuts, interspersed with second-growth forest and strips of remnant forest and where the crests of the ridges flanking the valley were still partly covered with degraded rain forest.

The number of individuals of this species cannot be very large, as the eastern rain forest has been reduced to 61,500 sq km (25,500 sq miles) and the total forested habitats that might be suitable for the kestrel comprise no more than 100,000 sq km (Jolly 1980). There might be several hundred to a thousand pairs at most. The future of this interesting, and still largely unknown, species will surely be determined by how much suitable forest mankind allows to remain in the humid east of Madagascar.

PLATE XXXVIII
Barred Kestrel
Falco zoniventris
Adult female
Map page 188

R. David Digby

Brown Falcon

(Brown Hawk)

Falco berigora

Тhe brown falcon of Australia, Tasmania, and New Guinea is an aberrant falcon, probably not closely related to any other species in the genus *Falco*. Structurally it has more the appearance of a buteonine or accipitrine species, although it retains most of the special characters that define falcons. Its habits are also rather unfalcon-like, and it seems to have evolved to occupy a convergent, buzzard-like ecological niche in Australia, where true buteonines, other than eagles, do not occur. For these reasons the brown falcon is of particular interest, and fortunately several fieldworkers in Australia are now studying the bird, so that we should know much more about it in a few years.

As the name denotes, this is a rather uniformly brownish species, but there are great variations in colour and pattern from individual to individual, as well as some regional differences. Males and females are alike. In the so-called "normal" or pale phase, the crown, nape and dorsal surfaces are rufous brown with blackish shaft-streaks on the head and paler rufous spots or bars in other areas. The tail is dark brown with many narrow, light rufous bars and tipped with whitish. A narrow eyebrow, the sides of face, and moustachial streak are black. The throat is buffy white with black shaft-streaks, and the rest of the underparts have feathers with buffy white basal parts and distal parts tipped or edged with darker brown. The thighs are darker brown with pale edgings to the feathers. There is a melanistic form which is almost uniformly dark brown to black above and below with some white showing on the throat, under the eye, in the midline of the belly and on the under surfaces of the primaries.

Every kind of intermediate condition between these two extremes occurs in the population. Brown falcons tend to be lighter and more rufous in colour in the dry interior of Australia, darker on the coast or in regions of high rainfall, and less spotted and with conspicuous black shaft-streaks above and below in New Guinea. First year birds are similar to adults in both the pale and melanistic plumages, and they are not easily told apart in worn condition.

The brown falcon is a medium-sized to largish falcon with a body length of 40–50 cm ($15\frac{1}{2}$–$19\frac{1}{2}$ in) and a wingspan of, 80–95 cm ($31\frac{1}{2}$–$37\frac{1}{2}$ in). It has long legs with greyish to bluish fleshy parts and a tarsometatarsus ranging from 70–75 mm ($2\frac{1}{2}$–3 in) – longer than for any other species of *Falco* – and it is quite adept at walking and running on the ground, somewhat like the chanting goshawks (*Milierax* spp) of Africa. The toes are thick and stubby, and the scales on the toes and bare tarsus are large and coarse. These features may be an adaptation related to catching snakes and other difficult ground quarry, as similar types of feet are found on other snake-eating raptors such as the laughing falcons (*Herpetotheres* sp), snake-eagles (*Circaetus*), and some others. The wing is rather rounded (P8 is longer than P9 or P7, and P10 is barely longer than P6) and broad with wide, flexible primaries and secondaries. The tail is moderately long in proportion to the wing (about 59 per cent of the standard wing measurement) and is decidedly graduated at the tip.

There is considerable difference in size between males and females. Males from the more humid parts of Australia have wings measuring from 319–355 mm ($12\frac{1}{2}$–14 in), or 89 per cent of female wing length, which ranges from 350–397 mm ($13\frac{1}{2}$–$15\frac{1}{2}$ in). (Data from Brown and Amadon 1968.) A similar set of measurements compiled by Rob Bierregaard (Ph.D. dissertation) gives 88 per cent, and his data also show

R. DAVID DIGBY.

other marked size differences between males and females.

Body weights vary greatly from season to season, as well as differing between males and females and between adults and juveniles. Brown and Amadon (1968) give a range of 387–512 g (13½–18 oz) for four males and 505–635 g (17½–22½ oz) for four females, while Serventy and Whittell (1967) give a range for males of 378–532 g (13½–18½ oz) and for females of 560–672 g (19½–23½ oz). Nick Mooney has, however, obtained the most significant series of weights for this species in Tasmania, with samples covering all months of the year, both sexes, and adults and juveniles, and his most interesting findings are summarized here with his generous permission.

The total range of individual weights for adult females is 520–842 g (18½–29½ oz), while monthly averages range from summertime lows of 618–641 g (October to January) to winter highs of 730–755 g (May to July). The range of individual weights for first year females is 490–720 g (17–25½ oz) with monthly averages declining from 601 g in January to 516 g in April and then increasing again to 598 g by September. The range of individual weights for adult males is 430–575 g (15–20 oz) with summer monthly averages of 425–440 g and winter highs of 539–551 g. Juvenile males range from 380–571 g (13½–20 oz) and decline from a monthly average of 458 g in January to 431 g in March and then increase to 497 g by June. If one compares a sample of males and females at the same time of year, then adult males weigh on average about 74 to 76 per cent of the average female weight, a degree of difference close to that seen in some of the bird-eating falcons and accipiters.

The brown falcon is ubiquitous and common to abundant throughout Australia and Tasmania, occurring in virtually every kind of habitat from arid, interior deserts to moist coastal forests, the northern tropical zones, and in the mountains of central eastern New Guinea, where it is the commonest diurnal raptor. It does show a preference for open country, especially when hunting, but perches within woods and forests and nests in trees (Brown and Amadon 1968).

Brown falcons are usually spaced out as individuals or pairs, but at times when local movements are under way they occur in flocks of up to 100 birds. They also tend to aggregate in districts where grasshopper or mouse plagues occur, especially the young of the year. The movements of this species are not well understood, and some populations may be regularly migratory, for example across the Bass Strait between Tasmania and Australia; but most adults appear to remain more or less resident and paired all year round in the areas where they nest, and movements may be undertaken mostly by juveniles and unmated, surplus adults (N. Mooney).

The brown falcon has a catholic diet consisting of insects, especially grasshoppers and large beetles, other terrestrial invertebrates (such as centipedes), occasional fish and frogs taken from shallow or drying pools, lizards (especially skinks), venomous snakes up to one metre in length, various kinds of birds – mostly ground-dwelling – up to 300 g (10½ oz) and more in weight, and various species of small mammals up to rabbits weighing one kilogram (2 lb 3 oz). It also feeds on carrion to a considerable extent and pirates food from other birds of prey (Brown and Amadon 1968, Serventy and Whittell 1967, Frith 1969, N. Mooney).

The diet varies considerably from season to season, locality to locality, and between adults and immatures, as Nick Mooney has learned from his detailed studies in Tasmania. During the breeding season (October to January) the adult diet, including the food brought to the young, consists of about 50 per cent birds (especially European starlings), 40 per cent mammals, 5 per cent insects, and 5 per cent carrion. During the summer (January to March) the diet shifts to insects (40 per cent) and reptiles (40 per cent), with birds and mammals making up 10 per cent and carrion 10 per cent. During winter the diet shifts back to small mammals (30 per cent), more carrion (30 per cent), birds (20 per cent), and insects and reptiles (15 per cent). The newly independent young depend heavily on concentrations of field crickets and grasshoppers, mouse plagues and on small reptiles, and it is at this season when they often aggregate into loose foraging flocks where food is locally abundant.

While brown falcons usually give the appearance of being rather lethargic hunters they are, in fact, remarkably versatile and opportunistic predators. They spend most of their time quietly perched, searching the ground for vulnerable prey, but they also hunt from a hovering position in air (especially the juveniles, which have lighter wing-loadings than adults), and they can fly quite fast when the occasion demands. They are also often attracted to disturbed prey at grass-fires. Nick Mooney has observed that brown falcons usually catch birds in a tail-chase, in which the falcons often enter dense cover in full pursuit like goshawks. Most birds are probably taken this way, or by surprise on the ground or just as they flush from the ground. Co-operative hunting between mates is also common, especially for birds: one, usually the male, chases or flushes prey from cover or harries a flock, while the other, usually the female, waits on above to attack any individual that becomes vulnerable. Brown falcons also pursue prey by walking or running on the ground, and at such times they may catch insects in their beaks as well as in their feet. The method of attacking venomous snakes has not been reported, but it is likely that these attacks are also from the ground, as in the case of other snake-catching raptors.

Brown falcons are highly aggressive toward other birds of prey, including eagles and other large falcons such as the peregrine. Steve K. Sherrod saw brown falcons regularly rob prey from caches around a peregrine eyrie in Victoria, and it is likely that they also force some raptors to yield their catches by harassing them aggressively in the air or on the ground.

The timing of reproduction is seasonal but somewhat variable from year to year and from one region to another, apparently in relation to favourable feeding conditions. Thus, over much of temperate Australia egg dates vary from June to November or even later, but most often the eggs are laid between September and November. In tropical northern Australia, on the other hand, laying takes place between December and March, which corresponds to the rainy season, an apparent adaptation to take advantage of the flush of insects and other animal life following the onset of the rains.

The two to five, usually three, eggs are often laid in the old stick nest of crows, ravens, Australian magpies, wattle birds, or other birds of prey, in trees at any height up to 50 m (160 ft) above ground. Brown falcons have been reported to construct their own nests on occasion, but as with other species of falcon this conclusion needs verification; however, they do reline old nests with fresh bark and add some sticks to the nest (N. Mooney). They also sometimes nest in hollows of trees (Serventy and Whittell 1967), and on the tops of termite mounds (Brown and Amadon 1968).

Both sexes incubate and sit very tightly, but according to Nick Mooney, when they are forced off by humans they defend by coming at the intruder in long, low swoops through the air, using heavy, measured wingbeats and uttering continually repeated squawks, quite unlike the fast, steep diving attacks of most falcons at their nests. Defence of the nest against other animals, especially other raptors, is extremely violent and persistent.

The young leave the nest at 40 to 42 days of age. They often branch out from the nest before they are capable of sustained flight and perch on adjacent limbs of the tree. Again like buteos, the fledglings remain with their parents for a relatively short time, and they can be independent of parental care within a few days after starting to fly. Nick Mooney reports that he has trapped hunting juveniles with incompletely grown tails and wings and still with down on their shoulders and heads. At first these young birds restrict their attention to insects and small skinks, but they begin chasing birds by eight weeks of age (*ca.* two weeks out of the nest).

The brown falcon is perhaps overall the commonest diurnal raptor in Australia; certainly it is no less common than the Australian kestrel. While it has undergone some local reduction in numbers around urban centres (for example Perth, according to Serventy and Whittell 1967), it remains abundant over most of its range. N. Mooney has found densities of one pair per 40 sq km (15 sq miles) in Tasmania, and in some wet temperate regions of Australia, densities average even higher, around one pair per 20 sq km (8 sq miles). Densities no doubt average considerably less in the arid interior, but with a total range exceeding 7.5 million sq km (2.9 million sq miles) there must be several hundred thousand brown falcons in existence. If half the range is occupied at a density of one pair per 20 sq km and the other half at one pair per 100 sq km, then the total breeding population would be around 225,000 pairs.

Maps

Solid blue areas on the maps indicate known breeding ranges. Migration ("wintering") ranges are separately indicated for six trans-equatorial migrants (hobby, Eleonora's falcon, sooty falcon, western and eastern red-footed falcons, and lesser kestrel). Populations of other northern species often migrate in winter into ranges that overlap their breeding ranges (see page 19); for three of these (gyrfalcon, saker and merlin) the southern limits of their usual winter migration ranges are shown.

1. PEREGRINE

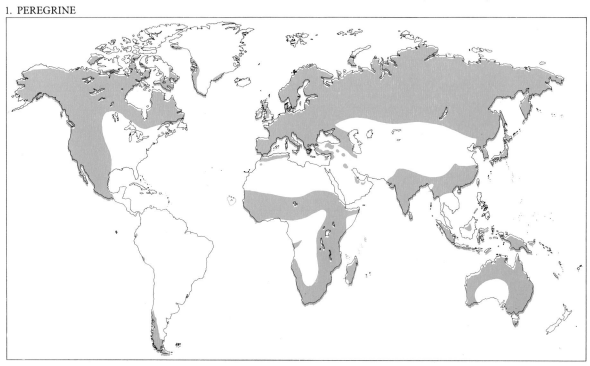

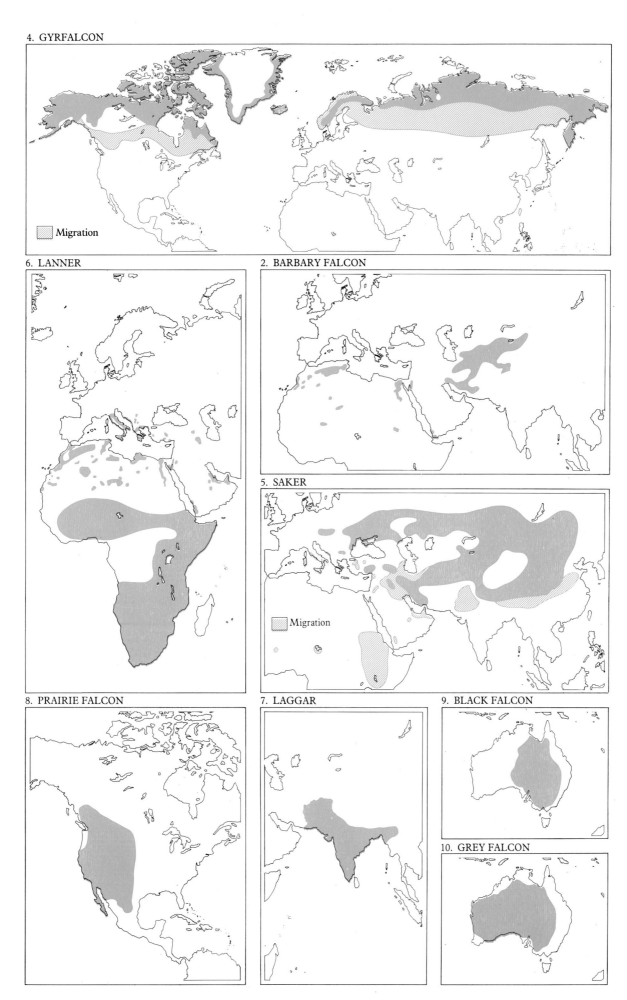

4. GYRFALCON

Migration

6. LANNER

2. BARBARY FALCON

5. SAKER

Migration

8. PRAIRIE FALCON

7. LAGGAR

9. BLACK FALCON

10. GREY FALCON

185

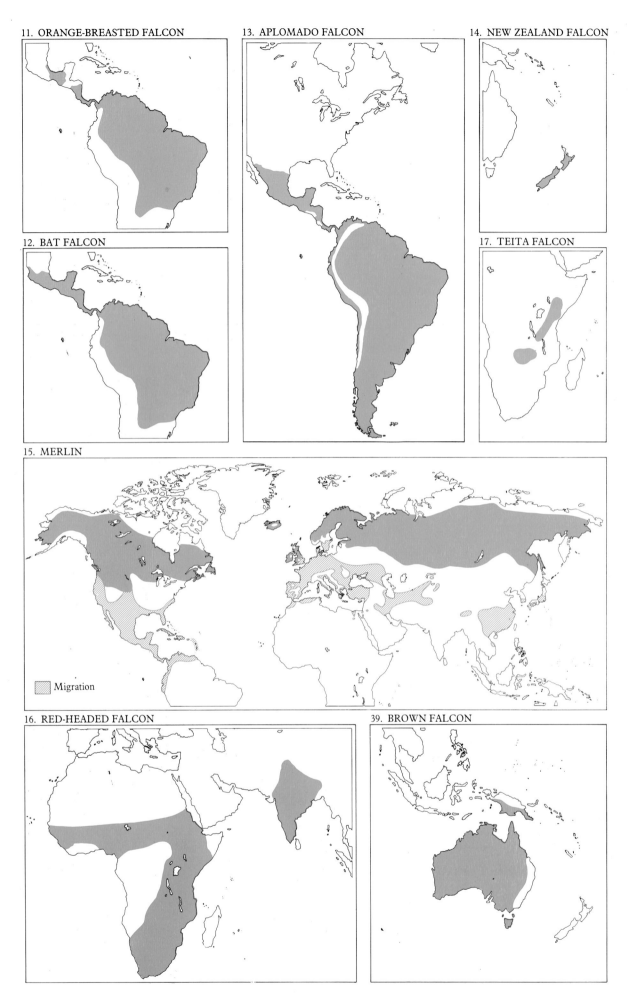

11. ORANGE-BREASTED FALCON

12. BAT FALCON

13. APLOMADO FALCON

14. NEW ZEALAND FALCON

17. TEITA FALCON

15. MERLIN

Migration

16. RED-HEADED FALCON

39. BROWN FALCON

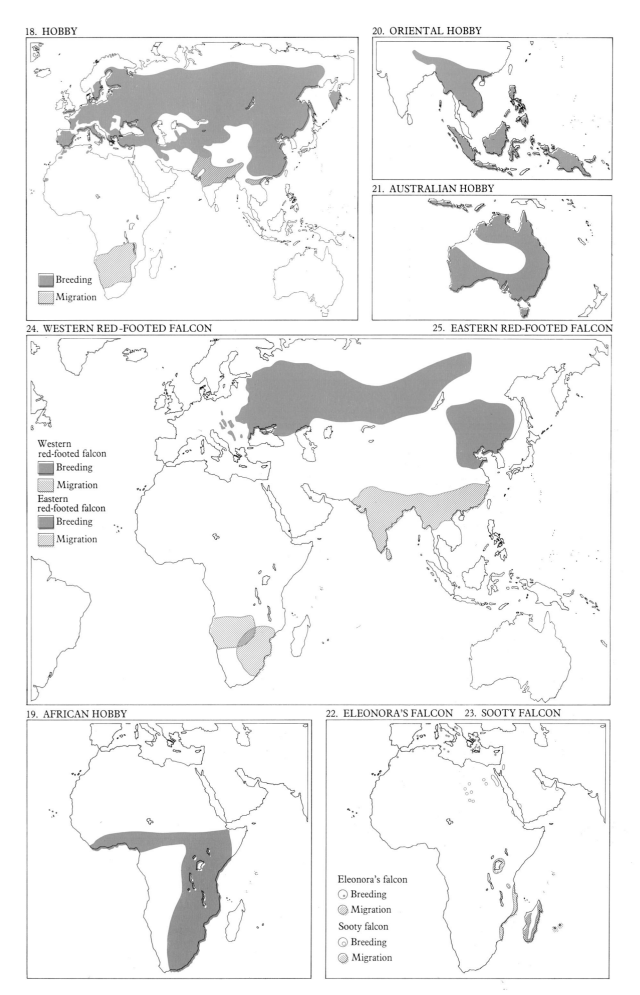

18. HOBBY

■ Breeding
▨ Migration

20. ORIENTAL HOBBY

21. AUSTRALIAN HOBBY

24. WESTERN RED-FOOTED FALCON

25. EASTERN RED-FOOTED FALCON

Western
red-footed falcon
■ Breeding
▨ Migration
Eastern
red-footed falcon
■ Breeding
▨ Migration

19. AFRICAN HOBBY

22. ELEONORA'S FALCON   23. SOOTY FALCON

Eleonora's falcon
⊙ Breeding
▨ Migration
Sooty falcon
◉ Breeding
▨ Migration

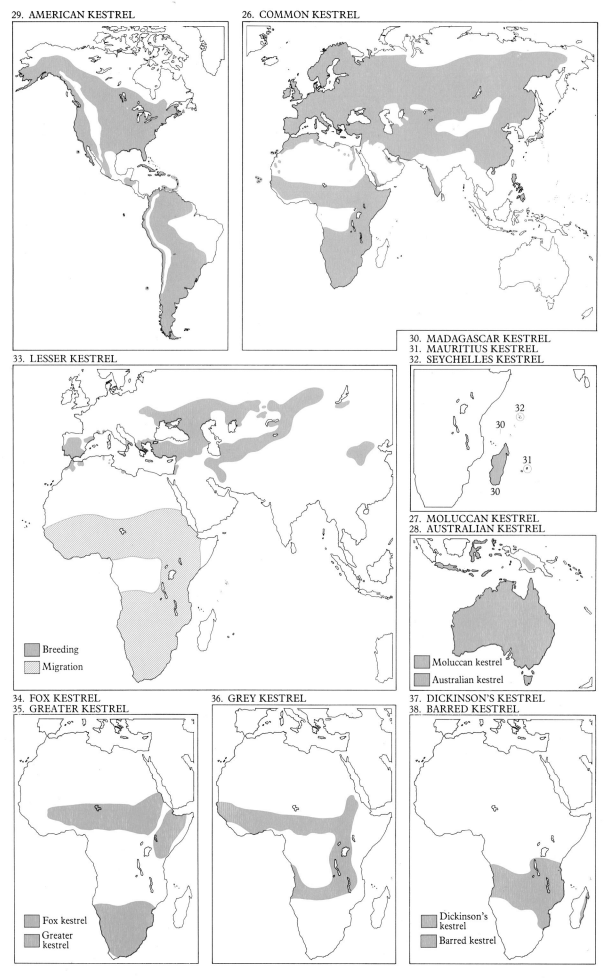

29. AMERICAN KESTREL

26. COMMON KESTREL

30. MADAGASCAR KESTREL
31. MAURITIUS KESTREL
32. SEYCHELLES KESTREL

33. LESSER KESTREL

Breeding

Migration

27. MOLUCCAN KESTREL
28. AUSTRALIAN KESTREL

Moluccan kestrel

Australian kestrel

34. FOX KESTREL
35. GREATER KESTREL

Fox kestrel

Greater kestrel

36. GREY KESTREL

37. DICKINSON'S KESTREL
38. BARRED KESTREL

Dickinson's kestrel

Barred kestrel

188

Bibliography

Ali, S. 1968. The book of Indian birds. Bombay Natural History Society.

Ali, S. 1977. The book of Indian birds. Revised edition. Bombay N.H.S.

Ali, S., and Ripley, S. D. 1978. Handbook of the birds of India and Pakistan. Vol.1. Oxford Univ. Press.

Allen, M. 1979. Falconry in Arabia. London: Orbis Publishing.

Amadon, D. 1959. The significance of sexual differences in size among birds. *Proc. Am. Phil. Soc.* 103: 531–536.

Amadon, D. 1975. Why are female birds of prey larger than males? *Raptor Research* 9: 1–11.

Amadon, D. 1977. Further comments on sexual size dimorphism in birds. *Wilson Bulletin* 89: 619–620.

Anderson, C. M., and Ellis, D. A. *Raptor Research* (in press).

Andersson, M., and Norberg, R. A. 1981. Evolution of reversed sexual size dimorphism and role partitioning among predatory birds, with a size scaling of flight performance. *Biol. J. Linnean Soc.* 15: 105–130.

Baker, J. A. 1967. The peregrine. London: Collins.

Balgooyen, T. G. 1976. Behavior and ecology of the American kestrel in the Sierra Nevada of California. *Univ. Calif. Publ. Zool.* 103: 1–83.

Baumgart, W. 1975. Die Bedeutung funktioneller Kriterien für die Beurteilung der taxonomischen Stellung paläarktischer Grossfalken. *Zool. Abh.* 33: 303–315.

Bedggood, G. W. 1979. Field notes on the black falcon. *Australian Bird Watcher* 8: 3–34.

Beebe, W. 1950. Home life of the bat falcon, *Falco albigularis albigularis*. Daudin. *Zoologica* 35: 69–86.

Bengston, S.-A. 1971. Hunting methods and choice of prey of gyrfalcons *Falco rusticolus* at Myvatn in northeast Iceland. *Ibis* 113: 468–476.

Bengston, S.-A. 1975. *Fauna och Flora*, Upps. 70: 8–12.

Benson, C. W., and Penny, M. J. 1971. The land birds of Aldabra. *Phil. Trans. Roy. Soc.* B26: 417–527.

Benson, C. W., and Smithers, R. H. N. 1958. The Teita falcon *Falco fasciinucha* at the Victoria Falls. *Ostrich* 29: 57–58.

Bent, A. C. 1938. Life histories of North American birds of prey (Part 2). *U. S. Natl. Mus. Bull.* 170.

Bierregaard, R. O. 1978. Morphological analyses of community structure in birds of prey. Ph.D. dissertation, University of Pennsylvania.

Bijleveld, M. 1974. Birds of prey in Europe. London: Macmillan Press.

Blaine, G. 1936. Falconry. London: Neville Spearman.

Booth, B. D. McD. 1961. Breeding of the sooty falcon in the Libyan desert. *Ibis* 103a: 129–130.

Boyce, D. A., Jr. 1980. Hunting and pre-nesting behavior of the orange-breasted falcon. *Raptor Research* 14 (2): 35–39.

Brooke, R. K., and Howells, W. W. 1971. Falcons at Birchenough Bridge, Rhodesia. *Ostrich* 42: 142–143.

Brosset, A. 1961. Ecologie des oiseaux du Maroc oriental. *Trov. Inst. scient. chérif.* Ser Biol. 22.

Brown, L. 1970. African birds of prey. London: Collins.

Brown, L. 1976. British birds of prey. London: Collins.

Brown, L., and Amadon, D. 1968. Eagles, hawks and falcons of the world.

Vol. 2. London: Country Life Books.

Burnham, W. A., and Mattox, W. G. *Meddel. om Grønland.* (in press).

Cade, T. J. 1954. On the biology of falcons and the ethics of falconers. *Falconry News and Notes* 1 (4): 12–19.

Cade, T. J. 1955. Experiments on winter territoriality of the American kestrel. *Wilson Bull.* 67: 5–17.

Cade, T. J. 1960. Ecology of the peregrine and gyrfalcon populations in Alaska. *Univ. Calif. Publ. Zool.* 63: 151–290.

Cade, T. J. 1965. Relations between raptors and columbiform birds at a desert water hole. *Wilson Bulletin* 77: 340–345.

Cade, T. J. 1967. Ecological and behavioral aspects of predation by the northern shrikes. *Living Bird* 6: 43–86.

Cade, T. J. 1968. The gyrfalcon and falconry. *Living Bird* 7: 237–240.

Cade, T. J. 1969. The status of the peregrine and other falconiforms in Africa. Pp. 289–321 in: Peregrine Falcon Populations, edited by J. J. Hickey. Univ. Wisconsin Press.

Cade, T. J. 1974. Plans for managing the survival of the peregrine falcon. Raptor Research Foundation, *Raptor Research Report* 3: 89–104.

Cade, T. J. 1980a. [Review of] Population ecology of raptors by Ian Newton. *Journal of Wild. Mngt.* 44 (4): 969–972.

Cade, T. J. 1980b. The husbandry of falcons for return to the wild. *International Zoo Yearbook* 20: 23–35.

Cade, T. J., and Dague, P. R. (Eds.) 1980. The Peregrine Fund Newsletter No. 8 Cornell Lab. of Ornithology.

Cade, T. J., and Dague, P. R. 1981. The Peregrine Fund Newsletter no. 9. Cornell Laboratory of Ornithology.

Cade, T. J., and Fyfe, R. 1970. The North American peregrine survey, 1970. *Can. Field-Nat.* 84: 231–245.

Cade, T. J., and Fyfe, R. 1978. What makes peregrine falcons breed in captivity? Pp. 251–262 in: Endangered Birds, Management Techniques for Preserving Threatened Species, edited by S. A. Temple. University of Wisconsin Press.

Cade, T. J., and Greenwald, L. 1966. Nasal salt secretion in falconiform birds. *Condor* 68: 338–350.

Cade, T. J., Lineer, J. L., White, C. M., Roseneau, D. C., and Swartz, L. C. 1971. DDE residues and eggshell changes in Alaskan falcons and hawks. *Science* 172: 955–957.

Cade, T. J., and Weaver, J. D. 1976. Gyrfalcon × peregrine hybrids produced by artificial insemination. *J. N. Am. Falconers' Asscn.* 15: 42–47.

Cade, T. J. and White, C. M., 1976. Alaska's falcons; the issue of survival. *Living Wilderness* 39 (132): 35–47.

Cade, T. J., White, C. M., and Haugh, J. R. 1968. Peregrines and pesticides in Alaska. *Condor* 70: 170–178.

Campbell, R. W., Carter, H., Paul, M. A., and Rodway, M. A. 1977. Tree-nesting peregrine falcons in British Columbia. *Condor* 79: 500–501.

Cavé, A. J. 1968. The breeding of the kestrel, *Falco tinnunculus* L., in the reclaimed area Oostelijk Flevoland. *Netherlands J. Zool.* 18: 313–407.

Cawkell, E. M., and Hamilton, S. E. 1961. The birds of the Falkland Islands. *Ibis* 103a: 1–27.

Clapham, C. S. 1964. The birds of the Dahlac Archipelago. *Ibis* 106: 376–388.

Clark, A. L., and Peakall, D. B. 1977.

Organochlorine residues in Eleonora's falcon *Falco eleonorae*, its eggs and its prey. *Ibis* 119: 353–358.

Clunie, F. 1972. A contribution to the natural history of the Fiji peregrine. *Notornis* 19: 302–322.

Clunie, F. 1976. A Fiji peregrine (*Falco peregrinus*) in an urban-marine environment. *Notornis* 28: 8–28

Cody, M. L. 1969. Convergent characteristics in sympatric bird populations: a possible relation to interspecific territoriality. *Condor* 71: 223–234.

Colebrook-Robjent, J. F. R. 1973. The breeding of the Madagascar banded kestrel. *Bull. Brit. Orn. Club* 93 (3): 108–111.

Colebrook-Robjent, J. F. R. 1977. The eggs of the Taita falcon. *Bull. Brit. Ornithol. Club* 97: 44–46.

Colebrook-Robjent, J. F. R., and Osborne, T. O. 1974. High density breeding of the red-necked falcon, *Falco chicquera*, in Zambia. *Bull. Brit. Ornithol. Club* 94: 172–176.

Collopy, M. W. 1973. Predatory efficiency of American kestrels wintering in northwestern California. *Raptor Research* 7: 25–31.

Compton, L. V. 1938. The pterylosis of the Falconiformes with special attention to the taxonomic position of the osprey. *Univ. Calif. Publ. Zool.* 42: 173–212.

Cooke, A. S. 1979. Changes in the egg shell characteristics of the sparrow-hawk (*Accipiter nisus*) and peregrine (*Falco peregrinus*) associated with exposure to environmental pollutants during recent decades. *Journal of Zoology*, London 187: 245–263.

Cover, D. 1977. Memories. *J. of the N. Am. Falconers' Assn.* 16: 17–20.

Cracraft, J. 1981. Toward a phylogenetic classification of the recent birds of the world (Class Aves). *Auk* 98: 681–714.

Craighead, J. J., and Craighead, F. C., Jr. 1956. Hawks, owls and wildlife. Harrisburg: The Stakpole Co.

Cramp, S., and Simmons, K. E. L. (Eds.) 1980. Handbook of the birds of Europe, the Middle East and North Africa. The birds of the western Palearctic. Vol. II. Hawks to Bustards. Oxford University Press.

Cummings, J. H., Duke, G. E., and Jegers, A. A. 1976. Corrosion of bone by solutions simulating raptor gastric juice. *Raptor Research* 10 (2): 55–57.

Cupper, J., and Cupper, L. 1980. Nesting of the grey falcon *Falco hypoleucos*. *Australian Bird Watcher* 8: 212–219.

Darlington, P. J. 1957. Zoogeography: the geographical distribution of animals. New York: John Wiley & Sons.

Dementiev, G. P. 1951. Order Falconiformes (Accipitres). Diurnal Raptors. Pp. 126–136 in Birds of the Soviet Union, vol. 1, edited by G. P. Dementiev and N. A. Gladkov. Translated from Russian by the Israel Program for Scientific Translations, for the Smithsonian Institution and the National Science Foundation.

Dementiev, G. P. 1957. On the shaheen *Falco peregrinus babylonicus*. *Ibis* 99: 477–482.

Dementiev, G. P. 1965. Quelques reflexions sur le faucon pelerin de Kleinschmidt, *Falco kreyenborgi*. *El Hornero* 10: 197–201.

Dementiev, G. P., and Iljitschev, V. D. 1961. Bemerkungen über die Morphologie de Wüsten-

Wanderfalken. *Falke* 8: 147–154.

Dharmakumarsinhji, R. S. (195-.) Birds of Saurashtra. Privately published at Dil Bahar, Bhavnagar, Saurashtra.

Dodsworth, P. T. L. 1913. Some notes on the nesting and plumage of the Shahin falcon (*Falco peregrinator*) and the black-cap falcon (*Falco atriceps*). *J. Bombay Nat. Hist. Soc.* 22: 197–198.

Downhower, J. F. 1976. Darwin's finches and the evolution of sexual dimorphism in body size. *Nature* 263: 558–563.

Dowsett, R. J. *Ibis* (in press). (Not 1980.)

Drent, R. 1975. Incubation. Pp. 333–420 in: Avian Biology, vol. 5, edited by D. S. Farner and J. R. King. New York: Academic Press.

Duke, G. E., Jegers, A. A., Loff, G., and Evanson, O. A. 1975. Gastric digestion in some raptors. *Comp. Biochem. Physiol.* 50A: 649–656.

Earhart, C. M., and Johnson, N. K. 1970. Size dimorphism and food habits of North American owls. *Condor* 72: 251–264.

Ellis, D. H., Anderson, C. M., and Roundy, T. B. 1981. *Falco kreyenborgi*; more pieces for the puzzle. *Raptor Research* 15 (2): 42–45.

Ellis, D. H., and Glinski, R. L. 1980. Some unusual records for the peregrine and pallid falcons in South America. *Condor* 82: 350–351.

Enderson, J. H. 1964. A study of the prairie falcon in the central Rocky Mountain region. *Auk* 81: 332–352.

Falxa, G. A., Ukrain, D. J., and Whitacre, D. F. 1977. The status and ecology of the bat falcon in southeastern Mexico. Paper presented to the 1977 meeting of the Raptor Research Foundation, Tempe, Arizona.

Feare, C. J., Temple, S. A., and Procter, J. 1974. The status, distribution, and diet of the Seychelles kestrel *Falco araea*. *Ibis* 116: 548–551.

Fennell, C. M. 1954. Notes on the nesting of the kestrel in Japan. *Condor* 56: 106–107.

Ferguson-Lees, I. J. 1951. The peregrine population of Britain, parts I & II. *Bird Notes* 24: 202–208; 309–314.

Ferguson-Lees, I. J. 1972. Kestrels nesting close together. *British Birds* 65: 257–258.

Fiuczynski, D. 1978. *Zool. Jb. Syst.* 105: 193–257.

Flint, V. E. (Ed.) 1978. Part II Birds. In: Red Data Book of USSR. Central Research Laboratory on Nature Conservation. Moscow: Lesnaya Promyshlennost Publishers.

Fox, N. 1976. Rangle. *Raptor Research* 10 (2): 61–63.

Fox, N. C. 1977. The biology of the New Zealand falcon (*Falco novaeseelandiae* Gmelin 1788). Ph.D. dissertation, University of Canterbury.

Fox, N. 1978. The distribution and numbers of New Zealand falcons. *Notornis* 25 (4): 317–331.

Fox, N. 1979. Nest robbing and food storing by New Zealand falcons. *Raptor Research* 13 (2): 51–56.

Franco, A., and Andrada, J. 1977. *Ardeola* 23: 137–187.

Friedmann, H. 1950. The birds of North and Middle America. Part XI. *U. S. Natl. Mus. Bull.* 50.

Frith, H. J. (Ed.) 1969. Birds in the Australian high country. Sydney: A. H. and A. W. Reed.

Fuertes, L. A. 1920. Falconry, the sport of Kings. *National Geographic Magazine* 38 (6): 429–460.

Fyfe, R. W., and Armbruster, H. I. 1977. Raptor research and management in Canada. Pp. 282–293 in: World Conference on Birds of Prey, Report of Proceedings, Vienna 1975, edited by R. D. Chancellor. ICBP.

Fyfe, R. W., Campbell, J., Hayson, B., and Hodson, K. 1969. Regional population declines and organochlorine insecticides in Canadian prairie falcons. *Canadian Field-Naturalist* 83: 191–200.

Fyfe, Richard, W., Risebrough, R. W., and Walker, Wayman II. 1976. Pollutant effects on the reproduction of the prairie falcons and merlins of the Canadian prairies. *Canadian Field-Naturalist* 90 (3): 346–355.

Fyfe, R. W., Temple, S. A., and Cade, T. J. 1976. The 1975 North American peregrine falcon survey. *Canadian Field-Naturalist* 90: 228–273.

Galushin, V. M. 1981. Changes in population status and nest range distribution of Falconiformes in the USSR since 1950. *Raptor Research* 15: 4–11. (Not 1977.)

George, U. 1970. Beobachtungen an *Pterocles senegallus* und *Pterocles natus* in der Nordwest-Sahara. *J. für Orn.* 111: 175–188.

Goslow, C. E., Jr. 1971. The attack and strike of some North American raptors. *Auk* 88: 815–827.

Gaymer, R., Blackman, R. A. A., Dawson, P. G., Penny, M. J., and Penny C. M. 1969. The endemic birds of Seychelles. *Ibis* 111: 157–176.

Glutz von Blotzheim, U. N., Bauer, K., and Bezzel, E. 1971. Handbuch der Vogel Mitteleuropas, Vol. 4. Frankfurt: Akademische Verlagsgesselschaft.

Greenewalt, C. H. 1962. Dimensional relationships for some flying animals. *Smithsonian Misc. Coll.* 144, No 2.

Grossman, M. L. and Hamlet, J. 1964. Birds of prey of the world. New York: Clarkson N. Potter, Inc.

Gudmundsson, F. 1970. The predator-prey relationship of the gyrfalcon and the rock ptarmigan in Iceland. *Proc. XV. Int. Orn. Congr.*

Gwinner, E. 1965. Über den Einfluss des Hungers und anderen Fuctoren auf die Versteck-Aktivitatdes des Kolkraben. *Die Vogelwarte* 23: 1–4.

Haak, B. A. and Denton, S. J. 1979. Sub-terranean nesting by prairie falcons. *Raptor Research* 13 (4): 121–122.

Hagen, Y. 1969. Norwegian studies on the reproduction of birds of prey and owls in relation to micro-rodent population fluctuations. *Fauna* 22: 73–126.

Hall, G. H. 1955. Great moments in action. The story of the Sun Life falcons. Montreal: Mercury Press. (see *Can. Field-Nat.* 84 (3), 1970.)

Hamerstrom, F., Hamerstrom, F. N., and Hart, J. 1973. Nest boxes: An effective management tool for kestrels. *J. Wildlife Mngmnt.* 37: 400–403.

Hangte, E. 1968. Beuteerwerk unserer Wanderfalken (*Falco peregrinus*). *Orn. Mitt.* 20: 211–217.

Harper, T. 1981. Peregrines' progress. *Defenders* 56: 7–11.

Hartman, F. A. 1961. Locomotor mechanisms of birds. *Smithsonian Misc. Coll.* 143 (1): 1–99.

Haverschmidt, F. 1962. Notes on the feeding habits and food of some hawks of Surinam. *Condor* 64: 154–158.

Hector, D. P. 1980. Our rare falcon of the desert grassland. *Birding* 12 (3): 93–102.

Hector, D. P. *Living Bird* (in press).

Hickey, J. J. 1942. Eastern population of the duck hawk. *Auk* 59 (2): 176–204.

Hickey, J. J. (Ed.) 1969. Peregrine falcon populations, their biology and decline. Univ. of Wisconsin Press.

Hickey, J. J., and Anderson, D. W. 1968. Chlorinated hydrocarbons and eggshell changes in raptorial and fish-eating birds. *Science* 162: 271–273.

Hill, N. P. 1944. Sexual dimorphism in the Falconiformes. *Auk* 61: 228–234.

Holliday, C. S. 1965. A note on the Teita falcon. *Puku* 3: 71–73.

Horváth, L. 1955. Redfooted falcons on Ohat-woods, near Hortobágy. *Acta Zool. Acad. Sc. Hungar.* 1: 245–287.

Horváth, L. 1956. The life of the red-legged falcon in the Ohat forest. *Proc. XI. Int. Orn. Congr.*, Basel 1954, pp. 583–587.

Horváth, L. 1975. Social pattern and behavior between two *Falco* species (Aves). *Ann. Historico-Naturales Musei Nationalis Hungarici* 67: 327–331.

Howell, T. R. 1965. New subspecies of birds from the lowland pine savanna of northeastern Nicaragua. *Auk* 82: 438–464.

Howell, T. R. 1972. Birds of the lowland pine savannah of northeastern Nicaragua. *Condor* 74: 316–340.

Howland, H. C. 1974. Optimal strategies for predator avoidance: the relative importance of speed and maneouvrability. *J. of Theoretical Biology* 47: 333–350.

Hudson, R. 1975. Threatened birds of Europe. London: Macmillan.

Hunter, N. D., Douglas, M. G., Stead, D. E., Taylor, V. A., Alder, J. R., and Carter, A. T. 1979. A breeding record and some observations of the Taita *Falco fasciinucha* in Malawi. *Ibis* 121: 93–94. (Not 1977.)

Jenkins, R. E. 1970. Food habits of wintering sparrow hawks in Costa Rica. *Wilson Bulletin* 82: 97–98.

Jenny, J. P., Ortiz, F. and Arnold, M. D. 1981. First nesting record of the peregrine falcon (*Falco peregrinus*) for Ecuador. *Condor* 83: 387.

Johnson, A. W. 1965. The birds of Chile and adjacent regions of Argentina, Bolivia and Peru. Vol I. B. Aires: Platt Establecimientos Graficos.

Jollie, M. 1953. Are the Falconiformes a monophyletic group? *Ibis* 95: 769–771.

Jollie, M. 1976–77. A contribution to the morphology and phylogeny of the Falconiformes. *Evol. Theory* 1: 285–298; 2: 115–300; 3: 1–141.

Jolly, A. 1980. A world like our own, man and nature in Madagascar. Yale University Press.

Jones, C. G. 1980. The Mauritius kestrel, its biology and conservation. Hawk Trust Annual Report 10: 18–29.

Kemp, A. C. 1978. Territory maintenance and use by breeding greater kestrels. *Proc. Symp. African Predatory Birds*, pp. 71–76. Pretoria: Northern Transvaal Ornithol. Soc.

Kenward, R. 1979. The numbers of birds of prey obtained and possessed by falconers in the United Kingdom. *The Falconer* 7 (3): 158–163.

Kiff, L. F., Peakall, D. B., and Hector, D. P. 1981. Eggshell thinning and organochlorine residues in the bat and aplomado falcons in Mexico. *Proc. XVII. Int. Ornithol. Conf.*, 1978.

King, W. 1977. The Red Data Book. Aves. Morges: IUCN/ICBP.

Kleinschmidt, O. 1929. *Falco kreyenborgi. Falco* 3: 33–35.

Kleinschmidt, O. 1958. Raubvogel und Eulen der Heimat. 3rd Ed., revised. Wittenberg-Lutherstadt: A. Ziemsen.

Koplin, J. R. 1973. Differential habitat use by sexes of American kestrels wintering in northern California. *Raptor Research* 7: 39–42.

Koplin, J. R., Collopy, M. W., Bammann, A. R., Levenson, H. 1980. Energetics of two wintering raptors. *Auk* 97: 795–806.

Lasiewski, R. C., and Dawson, W. R. 1967. A re-examination of the relation between standard metabolic rate and body weight in birds. *Condor* 69: 13–23.

Latham, S. 1615. Latham's falconry; or the faulcons lure and cure. London: Roger Jackson.

Lawrence, G. N. 1874. The birds of western and northwestern Mexico, based upon collections made by Col. A. J. Grayson . . . *Mem. Boston Soc. Nat. Hist.* 2: 265–319.

Lawson, R. 1930. The stoop of a hawk. *Bull. Essex County Orn. Club*, 1930, pp. 79–80.

Lewis, E. (E. Vasey, pseud.). 1938. In Search of the Gyr-Falcon. London: Constable.

Loosemore, E. 1963. *J. E. Af. Nat. Hist. Soc.* 24 (2): 67–70.

McAtee, W. L. 1906. The shedding of the stomach lining by birds. *Auk* 23: 346.

McLachlan, R. G., and Liversidge R. 1957. Roberts' birds of South Africa. Cape Times Limited.

McNulty, F. 1972. The falcons of Moro Rock. *The New Yorker*, 23.12.72.

Maclean, G. L. 1968. Field studies on the sandgrouse of the Kalahari desert. *Living Bird* 7: 209–235.

Macdonald, J. D. 1973. Birds of Australia, a summary of information. London: Witherby.

Maclean, G. L. 1970. An analysis of the avifauna of the southern Kalahari Gemsbok National Park. *Zoologica Africana* 5 (2): 249–273.

Maher, W. J. 1974. Ecology of pomarine, parasitic, and long-tailed jaegers in northern Alaska. *Pacific Coast Avifauna* no 37.

Mangold, O. 1946. Die Nase der segeln-den Vögel ein Organ des Strömungs-sinnes? *D. Naturwissenschaften* 33: 19–23.

Masterson, H. B. 1951. Nesting of Dickinson's kestrel in Southern Rhodesia. *Ostrich* 22: 202.

Mavrogordato, J. G. 1966. A falcon in the field. London: Knightly Vernon.

Mebs, T. 1972. Family: Falcons, in Grzimek, B. (Ed.), *Grzimek's Animal Life Encyclopedia*. Vol. 7. New York: Van Nostrand Reinhold Company.

Meinertzhagen, R. 1954. Birds of Arabia. London: Oliver and Boyd.

Meinertzhagen, R. 1959. Pirates and predators. Edinburgh & London: Oliver and Boyd.

Mendelssohn, H. 1972. The impact of pesticides on bird life in Israel. ICBP *Bull.* 11: 104. (Not 1971.)

Meyburg, B-U. 1974. Sibling aggression and mortality among nestling eagles. *Ibis* 116: 224–228.

Michell, E. B. 1900. The art and practice of hawking. London: Holland Press.

Miller, D. S., Kinter, W. B., and Peakall, D. B. 1976. Enzymatic basis for DDE-induced eggshell thinning in a sensitive bird. *Nature* 259: 122–124.

Milton, P. Petter, J.-J., and Randrianasolo, G. 1973. Faune de Madagascar. Vol. 35. Oiseaux. Tananarive and Paris.

Mills, G. S. 1976. American kestrel sex ratios and habitat separation. *Auk* 93: 740–748.

Monneret, R. J. 1974. Repertoire comportemental du faucon pélerin *Falco peregrinus*: Hypothèse explicative des manifestations adversives. *Alauda* 42: 407–428.

Moreau, R. E. 1966. The bird faunas of Africa and its islands. London: Academic Press.

Moreau, R. E. 1969. The sooty falcon *Falco concolor* Temminck. *Bull. Brit. Orn. Club* 89: 62–67.

Moreau, R. E. 1972. The Palearctic-African bird migration systems. London: Academic Press.

Mueller, H. C. 1971. Displays and courtship of the sparrow hawk. *Wilson Bulletin* 83: 249–254.

Mueller, H. C. 1974. Food caching behaviour in the American kestrel. *Zeit. für Tierpsychologie* 34: 105–114.

Mueller, H. C., Berger, D. D., and Allez, C. 1976. Age and sex variation in the size of goshawks. *Bird-Banding* 47: 316–318.

Mueller, H. C., Berger, D. D., and Allez, C. 1979. Age and sex difference in size of sharp-skinned hawks. *Bird-Banding* 50: 34–44.

Mueller, H. C., Berger, D. D., and Allez, C. 1981. Age sex, and seasonal difference in size of Cooper's hawks. *J. of Field Orn.* 52: 112–126.

Nagy, A. 1963. Population density of sparrow hawks in eastern Pennsylvania. *Wilson Bull.* 75: 93.

Nelson, R. W. 1977. Behavioural ecology of coastal peregrines (*Falco peregrinus pealei*). Ph.D. dissertation, University of Calgary.

Newton, Ian. 1973. Egg breakage and breeding failure in British merlins. *Bird Study* 20: 241–244.

Newton, I. 1979. Population ecology of raptors. Carlton: T. & D. Poyser Ltd.

Newton, Ian. 1979. The wild merlin. *The Falconer* 7 (3): 164–167.

Newton, I., Meek, E., and Little, B. 1978. Breeding ecology of the merlin in Northumberland. *British Birds* 71: 376–398.

Olendorff, R. R., and Stoddart, J. W., Jr. 1974. The potential of management of raptor populations in western grasslands. Pp. 47–88 in: F. N. Hamerstrom, Jr., B. E. Harrell, and R. R. Olendorff (eds). Management of raptors. *Raptor Res. Rept.* no. 2.

Oliphant, L. W., and Thompson, W. J. P. 1978. Recent breeding success of Richardson's merlin in Saskatchewan. *Raptor Research* 12 (1/2): 35–39.

Olrog, C. C. 1948. Observaciones sobre la avifauna de Tierra del Fuego y Chile. *Acta Zool. Lilloana* 5: 437–531.

Olsen, J., and Olsen, P. 1980. Observations of defence of the nest against humans by species of *Falco*. *Emu* 80: 163–165.

Olsen, J., Olsen, P., and Jolly, J. 1979. Observations on interspecific conflict in the peregrine, *Falco peregrinus* and other Australian falcons. *Australian Bird Watcher* 8 (2): 51–57.

Olsen, P., and Olsen, J. 1980. Observations on development, nesting chronology, and clutch and brood size in the Australian kestrel. *Aust. Wildl. Res.* 7: 247–255.

Olsen, P., Vestjens, W. J. M., and Olsen, J. 1979. Observations on the diet of the Australian kestrel *Falco cenchroides*. *Emu* 79: 133–138.

Ortega, J. 1972. Meditations on hunting. New York: Charles Scribners & Sons.

Orton, D. A. 1975. The speed of a peregrine's dive. *The Field*, 25.9.75.

Osborne, T. O. 1981. Ecology of the red-necked falcon, *Falco chicquera* in Zambia. *Ibis* 123: 289–297.

Page, G., and Whitacre, D. F. 1975. Raptor predation on wintering shorebirds. *Condor* 77: 73–78.

Parker, A. 1979. Peregrines at a Welsh coastal eyrie. *Brit. Birds* 72: 104–144.

Parkes, K. C. 1955. Notes on the molts and plumages of the sparrow hawk. *Wilson Bulletin* 67: 194–199.

Peakall, D. B. 1967. Progress in experiments on the relation between pesticides and fertility. *Atlantic Naturalist* 22 (2): 109–111.

Peakall, D. B., Cade, T. J., White, C. M., and Haugh, J. R. 1975. Organo-chlorine residues in Alaskan peregrines. *Pesticides Monitoring J.* 8: 255–260.

Peakall, D. B., and Kiff, L. F. 1979. Eggshell thinning and DDE residue levels among peregrine falcons: A global perspective. *Ibis* 121: 200–204.

Penny, M. 1974. The birds of Seychelles and the outlying islands. London: Collins.

Pennycuick, C. J. 1975. Mechanics of flight. Pp. 1–75 in Avian Biology, vol. 5, edited by D. S. Farner and J. P. King. New York: Academic Press.

Perdeck, A. C. 1960. Observations on the reproductive behavior of the great skua or bonxie, *Stercorarius skua skua* in Shetland. *Ardea* 48: 111–136.

Peterson, R. T. 1948. Birds over America. New York: Dodd, Mead & Co.

Platt, J. B. 1976. Gyrfalcon nest site selection and winter activity in the western Canadian Arctic. *Can. Field-Nat.* 90: 338–345.

Platt, J. B. 1977. The breeding behavior of wild and captive gyrfalcons in relation to their environment and human disturbance. Ph.D. thesis. Cornell University.

Porter, R. D., and Wiemeyer, S. N. 1970. Propagation of captive American kestrels. *Journal of Wildlife Mngt.* 34: 594–604.

Prestt, I. 1965. An enquiry into the recent breeding status of some of the smaller birds of prey and crows in Britain. *Bird Study* 12: 196–221.

Pruett-Jones, S. G., White, C. M., and Devine, W. R. 1981. Breeding of the peregrine falcon in Victoria, Australia. *Emu* 80 (Supplement): 253–269.

Rahn, H. Paganelli, C. V., and Ar, A. 1975. Relation of avian egg weight to body weight. *Auk* 92: 750–765.

Ralls, K. 1976. Mammals in which females are larger than males. *Quart. Rev. of Biol.* 51: 245–276.

Rand, A. L. 1936. The distribution and habits of Madagascar birds: A summary of the field notes of the Mission Zoologique Franco-Anglo-Americáine a Madagascar. *Bull. Amer. Mus. Nat. Hist.* 72: 143–499.

Rand, A. L. 1952. Secondary sexual characters and ecological competition. *Fieldiana Zoology* 34: 65–70.

Ratcliffe, D. A. 1967. Decrease in eggshell weight in certain birds of prey. *Nature* 215: 208–210.

Ratcliffe, D. 1980. The peregrine falcon. Carlton: T. & D. Poyser Ltd.

Rattray, R. H. 1919. The Indian peregrine falcon. *Ibis* 11: 369–371.

Reynolds, R. T. 1972. Sexual dimorphism in accipiter hawks: A new hypothesis. *Condor* 74: 191–197.

Richardson, F. 1972. Accessory pygostyle bones of Falconidae. *Condor* 74: 350–351.

Ripley, S. D., and Heinrich, G. H. 1966. Comments on the avifauna of Tanzania I. *Postilla* 96: 45.

Rockenbauch, D. 1968. Zur Brutbiologie des Turmfalken. *Anz. orn. Ges. Bayern* 8: 267–276.

Roest, A. I. 1957. Notes on the American sparrow hawk. *Auk* 74: 1–19.

Roseneau, D. G. 1972. Summer distribution, numbers, and food habits of the gyrfalcon (*Falco rusticolus*) on the Seward Peninsula, Alaska. M. S. thesis. University of Alaska.

Rowan, Wm. 1921–2. Observations on the breeding habits of the merlin. *British Birds* 15: 122–9; 194–202; 222–31; 246–53.

Rudebeck. G. 1950–1. The choice of prey and modes of hunting of predatory birds with special reference to their selective effect. *Oikos* 2: 65–88; 3: 200–231.

Rudebeck, G. 1963. Studies on some Palaearctic and Arctic birds in their winter quarters in South Africa. 4. Birds of prey. Pp. 418–453 in Hanstrom *et al.* (Eds.) South African animal life; results of the Lund Univ. expedition in 1950–51. Vol. 9.

Ruttledge, W. 1979. Merlins in the years between. *The Falconer* 7 (3): 174–179.

Salomonsen, F. 1951. Grønlands Fugle, vol. 3. Copenhagen.

Savile, D. B. O. 1957. Adaptive evolution in the avian wing. *Evolution* 11: 212–224.

Segnestam, M., and Helander, B. 1977. Birds of prey in Sweden. Pp. 170–178 in: World Conference on Birds of Prey, Report of Proceedings, Vienna, 1975, edited by R. D. Chancellor. ICBP.

Selander, R. K. 1966. Sexual dimorphism and differential niche utilization in birds. *Condor* 68: 113–151.

Selander, R. K. 1972. Sexual selection and dimorphism in birds. Pp. 180–230 in Sexual selection and the descent of man 1871–1971, edited by B. Campbell. Chicago: Aldine.

Serle, W. 1943. *Ibis* 85: 281.

Serventy, D. L., and Whittell, H. M. 1967. Birds of Western Australia. Perth: Lamb Publishing.

Short, L. L. 1975. A zoogeographical analysis of the South American Chaco avifauna. *Bull. Amer. Mus. Nat. Hist.* 154: 163–352.

Sibley, C. G., and Ahlquist, J. E. 1972. A comparative study of the egg-white proteins of non-passerine birds. *Peabody Mus. Nat. Hist., Yale Univ. Bull.* 39: 1–276.

Siegfried, W. R., and Frost, P. G. H. 1970. Notes on the Madagascar kestrel. *Ibis* 112: 400–402.

Siegfried, W. R., and Skead, D. M. 1971. Status of the lesser kestrel in South Africa. *Ostrich* 42: 1–4.

Smith, S. 1980. Henpecked males; the general pattern in monogamy? *Journal of Field Ornithology* 51: 55–64.

Smith, S. *Oikos* (in press).

Snyder, N. F. R., and Wiley, J. W. 1976. Sexual size dimorphism in hawks and owls of North America. *Ornithological Monographs* 20: 1–96.

Solomatin, A. O. 1974. *Byull. Mosk. Obch. Istp. Prir. biol.* 79: 40–51.

Sparrowe, R. D. 1972. Prey-catching behavior in the sparrow hawk. *Journal of Wildlife Management* 36: 297–308.

Starck, D. 1959. Neueine Ergelbnisse der vergleichenden Anatomie und ihre Bedeutung für die Taxonomie, er läutert an der Trigeminus – Muskulatur der Vögel. *J. Orn.* 100: 47–59.

Stegmann, B. 1933. On the relationship of South American and New Zealand falcons. *C. R. Acad. Sc. U.S.S.R.* 4: 172–175 (in Russian).

Stepanyan, L. S. 1969. Beobachtungen am Rotnackenshahin in Mittelasien. *Falke* 16: 124–130.

Stevens, R. 1956. The taming of Genghis. London: Faber and Faber.

Stinson, C. H., Crawford, D. L., and Lauthner, J. 1981. Sex differences in winter habitat of American kestrels in Georgia. *J. of Field Ornith.* 62: 29–35.

Storer, R. W. 1955. Weight, wing areas and skeletal proportions in three accipiters. *International Ornithological Congress*, 1954. 11: 287–290.

Storer, R. W. 1966. Sexual dimorphism and food habits in three North American accipiters. *Auk* 83: 423–436.

Stresemann, V. 1958. Sind die Falconidae ihrer Mauserweise nach eine einheitliche Gruppe? *J. für Ornith.* 99: 81–88.

Stresemann, E., and Amadon, D. 1963. What is *Falco kreyenborgi* Kleinschmidt? *Ibis* 105: 400–402.

Suschkin, P. 1905. Vergleichende der normalen Tagraubvogel (Accipitres) und die Fragen der Classification. *Nour. Mem. Soc. Imp. Naturalistes Moscou* 16.

Swann, H. K. 1936. A monograph of the birds of prey (order Accipitres). Part 14: 398–399. London. Wheldon and Wesley.

Swartz, L. G., Walker, W. II, Roseneau, D. G., and Springer, A. M. 1975. Populations of gyrfalcons on the Seward Peninsula, Alaska, 1968–1972. Pp. 71–71 in Proceedings of the Conference on Raptor Conservation Techniques, Part 6. *Raptor Research Report* no. 3.

Technau, G. 1936. Die Nasendrüse der Vögel. *J. Ornithol.* 84: 511–616.

Temple, S. A. 1974. Project 986 Western Indian Ocean Island Raptors – conservation. World Wildlife Yearbook 1973–74, pp. 201–204.

Temple, S. A. 1975. Project 986 Western Indian Ocean Raptors – ecology and conservation. World Wildlife Yearbook 1974–75. Pp. 210–212.

Temple, S. A. 1977. The status and conservation of endemic kestrels on Indian Ocean Islands. Pp. 78–82 in World Conference on Birds of Prey, Vienna 1975, edited by R. D. Chancellor. ICBP.

Temple, S. A. British Ornithologists' Union (in press).

Theide, W., and Theide, U. 1973. *Bonn zool. Beitr.* 24: 285–290.

Thiollay, J. M. 1975. Les rapaces d'une zone de contact Savane-Foret en Cote-d'Ivoire: Presentation du peuplement. *Alauda* 43: 75–10

Thiollay, J. M. 1976. Les rapaces d'une zone de contact Savane-Foret en Cote-d'Ivoire: Modalites et success de la reproduction. *Alauda* 43: 387–416.

Thiollay, J. M. 1977. Les rapaces d'une zone de contact Savane-Foret en Cote-d'Ivoire: Modes d'exploitation au milieu. *Alauda* 45: 197–218.

Tømmeraas, P. J. 1978. Kunstige reirplasser for jaktfalk *Falco rusticolus* og vandrefalk *Falco peregrinus*. *Var Fuglefauna* 1: 142–151.

Tordoff, H. B. 1955. Food-storing in the sparrow hawk. *Wilson Bull.* 67: 139–140.

Treleaven, R. 1980. High and low intensity hunting in raptors. *Zeitschrift für Tierpsychologie* 54: 339–345.

Tucker, V. A. 1971. Flight energergetics in birds. *American Zoologist* 11: 115–124.

Tucker, V. A., and Parrott, G. C. 1970. Aerodynamics of gliding flight in a falcon and other birds. *Journal of Experimental Biology* 52: 345–367.

Tyler, C. 1966. A study of the egg shells of the Falconiformes. *J. Zool.*, London 150: 413–425.

U. S. Dept. of the Interior, Bureau of Land Management. 1979. Snake River Birds of Prey Special Research Report to the Secretary of the Interior. BLM Boise District, Idaho. Snake River Birds of Prey Study Area, Summary Report, June 1979.

Vaughan, R. 1961. *Falco eleonorae*. *Ibis* 103a: 114–128.

Vaurie, C. 1961. Systematic notes on Palearctic birds. No. 44: Falconidae: The genus *Falco* (Part I, *Falco peregrinus* and *Falco pelegrinoides*). *Amer. Mus. Novitates* 2035.

Vincent, J. (Ed.) 1966. Red Data Book – Aves. Morges: IUCN.

Voous, K. H. 1973. List of recent Holarctic bird species non-passerines *Ibis* 115: 612–635.

Walter, H. 1979. Eleonora's falcon, adaptations to prey and habitat in a social raptor. Univ. of Chicago Press.

White, C. M., and Cade, T. J. 1971. Cliff-nesting raptors and ravens along the Colville River in Arctic Alaska. *Living Bird* 10: 107–150.

White, C. M., Pruett-Jones, S. G., and Emison, W. B. 1981. The status and distribution of the peregrine falcon in Victoria, Australia. *Emu* 80 (suppl.): 270–280.

White, C. M. N. 1945. The ornithology of the Kaonde-Lunda Province, Northern Rhodesia. Part II. Systematic list. *Ibis* 87: 185–202.

Willoughby, E. J., and Cade, T. J. 1964. Breeding behavior of the American kestrel. *Living Bird* 3: 75–96.

Willoughby, E. J., and Cade, T. J. 1967. Drinking habits of birds in the Central Namib Desert of South West Africa. Scientific Papers of the Namib Desert Research Station No. 31.

Wilson, Robbie. 1979. Lark-hawking today. *The Falconer* 7 (3): 180–184. (See also pp. 199–200).

Wink, M. von, Wink, C., and Ristow, D. 1978. Biologie des Eleonorenfalken (*Falco eleonorae*): 2. Zur Vererbung der Gefiederphasen (hell-dunkel). *J. für Orn.* 119: 421–428.

Woodin, N. 1980. Observations on gyrfalcons (*Falco rusticolus*) breeding near Lake Myvatn, Iceland, 1967. *Raptor Research* 14 (4): 97–124.

Wrege, P., and Cade, T. J. 1977. Courtship behavior of the large falcons in captivity. *Raptor Research* 11: 1–27.

Yanez, J. L., Nunez, H., Schlatter, R. P., and Jaksic, F. M. 1980. Diet and weight of American kestrels in central Chile, *Auk* 97: 629–631.

Zern, E. 1972. I am a hunter. *Audubon* 74 (1): 17–19.

Ziswiler, V. and Farner, D. S. 1972. Digestion and the digestive system. Pp. 343–430 in: Avian Biology, vol. 2, edited by D. S. Farner and J. R. King. New York: Academic Press.

Index

Page numbers in *italics* refer to plates.